WRITING

INSIDE

LANGUAGE, LITERACY, AND CONTENT

PROGRAM AUTHOR

Gretchen Bernabei

Acknowledgments

Grateful acknowledgment is given to the authors, artists, photographers, museums, publishers, and agents for permission to reprint copyrighted material. Every effort has been made to secure the appropriate permission. If any omissions have been made or if corrections are required, please contact the Publisher.

Appreciation

The Publisher gratefully acknowledges that ideas for the following lessons in this book have previously appeared in other works by Gretchen Bernabei and/or Barry Lane:

- What If Ideas Are Hard to Find? (page 50W–51W), Idea Organizers (pages 426W–427W), and Try Adding a Ba-Da-Bing (page 299W), are based on ideas in *Reviving the Essay*© 2005 Gretchen Bernabei and published by Discover Writing Press.
- Try Getting Into an Argument . . . with Yourself and Ways You Know Things (page 315W) are based on ideas in *Why We Must Run with Scissors*© 2001 Gretchen Bernabei and Barry Lane and published by Discover Writing Press.
- Try Adding Snapshots and Thoughtshots (page 171W) and Try Adding Meat to the Bones (page 347W) are based on ideas in *The Reviser's Toolbox*© 1999 by Barry Lane and published by Discover Writing Press.

Gretchen Bernabei and Barry Lane present open-enrollment seminars nationwide, and are available for inservice workshops with students and teachers. For more information, contact:

Discover Writing Press
1-800-613-8055
www.discoverwriting.com

Cover design: (tc) FusionPix/Corbis. (ml - mr) DLILLC/Corbis. DLILLC/Corbis. Brandon D. Cole/Corbis. Scot Frei/Corbis. Robert Glusic/Corbis. Colin Dutton/Grand Tour/Corbis.

Acknowledgments and credits continue at the back of the book.

Published by National Geographic School Publishing & Hampton-Brown
Sheron Long, Chief Executive Officer
Samuel Gesumaria, President

Editorial, Art, Design, and Production team acknowledgments can be found at the back of the book.

The National Geographic Society
John M. Fahey, Jr., President & Chief Executive Officer
Gilbert M. Grosvenor, Chairman of the Board

Manufacturing and Quality Management, The National Geographic Society

Christopher A. Liedel, Chief Financial Officer
George Bounelis, Vice President

National Geographic School Publishing
Hampton-Brown
www.NGSP.com

Printed in the United States of America
Quad/Graphics, Taunton, MA

ISBN: 978-0-7362-58630

ISBN (CA): 978-0-7362-59484

11 12 13 14 15 16 17 18 10 9 8 7

Contents

THE
Building
Blocks
OF WRITING

THE Writing Process

Project 5 **Use the Writing Process**

At Each Stage of the Writing Process–

THE Many Writers YOU ARE

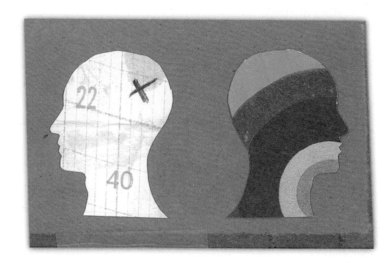

Project 6 **Write as a Friend**

Chapter 3, continued

Chapter 3, continued

Writer's Files

Handbooks

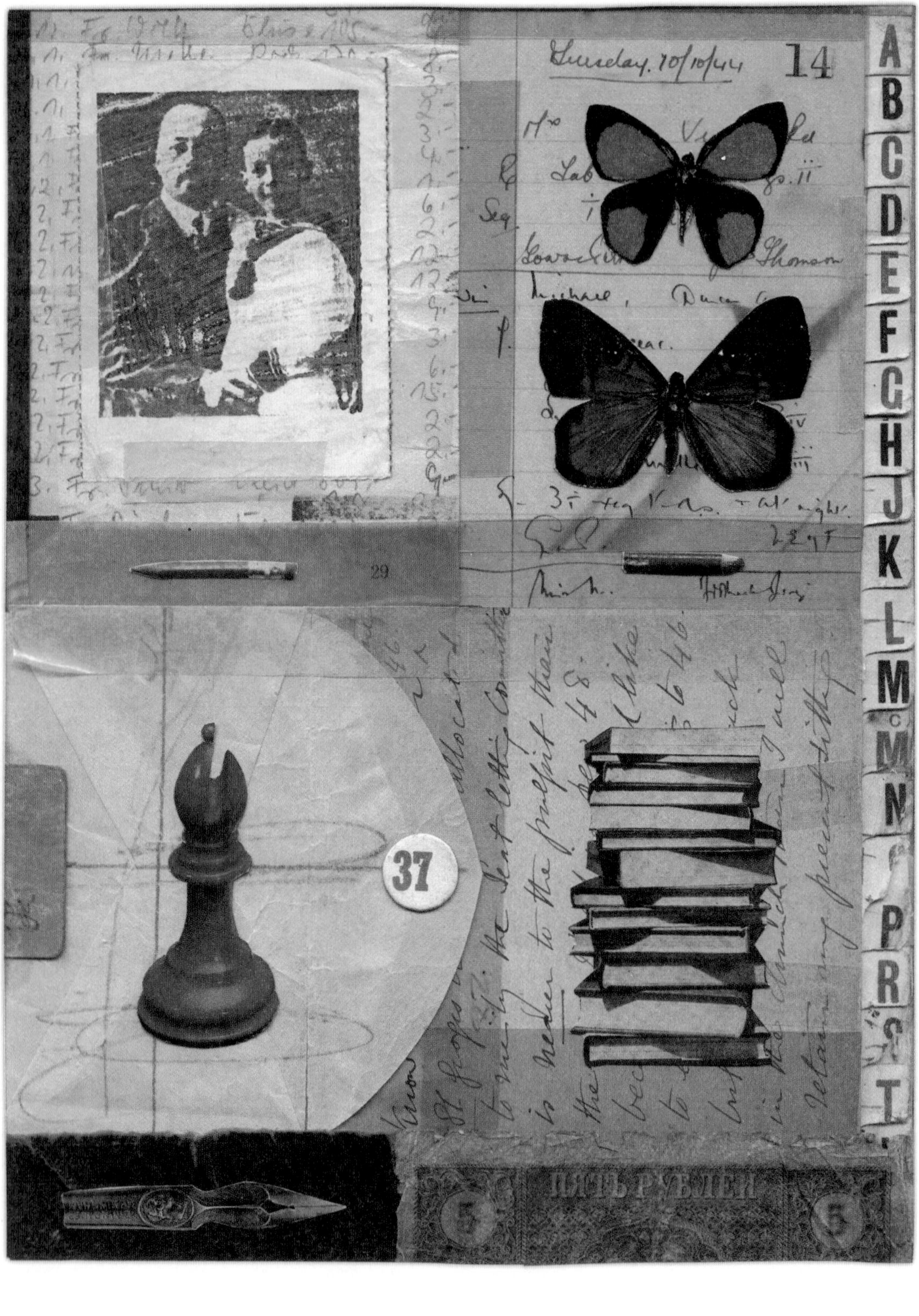
14
29
37
ПЯТЬ РУБЛЕЙ

THE
Building
Blocks
OF WRITING

Paragraph Structure:
Topic and Details

"Nothing helps me learn
something new like seeing
an example of it."
—Deion

Model Study

Sentences and Paragraphs

One great way to share ideas or express feelings is through writing. But how do you put your thoughts clearly on paper? You start with a **sentence**, a group of words that expresses a complete thought. There are four types of sentences:

Type of Sentence	Example
A **statement** tells something.	Danny is from Guatemala.
A **question** asks something.	Where is Guatemala?
An **exclamation** shows strong emotion.	Guatemala is so far away!
A **command** tells you to do something.	Come here. Watch out!

When you group sentences in an organized way, you have a **paragraph**. The sentences in a paragraph all tell about the same idea. One sentence gives the **main idea**. The other sentences offer **details** that support the main idea. Details might be examples that show the main idea is true. They might also describe parts of the "big picture" of the main idea.

PARAGRAPH

A well-developed paragraph

☑ has a topic sentence that states the main idea

☑ contains examples that tell more about the main idea.

Feature Checklist

California English–Language Arts Content Standards

Chapter 1 The Building Blocks of Writing

Project 1 Paragraph Structure: Topic and Details

4W–5W	**Writing Strategy: State a Topic Sentence**	• **Reading Comprehension 2.5** Distinguish the main idea and supporting details in expository text.
6W–7W	**Write a Paragraph with Examples: Plan and Write**	• **Writing Strategies 1.1a** Create a single paragraph: Develop a topic sentence. • **Writing Strategies 1.1b** Create a single paragraph: Include simple supporting facts and details. • **Writing Strategies 1.1** Select a focus, an organizational structure, and a point of view based upon purpose, audience, length, and format requirements. • **Writing Strategies 1.3** Use traditional structures for conveying information (e.g., chronological order, cause and effect, similarity and difference, posing and answering a question).
8W–9W	**Write a Paragraph with Examples: Revise**	• **Writing Strategies 1.10** Edit and revise selected drafts to improve coherence and progression by adding, deleting, consolidating, and rearranging text.
10W	**Write a Paragraph with Examples: Edit and Proofread**	• **Writing Strategies 1.2** Write legibly in cursive or joined italic, allowing margins and correct spacing between letters in a word and words in a sentence. • **Writing Strategies 1.4** Write fluidly and legibly in cursive or joined italic.
11W	**Write a Paragraph with Examples: Edit and Proofread Mechanics Workout**	• **Written and Oral English Language Conventions 1.1** Understand and be able to use complete and correct declarative, interrogative, imperative, and exclamatory sentences in writing and speaking. • **Written and Oral English Language Conventions 1.1** Use simple and compound sentences in writing and speaking.

Project 2 Paragraph Structure: Compare and Contrast

16W–17W	**Write a Comparison-Contrast Paragraph: Plan and Write**	• **Writing Strategies 1.1a** Create a single paragraph: Develop a topic sentence. • **Writing Strategies 1.1b** Create a single paragraph: Include simple supporting facts and details. • **Writing Strategies 1.3** Use traditional structures for conveying information (e.g., chronological order, cause and effect, similarity and difference, posing and answering a question).
18W–19W	**Write a Comparison-Contrast Paragraph: Revise**	• **Writing Strategies 1.10** Edit and revise selected drafts to improve coherence and progression by adding, deleting, consolidating, and rearranging text.
21W	**Write a Comparison-Contrast Paragraph: Edit and Proofread Mechanics Workout**	• **Written and Oral English Language Conventions 1.1** Understand and be able to use complete and correct declarative, interrogative, imperative, and exclamatory sentences in writing and speaking. • **Written and Oral English Language Conventions 1.1** Use simple and compound sentences in writing and speaking.

For coverage of additional standards, see the California standards maps in the Reading and Language book.

California English–Language Arts Content Standards, continued

Project 3 Paragraph Structure: Main Idea and Details

24W–25W	**Writing Strategy: Connect Main Idea and Details**	• **Reading Comprehension 2.5** Distinguish the main idea and supporting details in expository text.
26W–27W	**Write a Descriptive Paragraph: Plan and Write**	• **Writing Strategies 1.1a** Create a single paragraph: Develop a topic sentence. • **Writing Strategies 1.1b** Create a single paragraph: Include simple supporting facts and details. • **Writing Applications 2.2** Write descriptions that use concrete sensory details to present and support unified impressions of people, places, things or experiences. • **Writing Strategies 1.1** Select a focus, an organizational structure, and a point of view based upon purpose, audience, length, and format requirements.
28W–29W	**Write a Descriptive Paragraph: Revise**	• **Writing Strategies 1.10** Edit and revise selected drafts to improve coherence and progression by adding, deleting, consolidating, and rearranging text.
31W	**Write a Descriptive Paragraph: Edit and Proofread Mechanics Workout**	• **Written and Oral English Language Conventions 1.1** Understand and be able to use complete and correct declarative, interrogative, imperative, and exclamatory sentences in writing and speaking. • **Written and Oral English Language Conventions 1.1** Use simple and compound sentences in writing and speaking.

Project 4 Order of Events

36W–37W	**Write a Sequence Paragraph: Plan and Write**	• **Writing Strategies 1.1a** Create a single paragraph: Develop a topic sentence. • **Writing Strategies 1.1b** Create a single paragraph: Include simple supporting facts and details.
38W–39W	**Write a Sequence Paragraph: Revise**	• **Writing Strategies 1.10** Edit and revise selected drafts to improve coherence and progression by adding, deleting, consolidating, and rearranging text.
41W	**Write a Sequence Paragraph: Edit and Proofread Grammar Workout**	• **Reading 1.5** Demonstrate knowledge of levels of specificity among grade-appropriate words and explain the importance of these relations (e.g., *dog/mammal/animal/living things*).
42W	**Write a Sequence Paragraph: Edit and Proofread Spelling Workout**	• **Written and Oral English Language Conventions 1.8** Spell correctly one-syllable words that have blends, contractions, compounds, orthographic patterns (e.g., *qu*, consonant doubling, changing the ending of a word from -y to -ies when forming the plural), and common homophones (e.g., *hair-hare*).
43W	**Write a Sequence Paragraph: Edit and Proofread Mechanics Workout**	• **Written and Oral English Language Conventions 1.7** Capitalize geographical names, holidays, historical periods, and special events correctly.

Project 5 Use the Writing Process

52W–59W	Prewrite	• **Writing Strategies 1.1** Select a focus, an organizational structure, and a point of view based upon purpose, audience, length, and format requirements.
60W–67W	Draft	• **Writing Strategies 1.1a** Create a single paragraph: Develop a topic sentence. • **Writing Strategies 1.1b** Create a single paragraph: Include simple supporting facts and details. • **Writing Strategies 1.3** Use traditional structures for conveying information (e.g., chronological order, cause and effect, similarity and difference, posing and answering a question). • **Writing Applications 2.1a** Write narratives: Relate ideas, observations, or recollections of an event or experience.
68W–69W	Tech Manual: Creating, Saving, and Opening Documents	• **Reading Comprehension 2.7** Follow simple multiple-step written instructions (e.g., how to assemble a product or play a board game). • **Writing Strategies 1.9** Demonstrate basic keyboarding skills and familiarity with computer terminology (e.g., cursor, software, memory, disk drive, hard drive). • **Reading Comprehension 2.7** Follow multiple-step instructions in a basic technical manual (e.g., how to use computer commands or video games).
74W–75W	Writing Strategy: Revision in Action	• **Writing Strategies 1.10** Edit and revise selected drafts to improve coherence and progression by adding, deleting, consolidating, and rearranging text.
76W–77W	TechManual: How to Add and Delete Text	• **Reading Comprehension 2.7** Follow simple multiple-step written instructions (e.g., how to assemble a product or play a board game). • **Writing Strategies 1.9** Demonstrate basic keyboarding skills and familiarity with computer terminology (e.g., cursor, software, memory, disk drive, hard drive). • **Reading Comprehension 2.7** Follow multiple-step instructions in a basic technical manual (e.g., how to use computer commands or video games).
80W–81W	Writing Strategy: Edit and Proofread	• **Reading Comprehension 1.7** Use a dictionary to learn the meaning and other features of unknown words. • **Writing Strategies 1.3** Understand the structure and organization of various reference materials (e.g. dictionary, thesaurus, atlas, encyclopedia). • **Writing Strategies 1.7** Use various reference materials (e.g. dictionary, thesaurus, card catalog, encyclopedia, online information) as an aid to writing.
87W	Editing and Proofreading: Grammar Workout	• **Written and Oral English Language Conventions 1.2** Identify subjects and verbs that are in agreement and identify and use pronouns, adjectives, compound words, and articles correctly in writing and in speaking. • **Written and Oral English Language Conventions 1.4** Identify and use subjects and verbs correctly in speaking and writing simple sentences. • **Written and Oral English Language Conventions 1.3** Identify and use regular and irregular verbs, adverbs, prepositions, and coordinating conjunctions in writing and speaking.
88W	Editing and Proofreading: Spelling Workout	• **Written and Oral English Language Conventions 1.8** Spell correctly one-syllable words that have blends, contractions, compounds, orthographic patterns (e.g., qu, consonant doubling, changing the ending of a word from -y to -ies when forming the plural), and common homophones (e.g., hair-hare).
89W	Editing and Proofreading: Mechanics Workout	• **Written and Oral English Language Conventions 1.5** Punctuate dates, city and state, and titles of books correctly.

For coverage of additional standards, see the California standards maps in the Reading and Language book.

California English–Language Arts Content Standards, continued

Chapter 3 The Many Writers You Are

Project 6 Write as a Friend

98W–99W	**Friendly Letter: Prewrite**	• **Writing Strategies 1.1** Select a focus, an organizational structure, and a point of view based upon purpose, audience, length, and format requirements.
100W	**Friendly Letter: Draft**	• **Writing Applications 2.1c** Write narratives: Provide insight into why the selected incident is memorable. • **Writing Applications 2.3a** Write personal and formal letters, thank-you notes, and invitations: Show awareness of the knowledge and interests of the audience and establish a purpose and context. • **Writing Applications 2.3b** Write personal and formal letters, thank-you notes, and invitations: Include the date, proper salutation, body, closing, and signature. • **Writing Applications 2.1a** Write narratives: Relate ideas, observations, or recollections of an event or experience. • **Writing Applications 2.1d** Write narratives: Provide insight into why the selected event or experience is memorable.
101W	**TechManual: How to Change Font and Style**	• **Reading Comprehension 2.7** Follow simple multiple-step written instructions (e.g., how to assemble a product or play a board game). • **Writing Strategies 1.9** Demonstrate basic keyboarding skills and familiarity with computer terminology (e.g., cursor, software, memory, disk drive, hard drive). • **Reading Comprehension 2.7** Follow multiple-step instructions in a basic technical manual (e.g., how to use computer commands or video games).
102W–103W	**Friendly Letter: Revise**	• **Writing Strategies 1.10** Edit and revise selected drafts to improve coherence and progression by adding, deleting, consolidating, and rearranging text.
105W	**Friendly Letter: Edit and Proofread Grammar Workout**	• **Written and Oral English Language Conventions 1.2** Identify subjects and verbs that are in agreement and identify and use pronouns, adjectives, compound words, and articles correctly in writing and speaking.
106W	**Friendly Letter: Edit and Proofread Spelling Workout**	• **Written and Oral English Language Conventions 1.7** Spell correctly roots, inflections, suffixes and prefixes, and syllable constructions.
107W	**Friendly Letter: Edit and Proofread Mechanics Workout**	• **Writing Applications 2.3b** Write personal and formal letters, thank-you notes, and invitations: Include the date, proper salutation, body, closing, and signature. • **Written and Oral English Language Conventions 1.6** Use commas in dates, locations, and addresses and for items in a series.

Project 7 Write About Your Life

114W–117W	Writing Trait: Organization	• **Writing Strategies 1.4** Revise drafts to improve the coherence and logical progression of ideas by using an established rubric. • **Writing Strategies 1.10** Edit and revise selected drafts to improve coherence and progression by adding, deleting, consolidating, and rearranging text.
124W–125W	Personal Narrative: Prewrite	• **Writing Strategies 1.1** Select a focus, an organizational structure, and a point of view based upon purpose, audience, length, and format requirements.
126W–127W	Personal Narrative: Prewrite	• **Writing Strategies 1.1** Select a focus, an organizational structure, and a point of view based upon purpose, audience, length, and format requirements. • **Writing Strategies 1.3** Use traditional structures for conveying information (e.g., chronological order, cause and effect, similarity and difference, posing and answering a question).
128W–129W	Personal Narrative: Draft	• **Writing Applications 2.1c** Write narratives: Provide insight into why the selected incident is memorable. • **Writing Strategies 1.3** Use traditional structures for conveying information (e.g., chronological order, cause and effect, similarity and difference, posing and answering a question). • **Writing Applications 2.1a** Write narratives: Relate ideas, observations, or recollections of an event or experience. • **Writing Applications 2.1b** Write narratives: Provide a context to enable the reader to imagine the world of the event or experience. • **Writing Applications 2.1c** Write narratives: Use concrete sensory details. • **Writing Applications 2.1d** Write narratives: Provide insight into why the selected event or experience is memorable.
130W–131W	Personal Narrative: Revise	• **Writing Strategies 1.4** Revise drafts to improve the coherence and logical progression of ideas by using an established rubric. • **Writing Strategies 1.10** Edit and revise selected drafts to improve coherence and progression by adding, deleting, consolidating, and rearranging text.
133W	Personal Narrative: Edit and Proofread Grammar Workout	• **Written and Oral English Language Conventions 1.3** Identify and use regular and irregular verbs, adverbs, prepositions, and coordinating conjunctions in writing and speaking.
134W	Personal Narrative: Edit and Proofread Spelling Workout	• **Written and Oral English Language Conventions 1.7** Spell correctly roots, inflections, suffixes and prefixes, and syllable constructions.
135W	Personal Narrative: Edit and Proofread Mechanics Workout	• **Written and Oral English Language Conventions 1.4** Use parentheses, commas in direct quotations, and apostrophes in the possessive case of nouns and in contractions.
137W	Presentation Manual	• **Listening and Speaking 2.1a** Make brief narrative presentations: Provide a context for an incident that is the subject of the presentation. • **Listening and Speaking 2.1b** Make brief narrative presentations: Provide insight into why the selected incident is memorable. • **Listening and Speaking 2.3** Make descriptive presentations that use concrete sensory details to set forth and support unified impressions of people, places, things, or experiences. • **Listening and Speaking 2.1a** Make narrative presentations: Relate ideas, observations, or recollections about an event or experience. • **Listening and Speaking 2.1b** Make narrative presentations: Provide a context that enables the listener to imagine the circumstances of the event or experience. • **Listening and Speaking 2.1c** Make narrative presentations: Provide insight into why the selected event or experience is memorable.

For coverage of additional standards, see the California standards maps in the Reading and Language book.

Chapter 3 The Many Writers You Are, continued

Project 8 Write as a Storyteller

152W–155W	**Writing Trait: Voice and Style**	• **Writing Strategies 1.4** Revise drafts to improve the coherence and logical progression of ideas by using an established rubric. • **Writing Strategies 1.10** Edit and revise selected drafts to improve coherence and progression by adding, deleting, consolidating, and rearranging text.
156W–159W	**Writing Strategy: Use Effective Words**	• **Reading 1.5** Demonstrate knowledge of levels of specificity among grade-appropriate words and explain the importance of these relations (e.g., *dog/mammal/animal/living things*).
160W–161W	**Writing Strategy: Vary Your Sentences**	• **Written and Oral English Language Conventions 1.1** Use simple and compound sentences in writing and speaking.
162W–165W	**Writing Strategy: Combine Sentences**	• **Written and Oral English Language Conventions 1.2** Combine short, related sentences with appositives, participial phrases, adjectives, adverbs, and prepositional phrases.
166W–169W	**Rewrite a Story: Prewrite**	• **Writing Strategies 1.1** Select a focus, an organizational structure, and a point of view based upon purpose, audience, length, and format requirements.
170W–171W	**Rewrite a Story: Draft**	• **Writing Applications 2.1a** Write narratives: Provide a context within which an action takes place. • **Writing Applications 2.1b** Write narratives: Include well-chosen details to develop the plot. • **Writing Applications 2.1b** Write narratives: Provide a context to enable the reader to imagine the world of the event or experience. • **Writing Applications 2.1c** Write narratives: Use concrete sensory details.
172W–173W	**Rewrite a Story: Revise**	• **Writing Strategies 1.4** Revise drafts to improve the coherence and logical progression of ideas by using an established rubric. • **Writing Strategies 1.10** Edit and revise selected drafts to improve coherence and progression by adding, deleting, consolidating, and rearranging text.
175W	**Rewrite a Story: Edit and Proofread Grammar Workout**	• **Written and Oral English Language Conventions 1.2** Identify subjects and verbs that are in agreement and identify and use pronouns, adjectives, compound words, and articles correctly in writing and speaking. • **Written and Oral English Language Conventions 1.3** Identify and use regular and irregular verbs, adverbs, prepositions, and coordinating conjunctions in writing and speaking.
176W	**Rewrite a Story: Edit and Proofread Spelling Workout**	• **Written and Oral English Language Conventions 1.7** Spell correctly roots, inflections, suffixes and prefixes, and syllable constructions.
177W	**Rewrite a Story: Edit and Proofread Mechanics Workout**	• **Written and Oral English Language Conventions 1.4** Use parentheses, commas in direct quotations, and apostrophes in the possessive case of nouns and in contractions. • **Written and Oral English Language Conventions 1.6** Capitalize names of magazines, newspapers, works of art, musical compositions, organizations, and the first word in quotations when appropriate.
178W	**Presentation Manual**	• **Listening and Speaking 2.2** Plan and present dramatic interpretations of experiences, stories, poems, or plays with clear diction, pitch, tempo, and tone. • **Listening and Speaking 1.9** Use volume, pitch, phrasing, pace, modulation, and gestures appropriately to enhance meaning.

Project 9 Write as a Researcher

188W–191W	**Writing Trait: Focus and Unity**	• **Writing Strategies 1.4** Revise drafts to improve the coherence and logical progression of ideas by using an established rubric. • **Writing Strategies 1.10** Edit and revise selected drafts to improve coherence and progression by adding, deleting, consolidating, and rearranging text.
192W–195W	**Research Strategy: Plan Your Research**	• **Writing Strategies 1.1** Select a focus, an organizational structure, and a point of view based upon purpose, audience, length, and format requirements.
196W–197W	**Research Strategy: Locate Sources of Information**	• **Writing Strategies 1.7** Use various reference materials (e.g. dictionary, thesaurus, card catalog, encyclopedia, online information) as an aid to writing. • **Writing Applications 2.3c** Write information reports: Draw from more than one source of information (e.g. speakers, books, newspapers, other media sources).
198W–199W	**Research Strategy: Locate Sources of Information**	• **Writing Strategies 1.3** Understand the structure and organization of various reference materials (e.g. dictionary, thesaurus, atlas, encyclopedia). • **Written and Oral English Language Conventions 1.9** Arrange words in alphabetic order. • **Writing Strategies 1.7** Use various reference materials (e.g. dictionary, thesaurus, card catalog, encyclopedia, online information) as an aid to writing. • **Writing Applications 2.3c** Write information reports: Draw from more than one source of information (e.g. speakers, books, newspapers, other media sources).
200W–201W	**Research Strategy: Evaluate Sources**	• **Reading Comprehension 2.2** Use appropriate strategies when reading for different purposes (e.g. full comprehension, location of information, personal enjoyment)
202W–203W	**Research Strategy: Locate Relevant Information**	• **Reading Comprehension 2.1** Use titles, tables of contents, chapter headings, glossaries, and indexes to locate information in text. • **Reading Comprehension 2.2** Use appropriate strategies when reading for different purposes (e.g. full comprehension, location of information, personal enjoyment) • **Writing Strategies 1.3** Understand the structure and organization of various reference materials (e.g. dictionary, thesaurus, atlas, encyclopedia). • **Writing Strategies 1.6** Locate information in reference texts by using organizational features (e.g. prefaces, appendixes).
204W–207W	**Research Strategy: How to Take Notes**	• **Writing Strategies 1.5** Quote or paraphrase information sources, citing them appropriately. • **Writing Applications 2.3b** Write information reports: Include facts and details for focus.
208W–209W	**Research Strategy: How to Decide on a Central Idea**	• **Writing Applications 2.3a** Write information reports: Frame a central question about an issue or situation. • **Writing Applications 2.3c** Write information reports: Draw from more than one source of information (e.g. speakers, books, newspapers, other media sources).
210W–211W	**Research Strategy: How to Make an Outline**	• **Writing Applications 2.3b** Write information reports: Include facts and details for focus. • **Writing Applications 2.3c** Write information reports: Draw from more than one source of information (e.g. speakers, books, newspapers, other media sources).
212W–213W	**Information Report: Prewrite/Draft**	• **Writing Strategies 1.2a** Create multiple-paragraph compositions: Provide an introductory paragraph. • **Writing Strategies 1.2b** Create multiple-paragraph compositions: Establish and support a central idea with a topic sentence at or near the beginning of the first paragraph.

For coverage of additional standards, see the California standards maps in the Reading and Language book.

California English–Language Arts Content Standards, continued

Project 9 Write as a Researcher, continued

214W–215W	Information Report: Draft	• **Writing Strategies 1.2.c** Create multiple-paragraph compositions: Include supporting paragraphs with simple facts, details, and explanations. • **Writing Strategies 1.2.d** Create multiple-paragraph compositions: Conclude with a paragraph that summarizes the points. • **Writing Applications 2.3b** Write information reports: Include facts and details for focus.
216W–217W	Information Report: Draft	• **Writing Strategies 1.2c** Create multiple-paragraph compositions: Include supporting paragraphs with simple facts, details, and explanations. • **Writing Strategies 1.5** Quote or paraphrase information sources, citing them appropriately. • **Writing Strategies 1.7** Use various reference materials (e.g. dictionary, thesaurus, card catalog, encyclopedia, online information) as an aid to writing. • **Writing Applications 2.3b** Write information reports: Include facts and details for focus. • **Writing Applications 2.3c** Write information reports: Draw from more than one source of information (e.g. speakers, books, newspapers, other media sources).
218W–219W	Information Report: Revise	• **Writing Strategies 1.4** Revise drafts to improve the coherence and logical progression of ideas by using an established rubric. • **Writing Strategies 1.10** Edit and revise selected drafts to improve coherence and progression by adding, deleting, consolidating, and rearranging text.
221W	Information Report: Edit and Proofread Grammar Workout	• **Written and Oral English Language Conventions 1.3** Identify and use past, present, and future verb tenses properly in writing and speaking. • **Written and Oral English Language Conventions 1.3** Identify and use regular and irregular verbs, adverbs, prepositions, and coordinating conjunctions in writing and speaking.
222W	Information Report: Edit and Proofread Spelling Workout	• **Written and Oral English Language Conventions 1.7** Spell correctly roots, inflections, suffixes and prefixes, and syllable constructions.
223W	Information Report: Edit and Proofread Mechanics Workout	• **Written and Oral English Language Conventions 1.5** Use underlining, quotation marks, or italics to identify titles of documents. • **Written and Oral English Language Conventions 1.6** Capitalize names of magazines, newspapers, works of art, musical compositions, organizations, and the first word in quotations when appropriate.
225W	TechManual: Create a Multimedia Report	• **Writing Strategies 1.9** Demonstrate basic keyboarding skills and familiarity with computer terminology (e.g., cursor, software, memory, disk drive, hard drive).
228W–231W	Research Resources: Parts of a Book	• **Reading Comprehension 2.1** Use titles, tables of contents, chapter headings, glossaries, and indexes to locate information in text.
232W–241W	Research Resources: Types of Resource Books	• **Reading 1.7** Use a dictionary to learn the meaning and other features of unknown words • **Writing Strategies 1.3** Understand the structure and organization of various reference materials (e.g., dictionary, thesaurus, atlas, encyclopedia). • **Reading 1.5** Use a thesaurus to determine related words and concepts. • **Writing Strategies 1.7** Use various reference materials (e.g. dictionary, thesaurus, card catalog, encyclopedia, online information) as an aid to writing. • **Writing Strategies 1.8** Understand the organization of almanacs, newspapers, and periodicals and how to use those print materials.
242W–245W	Research Resources: Other Print Resources	• **Writing Strategies 1.8** Understand the organization of almanacs, newspapers, and periodicals and how to use those print materials.

Project 10 Write to Summarize

248W–249W	**Summary Paragraph: Prewrite**	
250W	**Summary Paragraph: Draft**	• **Writing Strategies 1.1a** Create a single paragraph: Develop a topic sentence. • **Writing Strategies 1.1b** Create a single paragraph: Include simple supporting facts and details. • **Writing Applications 2.4** Write summaries that contain the main idea of the reading selection and the most significant details.
251W	**Tech Manual: Formatting with Word Processors**	• **Writing Strategies 1.9** Demonstrate basic keyboarding skills and familiarity with computer terminology (e.g., cursor, software, memory, disk drive, hard drive).
252W–253W	**Summary Paragraph: Revise**	• **Writing Strategies 1.4** Revise drafts to improve the coherence and logical progression of ideas by using an established rubric. • **Writing Strategies 1.10** Edit and revise selected drafts to improve coherence and progression by adding, deleting, consolidating, and rearranging text.
255W	**Summary Paragraph: Edit and Proofread Grammar Workout**	• **Written and Oral English Language Conventions 1.2** Identify subjects and verbs that are in agreement and identify and use pronouns, adjectives, compound words, and articles correctly in writing and speaking.
256W	**Summary Paragraph: Edit and Proofread Spelling Workout**	• **Written and Oral English Language Conventions 1.7** Spell correctly roots, inflections, suffixes and prefixes, and syllable constructions.
257W	**Summary Paragraph: Edit and Proofread Mechanics Workout**	• **Written and Oral English Language Conventions 1.7** Capitalize geographical names, holidays, historical periods, and special events correctly. • **Written and Oral English Language Conventions 1.6** Capitalize names of magazines, newspapers, works of art, musical compositions, organizations, and the first word in quotations when appropriate.

For coverage of additional standards, see the California standards maps in the Reading and Language book.

Chapter 3 The Many Writers You Are, continued

Project 11 Write to Explain

270W–271W	Cause-and-Effect Essay: Prewrite	• **Writing Strategies 1.1** Select a focus, an organizational structure, and a point of view based upon purpose, audience, length, and format requirements. • **Writing Strategies 1.3** Use traditional structures for conveying information (e.g., chronological order, cause and effect, similarity and difference, posing and answering a question).
272W–273W	Cause-and-Effect Essay: Draft	• **Writing Strategies 1.3** Use traditional structures for conveying information (e.g., chronological order, cause and effect, similarity and difference, posing and answering a question). • **Writing Strategies 1.2.a** Create multiple-paragraph compositions: Provide an introductory paragraph. • **Writing Strategies 1.2.b** Create multiple-paragraph compositions: Establish and support a central idea with a topic sentence at or near the beginning of the first paragraph. • **Writing Strategies 1.2.c** Create multiple-paragraph compositions: Include supporting paragraphs with simple facts, details, and explanations. • **Writing Strategies 1.2.d** Create multiple-paragraph compositions: Conclude with a paragraph that summarizes the points.
274W–275W	Cause-and-Effect Essay: Revise	• **Writing Strategies 1.4** Revise drafts to improve the coherence and logical progression of ideas by using an established rubric. • **Writing Strategies 1.10** Edit and revise selected drafts to improve coherence and progression by adding, deleting, consolidating, and rearranging text.
277W	Cause-and-Effect Essay: Edit and Proofread Grammar Workout	• **Written and Oral English Language Conventions 1.2** Identify subjects and verbs that are in agreement and identify and use pronouns, adjectives, compound words, and articles correctly in writing and speaking.
278W	Cause-and-Effect Essay: Edit and Proofread Spelling Workout	• **Written and Oral English Language Conventions 1.7** Spell correctly roots, inflections, suffixes and prefixes, and syllable constructions.
279W	Cause-and-Effect Essay: Edit and Proofread Mechanics Workout	• **Written and Oral English Language Conventions 1.4** Use parentheses, commas in direct quotations, and apostrophes in the possessive case of nouns and in contractions.
281W	Tech Manual: How to Format your Essay	• **Reading Comprehension 2.7** Follow simple multiple-step written instructions (e.g., how to assemble a product or play a board game). • **Reading Comprehension 2.7** Follow multiple-step instructions in a basic technical manual (e.g., how to use computer commands or video games). • **Writing Strategies 1.9** Demonstrate basic keyboarding skills and familiarity with computer terminology (e.g., cursor, software, memory, disk drive, hard drive).

Project 12 Write to Describe

288W–291W	Writing Trait: Development of Ideas	• **Writing Strategies 1.4** Revise drafts to improve the coherence and logical progression of ideas by using an established rubric. • **Writing Strategies 1.10** Edit and revise selected drafts to improve coherence and progression by adding, deleting, consolidating, and rearranging text.
294W–295W	Writing Strategy: Choose an Organization	• **Writing Strategies 1.3** Use traditional structures for conveying information (e.g., chronological order, cause and effect, similarity and difference, posing and answering a question).
296W–297W	Descriptive Essay: Prewrite	• **Writing Strategies 1.1** Select a focus, an organizational structure, and a point of view based upon purpose, audience, length, and format requirements. • **Writing Strategies 1.3** Use traditional structures for conveying information (e.g., chronological order, cause and effect, similarity and difference, posing and answering a question).
298W–299W	Descriptive Essay: Draft	• **Writing Applications 2.2** Write descriptions that use concrete sensory details to present and support unified impressions of people, places, things, or experiences. • **Writing Strategies 1.3** Use traditional structures for conveying information (e.g., chronological order, cause and effect, similarity and difference, posing and answering a question). • **Writing Strategies 1.2a** Create multiple-paragraph compositions: Provide an introductory paragraph. • **Writing Strategies 1.2b** Create multiple-paragraph compositions: Establish and support a central idea with a topic sentence at or near the beginning of the first paragraph. • **Writing Strategies 1.2c** Create multiple-paragraph compositions: Include supporting paragraphs with simple facts, details, and explanations. • **Writing Strategies 1.2d** Create multiple-paragraph compositions: Conclude with a paragraph that summarizes the points.
300W–301W	Descriptive Essay: Revise	• **Writing Strategies 1.4** Revise drafts to improve the coherence and logical progression of ideas by using an established rubric. • **Writing Strategies 1.10** Edit and revise selected drafts to improve coherence and progression by adding, deleting, consolidating, and rearranging text.
303W	Descriptive Essay: Edit and Proofread Grammar Workout	• **Written and Oral English Language Conventions 1.3** Identify and use regular and irregular verbs, adverbs, prepositions, and coordinating conjunctions in writing and speaking.
304W	Descriptive Essay: Edit and Proofread Spelling Workout	• **Written and Oral English Language Conventions 1.8** Spell correctly one-syllable words that have blends, contractions, compounds, orthographic patterns (e.g., *qu*, consonant doubling, changing the ending of a word from -y to -ies when forming the plural), and common homophones (e.g., *hair-hare*).
305W	Descriptive Essay: Edit and Proofread Mechanics Workout	• **Written and Oral English Language Conventions 1.6** Use commas in dates, locations, and addresses and for items in a series. • **Written and Oral English Language Conventions 1.4** Use parentheses, commas in direct quotations, and apostrophes in the possessive case of nouns and in contractions.
307W	Tech Manual: How to Insert a Picture in a Document	• **Reading Comprehension 2.7** Follow simple multiple-step written instructions (e.g., how to assemble a product or play a board game). • **Reading Comprehension 2.7** Follow multiple-step instructions in a basic technical manual (e.g., how to use computer commands or video games). • **Writing Strategies 1.9** Demonstrate basic keyboarding skills and familiarity with computer terminology (e.g., cursor, software, memory, disk drive, hard drive).

For coverage of additional standards, see the California standards maps in the Reading and Language book.

California English–Language Arts Content Standards, continued

Project 13 Write to Persuade

310W–313W	**Persuasive Business Letter: Prewrite**	• **Writing Strategies 1.1** Select a focus, an organizational structure, and a point of view based upon purpose, audience, length, and format requirements.
314W–315W	**Persuasive Business Letter: Draft**	• **Writing Applications 2.3a** Write personal and formal letters, thank-you notes, and invitations: Show awareness of the knowledge and interests of the audience and establish a purpose and context. • **Writing Applications 2.3b** Write personal and formal letters, thank-you notes, and invitations: Include the date, proper salutation, body, closing, and signature. • **Writing Strategies 1.3** Use traditional structures for conveying information (e.g., chronological order, cause and effect, similarity and difference, posing and answering a question).
316W–317W	**Persuasive Business Letter: Revise**	• **Writing Strategies 1.4** Revise drafts to improve the coherence and logical progression of ideas by using an established rubric. • **Writing Strategies 1.10** Edit and revise selected drafts to improve coherence and progression by adding, deleting, consolidating, and rearranging text.
319W	**Persuasive Business Letter: Edit and Proofread Grammar Workout**	• **Written and Oral English Language Conventions 1.2** Identify subjects and verbs that are in agreement and identify and use pronouns, adjectives, compound words, and articles correctly in writing and speaking.
320W	**Persuasive Business Letter: Edit and Proofread Spelling Workout**	• **Written and Oral English Language Conventions 1.8** Spell correctly one-syllable words that have blends, contractions, compounds, orthographic patterns (e.g., qu, consonant doubling, changing the ending of a word from –y to –ies when forming the plural) and common homophones (e.g., hair-hare).
321W	**Persuasive Business Letter: Edit and Proofread Mechanics Workout**	• **Written and Oral English Language Conventions 1.2** Combine short, related sentences with appositives, participle phrases, adjectives, adverbs, and prepositional phrases.

Project 14 Write Social Notes

326W–327W	Invitation or Thank-You Note: Plan and Draft	• **Writing Strategies 1.1** Select a focus, an organizational structure, and a point of view based upon purpose, audience, length, and format requirements. • **Writing Applications 2.3a** Write personal and formal letters, thank-you notes, and invitations: Show awareness of the knowledge and interests of the audience and establish a purpose and context. • **Writing Applications 2.3b** Write personal and formal letters, thank-you notes, and invitations: Include the date, proper salutation, body, closing, and signature.
328W–329W	Invitation or Thank-You Note: Revise	• **Writing Strategies 1.4** Revise drafts to improve the coherence and logical progression of ideas by using an established rubric. • **Writing Strategies 1.10** Edit and revise selected drafts to improve coherence and progression by adding, deleting, consolidating, and rearranging text.
331W	Invitation or Thank-You Note: Edit and Proofread Grammar Workout	• **Written and Oral English Language Conventions 1.1** Understand and be able to use complete and correct declarative, interrogative, imperative, and exclamatory sentences in writing and speaking. • **Written and Oral English Language Conventions 1.1** Use simple and compound sentences in writing and speaking.
332W	Invitation or Thank-You Note: Edit and Proofread Spelling Workout	• **Written and Oral English Language Conventions 1.8** Spell correctly one-syllable words that have blends, contractions, compounds, orthographic patterns (e.g., *qu*, consonant doubling, changing the ending of a word from -y to -ies when forming the plural), and common homophones (e.g., *hair-hare*).
333W	Invitation or Thank-You Note: Edit and Proofread Mechanics Workout	• **Written and Oral English Language Conventions 1.5** Use underlining, quotation marks, or italics to identify titles of documents. • **Written and Oral English Language Conventions 1.6** Capitalize names of magazines, newspapers, works of art, musical compositions, organizations, and the first word in quotations when appropriate.

For coverage of additional standards, see the California standards maps in the Reading and Language book.

Chapter 3 The Many Writers You Are, continued

Project 15 Write About What You Read

344W–345W	**Literary Response: Prewrite**	• **Writing Strategies 1.1** Select a focus, an organizational structure, and a point of view based upon purpose, audience, length, and format requirements.
346W–347W	**Literary Response: Draft**	• **Writing Strategies 1.2a** Create multiple-paragraph compositions: Provide an introductory paragraph. • **Writing Strategies 1.2c** Create multiple-paragraph compositions: Include supporting paragraphs with simple facts, details, and explanations. • **Writing Strategies 1.2d** Create multiple-paragraph compositions: Conclude with a paragraph that summarizes the points. • **Writing Strategies 1.5** Quote or paraphrase information sources, citing them appropriately. • **Writing Applications 2.2a** Write responses to literature: Demonstrate an understanding of the literary work. • **Writing Applications 2.2b** Write responses to literature: Support judgments through references to both the text and prior knowledge.
348W–349W	**Literary Response: Revise**	• **Writing Strategies 1.4** Revise drafts to improve the coherence and logical progression of ideas by using an established rubric. • **Writing Strategies 1.10** Edit and revise selected drafts to improve coherence and progression by adding, deleting, consolidating, and rearranging text.
351W	**Literary Response: Edit and Proofread Grammar Workout**	• **Written and Oral English Language Conventions 1.1** Understand and be able to use complete and correct declarative, interrogative, imperative, and exclamatory sentences in writing and speaking. • **Written and Oral English Language Conventions 1.1** Use simple and compound sentences in writing and speaking.
352W	**Literary Response: Edit and Proofread Spelling Workout**	• **Written and Oral English Language Conventions 1.7** Spell correctly roots, inflections, suffixes and prefixes, and syllable constructions.
353W	**Literary Response: Edit and Proofread Mechanics Workout**	• **Written and Oral English Language Conventions 1.5** Use underlining, quotation marks, or italics to identify titles of documents. • **Written and Oral English Language Conventions 1.6** Capitalize names of magazines, newspapers, works of art, musical compositions, organizations, and the first word in quotations.
355W	**Presentation Manual**	• **Listening and Speaking Strategies 1.2** Connect and relate prior experiences, insights, and ideas to those of a speaker. • **Listening and Speaking Strategies 1.3** Respond to questions with appropriate elaboration.

For coverage of additional standards, see the California standards maps in the Reading and Language book.

I'm Many Different People
by Tony Sanchez

I can change in different situations. I speak Spanish at home with my family. I speak English at school. I am gentle with my little brother. I am more of a tough guy around my friends. I am many different people.

Student Model

The **topic sentence** states the writer's main idea.

The **details** tell more about the main idea.

Music
by Cathy Long

I like playing the violin. I want to play the piano. Maybe I want to play drums. Learning to play a new instrument takes time and practice.

Student Model

This paragraph has no topic sentence.

Playing Soccer
by Maria Mahadavi

I am a good soccer player. I practice every day. Soccer is popular in Brazil. Brazil has won five World Cups since 1930! Since I practice so much, I hope to make the school team.

Student Model

This **detail** doesn't go with the **main idea**. The main idea is about the writer, not Brazil.

State a Topic Sentence

What's It Like

Think about a tasty combination pizza with all the toppings. Yum! You may not know what all the toppings are when you hear the words "combination pizza," but you have a good sense of what to expect. A topic sentence is like the phrase "combination pizza." The topic sentence doesn't give away all of the details, but it tells readers about the main idea and helps them know what to expect.

What Is a Topic?

Before you begin writing, choose your **topic**. Your topic is what you will write about. Write your topic. Write as many details as you can about your topic. Then look to see how the details are all related. Draw lines to connect the details and the topic.

Once you see how the details fit together, write a topic **sentence**. The topic sentence is a statement that tells the main idea of the paragraph.

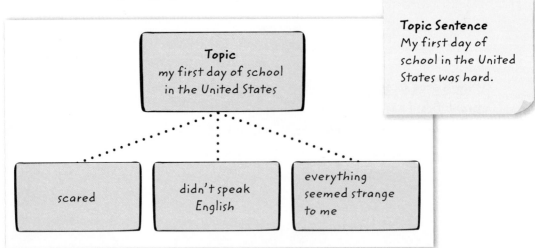

Topic
my first day of school in the United States

scared

didn't speak English

everything seemed strange to me

Topic Sentence
My first day of school in the United States was hard.

Plan for a Paragraph

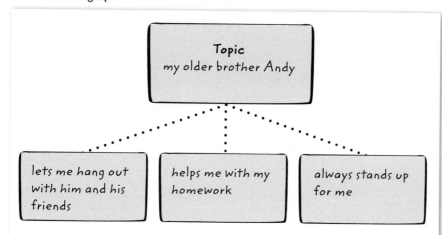

Topic
my older brother Andy

lets me hang out with him and his friends

helps me with my homework

always stands up for me

How do these details go together? How do they relate to the topic?

Plan for a Paragraph

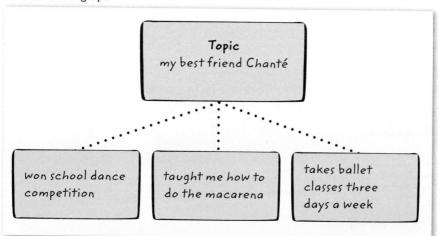

Topic
my best friend Chanté

won school dance competition

taught me how to do the macarena

takes ballet classes three days a week

What topic sentence would you write based on this plan?

Write a Paragraph

WRITING PROMPT How do you describe yourself? Maybe you love to draw and you want to be an artist someday. Perhaps you're great at taking care of younger kids. Or you might be a great athlete.

Think about how you want your classmates to think about you. Then write a paragraph that tells

- one important idea about who you are
- details that show this idea.

Plan and Write

Here are some ideas for how you can plan and then get started on your writing.

1 Choose a Topic

Decide what to emphasize. You can't tell everything about yourself, so what do you most want readers to know?

— great gamer
— good friend
— (adventurous)

2 Get Some Ideas on Paper

After you choose a topic, list related details. Your details will be examples of how you are this kind of person.

Adventurous
— try new foods
— not shy
— felt excited when we moved

3 Plan Your Paragraph

Use a graphic organizer to organize your thoughts. Write your main idea first. Then add details.

Paul's Plan for His Paragraph

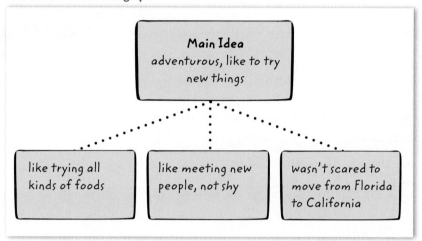

4 Write Your Topic Sentence

Think about how your details relate to one another and to the main idea. Connect the details with a single statement. That statement is your topic sentence.

I am adventurous because I like to try new things.

Paul's topic sentence connects his main idea and details.

5 Turn Your Examples into Sentences

Turn the details from your graphic organizer into sentences. Each sentence should be an example that helps to prove the main idea.

I will try any kind of food at least once.

Which section of Paul's graphic organizer does this sentence match?

Reflect

- Read your draft. Does your topic sentence clearly state your main idea?

- Does each of your details show that the main idea is true?

Revise

As you revise your work, think about your audience and your purpose for writing. Does your writing do what you want it to do? Will it connect with your audience?

1 **Evaluate Your Work**

Read your draft aloud to yourself to see what can be improved. As you read, ask yourself questions:

- **About the Topic** Does my paragraph have a clear topic sentence?

- **About the Details** Have I included enough examples to prove that my topic sentence is true?

Revision in Action

Paul's Draft

> I am adventurous because I like to try new things. I like meeting new people. I will try food at least once. I hope I get to try many new things this year.

Paul thinks:

" I don't have enough details. What examples can I add to prove my point?"

" This is not clear. I need to tell what kind of food I will try. I can add an example, too."

Maria's Draft

> You can learn a lot from reading. I am always at the library reading about different people and cultures. My brother is taking an art class, and I asked him to show me how to draw with charcoal. Also, my teacher knows French, so I asked her to teach me a few words.

Maria thinks:

" I don't have a topic sentence. It should tell my main idea—something about me!"

② Mark Your Changes

Add Text To show where you will add words or sentences, you use a mark called a **caret**. It looks like an upside-down v: ∧. Use this mark to add:

- a topic sentence that tells your main idea
- details that support your main idea
- words to make your ideas clear.

Revising Marks

MARK	∧
WHAT IT MEANS	Insert something.

Paul's Revised Draft

> I was not scared when my family moved. I was excited.
> I am adventurous because I like to try new things.∧
> new kinds of
> I like meeting new people. I will try∧food at least once.
> I even tried a kind of chicken that had chocolate in it.
> ∧I hope I get to try many new things this year.

Paul added more details to show that he is adventurous. He also added an example to make one detail clearer.

Maria's Revised Draft

> I am someone who loves to learn.
> ∧You can learn a lot from reading. I am always at the library reading about different people and cultures. My brother is taking an art class, and I asked him to show me how to draw with charcoal. Also, my teacher knows French, so I asked her to teach me a few words.

Maria added a topic sentence stating her main idea.

Edit and Proofread

Once your paragraph says what you want it to say, you need to read it carefully to catch mistakes. This is called **proofreading**. Then you **edit**. Editing is fixing the mistakes. Here are some things to look for when you edit and proofread:

- **Check the Grammar and Spelling** Make sure that you have used correct grammar and have spelled all words correctly. Use a dictionary to check your spelling.

- **Check the Mechanics** Errors in punctuation and capitalization can make your work hard to understand. In particular, check that your sentences begin with a capital letter and end with the correct punctuation mark. (See page 11W.)

- **Check Your Handwriting** If you're writing by hand, use clear, legible handwriting. (For more about good handwriting, see the Writer's File, page 470W.)

Use these marks as you edit and proofread your paragraph.

Editing and Proofreading Marks

MARK	WHAT IT MEANS	MARK	WHAT IT MEANS
∧	Insert something.	╱	Make lowercase.
∧	Add a comma.	ℛ	Delete, take something out.
∧	Add a semicolon.	⁋	Make new paragraph.
⊙	Add a period.	⬭	Spell out.
⊙	Add a colon.	⌄	Replace with this.
ⱽ ⱽ	Add quotation marks.	∼	Change order of letters or words.
ⱽ	Add an apostrophe.	#	Insert space.
≡	Capitalize.	‿	Close up, no space here.

Reflect

- What kinds of errors did you find? What can you do to keep from making them?

MechanicsWorkout

Check for Correct Sentences

- Use a capital letter at the beginning of each sentence.

    INCORRECT   their family is from Cuba.

    CORRECT   Their family is from Cuba.

- Use a period at the end of a statement or a polite command.

    EXAMPLES   Rachel enjoys riding on the train.

    David, please feed the cats.

- Use the proper punctuation mark at the end of other types of sentences.

    EXAMPLES   I love Thai food! (exclamation)

    Can we go to the mall today? (question)

    Be quiet! (command with strong feeling)

Find the Trouble Spots

I grew up speaking two languages. Ever since I was little, I could speak both English and Vietnamese. my parents are originally from Vietnam. they have lived in America for more than thirty years, but they still speak Vietnamese at home. sometimes my mother will ask me a question in Vietnamese and I will reply in English. My best friend Jennie thinks this is really cool

Find three more errors in capitalization or punctuation to fix.

"I compare and contrast all
the time during my favorite
activity—shopping!"
—Chelsea

Model Study

Comparison-Contrast Paragraphs

The way that a writer organizes a paragraph depends on what
he or she wants to say. When you write to compare or contrast
something, the topic sentence tells what you're comparing.
The details tell how things are alike or different.

Life in Japan
by Dan Naragi

Life in Japan is different from life in the United States in
many ways. Traditional Japanese food is mostly fish,
rice, and vegetables. Some traditional American foods are
hamburgers, hot dogs, and corn on the cob. School is also
very different. Japanese students often wear uniforms. Most
American students do not. The Japanese school year starts
in April. The American school year starts in September.

The **topic sentence** states the main idea.

The **details** support the main idea

COMPARISON-CONTRAST PARAGRAPH

A good comparison-contrast paragraph

✓ has a topic sentence that names two things and states
whether they are alike or different, or both

✓ contains details about the similarities and/or differences

✓ uses signal words to emphasize similarities and differences.

Feature Checklist

Some paragraphs use comparison or contrast. Some use both. To **compare** means to tell how two things are alike. To **contrast** means to tell how they are different.

Writers use **signal words** to show when they are comparing or contrasting. Signal words help the reader see that the writer is telling how things are alike or different.

Read the paragraphs below. One compares and one contrasts.

Comparison Paragraph

English and American Schools
by Karen McCarthy

The **topic sentence** names the two things being compared.

The **details** tell how the things are alike.

English and American schools are alike in many ways. English children must go to school from age five to age 16. American children must do the same. Most stay in school until age 18. English students study reading, writing, art, math, and science. American kids also learn these subjects. Both countries have public and private schools.

Signal words help to show that the two things are alike.

Contrast Paragraph

English and American Schools
by Joe Harper

The **topic sentence** names the two things being contrasted.

The **details** tell how the things are different.

School in England is different from school in the United States in some ways. Children go to primary and secondary school in England. But in the United States, they go to elementary, middle, and high school. English students take a test called the A-Levels to get into college. American students take different tests like the SAT or ACT.

Signal words help to show that the two things are different.

Signal Your Ideas

When you visit a new place, finding your way around can be tricky. A guide can tell you where to go. Signal words are like guides. They show your readers where they are heading next.

What Are Signal Words?

Signal words show the reader the connections between ideas. It's important to include signal words in your writing. Without them, your reader might get confused! Signal words also make your writing flow more smoothly.

Writers use signal words to show when two things are alike and when they are different. Here are some words you can use to signal the reader that you will compare or contrast:

Compare	Contrast
both	but
like	different
alike	differently
same	unlike
too	however
also	although
similar	while
similarly	in contrast
in the same way	on the other hand

Read the comparison-contrast paragraphs on page 15W. Which one is clear?

Chinese and American Families
by Carrie Lee

Families in China and the United States are alike in some ways and different in others. Many American households include just parents and their children. But Chinese households often include many other family members. Most Chinese families have only one child. However, American families often have two or three children. Both cultures teach respect for older people, but Chinese culture is strict about it. Families in China and the United States are similar because family members help each other.

The **signal words** show that a similarity or difference is being presented.

Chinese and American Families
by Carrie Lee

Families in China are similar to and unlike families in the United States. Families in China usually have only one child. Chinese households often include many family members. Many American households include only parents and their children. American families often have two or three children. The cultures teach respect for older people. Chinese culture is strict about it. In families in China and the United States, family members help each other.

Because this paragraph has few **signal words**, the reader must think hard and reread to try to follow the flow of ideas.

Write a Comparison-Contrast Paragraph

WRITING PROMPT Think about a place you can compare or contrast with the place where you live. Since you can't tell everything about the two places in one paragraph, choose an event or part of life in those places to focus on. Then write a paragraph that tells

- how things are alike in the two places
- how things are different.

Plan and Write

Here are some tips for planning your paragraph.

1 Organize Your Ideas

Use a **Venn diagram** like Enrique's. Choose an event or part of life to compare. Stay focused on this main idea.

Enrique's Plan for His Paragraph

Cinco de Mayo in Mexico

food, dancing, piñatas

celebrates an important victory over French forces

Both

celebrate overcoming oppression

celebrated with parades

national holidays

Fourth of July in the United States

picnics and fireworks

celebrates independence from Great Britain

Write details about differences in the two circles.

In the center, list what the two things have in common.

② Start with a Good Topic Sentence

Write a topic sentence to introduce what you are comparing. Name the two places. Signal to readers that you will tell how something in these places is similar and different.

> Although Mexico's Cinco de Mayo is like America's Independence Day in some ways, they are two very different holidays.

③ Add Supporting Details

Include details from your diagram. Show your readers how things are alike and different in the two places.

From Enrique's Draft

> Although Mexico's Cinco de Mayo is like America's Independence Day in some ways, they are two very different holidays. They are national patriotic holidays. However, Cinco de Mayo does not celebrate independence. It celebrates a famous victory over French forces.

④ Use Signal Words

Make sure you use signal words to alert the reader when things are being compared and contrasted. See the list on page 14W.

> Although Mexico's Cinco de Mayo is like America's Independence Day in some ways, they are two very different holidays.

Reflect

- How well does your topic sentence state your main idea?

- Could you use more or better signal words to show similarities and differences?

Revise

Does your writing show what you want it to show? Will it connect with your audience?

1 Evaluate Your Work

Read your draft aloud to yourself to see what can be improved. As you read, ask yourself questions:

- **About the Form** Have I included enough details so that readers can see the similarities and differences?

- **About the Organization** Did I start with a good topic sentence?

Revision in Action

Enrique's Draft

Although Mexico's Cinco de Mayo is like America's Independence Day in some ways, they are two very different holidays. They are national patriotic holidays. However, Cinco de Mayo does not celebrate independence. It celebrates a famous victory over French forces. I enjoy both holidays. It's hard to choose between fireworks and piñatas!

Enrique thinks:

" I should also use signal words to show that I am talking about differences or similarities. "

" How are the celebrations different? I need to add more details. "

2 Mark Your Changes

Add Text To help your readers understand the similarities and differences, you may need to add more details. You may also add signal words to show comparison or contrast. Use this mark: ∧.

Three friends wear ethnic costumes at a Cinco de Mayo festival in Minnesota. ▶

Reflect

- Read your paragraph. Does it include enough specific details to help readers understand?

- Where did you use signal words? How will they help readers?

Revising Marks

MARK	∧
WHAT IT MEANS	Insert something.

Revised Draft

Although Mexico's Cinco de Mayo is like America's Independence Day in some ways, they are two very different holidays. They are ∧both national patriotic holidays. However, Cinco de Mayo does not celebrate independence.∧ It celebrates a famous victory over Instead,
On Cinco de Mayo, people dance and break piñatas. On Independence
French forces.∧ enjoy both holidays. It's hard to Day, people choose between fireworks and piñatas! watch fireworks. They also have picnics.

Enrique added the signal words *both* and *instead*.

Enrique added more details about how the two holidays are different.

Edit and Proofread

Now that you're satisfied with your comparison-contrast paragraph, read your paper again to fix any language errors. This is what you do when you edit and proofread your work:

- **Check the Grammar** Make sure that your sentences are correct. Check your grammar.

- **Check the Spelling** Read your work carefully. If you need to check the spelling of a word, use a dictionary.

- **Check the Mechanics** Errors in punctuation and capitalization can make your work hard to understand. Check that your sentences begin with a capital letter. Check that all questions end with a question mark and that all statements end with a period. (See page 21W.)

Use these marks as you edit and proofread your paragraph.

Editing and Proofreading Marks

MARK	WHAT IT MEANS	MARK	WHAT IT MEANS
∧	Insert something.	╱	Make lowercase.
∧	Add a comma.	ℯ	Delete, take something out.
∧	Add a semicolon.	⁋	Make new paragraph.
⊙	Add a period.	⬭	Spell out.
⊙	Add a colon.	⌃	Replace with this.
˅ ˅	Add quotation marks.	∼	Change order of letters or words.
˅	Add an apostrophe.	#	Insert space.
≡	Capitalize.	‿	Close up, no space here.

Reflect

- What kinds of errors did you find? What can you do to keep from making them?

MechanicsWorkout

Check for Correct Sentences

- Use a capital letter at the beginning of each sentence.

  EXAMPLE   My parents speak Polish.

- Use a period at the end of a statement.

  EXAMPLE   Carmen is from Mexico.

- Use a question mark at the end of a question.

  EXAMPLE   When did you come to the United States?

Find the Trouble Spots

> How are Thai food and American food different? Many Thai dishes are hot and spicy and served over bland white rice. on the other hand, American food is not as spicy. Thai food uses a lot of herbs like basil and mint. American food does not use as many herbs. the cultures of China and India influenced what Thai food is like Americans eat foods from many cultures, like pizza, sushi, and tacos. What exactly is "American" food It is hard to say.

Find and fix three more errors in punctuation or capitalization.

Model Study

A Well-Organized Paragraph

A well-organized paragraph presents ideas in a clear, logical order. It includes a topic sentence that states the main idea. The other sentences give details or examples that relate to the main idea.

Often the topic sentence of a paragraph is a statement. Details support the statement. You can also write your topic sentence as a question. The details in your paragraph should answer the question.

Read the student models on page 23W. They show two examples of a well-organized paragraph.

A WELL-ORGANIZED PARAGRAPH

A well-organized paragraph

☑ has a topic sentence that states the main idea

☑ contains details or examples that tell more about the main idea

☑ presents all the ideas in the best order.

Feature Checklist

Paragraph

Buying Pupusas
by Ana Perón

I like to go downtown to get pupusas. They are a little bit like Mexican tamales. A man named Alejandro owns a pupusa shop in town. He knows my family and me from El Salvador. He gives us a discount whenever we buy his pupusas. I go to his shop often because his pupusas are so good! Sometimes I go three times a week!

The **topic sentence** gives the main idea.

This **detail** tells more about the main idea.

Paragraph

Making Pupusas
by Steve Sutton

How do you make pupusas? You start by mixing corn meal with water to make the dough. Then, you roll the dough into balls. To make the filling, mix a can of beans, some cheese, and spices together. Flatten the balls into discs. Put a spoonful of the bean mixture onto each disc. Wrap the dough around the mixture. Then put them in the oven and bake. Soon, you will have tasty pupusas!

This **topic sentence** presents the main idea as a question.

Each **detail** helps answer the question.

Connect Main Idea and Details

Would you want to eat spaghetti topped with tomatoes, meatballs, Parmesan cheese—and peanut butter? Of course not! That last ingredient just doesn't belong on spaghetti. Choosing details for your paragraph is like that. All of your details need to go with the main idea. Leave out details that don't belong.

What Makes a Good Paragraph?

In a good paragraph, the writer states the main idea in the topic sentence. The details tell more about the main idea.

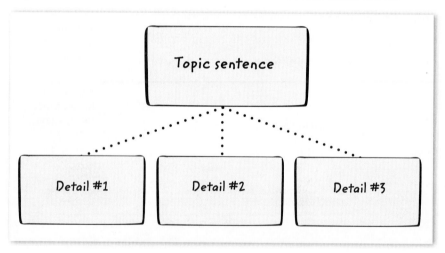

When you think of details to add, ask yourself:

- Does this detail go with the main idea?

- Where should I add this detail?

Look at the paragraph on page 25W to see how John decided which details to add and where to add them.

Where I Feel at Home
by John Nguyen

I feel at home in San Jose's Saigon Business District. I can understand people speaking Vietnamese on the street. Sometimes I stop at a street stall to get a bowl of pho, a soup that my mother also makes. I also can read the Vietnamese writing in the windows of stores.

The **topic sentence** states a strong main idea.

Hearing the language reminds me of my Aunt Linh and Uncle Tuan.

John thinks:

"I can add this detail after I talk about understanding people who speak Vietnamese."

None of my friends at school speak Vietnamese.

"I will leave out this detail. It doesn't go with my main idea."

I can find things in the shops that cannot be found anyplace else.

"I can add this detail at the end, after I talk about the shop windows."

Write a Paragraph

WRITING PROMPT What does the word *home* mean to you? For some people, home is anywhere their family and friends are.

Think about what *home* means. Then write a paragraph that tells

- what *home* means to you
- what things make home special
- what you like to do in the place you call home.

Plan and Write

Here are some ways to plan and write your paragraph.

1 **Think about the Question**

Take some time to think about what *home* means to you. Don't worry about finding the perfect idea right away. Just get your thoughts down on paper.

> What does <u>home</u> mean to me?
> —where everyone can belong
> —the place I know best
> —People there are friendly.

2 **Decide on Your Main Idea**

Your main idea sums up what home means to you.

> home = a place where everyone can belong = New York City

❸ Organize Your Main Idea and Details

Once you form a main idea, write down details that support it.

Stacy's Plan for Her Paragraph

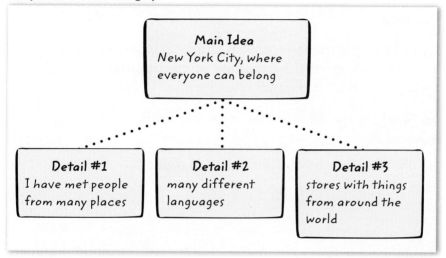

Main Idea
New York City, where everyone can belong

Detail #1
I have met people from many places

Detail #2
many different languages

Detail #3
stores with things from around the world

❹ Write Your Paragraph

Begin by turning your main idea into a topic sentence. You can write it as a statement or as a question.

New York City is like a home to the entire world.

Next, add your details in an order that makes sense. You might start with the most important detail and then add less important details.

Stacy's Draft

New York City is like a home to the entire world. I live in New York and so do people from many other countries. I have met people from China, Italy, Puerto Rico, and Ethiopia.

The **topic sentence** states Stacy's main idea.

Details support the main idea.

Reflect

• Does your topic sentence clearly state what *home* means to you?

• Did you organize details in a way that makes sense?

Revise

As you revise your work, keep in mind your audience and your purpose for writing. Does your writing do what you want it to do? What effect will it have on your audience?

1 **Evaluate Your Work**

Read your draft to a partner to see what can be improved. Ask your partner what he or she imagined when listening. Then, ask yourself and your partner questions:

- **About the Form** Do the details show what the word *home* means to me?

- **About the Organization** Are the details in an order that makes sense?

Revision in Action

Stacy's Draft

New York City is like a home to the entire world. I live in New York and so do people from many other countries. I have met people from Italy, Puerto Rico, China, and Ethiopia. You can find things from all over the world in the different shops in New York City. Sometimes I don't even recognize the vegetables at the corner store! You can take the subway to lots of different neighborhoods. I hear many different languages in New York. My friend taught me how to say "hello" in Chinese. No matter where you are from, you can make a home in New York. I feel at home there, and so do many other people.

Stacy's partner says:

" What does the subway have to do with your topic sentence?"

" You don't need to include the detail about your friend teaching you Chinese words."

2 **Mark Your Changes**

Delete Text To show where you will delete, or take out, words or sentences, you use a delete mark. A delete mark is just a line through the words, with a curlicue at the end: ⟿. You can use this mark to take out details that don't relate to your main idea.

◀ Many different people feel at home in New York City's markets.

Reflect

- Does your topic sentence state your main idea about what *home* means to you?

- Do you need to take out any details that don't belong?

Revising Marks

MARK	∧	⟿
WHAT IT MEANS	Insert something.	Take out.

Stacy's Revised Draft

New York City is like a home to the entire world. I live in New York and so do people from many other countries. I have met people from Italy, Puerto Rico, China, and Ethiopia. You can find things from all over the world in the different shops in New York City. Sometimes I don't even recognize the vegetables at the corner store! ~~You can take the subway to lots of different neighborhoods.~~ I hear many different languages in New York. ~~My friend taught me how to say "hello" in Chinese.~~ No matter where you are from, you can make a home in New York. I feel at home there, and so do many other people.

Stacy took out the details about the subway and her friend.

Edit and Proofread

Once you're satisfied with how you present your main idea and details, read your paragraph again with an eye for errors. This type of focused reading is what you do when you edit and proofread your work.

- **Check the Grammar** Read every sentence and make sure that your grammar is correct. Then read the sentences together and make sure that your grammar is consistent.

- **Check the Spelling** Read your work carefully. If you need to check the spelling of a word, use a dictionary.

- **Check the Mechanics** Errors in punctuation and capitalization can make your work hard to understand. Check that your sentences begin with a capital letter and end with the right punctuation mark. (See page 31W.)

Use these marks as you edit and proofread your paragraph.

Editing and Proofreading Marks

MARK	WHAT IT MEANS	MARK	WHAT IT MEANS
∧	Insert something.	/	Make lowercase.
∧	Add a comma.	℘	Delete, take something out.
∧	Add a semicolon.	¶	Make new paragraph.
⊙	Add a period.	◯	Spell out.
⊙	Add a colon.	⌃	Replace with this.
⌄ ⌄	Add quotation marks.	∼	Change order of letters or words.
⌄	Add an apostrophe.	#	Insert space.
≡	Capitalize.	◡	Close up, no space here.

Reflect

- What kinds of errors did you find? What can you do to keep from making them?

Mechanics Workout

Check Sentences and Paragraphs

Use a capital letter at the beginning of each sentence.

EXAMPLE   Do you speak French?

Use a punctuation mark at the end of each sentence.

- Use a period at the end of a statement or a polite command.

  EXAMPLES   Yael is from Israel.
  Tell me about life in Israel.

- Use a question mark at the end of a question.

  EXAMPLE   Where are you from?

- Use an exclamation mark at the end of a sentence that expresses a strong feeling. The sentence could be a command.

  EXAMPLES   I miss my friends back home!
  Send an e-mail right now!

Indent the beginning of each paragraph.

EXAMPLE   We are learning about India in class. More than one-sixth of the world's population lives in India.

Find the Trouble Spots

I love playing soccer. My buddies and I always played when I lived in Ghana. sometimes it got too hot to play, though. I moved to the United States last year. I didn't think anything would be the same But the kids in my neighborhood play soccer. they let me play with them.

Find and fix two more errors in capitalization or punctuation.

Model Study

Sequence Paragraph

A good paragraph includes a main idea and related details.
Sometimes the detail sentences tell about events in the order
in which they happened. This kind of paragraph is called a
sequence paragraph. The details flow in sequence, or **time order**.

Sequence paragraphs appear frequently in stories since writers
often tell the story events in the order in which they happened.

Read the model on page 33W. It shows the features of a good
sequence paragraph.

SEQUENCE PARAGRAPH

A good sequence paragraph

☑ has a topic sentence that states the main idea

☑ includes details that tell more about the main idea

☑ presents events in time order.

Feature Checklist

Riding the Waves
by Terrell Jones

Terrell tells the **main idea** in the first sentence of the paragraph.

Terrell gives **specific details** about what happened.

Chang and Kristen were on a boat crossing Lake Superior when the storm hit. The lake seemed as big as an ocean, and the kids couldn't see the other side. But they did see dark clouds coming their way. Soon there was a pounding rain, and they scrambled below deck. The winds tossed the boat on the waves, lifting it up and slamming it down. When it was over, Kristen said it was the worst twenty minutes she had ever experienced.

The events flow in **time order,** or the order in which they happened.

Student Model

Show the Sequence of Events

Waterfalls flow in one direction—down. Some paragraphs are like that, too. They have a clear direction and often present events in time order, starting with the first event and moving down to the last event.

How Can You Signal the Sequence?

"Sequence of events" means "the order in which things happened." Good writing makes it easy to follow what happened first, next, and last. You can tell what day or time of day something happened. You can also use special signal words called **time-order words** like the ones below to make your paragraph flow logically.

Time-Order Words			
after	during	next	as soon as
afterward	meanwhile	later	at last
before	finally	soon	eventually
while	immediately		

Look at the models on page 35W to see how well writers show sequence.

Teri and Rob had a surprise at the beach. They were in the water playing Marco Polo when they heard the first rumble of thunder. "Was that thunder?" Rob asked. Teri stopped and listened. Everyone else continued swimming and playing. It seemed that they hadn't heard anything. Teri thought it must have been her imagination. There was a loud crash of thunder, followed by a bolt of lightning. The lifeguard blew her whistle, and everyone got out of the water.

The story is hard to follow without time-order words.

With Time-Order Words

Teri and Rob had a surprise that afternoon at the beach. They were in the water playing Marco Polo when they heard the first rumble of thunder. "Was that thunder?" Rob asked. Teri stopped and listened. Meanwhile, everyone else continued swimming and playing. It seemed that they hadn't heard anything. Teri thought it must have been her imagination. Then there was a loud crash of thunder, followed immediately by a bolt of lightning. The lifeguard blew her whistle, and everyone got out of the water right away.

Time-order words make it easier to follow the sequence of events.

Where should the writer add more time-order words?

More thunder rumbled in the sky. Teri and Rob ran to their beach towels. Drying off, they put on their shoes. They collected their things and shoved their towels into their backpacks.

Write a Sequence Paragraph

WRITING PROMPT What kinds of stories do you like to tell your friends? Think about something that happened to you. Then write a sequence paragraph to tell what happened. Include

- a main idea about what happened
- details that tell more about the event
- time-order words that show the order of events.

Plan and Write

Here are some tips for planning and writing your sequence paragraph.

1 **Decide on the Main Event**

At the heart of every good story is an interesting event. What's the main event you want to write about? Sum it up in one sentence before you start writing.

> A kid almost drowns at the beach but gets rescued.

2 **Brainstorm and Organize Details**

You've got the idea for your paragraph. Now, list the events in order using a web like the one below.

Rafey's Web

③ Begin with the Main Idea

State the main idea of your paragraph in a topic sentence. Don't give the ending away! Tell just enough about the event to make people want to keep reading.

> Mandy and her brother Sam had an exciting day at the beach.

Rafey's topic sentence sums up the event and hooks the reader.

④ Add a Few Details

Tell your reader where and when the event takes place.

From Rafey's Draft

> Mandy and her brother Sam had an exciting day at Big Rock Beach. It was really hot that day. The cool blue water was a relief.

⑤ Tell the Events in the Order They Happened

Use your web to tell about the event from beginning to end. Use time-order words to help readers follow the story.

Rafey's Draft

> Mandy and her brother Sam had an exciting day at Big Rock Beach. It was really hot that day. The cool blue water was a welcome relief. Last year it had been cold when they went to the beach. Then Mandy noticed that Sam was out too far in the ocean. The waves were too big out there. He was starting to panic. Immediately Mandy waved her arms and called out to Uncle Ted to go get help. A woman swam out to Sam right away and soon brought him safely back to shore. Before long, Mandy and Sam were enjoying snacks from Mel's Surfside Diner and telling friends about the exciting rescue. They had two boxes of raisins and two sandwiches.

Rafey used **time order words** to make his paragraph flow smoothly.

Revise

As you consider how to revise your work, keep in mind your intended audience and your purpose for writing. Does your writing do what you want it to do? Will it connect with your audience?

1 **Evaluate Your Work**

Read your draft aloud to yourself to see what could be improved. As you read, ask yourself questions:

- **About the Form** Does my paragraph have a topic sentence?

- **About the Details** Do all of my details go with the main idea?

Revision in Action

From Rafey's Draft

Mandy and her brother Sam had an exciting day at Big Rock Beach. It was really hot that day. As they swam in the ocean, the cool blue water was a welcome relief. Last year it had been cold when they went to the beach. Then Mandy noticed that Sam was too far out in the ocean. The waves were too big out there. He was starting to panic. Immediately Mandy waved her arms and called out to Uncle Ted to go get help. A woman swam out to Sam right away and soon brought him safely back to shore. Before long, Mandy and Sam were enjoying snacks from Mel's Surfside Diner and telling friends about the exciting rescue. They had two boxes of raisins and two sandwiches.

Rafey thinks:

"The detail about last year doesn't go with my main idea. It just slows my paragraph down. I'll take it out."

"What they ate at Mel's doesn't relate to the topic. Readers don't need to know that detail. My ending will be better without that sentence."

2 Mark Your Changes

Delete Text To make your paragraph flow more smoothly, you may need to take out details that don't belong. You can use this mark: ◡◠.

Revising Marks

MARK	∧	◡◠
WHAT IT MEANS	Insert something.	Take out.

Revised Draft

Mandy and her brother Sam had an exciting day at Big Rock Beach. It was really hot that day. As they swam in the ocean, the cool blue water was a welcome relief. ~~Last year it had been cold when they went to the beach.~~ Then Mandy noticed that Sam was too far out in the ocean. The waves were too big out there. He was starting to panic. Immediately Mandy waved her arms and called out to Uncle Ted to go get help. A woman swam out to Sam right away and soon brought him safely back to shore. Before long, Mandy and Sam were enjoying snacks from Mel's Surfside Diner and telling friends about the exciting rescue. ~~They had two boxes of raisins and two sandwiches.~~

Rafey took out the detail about last year. Now the paragraph flows more smoothly.

The detail about what they ate is not important. Rafey took it out. The ending is better.

Edit and Proofread

Once you're satisfied with the content of your paragraph, read it again to fix language errors. This is what you do when you edit and proofread your work:

- **Check the Grammar** Make sure that you have used correct and conventional grammar throughout. In particular, check to see that you've used specific nouns, not general ones. (See page 41W.)

- **Check the Spelling** Spell-check can help, but it isn't always enough. For errors with plural nouns, you'll have to read your work carefully and perhaps use a dictionary to check how the plural is spelled. (See page 42W.)

- **Check the Mechanics** Errors in punctuation and capitalization can make your work hard to understand. In particular, check that you have capitalized all proper nouns. (See page 43W.)

Use these marks to edit and proofread your paragraph.

Editing and Proofreading Marks

MARK	WHAT IT MEANS	MARK	WHAT IT MEANS
∧	Insert something.	/	Make lowercase.
∧	Add a comma.	℘	Delete, take something out.
∧	Add a semicolon.	¶	Make new paragraph.
⊙	Add a period.	◯	Spell out.
⊙	Add a colon.	⌒	Replace with this.
⌄ ⌄	Add quotation marks.	∼	Change order of letters or words.
⌄	Add an apostrophe.	#	Insert space.
≡	Capitalize.	◡	Close up, no space here.

Reflect

- What kinds of errors did you find? What can you do to keep from making them?

Grammar Workout

Check for Specific Nouns

A noun names a person, place, thing, or idea. Use specific nouns instead of general ones. Specific nouns give your reader a clear picture of what you're describing.

EXAMPLES   GENERAL   A huge **bug** was crawling up my leg!

MORE SPECIFIC   A huge **spider** was crawling up my leg!

VERY SPECIFIC   A huge **tarantula** was crawling up my leg!

VAGUE   SHARP
general words   ▶ medium words   ▶ precise words

Bug   Spider   Tarantula

Find the Opportunities

I was looking forward to going to ~~the beach~~ all week. *White Sand Beach*
I was going to meet ~~my friend~~ there. The person on TV *Ernesto*
said that it would be sunny. But when I woke up that
morning, I saw rain.

Find two more general nouns to replace with specific nouns.

SpellingWorkout

Check Plural Nouns

A plural noun names more than one person, place, thing, or idea.

- To make most nouns plural, just add -s.

  EXAMPLES   book + s = books
  car + s = cars
  house + s = houses
  store + s = stores

- If the noun ends in s, z, sh, ch, or x, add -es.

  EXAMPLES   beach + es = beaches
  bus + es = buses
  flash + es = flashes
  box + es = boxes

Find the Trouble Spots

friends
I met three ~~friend~~ at one of our favorite ~~beachs~~. We
had sunglasses, a big blanketes, two bottles of water,
and some boxs of saltine crackers. It was so hot, and the
crackeres were so salty, that we drank all the water by
noon! Then we dove into the cold water and made huge
splashs.

beaches

Find and fix four
more misspelled
plural nouns.

MechanicsWorkout

Check Capitalization of Proper Nouns

Proper nouns name a specific person, place, or thing. When you use proper nouns, always capitalize them. Here are some examples:

- Capitalize people's names.

  EXAMPLES   Jane Wu   Joe   Kevin Johnson

- Capitalize the names of buildings, monuments, and streets. Also capitalize cities, states, and countries.

  EXAMPLES   Empire State Building   Washington Monument
  Magnolia Street   Los Angeles
  Illinois   Mexico

- Capitalize names from geography, such as bodies of water and natural landforms.

  EXAMPLES   Indian Ocean   Lake Huron
  Mount Shasta   Sonora Desert

Find the Trouble Spots

Last year I went to ocean city with my friend david epstein. His sisters, karen and debbie, came along too. Actually, I have been to two different cities with that name. One is in the state of maryland. The other is in new jersey, near atlantic city. I have never traveled to the pacific ocean, though.

Find six more proper names of people or places. Make sure they are capitalized.

A

Z

THE Writing Process

"Writing projects can seem overwhelming. But they're manageable if I take them step by step."

—Sylvia

Overview

Stages of the Writing Process

Plants and trees don't grow overnight. You start with a seed. You plant, feed, and water it to make it grow. Eventually, you might have to trim the plant a bit.

Writing is like that, too. You start with one little idea. If you give it time and attention and follow certain steps, it can grow into something amazing.

Writers often follow a writing process to make their writing the best it can be. The writing process usually involves five stages: prewriting, drafting, revising, editing and proofreading, and publishing.

1 **Prewrite**

When you prewrite, you get ready to write. You think about ideas and decide what you want to say. Then you make a plan—notes, an outline, or even drawings.

2 **Draft**

Then, you draft your paper. Your writing doesn't have to be perfect. You can make changes later.

3 **Revise**

Next, you revise your work. You rethink ideas, get feedback from other people, and make any big changes.

4 **Edit and Proofread**

When you edit and proofread, you work on the details. You fix mistakes in grammar, spelling, and mechanics.

5 **Publish, Share, and Reflect**

Finally, you publish and share your work. You also think back to reflect on what you have created.

Your Job as a Writer

Good writers have many trade secrets. One of them is using the writing process. Try it in this project.

Write Explanatory Paragraphs

WRITING PROMPT We are surrounded by water. We use it every day. It is used for farming, building, and many other things. Write two paragraphs to explain a topic that involves water. Each paragraph should include

- a main idea
- details that tell more about the main idea
- an organization that makes sense.

Prewrite: Collect Ideas

If you were invited to a costume party, who would you go as? Viking warrior? Pop-music diva? Popular action star? There are many choices. You would pick one and then start planning your costume. Prewriting is like that. Choose an idea and plan the best way to impress your readers.

Start Thinking

Where can you get ideas for your writing? Think about what you see, hear, and read every day. If you stay on the lookout for inspiration, you're sure to find it. Here's how you might come up with ideas about the topic of water.

Ways to Come Up with Ideas

Think about

- how water causes problems

- times during the day when you need to use water

- very large bodies of water that you've seen

- ways to save water

- different states of water (solid, liquid, gas)

- why water is important.

> **Ways to Save Water**
> 1. take shorter showers
> 2. don't water your lawn
> 3. make sure your dishwasher is full before running it
> 4. check for dripping faucets

Where to Keep Your Ideas

An "idea file" can help you keep your ideas together in one place. Any kind of container will do. Try these:

- Put your written ideas inside a cereal box or basket.

- Keep a journal of your thoughts and feelings.

- Fill a file folder with pictures, articles, and stories.

- Keep a notebook just for collecting writing ideas.

- Keep a special Writing Ideas file on your computer.

- Record your ideas with audio.

TechTIP

Many computers, cell phones, and other kinds of electronic devices include microphones. Find out how to make a recording. You can even save ideas on a voice mail system.

On-the-Go Inspiration

Sometimes you will want to write on the go. You might not have your idea collection with you. Try asking yourself questions about your topic:

- What would it be like to live underwater?

- If I could visit any body of water, what would it be?

- Why does the Nile River flow north?

- What water sports do I like?

- When was the last time I went to a lake?

- How do I waste water?

- How can I save water?

- How can I get other people to save water?

Prewrite: Collect Ideas, continued

What If Ideas Are Hard to Find?

Some things, like science or spelling, you know in your head. Other things, about people or the world, you know in your heart. That's your truth. When you need an idea to write about, look into your heart and find your truth.

Sometimes looking at a photograph can help you discover your truth. What truth would you add to this list?

<u>Truths</u>

1. Everyone needs help to learn new things.

2. Families spend time together.

3. Not everyone can get things right without some help.

4. People change as they get older.

5. There are many ways to define a family.

Something that is true for one person is not necessarily true for others. When you look at these photographs, does a different truth come to mind?

Working together is so much better than working alone.

Sometimes you just need a quiet moment to think.

Sometimes you have to look from a distance to see something clearly.

Shopping is like searching for treasure. You never know what you're going to bring home.

Prewrite: Choose Your Topic

You can use your idea collection to come up with a topic to write about. Make sure you narrow your topic.

A small, specific topic is easier to manage than a broad, general one. It is also much more interesting for readers. Look at how one writer narrowed the topic "Water."

The ocean
This topic would take pages and pages to cover. Why?

Broad

Cleaning up America's rivers
This is better, but still too broad for a couple of paragraphs. There are too many things to say.

Ways to save water
This topic is interesting. It's very specific. It would be easier to tell about ways we can save water.

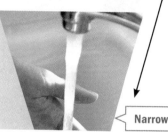

Narrow

Your Topic Is Too Broad When . . .

• you search the Internet and get thousands of hits.

• you search a library catalog and find hundreds of books.

• you have so many ideas, you don't know where to start.

Prewrite: Choose Your Audience

You have chosen a topic that interests you. Now you need to think about your audience—the people who will read your writing. The casual, informal tone you use when you e-mail your friends is different from the more formal tone you use for school papers. Knowing your audience will affect your tone.

Audience	Tone	Language
your best friend or someone your age	very informal	Hey, Karen— What's up? You going to Frank's pool party?
an older relative	somewhat informal	Hi, Dad, Will you drive me to Frank's house on Friday? He's having a pool party. Thanks.
your teacher	somewhat formal	Dear Mrs. Smith, I am sorry, but I will have to leave softball practice early on Friday. Thanks.
someone you do not know	very formal	Dear Swim-a-Lot Staff: Do you carry swimsuits in size 10? I would like to order one. Thank you.

Who is the audience for each of these e-mails?

Dear Swim-a-Lot Staff:
I am going to a pool party next weekend. I am looking for a swimsuit. Do you sell swimsuits in size 10? I can only pay $25. **I would appreciate** anything you could tell me. **Thank you for your time.**
Sincerely,

Tanika Jones

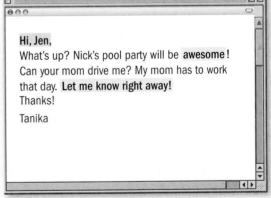

Hi, Jen,
What's up? Nick's pool party will be **awesome!** Can your mom drive me? My mom has to work that day. **Let me know right away!**
Thanks!

Tanika

The writer uses a formal greeting. The language gives the message a polite, formal tone.

The writer uses an informal, friendly greeting. Her words show strong feelings.

Prewrite: Choose Your Purpose

What do you want your audience to know or do? Maybe you're writing to make your audience think differently about your topic. Your reason for writing is your **purpose**. Choose your words to fit your purpose.

What is the writer's purpose in the e-mail below? What is the purpose in the journal entry?

E-mail

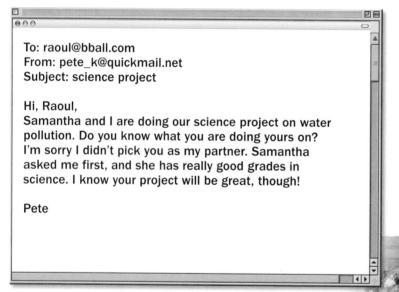

To: raoul@bball.com
From: pete_k@quickmail.net
Subject: science project

Hi, Raoul,
Samantha and I are doing our science project on water pollution. Do you know what you are doing yours on? I'm sorry I didn't pick you as my partner. Samantha asked me first, and she has really good grades in science. I know your project will be great, though!

Pete

Contaminated water pollutes rivers and streams. ▼

Journal Entry

Tuesday, 10/14
Yesterday I told Samantha I would be her partner for the science project. What a bad idea! Now Raoul is mad at me. He thought I would work with him. Raoul is my best friend, but whenever we do a project together, I end up doing most of the work.

Pete wrote the e-mail to inform Raoul why he was working with Samantha on his science project. Later, he wrote in his journal to express his feelings. What was his purpose for writing this letter to his friend Raoul?

Letter

October 16, 2008

Dear Raoul,
    Samantha and I have been talking, and we really want you to join our team. We have a lot to do on our science project and need your help! You are a great artist and could do some of the graphics. You're also really good at researching information on the Internet. What do you say? Let us know.

Are Your Audience and Purpose Connected?

Yes. Your audience and purpose are related to each other. Think about how you want your audience to react to what you say. That will help make your purpose clear.

If You Want Your Audience to...	Your Purpose Is...	For Quick Topic Ideas, List...
• learn something new • understand something better	to inform or explain	• ten things people can learn from you • ten ways to save water
• laugh • feel a deep feeling • enjoy reading your work	to entertain	• ten situations that made you laugh • ten situations in which you were scared
• believe something • do something • take action	to persuade	• five of your strongest opinions
• know how you feel • know what you think	to express yourself	• five of your favorite memories • ten ways you want to change the world

Prewrite: Choose Your Purpose, continued

You can change how and what you write to fit your purpose.
Look at the examples on these pages.

To Express

Write a journal entry to tell about your feelings.

> June 1, 2008
>
> The school picnic is coming up. The lake is really beautiful. I can't wait for everyone to get together and swim! Lucy and Carmella are excited too. We get to be in the sun and water all day!

Journal Entry

Write a note to share your feelings with a loved one.

> *Thank You*
>
> Dear Uncle Adam,
>
> Thank you for taking Carla and me out on the boat last weekend. I hope we all get to see you again soon.
>
> Love,
> Tina

Thank-You Note

To Inform or Explain

Give directions to explain how to do something.

> Directions to My Pool Party
> (from school)
> 1. Leave the parking lot. Turn right onto Hurffville Rd.
> 2. Go through two traffic lights.
> 3. Turn right onto Greentree Rd.
> 4. Turn left onto Haines Dr.
> 5. My house is number 20. It is the third on the left.

Directions

Write a paragraph to tell readers something they need to know.

> My house is at the end of the street. It's a red house with a brown roof. A brown station wagon is parked in front. There's a big empty lot next door.

Paragraph

In a newspaper editorial, give your opinion. Use words to convince people to agree with you.

Saving Water
How You Can Help

We haven't had much rain this year, so our town needs to find ways to save water. Everyone can help. For example, don't take really long showers. Don't run the dishwasher until it's full.

Editorial for School Newspaper

In an advertisement, you can convince someone to buy something.

Buy One
GET ONE FREE!

Corvey's Waterproof Mascara stays put in any weather. On sale now at selected Makeup-Mart stores.

Offer expires on August 31.

Advertisement

Write a paragraph that tells a funny story to make your readers laugh.

My tenth birthday was a big surprise. My mom got a fancy cake for the party. When she was carrying it to the table, she dropped it. The candles set fire to the edge of the tablecloth. Then, the smoke made the sprinklers go on. Everyone got wet!

Paragraph

Write a short story that's filled with suspense.

On the Boat

The bay was quiet and calm that morning. For days, Rob had been looking forward to the fishing trip with his dad. As he gazed across the water, a movement caught his eye. He looked again. "Um, Dad?" he asked. "There couldn't be any sharks out here, right?"

Short Story

Prewrite: Choose a Structure

You know your topic for your paragraphs. You have chosen an audience. You've also set a purpose for writing.

FATP Chart

Form: _explanatory paragraphs_

Audience: _classmates_

Topic: _water conservation_

Purpose: _to explain how a drought causes a lake to disappear_

Your next step is to organize your ideas. Start by choosing a good structure for your writing. To explain what happens to a lake when there is a drought, you could use time order to organize your ideas.

Process Step	What Happens
1.	An area experiences a drought when there is no rain and there are high temperatures.
2.	Water in lakes evaporates quickly due to hot, dry air.
3.	There is no rain to replace lost water.
4.	Water level gets lower and lower until the lake disappears.

Disappearing Lakes

When there is a drought, lakes can disappear completely! First, drought conditions set in: no rain and high temperatures. Then lake water begins to evaporate due to the hot, dry air. Since there is no rain to replace the lost water, lake levels get lower and lower. If the drought goes on long enough, the lake will finally disappear.

Maybe you want to compare a disappearing lake to the way it was before the drought. To organize your ideas in a compare-and-contrast structure, list qualities of the lake before the drought. Then list its qualities during the drought.

Lake Powell Reservoir	
Before the Drought	**During the Drought**
Water was 560 feet deep at the lake's deepest point.	Water is 430 feet deep at the lake's deepest point.
There were 6 marinas, or docks, on the water.	One marina has closed because it no longer reaches the water's edge.
Valleys in the canyon were buried underwater.	There is a ring along the canyon walls from low water levels.

Lake Powell: Now and Then

Lake Powell in Arizona has changed a lot since the drought. Before the drought, water was about 560 feet deep. Now the water is 430 feet deep at the lake's deepest point. There used to be six marinas around Lake Powell. Now one of them is closed because it no longer reaches the water's edge. A white ring along the canyon walls shows where the water level used to be. New valleys in the canyon are being discovered. These valleys used to be buried underwater.

Reflect

- Is your topic interesting and specific?

- Are you clear about why you are writing and to whom?

- What structure will you use? Does it suit your purpose?

Draft

Remember the first time you dove off a diving board into a pool? You were probably pretty scared, and you knew it wasn't going to be perfect on your first try. But you did it anyway. Drafting is like that. Your ideas aren't going to come out perfectly the first time you write them down, but you have to take that first scary jump to get the process started.

Taking the Leap

Here are some tips for how to take the leap into drafting:

- Collect your tools, including a pen or pencil, paper, and notes. Schedule time to use a computer if you need to.

- Find a good place to write. You don't have to be at a desk, but make sure that you are free from distractions.

- Start writing! Remember, your first draft isn't going to be perfect. Just get your ideas onto paper.

Look at Brodie's draft on page 61W. What makes it a good start? What should he work on next?

Lake Powell is located on the Utah-Arizona border. ▼

Saving a Disappearing Lake

by Brodie Williams

> Brodie wrote without worrying about little mistakes. Now he has a draft to work with.

Lake Powell is a reservoir. More than 20 million people depend on the water from Lake Powell! Millions more enjoy it's beauty every year. It is the second-largest reservoir in the country. But lately, the lake has been disappearing. A drout began in 1999. Since then, water levels in the lake have been dropping. Some people think the rest of Lake Powell should be drained.

The people in the three States who depend on lake Powell can help conserve water during the drought. The millions who visit glen canyon national recreation area every year should also help. After all, these familys enjoys the beauty of Lake Powell and should want to help. People can conserve water in many wayes. For example, each person can take a shorter shower. People can also turns the water off while brushing their teeth. Most people brush their teeth twice a day. Using water when it is needed will help conserve it. For example, people could stop washing their cars until things gets better. They could water their lawns on fewer dayes each month.

Drafting Checklist

In a good draft:

☑ the title shows the main idea.

☑ the writing has a clear beginning, middle, and ending.

☑ the message is clear, and the writing sticks to the topic.

☑ you quickly get down your ideas without worrying about spelling or grammar mistakes.

Tech*TIP*

On a draft written on a computer:

• Red squiggles show spelling mistakes.

• Green squiggles show grammar mistakes.

Draft, continued

No two people create a first draft in exactly the same way, and that's OK! What's important is that you get a good start. You can worry about improving your paper later. On the next few pages are some frequently asked questions and answers about drafting. Which of these ideas might help you?

Getting Started

Q: What do I need to get started?

A: After you find a comfortable place, you'll need paper and something to write with or a computer. You should also have your notes and graphic organizers close by. These materials will help you stay on track and give you ideas when you get stuck.

Q: What's the right way to start a draft?

A: Writers are like snowflakes. No two are exactly alike. While there's no single "right" way to start, here are a few possibilities:

- Jot down all of your ideas without stopping.

- Use your notes or graphic organizer to build your draft sentence by sentence. Spend more time on the topic sentence of each paragraph. That gives you a clear direction for what to write next.

- Work out of order if you need to. If you're not sure how to finish a paragraph, move on and come back to it later.

  Do whatever works best for you! The important thing is to just write.

How Do You Start Writing a Draft?

" I take five or ten minutes to write down anything about my topic, even if it sounds silly. Freewriting really helps me get my ideas out. "

—Karen

" I use pictures I've drawn of something that has to do with my topic. When I describe or explain something, my pictures help me visualize what I want to say. "

—Matthew

" I've usually talked to my friends about my paper first. Sometimes we talk in person and sometimes we instant-message our ideas. This really helps me figure out what I'm going to say when drafting. "

—Gilberto

" I look at lists or webs that I've made that relate to my topic. This gives me a lot of ideas to start with. "

—Sylvia

Draft, continued

Staying on Track

Q: Sometimes while I'm writing, I lose my train of thought. How can I stay on track?

A: Keep your notes and graphic organizers in front of you to remind you of your plan for your paper.

Another idea is to work with a writing partner—someone you trust. You can ask your partner to read your work and give you feedback.

Another trick is to write the most important parts down first. Write the main points without any details. See how this writer developed her main points with details in her first paragraph.

Alicia's Plan for Writing

| My brother and I went whitewater rafting. | → | The river was high and flowing fast. | → | We got turned over on a big rapid. | → | We grabbed the rocks and hung on. | → | Another raft came and rescued us. |

From Alicia's Draft

> When my brother and I decided to go whitewater rafting, we didn't expect to see the river so high or moving so fast! It had been raining a lot lately, and all that extra water had flowed down into the river. It looked scary!

Whitewater rafting can be dangerous.

How Do You Stay on Track?

" I need quiet when I write. I turn off my phone and the radio so that I won't be distracted. This helps me focus. "

—Fatima

" I write for five or ten minutes and then read what I've written. If I like it, I write for ten more minutes. If not, I take a short break. Then I decide how I want to fix it. "

—Mark

" Sometimes it helps to take a short break when I am having a hard time writing. The break helps me go back to my writing with fresh ideas. "

—Melanie

" After every couple of paragraphs, I like to read my writing to a friend. It helps to hear it out loud, and if the listener has any questions or gets confused, I know I'll hear about it! "

—Dean

Draft, continued

Knowing When You're Done

Q: How do I know when I'm finished with the draft and ready to begin the next step?

A: You are finished when all of your ideas are down on paper (or on your computer). Ask yourself:

- Does my writing say what I want it to say?

- Do I need to add anything? Do I need to get rid of anything?

- Does my paper come to a natural end, or does it seem like it ends all of a sudden? Will my reader be left with any unanswered questions?

The Truth About Drafting

FICTION: **You should always write your entire draft all at once.**
FACT: You might do that, but it's OK to take a break if you need to.

FICTION: **You should always use a pencil and lined notebook paper for drafting.**
FACT: Writers can draft using anything they want. You might use a pen and blank paper or type on a computer. Just be sure to follow your teacher's directions for writing your draft.

FICTION: **You should never, ever start a draft without doing some kind of prewriting first.**
FACT: Usually, it helps to do some prewriting to think of ideas and get them organized. But if you're feeling inspired, you can just write a draft. Then you can use that draft to plan a more polished piece.

FICTION: **As you write a draft, you have to stick to your original plan.**
FACT: Following your plan helps you stay on track. But as you write, new ideas might pop into your head. Don't be afraid to add them in. Be flexible, and change your plan if you need to.

What's One Truth About Drafting?

"You don't have to fill up the page. You just have to express your ideas well enough for your reader to understand."

—Greg

"Ideas can happen anywhere. You can be singing in the shower or eating ice cream when you think of a great idea. Just remember to write it down later!"

—Monica

"You *can* change your plan while you're drafting. I, for one, change my mind a lot while I'm drafting."

—Sam

"You don't have to use regular notebook paper for drafting. Some writers use journals that are pink with flower-scented paper, or type on their laptops. It doesn't matter how or where you write, just that you do!"

—Angela

Reflect

- What helps you get started with writing?

- What do you do when you get stuck with writing?

How to Create, Save, and Open Documents

To write using a computer, you will need to know how to create new documents, save documents, and open documents.

To create a new document

When you want to create a new piece of writing:

1. Open your word-processing program.

2. Click on the **File** menu.

3. Click on **New**.

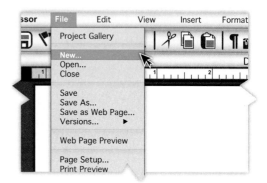

To save a document

When you are done writing and you are ready to save your work:

1. Click on the **File** menu.

2. Click on **Save As**.

3. A box labeled **File Name** will appear. In it, type a name for your document.

4. Click **Save**.

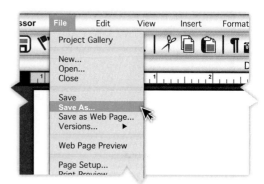

To open a document

When you want to open a document that you have already saved:

1. Click on the **File** menu.

2. Click **Open**.

3. Find the title of the document that you want.

4. Click on the title.

5. Click **Open**.

Revise: Gather Ideas

You've been looking forward to it for weeks—a perfect day at the beach. To make sure it turns out great, you check to be sure everything is ready: *Should we pack a lunch? Did we remember to bring sunscreen? Let's check the weather forecast so we don't get caught in the rain!* You also check up on things when you revise your writing. You ask for advice and you rethink your plans if you need to.

What Is Revising?

When you revise your draft, you improve your writing. Here are a few ways you might do that:

- make your main idea clearer

- add interesting details to support your main points

- add signal words to make your ideas flow better

- take out information that you don't really need.

Feedback from readers or listeners can help you improve your draft. Collect feedback from people you trust—a parent, teacher, or good friend.

Lake Powell is the second largest man-made lake in the U.S. ▶

How to Evaluate Your Work

How do you know what's good about your draft and what needs to be fixed? Try it out on some listeners. Reading your draft aloud will help you hear the strong and weak points. Plus, your listeners can give you great ideas to improve your draft. Try these techniques.

1 Read Your Paper Aloud to Yourself

The most important listener you can have is you. As you read your paper aloud to yourself, listen. Do you hear anything confusing? Do you have any questions about the information? Can you think of ways to make things sound better?

Saving a Disappearing Lake
by Brodie Williams

Lake Powell is a reservoir. More than 20 million people depend on the water from Lake Powell! Millions more enjoy it's beauty every year. It is the second-largest reservoir in the country. But lately, the lake has been disappearing. A drout began in 1999. Since then, water levels in the lake have been dropping. Some people think the rest of Lake Powell should be drained.

Brodie thinks:

" I should explain where Lake Powell is and who it affects."

" This is not related to my main idea. I should take it out."

Revise: Gather Ideas, continued

2 **Read Your Paper Aloud to a Partner**

Work with a partner in your class to get feedback. After you read, ask your partner to sketch what you wrote about. If your partner can "see" your ideas, you'll know that your writing is clear and easy to follow.

Next, ask your partner to write down three questions about your paper. This will help you find places to revise.

1. Where is Lake Powell?

2. How is this affecting people?

3. What can people do to help?

Brodie thinks:

" I need to explain what this means to people who live there."

> Lake Powell is a reservoir. More than 20 million people depend on the water from Lake Powell! Millions more enjoy it's beauty every year. It is the second-largest reservoir in the country. But lately, the lake has been disappearing. A drout began in 1999. Since then, water levels in the lake have been dropping. Some people think the rest of Lake Powell should be drained.

3 **Read Your Paper Aloud to Different People**

Share your work with at least one adult and one friend or classmate. Use some of these questions to ask your listeners for feedback.

Questions to Ask for Feedback

1. What part do you remember best?
2. Which part could you see most clearly?
3. What part is hard to picture or to understand?
4. What part confused or surprised you?

5. Which part was the most interesting?
6. What questions do you have about my paper?
7. Are there any parts that don't "flow" well?
8. Does this remind you of anything that you are familiar with? What?

④ Get a Reader

Let others read your draft. You can get great feedback from readers, too.

- Have family members and friends read your draft. What did they like most? What do they want to know more about?

- Post your writing on your school's Web site or your blog. Ask for comments.

- Share your draft during a peer conference. As you hear ideas, take notes. You might not do everything your reader suggested. That's OK, but think about *why* your reader suggested the change.

How to Have a Peer Conference

GETTING FEEDBACK	GIVING FEEDBACK
• Don't explain your paper before you begin. Let it speak for itself.	• As you read, look for the main idea. Do all details relate to that main idea?
• Ask for your reader's overall opinion. What were the strongest and weakest points? Were any parts confusing?	• Give your overall opinion. Did you understand every part? Which parts did you like the most or least? Why?
• Ask for specific suggestions. What does your reader want to know more about? Which parts can be cut?	• Give specific suggestions for improvement. Which parts need more detail? Which can be cut?
	• Be polite but honest. Help your partner improve the work.
	• Don't focus just on problems.

Revision in Action

As you decide how to improve your paper, don't lose track of your audience and your original purpose for writing.

1 **Evaluate Your Work**

Let several classmates read your draft. Then gather their ideas for what needs improvement. Be sure you ask these questions:

- **About the Form** Are the ideas presented in the best way to match my purpose? Can you identify the main idea and details of each paragraph?

- **About the Organization** Can you easily follow the flow of ideas?

> ## *Revision in Action*
>
> **From Brodie's Draft**
>
> The people living in three States who depend on lake Powell can help conserve water during the drought. The millions who visit glen canyon national recreation area every year should also help. People can conserve water in many ways. For example, each and every person can take a shorter shower and spend less time with the water on. People can also turn the water off while brushing their teeth. Using water when it is needed will help conserve it. For example, people could stop washing their cars until things get better. They could water their lawns on fewer days each month.
>
> **Brodie thinks:**
>
> " Some of these phrases say the same thing. I can get rid of them."
>
> " This sentence is not clear. I need to add something here."
>
> " I need a better ending. I should add a sentence."

❷ Mark Your Changes

Add Text Adding information can help your readers better understand your topic. For example, you might add:

- transition words or other words that improve flow and meaning
- sentences that give more details.

Delete Text Your readers can also be confused if you give too much information. That's right—if you have included details that don't support the main idea, your readers might think, "Huh?" Take that extra information out!

Brodie used these marks to make changes on his draft.

Reflect

- What additional information could help your readers understand your ideas better?

- Are there any details you should delete?

Revising Marks

MARK	∧	⤶
WHAT IT MEANS	Insert something.	Take out.

Revised Draft

The people living in three States who depend on lake Powell can help conserve water during the drought. The millions who visit glen canyon national recreation area every year should also help. People can conserve water in many ways. For example, each ~~and every~~ person can take a shorter shower ~~and spend less time with the water off~~. People can also turn the water off while brushing their teeth. Using water only when it is needed will help conserve it. For example, people could stop washing their cars until things gets better. They could water their lawns on fewer days each month. All of these small changes would help save water.

Brodie took out extra words and added an important word.

Brodie added a sentence to improve his ending.

How to Add and Delete Text

Revising your work involves adding and deleting text. Here's how to use a computer to make these changes:

To add text

When you want to add, or insert, characters, words, or spaces:

1. Put your cursor where you want to insert something.

2. Click the mouse once. The cursor will start to flash.

3. Type what you want to add.

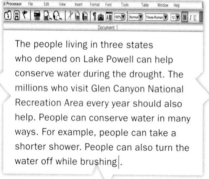

The people living in three states who depend on Lake Powell can help conserve water during the drought. The millions who visit Glen Canyon National Recreation Area every year should also help. People can conserve water in many ways. For example, people can take a shorter shower. People can also turn the water off while brushing|.

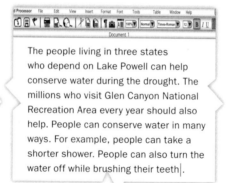

The people living in three states who depend on Lake Powell can help conserve water during the drought. The millions who visit Glen Canyon National Recreation Area every year should also help. People can conserve water in many ways. For example, people can take a shorter shower. People can also turn the water off while brushing their teeth|.

To delete text

To delete, or take out, a character or a space between characters:

1. Place your cursor just after the character or space.

2. Press the **Delete** key. The cursor will move backward and "erase" whatever was before it.

To delete a whole word:

1. Place your cursor anywhere on the word.

2. Click the mouse twice to highlight the word.

3. Press the **Delete** key. This erases the whole word.

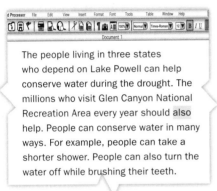
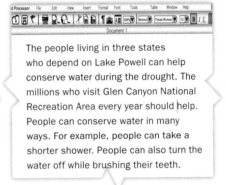

To delete more than one word:

1. Click and drag to highlight the words you want to delete.
   To do this, click on the mouse and hold it down as you
   slide it over the words.

2. Press the **Delete** key. This will erase everything you highlighted.

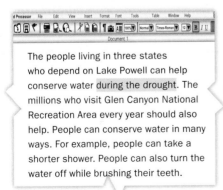
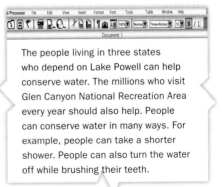

Edit and Proofread

When you swim in a pool, the water is clean because it's been filtered. Pool water is filtered to keep out bugs, leaves, twigs, and other things that you don't want to see while you're swimming. Editing is like putting your writing through a filter. You make sure it's free of mistakes that might distract the reader.

Make Your Paper Ready for Your Readers

You've worked hard writing and revising your draft. Now is the time to edit it carefully to make sure your writing is the best it can be.

- Look for errors in grammar, spelling, and mechanics as you read your writing carefully to yourself. Or, listen carefully as you read it aloud to a partner or a group.

- If something looks or sounds wrong, but you're not sure, check it out. Get help from a dictionary or your teacher.

- Fix any errors on your draft. Then, make a clean copy of your writing.

Look at the edited paragraph below. What types of changes is the writer making?

Edited Draft

Saving a Disappearing Lake
by Brodie Williams

Lake Powell is a reservoir that supplies water to Nevada, Arizona, and California. More than 20 million people depend on the water from Lake Powell! Millions more enjoy it's beauty every year. It is the second-largest reservoir in the country. But lately, the lake has been disappearing. A drout began in 1999. Since then, water levels in the lake have been dropping.

Editing and Proofreading Marks

MARK	WHAT IT MEANS	MARK	WHAT IT MEANS
∧	Insert something.	/	Make lowercase.
∧	Add a comma.	℘	Delete, take something out.
∧	Add a semicolon.	¶	Make new paragraph.
⊙	Add a period.	◯	Spell out.
⊙	Add a colon.	∧	Replace with this.
∨ ∨	Add quotation marks.	∼	Change order of letters or words.
∨	Add an apostrophe.	#	Insert space.
≡	Capitalize.	◡	Close up, no space here.

Lake Powell near Page, Arizona

Edit and Proofread, continued

Tools: The Dictionary

Editing and proofreading are like everything else—they're a lot easier to do if you have the right tools. The dictionary is a basic tool. It can help you check the spelling of a word, of course. But it can also tell you how to use words correctly—and much more!

Pronunciation: how to say the word

Part of speech

Origin: where the word comes from

Guide words: first and last entries on the page

Synonyms: words with a similar meaning

Different forms of the word

Pronunciation key: helps you say the word

farrier • fastball

far·ri·er \'far-ē-ər\ n : a blacksmith who shoes horses [Medieval French *ferrour*, derived from Latin *ferrum* iron]

¹**far·row** \'far-ō\ vb : to give birth to pigs [Middle English *farwen*, derived from Old English *fearh* "young pig"]

²**farrow** n : a litter of pigs

far·see·ing \'fär-'sē-ing\ adj : FARSIGHTED 1

Far·si \'fär-sē\ n : PERSIAN 2b

far·sight·ed \-'sīt-əd\ adj **1 a** : seeing or able to see to a great distance **b** : able to judge how something will work out in the future **2** : affected with hyperopia — **far·sight·ed·ly** adv — **far·sight·ed·ness** n

¹**far·ther** \'fär-thər\ adv **1** : at or to a greater distance or more advanced point **2** : more completely [Middle English *ferther*, alteration of *further*]

usage Farther and *further* have been used more or less interchangeably throughout most of their history, but currently they are showing signs of going in different directions. As adverbs, they continue to be used interchangeably whenever distance in space or time is involved, or when the distance is metaphorical. But when there is no notion of distance, *further* is used ⟨our techniques can be *further* refined⟩. *Further* is also used as a sentence modifier ⟨*further*, the new students were highly motivated⟩, but *farther* is not. A difference is also appearing in their adjective use. *Farther* is taking over the meaning of distance ⟨the *farther* shore⟩ and *further* the meaning of addition ⟨needs no *further* improvement⟩.

²**farther** adj **1** : more distant : REMOTER **2** : ³FURTHER 2, ADDITIONAL

far·ther·most \-,mōst\ adj : most distant : FARTHEST

¹**far·thest** \'fär-thəst\ adj : most distant in space or time

²**farthest** adv **1** : to or at the greatest distance in space or time : REMOTEST **2** : to the most advanced point **3** : by the greatest degree or extent : MOST

far·thing \'fär-thing\ n : a former British monetary unit equal to ¼ of a penny; *also* : a coin representing this unit [Old English *feorthung*]

far·thin·gale \'fär-thən-,gāl, -thing-\ n : a support (as of hoops) worn especially in the 16th century to swell out a skirt [Middle French *verdugale*, from Spanish *verdugado*, from *verdugo*

Word History The English words *fascism* and *fascist* are borrowings from Italian *fascismo* and *fascista*, derivatives of *fascio* (plural *fasci*), "bundle, fasces, group." *Fascista* was first used in 1914 to refer to members of a *fascio*, or political group. In 1919 *fascista* was applied to the black-shirted members of Benito Mussolini's organization, the *Fasci di combattimento* ("combat groups"), who seized power in Italy in 1922. Playing on the word *fascista*, Mussolini's party adopted the fasces, a bundle of rods with an ax among them, as a symbol of the Italian people united and obedient to the single authority of the state. The English word *fascist* was first used for members of Mussolini's *fascisti*, but it has since been generalized to those of similar beliefs.

Fa·sci·sta \fä-'shē-stä\ n, pl -**sti** \-stē\ : a member of the Italian Fascist movement [Italian]

¹**fash·ion** \'fash-ən\ n **1** : the make or form of something **2** : MANNER, WAY ⟨behaving in a strange *fashion*⟩ **3 a** : a prevailing custom, usage, or style **b** : the prevailing style (as in dress) during a particular time or among a particular group ⟨*fashions* in women's hats⟩ [Medieval French *façun, fauschoun*, "shape, manner," from Latin *factio* "act of making, faction"] — **after a fashion** : in a rough or approximate way ⟨did the job *after a fashion*⟩

synonyms FASHION, STYLE, MODE, VOGUE mean the usage accepted by those who want to be up-to-date. FASHION may apply to any way of dressing, behaving, writing, or performing that is favored at any one time or place ⟨the current *fashion*⟩. STYLE often implies the fashion approved by the wealthy or socially prominent ⟨a superstar used to traveling in *style*⟩. MODE suggests the fashion among those anxious to appear elegant and sophisticated ⟨muscled bodies are the *mode* at this resort⟩. VOGUE applies to a temporary widespread style ⟨long skirts are back in *vogue*⟩.

²**fashion** vt **fash·ioned; fash·ion·ing** \'fash-ning, -ə-ning\ : to give shape or form to : MOLD, CONSTRUCT — **fash·ion·er** \'fash-nər, -ə-nər\ n

fash·ion·able \'fash-nə-bəl, -ə-nə-\ adj **1** : following the fashion or established style : STYLISH ⟨*fashionable* clothes⟩ **2** : of or relating to the world of fashion : popular among those who

fas·cism \'fash-,iz-əm\ n, often cap : a political philosophy, movement, or regime that promotes nation and often race above individual worth and that supports a centralized autocratic government headed by a dictator, severe economic and social regimentation, and forcible suppression of opposition [Italian *fascismo*, from *fascio* "bundle, fasces, group," from Latin *fascis* "bundle" and *fasces* "fasces"] — **fas·cist** \'fash-əst\ n or adj, often cap — **fas·cis·tic** \fa-'shis-tik\ adj, often cap

curving downward slope to the rear; *also* : an automobile with such a roof

fast·ball n : a baseball pitch thrown at full speed

\ə\ abut	\aů\ out	\i\ tip	\ó\ saw	\ů\ foot
\ər\ further	\ch\ chin	\ī\ life	\ói\ coin	\y\ yet
\a\ mat	\e\ pet	\j\ job	\th\ thin	\yü\ few
\ā\ take	\ē\ easy	\ng\ sing	\t͟h\ this	\yů\ cure
\ä\ cot, cart	\g\ go	\ō\ bone	\ü\ food	\zh\ vision

Tools: Spell-Check

Most computers have a spell-check feature. This feature checks your words against the words it is programmed to recognize. Then it points out misspelled words and suggests other spellings.

When the program makes suggestions, choose the one that best fits your meaning.

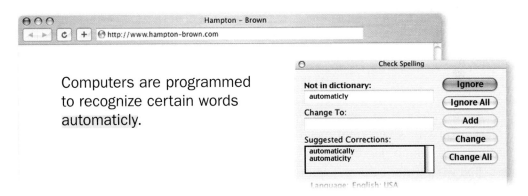

Spell-check programs may miss some mistakes. That's because the program cannot understand the meanings of the words. If you spell a word correctly but use it the wrong way, a spell-check program will not catch the mistake.

Even if you use a spell-check program, you should still proofread your paper carefully.

Edit and Proofread, continued

Tools: Your Own Checklist

The English language can be tricky! It might seem like there are a million mistakes you can make. Actually, most people make the same few mistakes over and over.

Look at other papers you have written. What errors are marked most often? Talk with your teacher if you're not sure.

What kinds of errors does Noah repeat in these papers?

Noah Rich
Grade 6
1/4/08

Down the Rapids

Have you ever seen water move so fast it looks white? I haven't just seen it, I've ridden it. steering a boat in white water is called whitewater rafting. I went whitewater rafting on the merrimac river with my family. I was scared at first. sometimes, it was just a peaceful trip down the river. But when we got to the rapids, it got a lot more exciting. "Rapid" means "fast," and that's how the water water moves there. we had to steer through the rapids. It was quite a ride. When we got out of the raft, I asked if we could come back soon.

Whitewater rafters wear protective clothing.

Noah Rich
Grade 6
3/31/08

The Worst Rain I Ever Saw

Rain isn't scary most of the time. But one time, riding in the car on pinetree road, I saw more rain than ever before. it just drizzled at first. Soon there was so much rain we couldn't see. I felt like I was in a car wash! My dad was driving. he said it wasn't safe. We had to stop and wait until the rain wasn't so heavy. Then we kept kept going. Most rain isn't that scary. But it's not that interesting, either. I'm glad I have a good story to tell. I'm also glad we got home safely.

You can use your past work to help you create a checklist for editing. List the mistakes you make the most, and watch out for those errors. Keep changing your list over time. Take off mistakes that you learn to avoid, and add new things to look for.

Noah Rich's Editing Checklist (4/1/08)

☑ **Remember to capitalize**
  - **the first word of a sentence**
  - **proper nouns**

☑ **Punctuation**
  - **End every sentence with a period, question mark, or exclamation mark.**

☑ **Extra words**
  - **Make sure I don't type a word twice when I'm writing fast.**

Edit and Proofread, continued

How to Catch and Correct Your Mistakes

When you proofread, it can be hard to find your mistakes. Errors in grammar, spelling, and mechanics are small details. They are easy to miss. Here are some tips to help you find your mistakes.

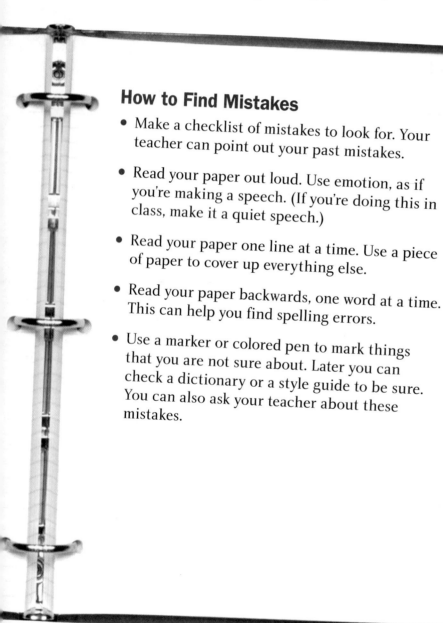

How to Find Mistakes

- Make a checklist of mistakes to look for. Your teacher can point out your past mistakes.

- Read your paper out loud. Use emotion, as if you're making a speech. (If you're doing this in class, make it a quiet speech.)

- Read your paper one line at a time. Use a piece of paper to cover up everything else.

- Read your paper backwards, one word at a time. This can help you find spelling errors.

- Use a marker or colored pen to mark things that you are not sure about. Later you can check a dictionary or a style guide to be sure. You can also ask your teacher about these mistakes.

Use Proofreading Marks

This paper is edited using some common proofreading marks. Look at the model to see how these marks are used.

How I Learned to Proofread

I used to think that editing a paper just meant using spell-check. I would run the program and make all the changes the computer suggested. Now I ^know no better. A computer will not find words that ^are our spelled right but used incorrectly. In ≡english class my teacher taught us how to use proofreader's marks. You use these marks ^to correct mistakes like words that need to be capitalized or made /Lowercase.

If you type a word twice, use the delete mark to remove the extra ~~extra~~ word. You can use a similar mark to cross out words or phrases.

Finally, know what marks to use to move letters or words that are in the (order wrong). Practice your proofreading skills, and soon your writing will be letter-perfect!

Editing and Proofreading Marks

MARK	WHAT IT MEANS	MARK	WHAT IT MEANS
∧	Insert something.	/	Make lowercase.
⩲	Add a comma.	ℰ	Delete, take something out.
⌃;	Add a semicolon.	¶	Make new paragraph.
⊙	Add a period.	⬭	Spell out.
⊙	Add a colon.	∧	Replace with this.
ⱽ ⱽ	Add quotation marks.	~	Change order of letters or words.
ⱽ	Add an apostrophe.	#	Insert space.
≡	Capitalize.	‿	Close up, no space here.

Editing and Proofreading in Action

Once you're satisfied with the content of your paragraphs, read your draft again to fix language errors. This is what you do when you edit and proofread your work:

- **Check the Grammar** Make sure that you have used correct and conventional grammar throughout. In particular, check to see that each action verb agrees with its subject. (See page 87W.)

- **Check the Spelling** Spell-check can help, but it isn't always enough. For errors with plural nouns, you'll have to read your work carefully and perhaps use a dictionary to check how the plural is spelled. (See page 88W.)

- **Check the Mechanics** Errors in punctuation and capitalization can make your work hard to understand. In particular, check that you have capitalized place names and used correct abbreviations when needed. (See page 89W.)

Use these marks to edit and proofread your paragraphs.

Editing and Proofreading Marks

MARK	WHAT IT MEANS	MARK	WHAT IT MEANS
∧	Insert something.	／	Make lowercase.
∧	Add a comma.	ℯ	Delete, take something out.
∧	Add a semicolon.	¶	Make new paragraph.
⊙	Add a period.	◯	Spell out.
⊙	Add a colon.	⌒	Replace with this.
ᵛ ᵛ	Add quotation marks.	∼	Change order of letters or words.
ᵛ	Add an apostrophe.	#	Insert space.
≡	Capitalize.	◡	Close up, no space here.

Reflect

- What kinds of errors did you find? What can you do to keep from making them?

Grammar Workout

Check Subject-Verb Agreement

When you write about what someone or something does, you use action verbs. Each action verb must agree with its subject.

- Add **-s** to the end of an action verb that tells what one other person or thing does.

  EXAMPLES The canoe slips quietly through the water.
  A child waves to us from the shore.

- Do not add **-s** to an action verb when the subject names more than one person or thing.

  EXAMPLES The ships blow their foghorns.
  The whales jump out of the water.

Find the Trouble Spots

One of my favorite things to do on weekends is to go on fishing trips with my brother Jamal. It is so quiet and peaceful. Our boat ~~drift~~ *drifts* calmly on the water. Little waves ~~laps~~ *lap* at the side of the boat. Sometimes, other people are there fishing, too. They calls out to us in a friendly way. Other times, we have the lake to ourselves. The sun shine on the water. The breeze make ripples. I feel relaxed and at peace.

Find three more action verbs that should be corrected to agree with their subjects.

Edit and Proofreading in Action, continued

> ## Spelling Workout

Check Plural Nouns

A plural noun names more than one person, place, thing, or idea.

- Add **-s** to form the plural of a noun ending in a vowel followed by **y**.

  EXAMPLES boy + -s = boys   toy + -s = toys

                       day + -s = days   guy + -s = guys

- Change the **y** to an **i** and add **-es** if there is a consonant before the **y**.

  EXAMPLES bab*i*y + -es = babies   lad*i*y + -es = ladies

                       cit*i*y + -es = cities   countr*i*y + -es = countries

Find the Trouble Spots

      A few ~~dayes~~ *days* ago, I brought my camera to the lake to take pictures. I like taking pictures of the flowers, trees, sailboats, and ~~butterflys~~ *butterflies* there. At the lake I saw a pair of dragonflys buzzing above the water. I took a picture of them and it came out great. I heard that my school is having a photography contest. In the hallway, there are displays of photographs that won prizes in the past. I think that my picture will be one of the entrys this year.

Find and fix three more spelling errors.

Mechanics Workout

Check Abbreviations

Abbreviations are shortened forms of words. These shortened forms are usually followed by a period.

- You can use abbreviations for people's titles.

  EXAMPLES Mister = Mr.

  Senator = Sen.

  Doctor = Dr.

  For additional examples, see page 459W.

- You can use abbreviations in addresses—for streets, places, states, and countries.

  EXAMPLES 300 Fairmount Avenue = 300 Fairmount Ave.

  Apartment 912 = Apt. 912

  Fort Worth, Texas = Ft. Worth, TX

  United States of America = USA

Notice that state and country names are abbreviated with capital letters and are not followed by a period.

Find the Opportunities

Dr.

~~Doctor~~ Lucinda Reyes

416 Ocean Avenue, Apartment B-5

Treasure Point, Florida 33135

Change the address. Use as many abbreviations as possible.

Publish, Share, and Reflect

You've taken a great shot with your new camera. You're pretty proud of the way it turned out. You pick a nice frame and put the picture in carefully. That way, you can show it to the world in the best possible light. That's how you publish a piece of writing: you "dress it up" to make sure it looks its best when it faces the public.

How Do Writers Share Their Writing?

Once you're done with your writing, what happens next?

- Collect your writing in a folder or binder to keep it organized.

- Don't stop thinking about what you've written. Reflect on what you're pleased with. Decide what areas you'd like to improve.

- Decide how you'll publish your writing and who will read it. Will you send your writing to a close family member? Will you present it to others as a speech?

Think about the ideas on page 91W. Which sound best to you?

Keeping It Personal

You "publish" your writing when you share it with others—with just a few people or with a large audience. If you don't want to show it to the whole world just yet, here are some more personal ways to share it.

- Write a letter to a friend or family member asking him or her to read your writing. Put a copy of your final draft in the envelope. You can also send your writing attached to an e-mail.

- Another cool way to share your writing is to present it as a special message. For instance, you could give this person a framed copy of your paper typed or neatly written by hand on colored paper.

Entering the Public Eye

Are you ready to share your writing with a larger audience? If so, here are a few ways you can make it public:

- Publish an article in your school newspaper.

- Send your paper to the Letters-to-the-Editor section of a local newspaper.

- Look for writing contests in your favorite magazines.

- Find out if you can publish school assignments on your school's Web site, or post a video of yourself reading your paper.

TechTIP

Keep safety in mind when publishing your work—especially when publishing online. Review the Acceptable Use Policy for your school before going online.

Publish, Share, and Reflect, continued

Make Your Work More Exciting With Graphics

Adding graphics or photographs can help your work come alive for readers. Whether you write out your paper by hand or work on a computer, there are many ways you can use graphics:

- Add charts and tables to a science or social studies report.

- If you're writing a book report, scan the book's front cover and insert the image in your report.

- If you're writing about something personal, scan a drawing or photograph to insert.

Reflect

- How will you choose to share your work?

- What can you do to make your work especially right for your audience?

Ready for Publishing

Lake Powell, on the
Utah-Arizona border

Saving a
Disappearing Lake
by Brodie Williams

Lake Powell is a reservoir that supplies water to Nevada, Arizona, and California. More than 20 million people depend on the water from Lake Powell! Millions more enjoy its beauty every year.
It is the second-largest reservoir in the country. But lately, the lake has been disappearing. A drought began in 1999. Since then, water levels in the lake have been dropping.

The people in the three states who depend on Lake Powell can help conserve water during the drought. The millions who visit Glen Canyon National Recreation Area every year should also help. People can conserve water in many ways. For example, each person can take a shorter shower. People can also turn the water off while brushing their teeth. Using water

Reflect on Your Writing

Finishing a piece of writing doesn't mean you forget about it. Reflect on your writing by asking questions about it.

Reflection Questions

1. What part of my writing makes me really proud?

2. What did I learn from writing this paper?

3. What was hard about writing this paper?

4. What other topics would I like to write about?

5. What other kinds of writing would I like to try?

6. How did getting feedback from other people help me?

7. What are some things I can work on? How can I improve my work?

8. How have I become a better writer? What am I getting really good at?

Make a Portfolio

A portfolio is a place where you can store and organize your work. You might want to decorate a folder or binder. Then, put in the work you're most proud of. You can include old drafts, also, to show how your writing has changed over time.

Whether you share your work is up to you. You might want to share your portfolio with your family or friends. If so, keep private writing (such as journal entries) in a separate place.

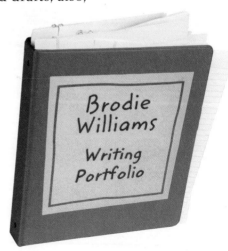

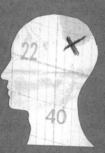

cell body, w
cts impulses away
gated dendrite is calle
ectively called nerve fib
d, cytoplasmic tubes,
sulating sheath of fatty
usually in the brain (P
dendron extends the
pine down to the
erve fibre has
electrical impu
them on to the

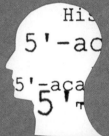

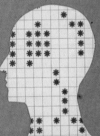
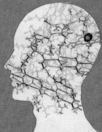

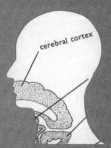
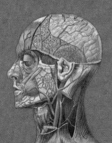

cerebral cortex

MOTHER

THE Many Writers YOU ARE

"E-mail is great, but there's nothing like getting a real letter from a friend."

—Jim

Model Study

Friendly Letter

Writing a letter is a great way to communicate with other people. In a friendly letter, you write to someone you know—like a close friend or a relative—in an informal way.

Often, a friendly letter tells about recent events in the writer's life. It might include a narrative paragraph telling about something that happened, in the order in which events happened.

Sometimes, you can describe the events in one paragraph. Other times, you need more than one paragraph to give your reader the whole story.

The student model on page 97W shows the features of a good friendly letter.

FRIENDLY LETTER

A good friendly letter

☑ begins with the date in the upper right corner

☑ includes a greeting

☑ uses an informal tone to tell about personal things

☑ asks about your friend's life

☑ includes a closing before the signature.

Feature Checklist

July 18, 2008

Dear Denise,

How are you? My family and I just got back from our trip to Hawaii last night. It was a long flight, but we had an amazing time!

The highlight of the trip (besides seeing my aunt and my cousins again, of course) was visiting the Hawaii Volcanoes National Park. First, we drove up to the summit of Kilauea volcano. On the way we drove through a rain forest! We were even lucky enough to watch a slow-moving lava flow. Later, we ended the day walking on Waldron Ledge, which was a road destroyed by a big earthquake in 1983.

This whole trip was so much fun. Write me back and let me know how your summer went. Hopefully we can see each other before the beginning of school!

Your friend,
Mary

Mary starts with the **date**.

In the body of the letter, Mary tells about recent events in her life.

Mary uses **friendly, informal language**.

Mary shows interest in what her friend is doing.

Mary includes a **closing** before her signature.

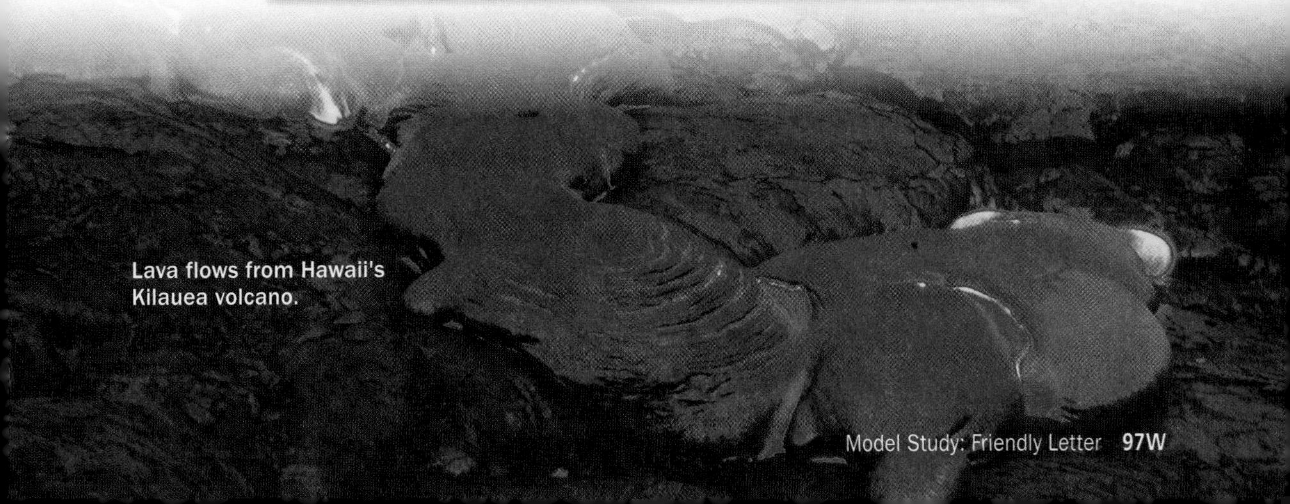

Lava flows from Hawaii's Kilauea volcano.

Write a Friendly Letter

WRITING PROMPT You can write a friendly letter to tell a pal about what's exciting in your life. What did you do over summer vacation? What cool things have you learned about? Have you visited any fun places lately? Write about something that's interesting to *you*.

Think about a recent experience you'd like to share with a friend or family member. Then write a friendly letter that includes

- the date in the upper right corner
- a greeting to your friend or relative
- a body paragraph or more about something interesting that's happened to you recently. Ask about your friend's life, too.
- a friendly closing before your signature.

Prewrite

Here are some tips for planning and preparing before you write your letter.

1 Choose One Experience to Write About

For a short friendly letter, it's best to focus on just one experience. Think about fun things you've done lately and pick one to write about.

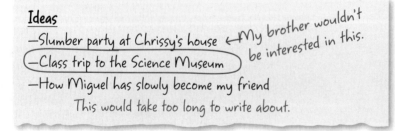

Ideas
—Slumber party at Chrissy's house ← My brother wouldn't be interested in this.
—Class trip to the Science Museum
—How Miguel has slowly become my friend
    This would take too long to write about.

TechTIP
If your computer has a calendar program, you can use it to keep an e-journal. That way you'll always have material to write to your friends about.

2 Think About Your Audience and Purpose

Choose your details based on what will interest your audience. Your purpose will also determine how you write. Do you want to just give information, or do you want to entertain the reader, too?

FATP Chart

Form: *friendly letter*

Audience: *my brother Dave*

Topic: *the Pompeii exhibit at the Science Museum*

Purpose: *to tell him about what I learned*

3 Organize Your Main Ideas and Details

Before you start writing, organize your ideas. Use a graphic organizer like the one below to put your topic sentence and details in order.

Theresa's Plan for Her Friendly Letter

> **Main Idea**
> Science Museum—learned a lot about Pompeii

> **Detail 1**
> museum guide explained how eruption buried the city

> **Detail 2**
> watched computer-animated illustration of the eruption

> **Detail 3**
> looked at lots of objects preserved from Pompeii, like body casts

▲ This is a body cast of a victim from Pompeii.

Reflect

- Do you have a main idea about your topic?

- Are your details in the order in which they happened?

Draft

Once you know what you want to say, you can start writing! You'll use your plan to help you write the letter.

- **Use the Right Form** Set up your letter with the date and a greeting.

> October 18, 2008
>
> Dear Dave,
>
> How are you? How is college? I am doing fine. We've been doing some interesting stuff in school lately.

Theresa starts out her letter with the date and a greeting.

- **Use Your Organizer** When you talk about what's been going on in your life, you'll want to keep details organized. Use your plan to stay on track. Start with your topic sentence and then add details.

From Theresa's Draft

> Last week we went on a class trip to the Science Museum. There was an exhibit about Pompeii and we learned a lot! First, our guide explained that Pompeii was an ancient Roman city (but I already knew that). It was buried when a volcano called Mount Vesuvius erupted. Next, we saw a computer animation of the eruption. It was really cool! We looked at lots of objects preserved from Pompeii, including body casts. It was like traveling back in time.

Theresa used her plan to draft this paragraph about her class trip.

Reflect

- Read your draft. Did you include all the parts of a friendly letter?

- Do your details flow smoothly from your topic sentence?

TechManual

How to Change Font and Style

The word *font* refers to how letters look on the screen or on the printed page. There are thousands of different fonts, with names like Arial and Times Roman. Within each font, there are also several **styles,** such as *italics,* **boldface,** and <u>underscore</u>.

To change your font or style:

1. Highlight the words you want to change by clicking and dragging your cursor.

2. Go to the **Format** menu and click **Font.**

3. Choose the font you want to use.

4. To make the font bold or italic (or both), select **Bold, Italic,** or **Bold Italic** under the **Font Style** menu.

5. To underline words, select the straight, unbroken line under the **Underline Style** menu.

6. When you've chosen the options you want, click **OK.**

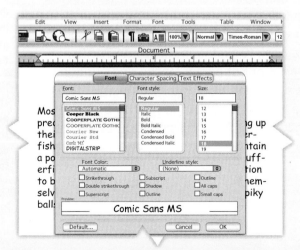

Revise

As you revise your letter, keep in mind your audience (the person who is going to receive it) and your purpose for writing the letter.

1 Evaluate Your Work

Try to look at the draft of your letter as if someone else has written it. Ask yourself these questions:

- **About the Form** Does my draft look and feel like a friendly letter? Is the tone friendly and informal?

- **About the Organization** Do the sentences in my paragraphs flow smoothly? Are the details in the right order? In your head, try to "play a movie" of the events—does it make sense?

> **Revision in Action**

From Theresa's Draft

Theresa thinks:

By the way, thank you for that book on volcanoes. I'm learning a lot. It was a great birthday present.

I'm using it to build a model of a volcano for science class. I chose Anak Krakatau in the South Pacific. I made the volcano out of papier-mâché and put it in the middle of a tub with blue water all around. Then maybe smoke will come out of the top. My brother showed me how to put dry ice inside. Do you have a better idea?

Love,
Theresa

"The last sentence doesn't really flow into the next paragraph. I'll move it."

"These sentences are out of order. It's not clear what caused the volcano to explode."

2 Mark Your Changes

Rearrange Text Sometimes, you will need to rearrange sentences to improve the flow of ideas in a paragraph. Use this mark: ⌒. Also use this mark to move paragraphs that are out of order.

Anak Krakatau volcano spews smoke and lava in the South Pacific. ▶

Reflect

- Does each sentence flow from the one that came before it?

- Do you need to move sentences to make your writing clearer?

Revising Marks

MARK	∧	⌒	⌐	⌿
WHAT IT MEANS	Insert something.	Move to here.	Replace with this.	Take out.

Revised Draft

By the way, thank you for that book on volcanoes. I'm learning a lot. (It was a great birthday present.)

I'm using it to build a model of a volcano for science class. I chose Anak Krakatau in the South Pacific. I made the volcano out of papier-mâché and put it in the middle of a tub with blue water all around. Then maybe smoke will come out of the top. (My brother showed me how to put dry ice inside.) Do you have a better idea?

Love,
Theresa

Theresa moved the last sentence to make ideas flow more smoothly.

Theresa moved this sentence to make the order of events clear.

Edit and Proofread

After you're satisfied with the content of your letter, read it again to fix language errors. This is what you do when you edit and proofread your work:

- **Check the Grammar** Make sure that you have used correct and conventional grammar throughout. In particular, check that you have used pronouns correctly and clearly in your writing. (See page 105W.)

- **Check the Spelling** Spell-check can help, but it isn't always enough. To spell compound words correctly, you need to read your work carefully and perhaps use a dictionary. (See page 106W.)

- **Check the Mechanics** Errors in punctuation and capitalization can make your work hard to understand. In particular, check that you have used commas correctly in the date, greeting, and closing of your letter. (See page 107W.)

Use these marks to edit and proofread your friendly letter.

TechTIP
Try using an online dictionary.

Editing and Proofreading Marks

MARK	WHAT IT MEANS	MARK	WHAT IT MEANS
∧	Insert something.	/	Make lowercase.
∧	Add a comma.	℘	Delete, take something out.
∧	Add a semicolon.	¶	Make new paragraph.
⊙	Add a period.	◯	Spell out.
⊙	Add a colon.	⌒	Replace with this.
⌄ ⌄	Add quotation marks.	∼	Change order of letters or words.
⌄	Add an apostrophe.	#	Insert space.
≡	Capitalize.	⌣	Close up, no space here.

Reflect
- What kind of errors did you find? What can you do to keep from making them?

Grammar Workout

Check Pronouns

- Use *he* to refer to a man or a boy. Use *she* to refer to a woman or a girl. Use *it* to refer to a thing.

  EXAMPLE   Luis lives in Washington. He remembers the
  eruption in 1980 of Mount St. Helens. It was awful.

- Use *he, she,* or *it* when referring to only one person. Use *they* when referring to more than one person.

  EXAMPLE   Luis and Maria, his wife, saw ash pour into the

  sky. They said that the sky looked black.

- Be sure the pronoun is not confusing.

  CONFUSING   Luis told Richard that there was a radio

  program about the eruption. He had heard it.

  CLEAR   Luis told Richard that there was a radio program about
  the eruption. Richard had heard the report.

Find the Trouble Spots

The eruption happened in the morning. ~~He~~ *It*
surprised many people. ~~It~~ *They* had never experienced
anything like that in their lives. My aunt lived in the
area of Mount St. Helens. He could see the mountain
from a distance. She said that they looked peaceful
in the morning. Then she heard a loud explosion.

Find two more
pronoun errors
to fix.

Edit and Proofread, continued

> ## SpellingWorkout

Check Compound Words

Some longer words, called **compound words**, are made up of two smaller words.

EXAMPLES			
basketball	= basket + ball	flashlight	= flash + light
keyboard	= key + board	rainbow	= rain + bow
sidewalk	= side + walk	toothbrush	= tooth + brush

To spell a compound word, say and spell the first smaller word. Then say and spell the other smaller word without putting a space in between.

A few compound words like the ones below are written with a space or a hyphen. Check the dictionary to be sure.

ice cream   hundred-meter dash

peanut butter   first-class ticket

Find the Trouble Spots

Coming back from our class#trip took forever! Our school⌒bus was stuck in traffic. It was almost night⌒time before we got home. The bus#driver used his cellphone to call the middle school and say we would be late. I was worried about missing soccer practice, but then there was a thunder-storm anyway. Our coach rescheduled practice for the week end.

Find and fix three more errors with compound words.

Mechanics Workout

Check Commas and Capitalization

Check the greeting, the closing, and any dates in your letter.

- When you write the date, use a comma (,) between the day and the year. Of course, capitalize the name of the month.

  EXAMPLE December 28, 2008

- Capitalize the first word of the greeting, and use a comma at the end.

  EXAMPLES Dear Marian,   Hey, Gary,
                           How are you?   How's it going?

- Capitalize the first word of the closing, and use a comma at the end.

  EXAMPLES Your friend,   Love,
                           Julie   David

Find the Trouble Spots

November 1, 2008

dear Dave

    We are still learning about volcanoes in school. Did you know that a volcano formed an island called Surtsey near Iceland? On November 14 1963, a fisherman saw smoke coming up from the water. The volcano was erupting out of the ocean! The lava built up to form a small island. I think that's amazing!

                love
                Theresa

Find and fix four errors with commas and capitalization.

Model Study

Personal Narrative

You tell personal narratives all the time. You might tell a classmate about what you did after school. You might tell friends about someone you met or something that made you happy.

Think about the last story you told about yourself. How did you make that story interesting? How did you make it easy to understand?

When you write a **personal narrative**, you tell a story about something that happened to you. Because the story is about you, you will be writing in the **first person**. That means you will use words like *I, we, me,* and *my* a lot.

Read the student model on page 109W. It shows the features of a good personal narrative.

PERSONAL NARRATIVE

A good personal narrative

☑ has a beginning, a middle, and an end

☑ includes real events, people, and places

☑ uses specific details that let the reader "see and feel" what's happening

☑ expresses the writer's feelings.

Feature Checklist

A Scary Day

by Jessica Alvarez

The beginning gets the reader's attention and tells what the event was.

I never thought so much water could fall out of the sky so fast. The day the tornado hit was the scariest day of my life! Okay, I wasn't really in the tornado, but we could see it. That was scary enough for me!

The writer tells her **feelings** about the event.

Every summer, I spend some time with my father in Miami Beach. His apartment building has a pool, and we can walk to the beach if we want to.

The middle gives details about the event.

The day started out as a normal, sunny day in Florida. It was hot, as usual, with tall clouds that looked like cauliflower. We were at the beach, when suddenly the sky got very dark, like night was falling.

The writer gives **specific details** that let the reader "see and feel" what's happening.

Dad said, "We'd better head home." We were still gathering our things when a big gust of wind blew away my hat. Big, fat drops of water hit us hard. In less than a minute we were soaked.

We ran to the nearest building. It was a hotel on the beach. From the big picture window, we could see a cloud with a long tail coming down. Dad said that was a tornado. Luckily, it didn't last very long, and the tail didn't touch the ground.

The end tells what finally happened.

We were able to make it home after an hour or so. The weather was sunny again the next day, but we didn't go back to the beach for a couple of weeks after that!

Student Model

109W

Organization

What's It Like?

After a hurricane, relief workers need to get organized to help as many people as possible. Signs and announcements need to be clear so that people know where to go and what to do first. Organizing your writing is kind of like that. You want your reader to understand right away what's important, without you having to be there to explain.

Why Does Organization Matter?

When a paper is well organized, it's easy to see how the ideas go together. One idea flows right into the next.

Writers organize their ideas in a way that fits their purpose for writing. Below, the writer wants her readers to understand when things happen. So she chooses to present her ideas in time order.

> It had been raining for almost a week, and the ground was squishy and soggy. But the morning of the flash flood it was sunny and beautiful.
>   By lunchtime, though, it was cloudy, dark, and windy. In the afternoon, without warning, there was a big crash of thunder and the rain started. It came down hard, as if somebody had turned a hose full on.

Transition words link one idea to the next.

Study the rubric on page 111W. What is the difference between a paper with a score of 2 and one with a score of 4?

Organization

	Does the writing have a clear structure, and is it appropriate for the writer's purpose?	How smoothly do the ideas flow together?
4 Wow!	The writing has a clear structure that is appropriate for the writer's purpose.	The ideas progress in a smooth and orderly way. • The **ideas** flow well from **paragraph** to **paragraph**. • The ideas in each paragraph flow well from one **sentence** to the next. • Meaningful and effective **transitions** connect ideas.
3 Ahh.	The writing has a structure that is <u>generally</u> clear and appropriate for the writer's purpose.	<u>Most</u> of the ideas progress in a smooth and orderly way. • Most of the **ideas** flow well from **paragraph** to **paragraph**. • Most of the ideas in each paragraph flow well from one **sentence** to the next. • Meaningful and effective **transitions** connect most of the ideas.
2 Hmm.	The structure of the writing is not clear or not appropriate for the writer's purpose.	<u>Some</u> of the ideas progress in a smooth and orderly way. • Some of the **ideas** flow well from **paragraph** to **paragraph**. • Some of the ideas in each paragraph flow well from one **sentence** to the next. • Meaningful and effective **transitions** connect some of the ideas.
1 Huh?	The writing does not have a structure.	<u>Few or none</u> of the ideas progress in a smooth and orderly way. The ideas in the paragraphs and sentences do not flow well together and are not connected with transitions.

Organization, continued

Compare Writing Samples

A well-organized narrative has good order and good transitions. Study the two examples of a personal narrative on this page.

Well Organized

First Things First

Paragraphs are placed in an effective order.

Focus on your responsibility. That's the lesson I learned the other day when I was babysitting my little sister.

I was playing my video game, Escape. I was focused on getting to the game's seventh level. That's all I cared about.

Transitions connect ideas from one sentence to another.

Suddenly, I heard a BOOM! Then I heard my sister Emily cry. So I ran to her room. Lightning had struck the tree outside of her window, and the tree was split open and smoking.

I grabbed Emily and brought her to the living room. I held her close to comfort her. We were both shaking. "I'll keep you safe, Emily," I whispered. I didn't let her go until my mom came home.

Not So Well Organized

Video Games

Paragraphs are not placed in an effective order, making the story hard to follow.

I was focused on getting to the game's seventh level. That's all I cared about. I was playing my video game, Escape.

I heard a BOOM! I heard my sister Emily cry. Lightning had struck the tree outside of her window, and the tree was split open and smoking. Right away, I ran to her room.

Without transitions, ideas don't flow as well from one sentence to another.

Focus on your responsibility. That's the lesson I learned the other day when I was babysitting my little sister.

I grabbed Emily and brought her to the living room. I held her close to comfort her. We were both shaking. I didn't let her go until my mom came home. "I'll keep you safe, Emily," I whispered.

Evaluate for Organization

Now read carefully the personal narrative below. Use the rubric on page 111W to score it.

What's the Right Thing to Do?
by Todd Gonzalez

Are the paragraphs in the best order? How would you change them?

Patrick and I were watching TV. Suddenly, we heard thunder. That's why we started counting the seconds during the commercials.

In school we had been learning that you can tell how far away a thunderstorm is if you count the seconds between the light and the sound. Five seconds from lightning to thunder means the storm is one mile away. This is all approximate.

Is the order of events clear? What transitions might help?

It was like 8 seconds—almost 2 miles away. It started getting closer and closer. We turned down the sound on the TV and counted again. It was closer to 3 seconds or about half a mile.

Dad was away on a trip. I was at home with my twin brother, Patrick. Mom was working late.

Another thing we learned is that during a thunderstorm you should stay away from electrical equipment, like TVs and computers. You should also stay away from the phone, unless it's an emergency.

The phone rang. We were almost sure it was Mom. But should we pick up the phone with the lightning only a half-mile away? We started arguing. Patrick thought we should, but I said no.

When Mom finally got home she said I was right, even though she had worried.

Raise the Score

These papers have been scored using the **Organization Rubric** on page 111W. Study each paper to see why it got the score it did.

Overall Score: 4

The Day of the Flood

Mark Smith

The **beginning** tells what the writer **will write about**.

I live near Fargo, North Dakota, which is near the Red River. When I was in second grade, I spent a very difficult day at school because of flooding.

The writer uses many **time words** to show the order of events.

Mom took me to school that morning, as usual. By noon, a voice over the P.A. system announced a flood warning. My family and I live far beyond the river, but the road to my house goes past it. I hoped the flooding wouldn't be anything major.

The **middle** gives more details about the event.

After school let out, I sat and waited for my mother for two hours. She didn't call, and I began to worry. "What if she's caught in the flood?" I wondered.

At 5:30, there was another announcement saying that the flooding had blocked a major road in town. Just then my mother arrived. She explained that her car had almost gotten stuck in the flood waters. Fortunately, two police officers helped get her car onto higher ground so she could continue driving.

Transitions show connections between ideas.

The **end** tells what finally happened and how it made the writer feel.

Finally, around 7:00, we received news that the waters had gone down at last. We left the school and arrived home shortly afterward. At the end of that long day, I knew we had been very lucky.

The Day of the Flood

I live near Fargo, North Dakota. Fargo is close to the Red River. I once spent a very difficult day at school because of flooding.

Mom took me to school that morning. By noon, a voice over the P.A. system announced a flood warning. My family and I live far beyond the river, but the road to my house goes past it. I hoped the flooding wouldn't be anything major.

I waited for over two hours for my mother to pick me up. She didn't call, and I began to worry that she was caught in the flood.

I heard another announcement saying that the river had blocked a major road in town. Just then my mother arrived. She said that her car had almost gotten stuck in the flood waters. The officers got her car onto higher ground so she could continue driving. Luckily, two police officers were there to help.

We received news that the waters had gone down. We drove home. We were very lucky that day.

The **structure** is still generally clear and appropriate.

The writer uses some **time words**, but the order is not always clear.

Most of the sentences in this paragraph flow smoothly, but the last one is out of order.

A **transition** is missing at the beginning of the last paragraph.

RAISING THE SCORE

This writer needs to improve the flow of ideas in her paragraphs and sentences. What should she do?

Raise the Score, continued

The Day of the Flood

The **structure** of the writing is not clear. The events are jumbled.

The Red River is near Fargo, North Dakota. That's where I live. One day I had a long day at school because of flooding.

We live beyond the Red River, so I never think about flooding causing a problem. The road to my house goes right past it. But that day was different.

I was waiting for my mother to pick me up after school. There had been a flood warning. Mom didn't call. I began to worry that she was caught in the flood. At that time, I didn't know that the river had blocked a major road in town.

The writer uses a few **time words**, but the order of events is not clear.

These paragraphs are out of order.

Soon the waters went down. Mom arrived. We drove home safely. We were lucky!

Mom explained to me that her car had almost gotten stuck in the flood waters. Some police officers stopped. They helped Mom get the car to higher ground. That's how she got to school to pick me up.

The sentences do not flow smoothly. Only some of the ideas are connected with **transitions**.

▲ RAISING THE SCORE

The writer needs to fix the organization of her writing. How can she improve the order and flow of ideas in the third paragraph?

The Day of the Flood

The Red River is near Fargo, North Dakota. One day it flooded while I was at school.

Mom didn't call to say she would be late. I waited and waited for her to pick me up. There had been a flood warning. I was worried. I thought maybe she was caught in the flood.

My family and I live beyond the Red River. The road to my house goes right past it. I have never seen it flood before. A major road had been blocked by the river. I didn't know that at the time.

The waters went down. Mom arrived to get me, and we drove home.

Some police officers stopped to help my mom. Mom said that her car had almost gotten stuck in the flood waters. They helped her get the car back on the road to the school.

It's hard to make sense of the writing. It lacks **structure**.

The writer uses very few **time words**. It is hard to tell exactly when things happened.

The sentences do not flow in a smooth and orderly way.

Transitions are missing. The ideas within and between paragraphs are not connected.

RAISING *THE SCORE*

The writers needs to put the sentences and paragraphs in better order. How should she rearrange the sentences and paragraphs?

Use Transitions

What's It Like

Transitions are like those highway signs that tell you what's coming ahead. They help your reader be prepared for the "turns" in your thinking.

Many Ways to Use Transitions

You can use transitions for different purposes such as:

- to show contrast

> New Orleans had been hit by hurricanes and flooding in
> **But**
> the past. ∧Hurricane Katrina brought destruction never
> seen before.

- to point out cause-and-effect relationships

> The levees were weak and collapsed when the
> **As a result,**
> water rose. ∧Lake Pontchartrain poured into the city.

- to introduce examples

> Many neighborhoods were severely damaged.
> **For example,**
> ∧St. Bernard Parish was covered in 20 feet of water.

Look at some transitions in action in the following passage.

All Was Not Lost
By Levon James

I expected the worst. But when I finally saw our house, I was shocked by how bad it was.

It was a mess. For example, there was mud everywhere, the furniture was all out of place, and smaller items were scattered around like trash. In fact, it looked like the place had been hit by a hurricane and an earthquake.

Floodwater had entered the house. As a result, everything was water-damaged and smelly, too. I could tell how high the water had been by looking at the stained walls.

I checked my room. I have never cared much about "things." So, I didn't have much in my room that could be damaged or lost. That's good, because I lost nearly everything I had. The only thing I took from the room was my football trophy for Most Valuable Player.

It was bad. Still, it could have been worse. At least we're all alive and unhurt. This storm has destroyed our neighborhood. But it hasn't destroyed our spirit.

These transitions show **contrast**.

This transition introduces **examples**.

These transitions point out **cause and effect**.

Without transitions, the passage would seem dull and choppy. The reader would not get as clear a sense of how the ideas are connected.

▼ This New Orleans neighborhood was damaged by the hurricane and flooding.

Use Transitions, continued

Show Contrast

You can use transition words to show how two or more things or ideas are different. Read the transition words. Then study the passage.

but	still	in contrast
yet	however	on the other hand

> There are many things people can do to prepare their homes for a big storm or hurricane. But even if people prepare, the storm may destroy their homes.
>
> Some people might worry too much. On the other hand, some people think that they shouldn't bother doing anything at all. Still, it is usually a good idea to try to protect your home. A powerful storm may damage your home. However, if you board up windows and take other steps to secure it, your home may not be too badly damaged.

Show Cause and Effect

The words below show how one event leads to another or how ideas are connected. Read the words and study the passage.

because	so	as a result
due to	since	therefore

> Due to the hurricane, the water level in the levees rose higher than it ever had before. The levees were not strong enough. As a result, they collapsed when the water rose. Because St. Bernard Parish was near a broken levee, it was flooded with 20 feet of water.
>
> In flooded neighborhoods, most of the homes had to be evacuated. Therefore, many people were left homeless. Other neighborhoods were on higher ground. So, these neighborhoods were not flooded, and the people did not have to leave.

Introduce Examples or Lists

You can also use transitions to introduce examples or lists that support your ideas. Read the transitions. Then study the passage.

for example   **for instance**   **such as**   **including**

There were problems helping the flood victims. For example, some people waited a long time to be rescued from their flooded homes. Others waited too long to be moved to shelter. For instance, some groups of people waited hours or days for buses to arrive.

Some frightened and hungry people committed crimes, such as stealing food.

Many people blamed leaders and organizations, including the government, for causing some of the problems.

▼ Hurricane Katrina caused widespread flooding in the Gulf Coast.

More On Transitions

Some time words and some order words can serve as transitions. You can use these transitions to help you:

- show time

  > People stayed home that afternoon, not realizing that
  > their neighborhood was in danger. Soon Floodwater rushed
  > into the streets.

- show events or ideas in sequence

  > I waded through the house and searched for her
  > everywhere. Finally, I found her upstairs in her room.

Study the transitions in this passage.

Narrative with Transitions

Helping Out an Old Friend
Alyx Del Lago

   When I think about it today, it seems foolish. But back then I did not hesitate to do it.

   After I left school, I rode the bus as far as I could. Then I got out and walked toward my home. Later I had to wade through water. By early afternoon, I reached my doorstep.

   First, I called her name as I searched everywhere downstairs. Next, I searched the yard and garage. Meanwhile, I heard helicopters overhead and sirens.

   I went upstairs and finally found my cat, hiding under my bed.

These transitions **show when events occur**.

These transitions **show the order of events or steps in a process**.

Without transitions, the reader would not get a clear sense of the order of events.

Show Time

Read these time words that can work as transitions to show when events happen. Then study the passage.

now	soon	back then	meanwhile	recently
today	after	never	in the future	in the past

For some cities near large rivers, flooding has been a problem in the past. Today, however, flooding can be an even greater danger.

Recently, climate changes have produced stronger storms, and more of them. As a result, major floods are more common now.

Also, many of the cities have grown. Since a lot more people are living in these areas, more people are at risk from floods.

Not all of these cities have built systems that protect against flooding. In the future, these cities will have to plan and build systems that control flooding as much as possible.

Show Events or Ideas in Sequence

These order words can work as transitions to show the order of events or the steps in a process. Study the words and the passage.

first	third	second	next	last	finally

It's not easy to build a system to control flooding, especially in large, older cities. Engineers face many challenges.

First, engineers must find ways to protect a city that was built long ago, long before anyone thought about flood-control planning.

Second, they must consider how the structures will look. Citizens sometimes don't agree with the changes engineers want to make.

Next, they must think about cost. It can be difficult to find money to pay for an advanced flood-control system.

Finally, engineers must get approval for planned changes.

Write a Personal Narrative

WRITING PROMPT Nature can be scary sometimes. Have you ever experienced a big storm or an earthquake? Or maybe it was just a really tall wave at the beach that made you feel like you were about to drown? Think of an experience you'd like to share with your classmates. Then write a personal narrative that tells

- what happened in the beginning, middle, and end
- what you saw, heard, and experienced
- how you felt while it was happening
- what made the event memorable for you or what life lesson you have learned from it.

Prewrite

Here are some tips for before you start writing.

1 **Choose a Topic**

It works best to choose an event that

- was exciting, unusual or interesting
- you remember well, so you can include enough details.

It helps to write down several ideas and then choose the best. Josh used a chart like this to choose a topic.

Ideas	Good and Bad Points
The time the wave came into the whale-watching boat.	Exciting! Can't remember very well— I was just a baby.
The Loma Linda earthquake in second grade.	That was exciting for sure! I can remember it pretty well.
The time the lights went out and I got scared of thunder.	Not interesting enough to others.

❷ Narrow Your Topic

Make sure you limit your topic so that it is not too broad for the kind of writing you want to do. Some topics take a whole book to do well! A smaller, more specific topic is easier to write about and will be much more interesting. Study how Josh narrowed his topic.

How Josh Narrowed His Topic

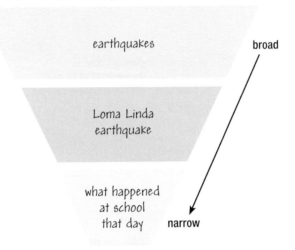

earthquakes — broad

Loma Linda earthquake

what happened at school that day — narrow

Strong earthquakes can damage buildings. ▼

❸ Gather Details

Next, gather details about the experience. Take notes to help you later as you draft. One way to gather specific sensory details is with a **five-senses diagram**.

Five-Senses Diagram

I saw . . .	• scared look on people's faces • kids crouching under desks • books all over the floor
I heard . . .	• kids crying • blocks clattering off shelves
I smelled . . .	• the fabric of my backpack • dust in the air
I tasted . . .	• the salt of my own tears!
I touched or felt . . .	• the rough underside of the desk • my friend's hair in my face

Prewrite, continued

4 Organize Ideas

Once you've chosen your topic and gathered some details, it's time to plan how you will build your narrative. One way to make a plan is to use a graphic organizer. Since personal narratives usually include a series of events, a **sequence chain** is a good graphic organizer to use for your plan.

Sequence Chain

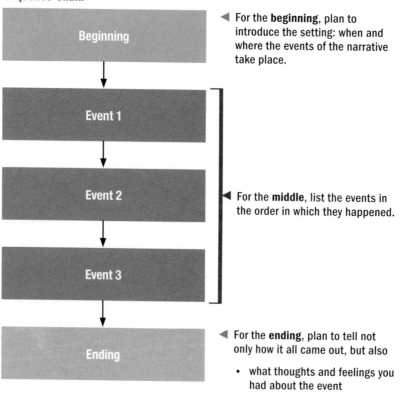

Beginning

◄ For the **beginning**, plan to introduce the setting: when and where the events of the narrative take place.

Event 1

Event 2

◄ For the **middle**, list the events in the order in which they happened.

Event 3

Ending

◄ For the **ending**, plan to tell not only how it all came out, but also

- what thoughts and feelings you had about the event

- why you find this experience memorable.

Aerial view of a residential area in Izmit, Turkey, following an earthquake in August, 1999. ►

Here's the plan that Josh made for his personal narrative about the earthquake.

Josh's Plan for His Personal Narrative

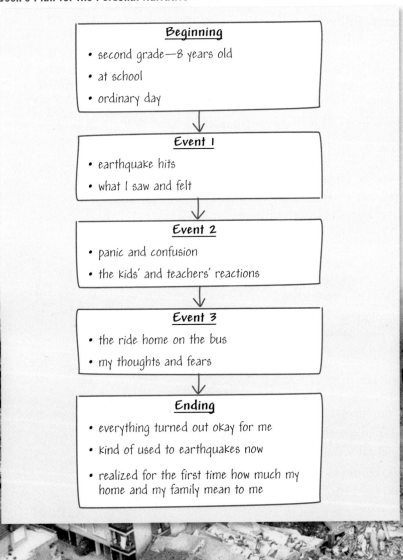

Beginning
- second grade—8 years old
- at school
- ordinary day

↓

Event 1
- earthquake hits
- what I saw and felt

↓

Event 2
- panic and confusion
- the kids' and teachers' reactions

↓

Event 3
- the ride home on the bus
- my thoughts and fears

↓

Ending
- everything turned out okay for me
- kind of used to earthquakes now
- realized for the first time how much my home and my family mean to me

Reflect
- Is your topic specific enough?
- Does your sequence chain show clearly the order of events?

Draft

Got a plan? Now it's time to start writing! Your draft doesn't have to be perfect, but you don't want to waste all that time you spent planning.

- **Use Your Organizer** Follow your writing plan. That way your narrative as a whole will have shape and organization.

> It started out as a day like any other for an 8-year-old boy. Before breakfast, I got dressed in my school uniform. Then I quickly ate so that I wouldn't miss the bus.

Josh used the top box of his Sequence Chain to draft this beginning paragraph.

- **Add Plenty of Details** Details can make any personal narrative rich and interesting. Give enough details to make your reader almost experience the events.

Five-Senses Diagram

I saw . . .	• scared look on people's faces • kids crouching under desks • books all over the floor
I heard . . .	• kids crying • blocks clattering off shelves

From Josh's Draft

> All of a sudden, the earthquake hit and the day stopped being normal. When the shaking started, I put my head down on my desk and covered it with my arms. I heard the sound of books and blocks falling off the shelves.
>
> Then I looked up. I was scared. The scared look on my teacher's face scared me even more!

Reflect

- Read your draft. Do you have enough details?

- Does it have a clear beginning, middle, and end?

DRAFTING TIPS
Trait: **Organization**

If Your Writing Wanders . . .
Sometimes you get your writing going and it starts going too many places. You have so many ideas that you don't know which one to stick with. The result is that your writing wanders and appears disorganized.

Try Writing a Skeleton Narrative First
This is not a narrative about a skeleton! A **skeleton narrative** is just a super-quick pre-draft that shows just the main points of your narrative, without any details.

Here's an example for Josh's paper.

Skeleton Narrative

Then, for his actual draft, Josh "exploded" each sentence by adding details about what he experienced, what he thought, and how he felt.

Revise

As you revise your work, keep in mind your audience and your purpose for writing. Does your writing do what you want it to do? Will it connect with your audience?

1 Evaluate Your Work

Read your draft aloud to yourself. Listen as if you were somebody else, to see what can be improved. As you read, ask yourself questions:

- **About the Form** Would my readers be able to picture the event and know how I felt about it?

- **About the Organization** Is the order of events clear? Do the ideas flow well together?

Revision in Action

Draft

The writer thinks:

The quake hit. The kids were really scared. The teacher was scared too. She told us to get under our desks.

" This event isn't clear. It's hard to 'see' what's happening "

I remember that I looked right away for my friend Frank. I think we both were expecting explosions and flames and stuff, like in a movie. But nothing like that happened. He usually sat at the desk next to mine, but he was in a different science group. He was on the other side of the room.

" How could I know what Frank was expecting? I wasn't with him yet. "

I ran over to get Frank. We grabbed our backpacks and huddled under our desks.

" The last sentence in this paragraph doesn't flow from the one before. "

2 Mark Your Changes

Add Text You may need to add text to make your writing clearer. Use this mark ∧ to add:

- details to help readers picture the event
- transitions to help improve your idea flow.

Rearrange Text To improve your organization, you may need to change the order of sentences and paragraphs. Circle the text and draw an arrow to where you want to move it.

Reflect

- Does the order of your paragraphs make sense?

- Do you need to add any more transitions?

Revising Marks MARK	∧	↶	⌐	─ℓ	⁋
WHAT IT MEANS	Insert something.	Move to here.	Replace with this.	Take out.	Make a new paragraph.

Revised Draft

Suddenly,   Books fell off the shelves. Boom! Boom!
The quake hit. The kids were really scared.
Most of them were crying.   , but she tried to sound calm
The teacher was scared too. She told us to get under
  and everyone did, without any argument
our desks.

I remember that I looked right away for my friend
Frank. (I think we both were expecting explosions and
flames and stuff, like in a movie. But nothing like that
happened.) He usually sat at the desk next to mine,
but he was in a different science group. So He was on
the other side of the room.

I ran over to get Frank. We grabbed our backpacks
and huddled under our desks. ∧

The writer added more details.

The writer rearranged the text to clarify when things happened.

The writer added a transition word to improve the flow of ideas.

Edit and Proofread

After you're satisfied with the content of your personal narrative, read your paper again to fix language errors. This is what you do when you edit and proofread your work:

- **Check the Grammar** Make sure that you have used correct and conventional grammar throughout. In particular, check for correct use of helping verbs. (See page 133W.)

- **Check the Spelling** Spell-check can help, but it isn't always enough. For errors with suffixes, you'll have to read your work carefully and remember a few rules. (See page 134W.)

- **Check the Mechanics** Errors in punctuation and capitalization can make your work hard to understand. In particular, check that your apostrophes are correct. (See page 135W.)

Use these marks to edit and proofread your narrative.

Editing and Proofreading Marks

MARK	WHAT IT MEANS	MARK	WHAT IT MEANS
∧	Insert something.	/	Make lowercase.
∧	Add a comma.	℘	Delete, take something out.
∧	Add a semicolon.	¶	Make new paragraph.
⊙	Add a period.	⬭	Spell out.
⊙	Add a colon.	⌒	Replace with this.
∨ ∨	Add quotation marks.	∼	Change order of letters or words.
∨	Add an apostrophe.	#	Insert space.
≡	Capitalize.	⌣	Close up, no space here.

Reflect

- What kind of errors did you find? What can you do to keep from making them?

GrammarWorkout

Check Helping Verbs

- A helping verb is a verb that works together with another verb. The main verb shows the action or state of being. The helping verb supports the main verb's meaning.

    EXAMPLE   An earthquake can shatter windows.

- *Can, could, may,* and *might* are helping verbs. Use *can* to tell what someone or something is able to do. Use *could, may,* or *might* to tell what is possible.

    EXAMPLES   We can prepare for a quake. A quake could hit our area.
    It may happen soon.

- *Can, could, may,* and *might* are always spelled the same way. They do not change with different subjects.

    EXAMPLES   We might see a film about earthquakes.
    Our teacher might show it during science class.

Find the Opportunities

I plan to write a report about earthquakes. Our
school library ~~has~~ *might have* some newspaper articles about last
year's quake. It is best to use more than one source, so I
could try to find three or four. My teacher offers her help, too.
I ask her for some ideas if I get stuck. I get a really good
grade on this report if I work hard!

Check the verbs. Where could you add a helping verb to make the meaning more precise? (You may have to change the main verb.)

Edit and Proofread, continued

Spelling Workout

Check Suffixes

A suffix is added at the end of a word. It changes the word's meaning. Study the suffixes in the chart.

Suffix	Meaning
-ful	full of
-hood	quality of
-ive	having qualities of
-less	without
-ly	in a certain way
-ment	an action or process
-ness	state of
-y	having the quality of

Sometimes you have to change the spelling of the base word when you add a suffix.

- If the base word ends in **e,** drop the final **e** when the suffix starts with a vowel. Keep the final **e** when the suffix starts with a consonant.

  EXAMPLES   love ⟶ lovable   love ⟶ lovely

- If the base word ends in a consonant plus **y,** change the **y** to an **i** before adding the suffix. If the base word ends in a vowel plus **y,** do not make a change.

  EXAMPLES   happy ⟶ happiness   play ⟶ playable

- Some base words end in a short vowel plus a consonant. Double the consonant when the suffix starts with a vowel. Do not double the consonant when the suffix starts with a consonant.

  EXAMPLES   sun ⟶ sunny   glad ⟶ gladly

Find the Trouble Spots

> My great-grandmother was in the big San Francisco quake in 1906. Her neighborhood was ~~heavyly~~ ^heavily^ damaged, so she and her family had to camp outside in a park. One ^sunny^ ~~suny~~ day, a puppy wandered into my great-grandmother's tent. He was adoreable. His sillyness and playfulness cheered everyone up.

Find and fix two more misspelled words with suffixes.

Mechanics Workout

Check Apostrophes in Contractions

When two words are joined into one, you have a **contraction**.

EXAMPLES   I + am ⟶ I'm   is + not ⟶ isn't

- Many contractions are formed with a pronoun and the verb
  am, are, or **is**. In this kind of contraction, an apostrophe
  replaces the first letter of the verb.

  EXAMPLES   you + are ⟶ you͜are ⟶ you're
              she + is ⟶ she͜is ⟶ she's

- Many other contractions are formed with a verb and the
  word **not**. To make this kind of contraction, an apostrophe
  replaces the **o** in **not**.

  EXAMPLES   could + not ⟶ couldn͜ot ⟶ couldn't
              are + not ⟶ aren͜ot ⟶ aren't

  EXCEPTIONS   can + not ⟶ can't [just one *n*]
               will + not ⟶ won't [a pretty different word!]

Find the Trouble Spots

Most people don͜t think about earthquake insurance.
But if you͜are in "earthquake country," a quake can
quickly destroy your home. If it isnt insured, you willn't
get money to rebuild. Some people do'not have enough
insurance. Theyre hoping their homes arent damaged.

Can you find the
problems with
the apostrophes
in the passage?

Publish, Share, and Reflect

You've worked hard to craft a personal narrative that is organized, full of interesting details, and correctly written. Don't keep it to yourself—share it!

1 **Publish and Share Your Work**

When you publish your writing, you put it in final form and make a conscious decision to share it with others. The way you publish your work will depend on whom you want to share it with.

If you want to share with the whole world, you might publish your personal narrative in

- a blog
- a school or town newspaper
- a local magazine for young writers
- a local radio show.

If you only want to share with family or a few friends, you might try one of the following:

- Desktop publish your narrative, enhancing it with photos and graphics. Then make multiple copies and pass them out to family and friends.
- Arrange a private reading, where you can gather a small audience and read your personal narrative aloud (see page 137W).

2 **Reflect on Your Work**

Publishing and sharing a piece of writing doesn't mean you stop thinking about it. Think back on what you have written. Ask yourself questions to pinpoint what you did well and what you want to improve.

TechTIP

Practice for an oral presentation by recording yourself on a computer. You'll need a built-in mike or be able to hook one up.

Reflect

- What did I discover about myself when I wrote?

- How did my feelings about this experience change as a result of my writing about it?

How to Hold a Private Reading

If you want to share your work only with family and a few friends, a private reading will do the trick. It can provide just the right mix of "formal" and "informal."

To hold a private reading:

1. Invite everyone over to your house or another convenient location. (Public libraries often have conference rooms that you can reserve.) You can also wait for a natural gathering, such as a birthday party or a wedding.

2. Plan for snacks or refreshments, if you like.

3. Invite other people to also bring materials to read, or be the star of the show all by yourself.

4. When it comes time for you to read, introduce your narrative. Explain why the event is particularly memorable or how it affected your life.

5. Read your work slowly, clearly, and with feeling and expression. Make eye contact with your audience. Think of yourself as an actor and not just a reader.

6. Give your audience a chance to respond to your reading.

" I remember this story very clearly because it was kind of my first big adventure. It also made me aware for the first time of how much my home and my family mean to me."

"I love to tell stories. I just
let my imagination run wild!"
—Melissa

Model Study

Short Story

Writers create stories to entertain their readers. They use
what they know and their imaginations to make their stories
interesting and exciting.

Stories can be about almost anything, but they have certain
elements in common: a **setting, characters,** and a **plot**.

- **Setting** The setting is the time of the story and the
  place where it happens.

- **Characters** Characters are the people or animals that
  take part in the plot.

- **Plot** The plot is what happens in a story.

Read the student model on page 139W. It shows the features
of a good short story.

SHORT STORY

A good short story

☑ provides background about the setting

☑ has a plot that makes sense and keeps readers' interest

☑ has one or more characters

☑ usually has dialogue between characters.

Feature Checklist

Another Saturday Morning

by Melissa Lopez

Melissa includes details about the **setting**.

Alex was eating breakfast Saturday morning when Luis knocked on the door to Alex's apartment.

'Hey, Alex," he said. "I was walking by Monster Sports. They're having a drawing for a custom skateboard. I put my name in and your name, too."

"Sounds awesome. I hope one of us wins," Alex said.

"We'll need to stop by the store this afternoon," explained Luis. "They are going to post the winner's name in the front window at 3 p.m."

Melissa builds her **plot** around a single event.

"It might happen, but you boys shouldn't get your hearts set on winning," said Mom as Luis left.

Alex read for a while and almost forgot about the skateboard. Then he went outside to hang out with Luis.

"Let's go to Monster Sports and check out the window," Luis said.

When the boys walked in, the first thing they saw was a huge sign that said: *Skateboard Winner: Alex Sanchez.* "I don't believe it!" exclaimed Alex.

The next day, Alex's name and photograph were in a newspaper ad for Monster Sports. There he was, holding a skateboard with a custom-drawn Frankenstein's Monster on it. *Anything is possible on a Saturday morning,* thought Alex.

Melissa's short story features just a few **characters**.

Melissa includes **dialogue** between characters.

Student Model

Focus on Character

An author can develop characters in four ways:

- a description of what the character looks like

- the character's actions

- the character's words

- how others think about or act toward the character.

Description

One of the quickest ways for writers to introduce a character is through description. Read this description from the story *Frankenstein* by Mary Shelley.

> I remember the moment his black lips moved. His skin, stretched and sewn together, quivered. He took a rasping breath and opened his watery, yellow eyes.

The writer carefully chose details such as the creature's "rasping breath" and sewn-together skin to show how frightening the creature is.

Character's Actions

How a character behaves can also tell us about his or her personality. What can you learn about the creature from his actions?

> The creature terrorized me for many years. First he found and killed my dear brother. Then he killed my best friend. Finally he killed my sweet bride on our wedding night.

Character's Words

Sometimes, writers reveal a character through the character's words. The question at the end of this passage shows how scared and guilty the creature's creator, Victor, feels.

> Instead of feeling proud, I was disgusted. I could not even stand to look at him. So I ran away, asking myself, *What have I done?*

Reactions of other Characters

Finally, a writer uses other characters' reactions to show what a character is like.

> People who saw him were terrified. Some people ran away screaming. Others threw stones and bricks at him. One man shot him in the arm.

These reactions to the creature emphasize that he is an outsider whose appearance terrifies people.

Put It All Together

When you create a character for a story, try starting with a character map.

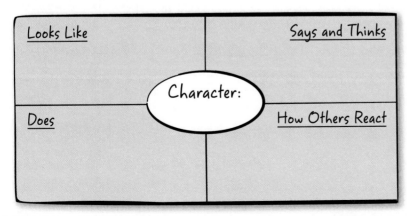

Focus on Setting

The **setting** of a story is the *time* and *place*. When and where do the events occur? That's up to you.

Plan Your Setting

The time and place for your story affect how your characters behave and what happens.

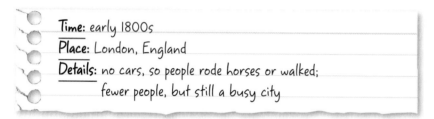

> Time: early 1800s
> Place: London, England
> Details: no cars, so people rode horses or walked;
>   fewer people, but still a busy city

Plan How the Setting Affects the Story

Think carefully about the details of your setting. What's it like to live in the time and place you chose? What things do people do for fun? What problems might come up? Determine how the setting will affect the characters and action.

> Time: 1700s
> Place: a ship in the Arctic
> How it affects the characters:
> —Few people are there so people are lonely.
> —Characters must have a really strong reason for going to such
>   a cold, distant place.
> How it affects the action:
> —There are no radios, cell phones, or ways to communicate.
> —People have to write letters.
> —It is a challenge to survive.

TechTIP

Go online and use a search engine to find images. Use images for inspiration when picking and writing about setting.

Use Specific, Sensory Words

Once you've got some basic ideas down, think of specific sensory details related to your setting. What do people see, hear, and feel there? Use precise words to make the setting come alive.

Time: 1700s

Place: a ship in the Arctic

Sights: the large expanse of ocean; ice floes and icebergs floating among the waves

Sounds: the sloshing of water and grinding of ice against the ship

Feelings: the bitter wind blowing

Put It All Together

After you've planned your setting, try putting all the details together. Don't worry about figuring out exactly what happens in the story. Just try to "get into" the time and place. Here's how one student wrote about England in the early 1800s:

Setting Description

Amelia rested her face across the soft, red velvet curtains as she gazed out at the dark gray sky. She sighed with boredom. The house was dead silent. It was still snowing heavily outside, and there was nothing—absolutely nothing—to do.

All week, she had looked forward to visiting her cousin. But the snowstorm had spoiled that. Elizabeth lived in a small village thirty miles away, and the roads out of London were impassable. She'd begged her father to try, but he had refused.

The writer includes **sensory words and details**.

The writer shows **how the setting affects the action**.

Focus on Plot

When you write a short story, you create characters and put them in a setting. The **plot** unfolds as you tell about a problem the characters face and how they try to solve it.

The Characters

Mary Shelley might have planned out the story for *Frankenstein* by first imagining characters:

- Victor Frankenstein, a scientist who wants to create life
- a creature that Frankenstein made

The Setting

She also had to choose a setting. In longer stories, the action might occur in more than one place, and the story might jump back and forth in time.

- a ship in the Arctic in the 1700s
- back in time in Frankenstein's lab and home city

A 1931 film version of *Frankenstein* featured Colin Clive as Victor Frankenstein. ▼

The Problem Starts the Story

How did Mary Shelley come up with a plot? Good plots center on a problem. If a scientist built a living creature, what problems might he face?

> Frankenstein discovers how to create life. He brings a creature to life, but then regrets what he has done. The creature won't leave him alone.

What Happens Next?

Victor Frankenstein's problem is what pushes the plot of *Frankenstein* forward. With each event, the problem gets worse until it builds to a **turning point**. After that, the problem is solved and the story ends.

Put It All together

You can use a diagram to organize the plot of a story.

Plot Diagram

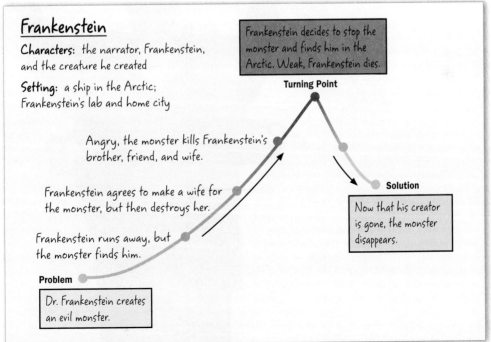

Frankenstein

Characters: the narrator, Frankenstein, and the creature he created

Setting: a ship in the Arctic; Frankenstein's lab and home city

Frankenstein decides to stop the monster and finds him in the Arctic. Weak, Frankenstein dies.

Turning Point

Angry, the monster kills Frankenstein's brother, friend, and wife.

Frankenstein agrees to make a wife for the monster, but then destroys her.

Frankenstein runs away, but the monster finds him.

Problem

Dr. Frankenstein creates an evil monster.

Solution

Now that his creator is gone, the monster disappears.

Focus on Point of View

When you write a story, you choose a **point of view**:

- When you use **first-person** point of view, you write in the voice of one of your characters, as if you're right inside the story. You describe events using words like *I, me, we,* and *us* to tell about "yourself" and the people "you" know.

  " My name is
    Victor Frankenstein."

- In **third-person** point of view, you write as if you're watching events from a distance. As a writer, you're separate from your characters, so you use words like *he, she, they,* and *them* to tell what happens.

  " His name is
    Victor Frankenstein."

The point of view you choose depends on your purpose and audience.

Hollywood created this version of Mary Shelley's tragic monster. ▶

Compare the passages below. The first one is straight from *Frankenstein*. The second tells the story from a different point of view. How does that change the story?

I hid in my room and nervously paced the floor, trying to determine what to do. But, because I had been hard at work for so long, I had not slumbered for many days, and I soon fell onto my bed and slept.

An odd, gurgling noise woke me up. The terrible creature was standing over me, grinning and making baby noises. He came closer and reached out one of his enormous hands to touch me. I leapt up and ran until I crumpled onto the street.

These **pronouns** are clues to first-person point of view. The writer tells the story in Victor's voice.

Dr. Frankenstein hid in his room and nervously paced the floor, trying to determine what to do. But, because he had been hard at work for so long, he had not slumbered for many days, and he soon fell onto his bed and slept.

An odd, gurgling noise woke him up. The terrible creature was standing over him, grinning and making baby noises. He came closer and reached out one of his enormous hands to touch Frankenstein. The scientist leapt up and ran until he crumpled onto the street.

The writer uses Frankenstein's name and these **pronouns** to tell the story in third-person point of view.

Readers may connect better with a character when the story is told in first-person. They get a good sense of how the character feels.

When the story is told in third-person, readers may get more information about all the characters. The writer is not limited to what one character knows.

Voice and Style

What's It Like ?

Have you ever gone to a costume party? People choose costumes to express themselves and show their personal style. Writers do the same thing. You express your own personal style through the words you choose and the way you put them together.

Why Do Voice and Style Matter?

Voice and style are what make your writing sound like you. You may use a different voice when you write different things. Your voice in a short story is different from your voice in a social studies report. Use these strategies to write with a strong voice and style:

- Use powerful words to help readers see and feel the action.

- Vary your sentences to keep the reader engaged.

- Remember your purpose, audience, and form.

To entertain readers, the writer of the story below has chosen powerful words. He also varies the length of his sentences.

The mummy felt dreadful. One of its long strips of winding cloth had been snagged on the door of its tomb. The creature struggled to free itself. First, it tugged gently, and then it yanked hard. Still, it could not get loose. And it was already late for the werewolf's birthday party. It was in BIG trouble!

Using both **short and long sentences** makes the writing varied.

Specific words help readers picture the scene.

Study the rubric on page 149W. What is the difference between a paper with a score of 2 and one with a score of 4?

Voice and Style

	Does the writing sound real, and is it unique to the writer?	How interesting are the words and sentences? How appropriate are they to the purpose and audience?
4 Wow!	The writing fully engages the reader with its individual voice and style. The tone is consistent throughout.	The words and sentences are interesting and appropriate to the purpose and audience. • The words are powerful and engaging. • The sentences are varied and flow together effectively.
3 Ahh.	<u>Most</u> of the writing engages the reader with a voice and style that are unique. The tone is mostly consistent.	<u>Most</u> of the words and sentences are interesting and appropriate to the purpose and audience. • Most words are powerful and engaging. • Most sentences are varied and flow together.
2 Hmm.	<u>Some</u> of the writing engages the reader, but the voice and style are not unique.	<u>Some</u> of the words and sentences are interesting and appropriate to the purpose and audience. • Some words are powerful and engaging. • Some sentences are varied, but the flow could be smoother.
1 Huh?	The writing does <u>not</u> engage the reader.	<u>Few or none</u> of the words and sentences are appropriate to the purpose and audience. • The words are often vague and dull. • The sentences lack variety and do not flow together.

Voice and Style, continued

Compare Writing Samples

A strong voice and style engage the reader with powerful words. The tone is consistent. Good writing is consistent—it stays the same throughout the story. Compare the opening paragraphs of two short stories on this page.

Strong Voice and Style

At last, my experiment was ready. An enormous, lifeless creature lay on the table in my lab. I thought my creation would show the world what a great scientist I was. I did not know how wrong I was!

That cold November night, I brought my creature to life. I remember the moment his black lips moved. His skin, stretched and sewn together, quivered. He took a rasping breath and opened his watery, yellow eyes. Then that repulsive creature sat up and looked at me.

The writer uses **colorful words** that fit the subject.

Sentences are varied and flow together.

Weak Voice and Style

My experiment was ready. A creature lay on the table in my lab. I thought my creation would show the world what a great scientist I was. I was wrong!

I brought my creature to life on a November night. I remember the moment his black lips moved. I remember when his skin shook. I remember when he took a breath and opened his eyes. I remember when the creature sat up and looked at me.

The **choice of words** is less specific and less interesting.

The **sentences** are boring because they all follow the same pattern.

Evaluate for Voice and Style

Carefully read the short story below. Use the rubric on page 149W to score it.

The Incident at the Door

by Ricky Colacino

The screaming could be heard for miles.

Paul Bunyan and his pet blue ox were watching TV. He liked the volume turned all the way up. He always turned it up during scary movies. He knew the neighbors wouldn't complain. No one had bothered him in years.

Paul was a great-great-great-great grandson of the original Paul Bunyan. Like the original Bunyan, he was a giant. Unlike the original Bunyan, he was grumpy and unpleasant. The neighbors kept their distance.

At the end of summer, someone new moved in next door. The name on the mailbox was Polyphemus. The locals recognized the name and shuddered. The new neighbor was a Cyclops—a one-eyed giant monster from Greek myths.

The Cyclops did not like the noise coming from Paul Bunyan's house. He knocked on Bunyan's door with his heavy wooden club.

"Turn down that noise or get headphones," he said. "I came to this valley for peace."

Angry, Bunyan opened the door. Then he saw just who was outside. He looked at the Cyclops up and down. He looked at the Cyclops side to side. He looked straight into the Cyclops's single eye.

Then Bunyan backed down. He slowly walked into the living room and lowered the volume.

Do the sentences all sound the same, or are they varied? Which ones would you change?

Does the language fit the subject?

How could you improve the writer's word choice?

Raise the Score

These papers have been scored using the **Voice and Style Rubric** on page 149W. Study each paper to see why it got the score it did.

Overall Score: 4

The writer uses **varied sentences**, mixing short and long sentences and different sentence types.

The writer uses many **specific, colorful words** and includes **figurative language**.

The Art Show
Chie Nakamura

Before dismissing class, Mrs. Barns reminded students of the school art show on Monday. Ben didn't need reminding. He had been working on his drawing for two weeks!

The class had been reading *Frankenstein*, and Ben decided to draw a portrait of the creature with all the gory details. He drew red blood oozing from its jagged stitches. He sketched the mounds of wrinkles on its massive forehead. Ben's hand was cramped up like a crab's claw!

On Monday night, Ben lingered near his drawing, eager to hear comments. But parents just breezed by, looking for their own children's work. Even worse was the reaction from Katie Trimble, a girl he had hoped to impress. She just muttered, "Gross," and walked away.

When Mrs. Barns walked over, she gasped. "Ben, this is amazing! I love how you made the bolts in its neck so realistic." Finally someone appreciated all of Ben's hard work.

After the show, Mrs. Barns put Ben's drawing in the library display case. Some of his classmates think it's creepy, but now he takes that as a compliment.

The **informal language** shows the writer's voice and style and goes with the story.

The Art Show

Before dismissing class, Mrs. Barns reminded students of the school art show on Monday. Ben didn't need reminding. He had been working on his drawing for two weeks!

He had just finished reading *Frankenstein*, and Ben decided to draw a picture of the creature. He was sure to include all of the details. He used a marker to draw red blood flowing from its uneven stitches. Then, he took a charcoal pencil and drew wrinkles on its huge forehead. Ben worked so hard, his right hand was cramped up like a crab's claw.

On Monday night, Ben waited where his drawing was displayed. He was eager to hear people's comments. But other kids' parents just walked by. Even worse was the reaction from Katie Trimble. He wanted her to like his drawing, but she just said, "Gross," and walked away.

When Mrs. Barns walked over, she gasped. "Ben, this is amazing," she said. He was happy that someone appreciated his hard work.

After the art show, Mrs. Barns picked Ben's drawing to be placed in the library display case. Some of his classmates don't like it, but now he takes that as a compliment.

*The writer **varies the length of sentences**.*

*The writer uses some **specific, colorful words** and includes **figurative language**.*

*The writer could include more examples of **informal language** like this.*

RAISING THE SCORE

The writing needs to be more varied and specific. Which statements could be changed to questions? Where could the writer be more specific?

Raise the Score, continued

Overall Score: 2

The writer uses many statements of the same length. That's dull.

The writer uses **vague words** that don't provide a clear picture of what's happening.

The writer **repeats the same phrases**, which makes the writing boring.

The Art Show

Mrs. Barns dismissed her class with a reminder. The sixth-grade art show was on Monday. Mrs. Barnes didn't need to remind Ben. He was almost done with his drawing.

He had just finished reading *Frankenstein*. He wanted to draw the creature. He was sure to include all of the details. He included blood and stitches. Then, he used a pencil to draw lines on its forehead. Ben worked really hard on the drawing.

On Monday night, Ben stood near his drawing. Parents just walked by. The reaction from Katie Trimble was even worse. She didn't like it at all.

When Mrs. Barns walked over, Ben's drawing got her attention. "It's amazing," she said. Ben was so happy that she liked it.

After the art show was over, Mrs. Barns picked Ben's drawing to be placed in the library display case. Some of his classmates don't like it very much, but he takes that as a compliment.

RAISING THE SCORE

This writer needs to add more variety. Which sentences could be shortened or lengthened? Which words could be replaced by more colorful words?

The Art Show

Mrs. Barns dismissed her class. She reminded them about the art show. It was on Monday. Ben's drawing was almost finished. It was pretty good.

He read *Frankenstein* in Mrs. Barns's class. He wanted to draw the creature. He included lots of details. He included stitches and wrinkles. He worked really hard.

The art show was on Monday night. Ben's drawing was on the wall. People just walked by. Katie Trimble saw it. She didn't like it.

Mrs. Barns said, "It's amazing." Ben felt better.

The art show was over. Mrs. Barns picked Ben's drawing to be placed in the library display case. Some people like it. Other people don't.

The writer uses too many short statements that start with a subject and a verb.

The writer uses **general words**. That makes the writing dull.

The writer starts these sentences the **same way**, which sounds boring.

RAISING *THE SCORE*

The writer needs to create a more interesting, personal voice. How could the writer make the story more colorful and personal?

Use Effective Words

What's It Like

Have you ever had bad reception on your TV? It was probably hard to tell exactly what was going on, even though you could get the general idea. In the same way, vague or dull words make it hard for your reader to get the full story. Use effective words to make sure the picture is clear.

Choosing Descriptive Nouns

By using specific nouns, you help your reader understand exactly who and what you're writing about. See how the nouns become more descriptive and interesting in this example.

VAGUE ── SHARP

general words   ▶ medium words   ▶ precise words

movie   horror film   **1931 film version of *Frankenstein***

Choosing Descriptive Verbs

Verbs help readers see the action! The more descriptive your verbs, the clearer the picture will be. Check these out.

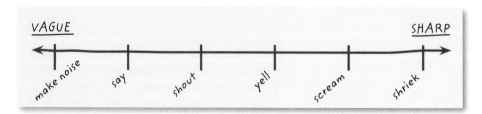

VAGUE ←─────────────────────────────────────→ SHARP

make noise   say   shout   yell   scream   shriek

Choosing Descriptive Adjectives and Adverbs

Adjectives and adverbs are great tools for writing with a powerful voice and style. Adjectives and adverbs help you describe, or give more information.

Adjectives tell more about nouns:

> The yellow flames flickered in the cold night air.

Adverbs tell more about verbs:

> The campers briskly rubbed their hands together and coughed nervously.

Read these examples. Which of the descriptions below helps you picture Marc better?

> Marc's eyes stared at the ground. He wore a shirt, jeans, and boots. His hair was covered by a hat, and he held a bag in his hands.

> Marc's bloodshot eyes stared at the ground. He wore an old, torn shirt, dirty blue jeans, and mud-covered boots. His tangled hair was covered by a dusty, bent black baseball cap, and he loosely held a crumpled paper bag in his rough hands.

Use Effective Words, continued

Finding the Right Balance

Some commonly used adjectives really aren't very descriptive.
Stay away from these vague words and choose words that are
more specific.

Overused Adjective	Better Alternative
big	enormous, massive, immense
small	tiny, petite, slight
dark	shady, murky, dim, gloomy
bright	sunny, radiant, brilliant
slow	sluggish, deliberate, leisurely
fast	rapid, swift, hasty, quick

Finally, it may be tempting to use as many adjectives and
adverbs as possible, but be careful. Too many can overwhelm
your reader!

Too Little	Just Right	Too Much
The kids watched the movie.	The curious kids eagerly watched the old movie.	The curious, excited kids eagerly watched the old, silent, black-and-white movie.

If your writing is overloaded with adjectives and adverbs,
think about whether a more specific noun or verb would help
get your meaning across.

*Tech*TIP

Set up a file and keep a bank of great words. Open your word-bank file when you need inspiration while writing.

Figurative Language: Description with a Twist

Choosing specific words isn't the only way to make your writing more descriptive. You can also use figurative language.

Similes use "like" or "as" to compare two things. Often they compare things that seem different but have hidden similarities. Similes add color to your writing.

Without Similes

> Frankenstein could not get rid of his sense of guilt.

With Similes

> Frankenstein's guilt was like a shadow, following him everywhere.

Guilt is compared to a **shadow**.

The word **"like"** connects the two things being compared.

Metaphors make comparisons without using "like" or "as."

Without Metaphor

> Frankenstein could not get rid of his sense of guilt.

With Metaphor

> Frankenstein's guilt was a shadow that followed him everywhere.

Guilt is compared to a **shadow**.

In a metaphor, you do not use "like" or "as" to make the connection.

Putting It All Together

Descriptive nouns, verbs, adjectives, adverbs, and figurative language make your writing come alive for your readers.

Nightmare

The yellow flames of the campfire flickered in the cold night air. The campers briskly rubbed their hands together and coughed nervously. Somewhere in the darkness, a creature screamed in anger and fear, like a wild caged beast. The campers sprinted through the dark forest, trying to escape.

Dane awoke suddenly in his bed, covered in cold sweat and breathing heavily. *I shouldn't have watched that old horror film before going to sleep,* he thought.

Does this writer use vivid, specific words? Find some examples.

Where does the writer use figurative language?

Vary Your Sentences

Actors in a play don't just say their lines. They speak with expression. They vary their tone, volume, and rhythm to make the performance exciting. Writers also use a variety of techniques to hold readers' interest. Varying the kinds of sentences you use keeps your writing lively.

Avoid Boring Writing

Don't bore your reader with sentences that all sound the same—mix it up a bit. Ask yourself these questions:

- Are all of my sentences statements?

- Are all of my sentences about the same length?

- Do all of my sentences start the same way?

If you answered "yes" to any of the above questions, you need to change things! Read on for a few tricks.

Use Different Sentence Types

One way to vary your sentences is to make sure you use a mix of statements, exclamations, and questions.

Boring

The angry mob trapped the creature in the town square. They yelled at him and threw stones. The creature cried out in fear. He didn't understand why everyone hated him so much.

Better

The angry mob trapped the creature in the town square. How they yelled at him! They even threw stones! The creature cried out in fear. Questions plagued his mind. Why did everyone hate him so much?

Use Different Sentence Lengths

Another way to keep your reader interested is to use a mix of sentence lengths. For example, follow a long sentence with a very short one.

Boring

> Dr. Frankenstein was scared. He didn't want to go home. He knew he would have to eventually. What if the creature was there? What if it was waiting for him? Frankenstein shuddered at the thought.

Better

> Dr. Frankenstein was scared. He didn't want to go home, but he knew he would have to eventually. What if the creature was there, waiting for him? He shuddered.

Start Your Sentences in Different Ways

Sentences that all start the same way get boring fast. Try to avoid starting too many sentences in a row with the same subject and verb.

Boring

> Chandra Pierce is a makeup artist. She can turn anyone into a monster using all kinds of materials. She uses rubber, plastic, foam, and paint as well as regular makeup. She made a young girl look like an 80-year-old man once!

Better

> Chandra Pierce is a makeup artist. Using all kinds of materials, she can turn anyone into a monster. In addition to regular makeup, she uses rubber, plastic, foam, and paint. Once, she made a young girl look like an 80-year-old man!

A makeup artist works her magic. ▶

Combine Sentences

What's It Like

Frankenstein's creature moved very awkwardly because he was made of parts that didn't fit together well. Writing can also be awkward if you have too many short sentences that don't work well together. By combining sentences, you can make your writing move smoothly.

Make Your Sentences Smoother

Too many short sentences can make your writing sound choppy and disconnected. They also make it harder for your reader to understand the connections between ideas. Study the writing sample below.

Choppy, Disconnected Sentences

> My teacher told me to write a new version of *Frankenstein*. I didn't really know where to start. Everyone knows the story of the crazy scientist. He creates a creature out of dead body parts. The creature tries to fit in. Everyone hates him. He gets angry. He kills several people. How could I write a new version?

On pages 163W–165W, you'll study a few ways to fix this problem:

- Join sentences that are next to each other.

- Move details from one sentence into another.

- Use fewer words to say the same thing.

Join Sentences That Are Next to Each Other

Sentences about related ideas that are right next to each other can often be combined. You can join the sentences using the words *and, but,* or *or.*

- Use *and* to join sentences that have related ideas.

- Use *but* to join sentences that show differences.

- Use *or* to join sentences that offer different ideas or possibilities.

> I was supposed to write a new version of
> Frankenstein ^and^ I was stuck. I liked Frankenstein okay ^but^
> I just didn't want to rewrite it. Did I have to work
> with this story? ^or^ Could I choose something different?

Sometimes, two sentences have closely related ideas, but one sentence is more important. You can use different kinds of words to combine the sentences.

- Join sentences with time words like *while, when, as, before,* and *after.*

> ^When^
>   My teacher told me to write a new version of
> Frankenstein ^,^ I didn't really know where to start.

- Join sentences with words that show how one thing caused another, such as *because, since, as,* and *so.*

> ^Since^
>   I had always been interested in this story ^,^ I decided
> to write a new version.

Combine Sentences, continued

Join Sentences With Repeated Ideas

Some sentences in your writing might repeat ideas without giving much new information. If that's the case, you can combine sentences and eliminate some of the repetition.

> I thought about ~~it. I wondered~~ what it was like to be that creature. It must have been hard knowing that you were so ugly, ~~It must have been hard knowing~~ everyone who saw you hated you. ~~They all~~ wanted you dead, ~~too.~~ I decided to write my new version from the creature's point of view.

Move Details from One Sentence Into Another

You can also turn the most important part of one sentence into a detail within another sentence.

> *Desperate and ashamed, Frankenstein*
> ~~Frankenstein was ashamed of what he had created. He was desperate to get away from the creature. He~~ abandoned the creature. The creature harmed Frankenstein's loved ones. Frankenstein then traveled all over the world ~~to find~~ *and* ~~him. He~~ finally met with the creature again in the Arctic.

In Mary Shelley's novel, the creature kills Victor's brother, his best friend, and his wife. ▶

Use Fewer Words to Say the Same Thing

Cut out unnecessary words so your writing gets to the point.

Too Wordy

> Who would think that sitting around telling ghost stories could lead to a book, movies, and even comic books? That happened with one ghost story, *Frankenstein*. It all started when Mary Shelley was visiting friends one summer. The weather that summer was rainy. The group needed to find a way to entertain themselves. One friend suggested a storytelling contest.

Just Right

> Who would think that telling ghost stories could lead to a book, movies, and even comic books? That happened with *Frankenstein*. It all started when Mary Shelley was visiting friends one rainy summer. The group needed to entertain themselves, so one friend suggested a storytelling contest.

Try condensing sentences into just a word or a phrase.

Too Wordy

> Mary Shelley's novel has inspired many other artists. It was first published nearly 200 years ago in 1818. There have been many films based on *Frankenstein*. Hollywood made a famous film version in 1931. The film starred Boris Karloff.

Just Right

> Mary Shelley's novel, first published in 1818, has inspired many other artists. There have been many films based on *Frankenstein*. Hollywood made a famous film version in 1931 starring Boris Karloff.

Tech*TIP*

Use **Save As** in the file menu to create a new version of your document. That way, you can go back to the original if you cut too much.

Rewrite a Story

WRITING PROMPT What if the creature from *Frankenstein* sat next to you in math class? When you write your own version of a story, the details are up to you. Create your own version of the Frankenstein story. Let your imagination run wild! You might

- rewrite it with a different setting—the present time or far into the future; another country or another planet
- change the character of Frankenstein's creature into a lovable beast who gets the wife he wants
- change what happens in the plot.

Prewrite

Here are some ideas for how you can get started writing.

1 Decide What to Change

Decide what elements to change in your version of the story. Don't change everything, or it will be a completely different story. It helps to create a chart to compare the original story with your new version. Study this plan:

	Original Story	My Story
Characters	narrator, Victor Frankenstein, his creature	Victor Frankenstein, the robot he builds, the woman the robot tries to befriend
Setting	Old-fashioned lab	Modern lab
Plot	Frankenstein creates a creature but abandons it. The creature seeks revenge on him. Frankenstein dies trying to stop him.	Dr. Frankenstein makes a robot. Robot tries to make a friend, but hurts someone. Frankenstein destroys the robot.
Point of View	Frankenstein narrates.	Frankenstein narrates.

② Plan Your Characters

How will your characters be the same as the characters in the original version? How will they be different? Create a web for each important character, and write down any details that come to mind.

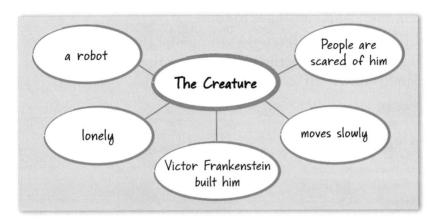

③ Plan Your Setting

Think about your setting the same way you planned your characters. Fill out a web with details about where and when your version of the story takes place.

Prewrite, continued

4 Plan Your Plot

What will happen in your version of *Frankenstein?* You can work from the events in the original story or strike out in a new direction. Either way, make sure your plot centers on a problem that characters have to solve.

Use a plot diagram to help develop a strong plot that will keep readers engaged. Here's the Plot Diagram that Isaiah made to plan his rewritten story.

Isaiah's Plot Diagram

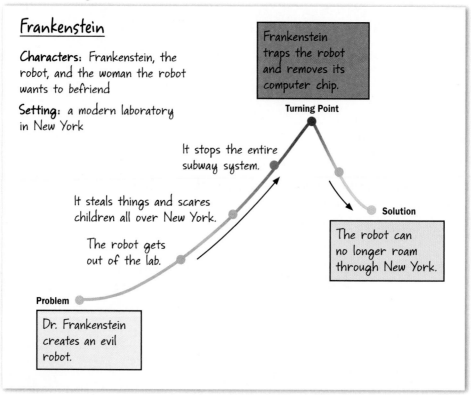

Frankenstein

Characters: Frankenstein, the robot, and the woman the robot wants to befriend

Setting: a modern laboratory in New York

Frankenstein traps the robot and removes its computer chip.

Turning Point

It stops the entire subway system.

It steals things and scares children all over New York.

The robot gets out of the lab.

Solution

The robot can no longer roam through New York.

Problem

Dr. Frankenstein creates an evil robot.

5 **Choose a Point of View**

Will you tell the story from an outsider's point of view (third person)? Or, will you use the voice of one of the characters (first person)? Try a few different points of view and decide which is the most interesting. Remember, a narrator can only tell what he or she knows.

Outsider's Point of View

> Victor's robot was almost complete. It just needed a brain and a left foot. He got an empty tuna can from the kitchen. That solved the foot problem.

Victor's Point of View

> My robot was almost complete. All it needed was a brain. Oh, and a left foot. What good was a walking robot that tripped all the time? Maybe that empty tuna can in the kitchen would work. I just hoped it wouldn't smell.

The Creature's Point of View

> When Victor put me together, I didn't know what was happening. After all, I didn't have a brain yet. But I'm glad he remembered to give me a left foot. I wouldn't have wanted to fall over when I took my first step.

Reflect

• Does your story have an exciting plot?

• Is your version different in an interesting way?

Draft

Now that you know the overall direction of your story, you can start writing. Use your plans to start crafting your story.

- **Use Your Plot Diagram** Follow the plan you laid out in your plot diagram to keep your story organized. But be flexible—you might think of some additional plot twists as you write.

From Isaiah's Draft

> It was just another day in my lab. What should I explore today? Soon, I thought of a question that had been bothering me. What made people think and move? Could I make something that could do what people did?
>
> There was only one way to find out. I had to build a robot.

- **Add Character and Setting Details** Don't waste the work you did planning your characters and setting. Give plenty of details to bring your story to life.

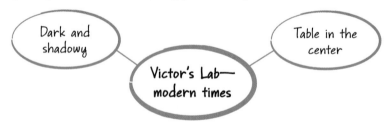

From Isaiah's Draft

> It was just another day in my dark and shadowy lab. What should I explore today? I leaned on the table and played with the sleeve of my lab coat. Soon, I thought of a question that had been bothering me. What made people think and move? Could I make something that could do what people did?
>
> There was only one way to find out. I had to build a robot.

Reflect

- Read your draft. Are you building your plot to an exciting turning point?

- Do you need to add any more details about the setting or characters?

DRAFTING TIPS
Trait: **Voice and Style**

If You Need More Details . . .
Maybe you've followed your plan, but your writing seems boring.

Try Adding Snapshots and Thoughtshots
- Read your draft. Pick one important moment and picture it in your mind. What does the character see, hear, smell, and taste? Write these details to create a snapshot of that moment.

- Think about that same moment. This time write down what the character might think. This description is called a thoughtshot.

Here are some snapshots and thoughtshots for Isaiah's story.

Snapshots	Thoughtshots
Where was Victor Frankenstein?	What inspired him to create the robot?
What was he doing?	How did he feel when the robot first moved?

In his draft, Isaiah used the questions to add vivid details and interesting insights into his character's mind.

> Frankenstein was in his dark lab, which smelled faintly of sulfur. Sparks occasionally flew from the electronic equipment that lined the walls. Frankenstein was about to flip the switch that would bring his robot to life. He had wanted to be famous as the first scientist to manufacture life. But now, as the robot stirred, Frankenstein's excitement was mixed with fear.

Revise

As you revise, keep in mind your audience and purpose for writing. Do you want to scare your friends, or make them laugh?

① Evaluate Your Work

Read your draft aloud to a partner. Have your partner sketch while listening to the story. Look at the sketch. Did he or she draw what you had imagined? Discuss these questions:

- **About the Form** Was the story interesting? Are any parts of the story confusing?

- **About the Voice and Style** Did it sound like me? Will the language hold readers' interest?

Revision in Action

From Isaiah's Draft

"Is it alive?" Ygor asked. He asked this question in a very impressed tone. He sounded in awe of the robot.

"It's moving—look out!" Ygor screamed.

The robot was off the table. The robot was coming toward us. It looked as if it was about to grab us. We were scared.

Its cold metallic hand reached toward me. I moved out of the way. What had I gotten myself into?

Isaiah's partner thinks:

" Some of your sentences are boring. Combine them."

" You can vary your sentences more"

" You can use more specific words to make the language more interesting."

2 Mark Your Changes

Add Text To make your writing livelier, you might add text using a caret: ∧. Use this mark to add

- effective, specific, colorful words
- words needed to combine sentences.

Delete Text Use the delete mark ⸎ to take out text. Use this mark to take out

- repeated ideas and unnecessary details
- words you get rid of when you combine sentences.

Rearrange Text Finally, you might rearrange some words for a better effect. Use this mark: ⟿.

Reflect

- Are your plot, settings, and characters engaging and clear?
- Have you used lively words and sentences?

Revising Marks **MARK**	∧	⟿	⌃	⸎	¶
WHAT IT MEANS	Insert something.	Move to here.	Replace with this.	Take out.	Make a new paragraph.

Revised Draft

"Is it alive?" Ygor asked. ~~He asked this question~~ in a very∧ impressed ~~tone.~~ He sounded in awe of the robot.
√"It's moving—look out!" ⟨Ygor screamed.⟩
The robot was off the table. ~~The robot was coming~~
lumbering
∧toward us. ~~It looked~~as if it was about to grab us. We
terrified
∧
were ~~scared.~~
clawed its way   dashed
Its cold metallic hand ∧~~reached~~ toward me. I ∧~~moved~~
out of the way. What had I gotten myself into?

Isaiah combined sentences to keep them from sounding dull.

Isaiah changed this sentence to add variety.

Isaiah used more specific, colorful verbs and adjectives.

Edit and Proofread

Once your story is as clear and interesting as you hoped it would be, read it again to fix language errors. This is what you do when you edit and proofread your work.

- **Check the Grammar** Make sure that you have used correct and conventional grammar throughout. In particular, check for correct use of adjectives and adverbs. (See page 175W.)

- **Check the Spelling** Spell-check can help, but it isn't always enough. For errors with adverbs ending in *-ly*, you'll have to read your work carefully and remember a few rules. (See page 176W.)

- **Check the Mechanics** Errors in punctuation and capitalization can make your work hard to understand. In particular, check that you've punctuated dialogue correctly. (See page 177W.)

Use these marks to edit and proofread your story.

Editing and Proofreading Marks

MARK	WHAT IT MEANS	MARK	WHAT IT MEANS
∧	Insert something.	∕	Make lowercase.
∧	Add a comma.	℘	Delete, take something out.
∧	Add a semicolon.	¶	Make new paragraph.
⊙	Add a period.	◯	Spell out.
⊙	Add a colon.	∧	Replace with this.
⌄ ⌄	Add quotation marks.	∼	Change order of letters or words.
⌄	Add an apostrophe.	#	Insert space.
≡	Capitalize.	◡	Close up, no space here.

Reflect

- What kind of errors did you find? What can you do to keep from making them?

Grammar Workout

Check for Adjectives and Adverbs

Adjectives are words that describe nouns—people, places, things and ideas. You can use adjectives to add color and richness to your writing.

PLAIN   Ygor was wearing a coat.

ENRICHED   Young Ygor was wearing a coarse brown coat.

Adverbs can also add details and bring life to your writing.

- You can use an adverb to describe a verb, telling *how, when,* or *where*. Many adverbs end in **-ly**.

  EXAMPLES   The robot moved quickly toward Miss Petal.

  She immediately jumped back.

- You can also use adverbs to modify an adjective or another adverb.

  EXAMPLES   Miss Petal was rather rude to the robot.

  She ran quite frantically.

Find the Opportunities

> I stopped to take a ^*deep* breath as I ran ^*quickly* after the robot. Its feet pounded on the smooth tile floor. The robot stopped. It stared at me. Although I knew it wasn't human, the look in its eyes frightened me. "Why won't anyone talk to me?" it howled.

Where else could you add adjectives or adverbs to enrich the writing?

Edit and Proofread, continued

Spelling Workout

Check Adverbs Ending in *-ly*

When you form an adverb by adding *-ly* to an adjective, you may have to change the spelling of the base word. Follow these rules:

- For adjectives that end in *-y*, change the *y* to an *i* before you add *-ly*.

  EXAMPLE   happy + -ly ⟶ happily

- For adjectives that end in *-l*, keep the *l* at the end of the root word and add *-ly*.

  EXAMPLE   real + -ly ⟶ really

- For adjectives that end in a consonant plus silent *-e*, the spelling stays the same when you add *-ly*.

  EXAMPLE   late + -ly ⟶ lately

- For adjectives that end in a long vowel followed by *-e*, drop the *e* before you add *-ly*.

  EXAMPLE   true + -ly ⟶ truly

Find the Trouble Spots

It was the scariest thing I had ever seen. The robot stomped toward Miss Petal. "Friend?" he repeated ~~mechanicaly.~~ *mechanically*

He just wanted to be her friend, but she didn't care. She kept moving *daintily* ~~daintyly~~ away. "No, I am not your *friend*," she said nastly. She gazed cooly at him.

Find two more spelling errors to fix.

> # Mechanics Workout

Check Punctuation in Dialogue

Writers use dialogue to make stories come alive for readers. Here are a few simple rules for punctuating dialogue:

- Use quotation marks to show where a quotation begins and ends. Begin the quotation with a capital letter:

  EXAMPLE "Is it alive?" asked my friend.

- Dialogue often includes tags such as *John said* or *Elizabeth replied*. When a dialogue tag comes before a quote, include a comma between it and the opening quotation marks.

  EXAMPLE I yelled, "Let's get out of here!"

- When a dialogue tag comes after a quote, include a comma inside the ending quotation marks, unless the quote ends in a question mark or exclamation mark. These dialogue tags are not capitalized.

  EXAMPLES "What have you done?" asked Ygor.
  "I just don't know," replied Victor.

Find the Trouble Spots

  The robot pushed through the door. My next-door neighbor, Miss Petal, saw him and asked What is that? Friend? asked the robot.
  But Miss Petal didn't notice. She was backing slowly away. What is that *thing*? she hissed. I shook my head.
  Oh no, I whispered.

Find and fix two other places where quotations aren't correctly punctuated.

Publish, Share, and Reflect

You've worked hard to rewrite a story in your own unique voice. Now it's ready to share with other readers.

1 Publish and Share Your Work

Publishing your writing means making it public—that is, sharing it with other people. How you do so is up to you.

If you want many people to read your story, you might try these ways of publishing it:

- Have a teacher post it on your school's website.

- Send it in to your school's literary magazine.

- Do a dramatic reading for the class.

If you want to share your story with fewer people, try one of these ideas:

- Maybe you'd like to include your own art, but you're not comfortable showing it to everyone. You can scan and insert your art or photos into your story, and then copy it and share with friends and family.

- Practice doing a dramatic reading of your story to a few friends. Have them suggest ways you can improve your reading.

2 Reflect on Your Work

Don't stop thinking about your story just because it's finished. You might find that you want to go back to it and work with it some more. Ask yourself questions to think about what went well and what other creative writing projects you'd like to do.

Tech*TIP*

"Dress up" your final paper! Draw and scan pictures, or use your computer to create illustrations.

Reflect

- What was fun about rewriting a story? Are there other stories I could rewrite?

- How did I put my own personal stamp on the story?

How to Do a Dramatic Reading

Entertain a group with your story. Reading it aloud will bring the characters and events to life! Don't tell your listeners what parts are sad or frightening or funny—show them:

1. Give a brief introduction to your story. You might explain how it is similar and different from the original story and give any background information your listeners will need to understand the events, setting, and characters.

2. Practice speaking with **diction**. Pronounce each word clearly. Practice saying difficult words until you can say them quickly and clearly.

3. Vary the **tone** and **pitch** of your voice to fit different parts of your story. Create one "voice" for each character and use it every time.

4. Plan and rehearse your **tempo**. Which parts will you read quickly? Slowly? Highlight those in different colors. Where will you pause to give your audience time to think? Mark those points with a large dot and write *pause* in the margin.

5. Be an actor! Use **gestures** and facial **expressions** to communicate as you read. Practice your gestures in front of a mirror or a friend, or videotape yourself and watch your performance.

" **Victor, Victor, how could you create me and then abandon me?!** "

"Doing research can actually be a lot of fun! I like digging for information."

— Brian

Model Study

Information Report

What's the best way to become an expert on a topic? Do some research and use the ideas and facts you find to write an **information report**! You will discover many new things when you

- gather information about the topic from books, articles, and other sources

- record the facts and details on note cards

- turn the notes into an outline to plan your report

- use the outline to write each part of the report: the introduction, body, and conclusion.

Analyze the student model on pages 181W–183W. Look for the features of an information report.

INFORMATION REPORT

A good information report

☑ tells about a topic in an interesting way

☑ has an introduction, body, and conclusion

☑ has a clear central idea

☑ uses facts and details to support the central idea.

Feature Checklist

Discovering Life on Mars
by Jamie Choi

The **title** and **introduction** get the reader's attention and tell what the report is about.

Do aliens exist only in books, movies, and on TV—or is there really life in outer space? People are especially curious about life on Mars, one of Earth's nearest neighbors. Although scientists have not discovered life on the surface of Mars, it's possible that life may have existed there in the past and might presently exist underground. Perhaps one day we will discover the answer.

The introduction also presents the **central idea**.

The **body** of the report presents information from the writer's research.

Scientists began to seriously consider the possibility of life on Mars over 100 years ago. In the late 1800s, some astronomers noticed complicated patterns of lines on the planet's surface (Simon, 28). They believed the lines were canals that intelligent living creatures had built (Simon, 29). The idea gripped people's imagination.

Each paragraph begins with a **main idea**. **Facts** and **details** support the main idea.

In the mid-1960s, spacecraft began to explore Mars. At first, spacecraft could only fly by the planet. Later, they could orbit Mars (Jordan, 35). By the early 1970s, the first spacecraft had landed on Mars to gather information (Jordan, 50). But the spacecraft did not find any signs of life, or canals. However, scientists have made more discoveries about Mars from later space missions.

Early space missons found little evidence of life on Mars.

Information Report, continued

Missions such as Viking and Pathfinder have found similarities between Mars and Earth. This is one reason some people think life could exist there. Mars has some of the same land features, such as volcanoes, giant canyons, and polar ice caps (Eng). It has clouds, winds, and seasons. Its surface temperature ranges from about -200° to 80° Fahrenheit (Eng). That's not so cold life couldn't exist. Most importantly, Mars may also have water (Eng).

Scientists are very interested in whether there is, or ever was, liquid water on the surface of Mars. We know living creatures on Earth need water. If there is water on Mars, there may be life there, too. In many places, it appears that water may have carved channels in Mars's surface (Eng). Therefore, some scientists believe there may once have been liquid water on the surface, even though Mars appears dry now. Pools of water—and life—may still exist underground.

Was there life on Mars in the past? In 1996, David McKay and his team of scientists thought so when they found signs of ancient Martian life in a meteorite. It had crashed into Antarctica thousands of years ago (White, 4). Inside it, they discovered tiny grooves that seemed to be fossil bacteria (White, 5)!

The Viking missions explored Mars in the 1960s and 1970s.

McKay's team believed they had found fossils of Martian bacteria. The grooves were deep inside the meteorite. Bacteria could not have gotten that far into it after it fell to Earth (Simon, 40). It also had chemicals and minerals often found where there is life (Jordan, 28). Finally, it was over 4 billion years old (Jordan 28). It came from a time when there was probably water on Mars's surface.

Many scientists have questioned McKay's claim. They say the grooves are much too small to be fossils of once-living creatures (White, 5). Any creature that tiny wouldn't be able to carry out basic life functions. Also, some of the same chemicals and minerals are found in many other asteroids, comets, and meteorites (White, 5). Their presence in a meteorite doesn't prove there was life there.

No one knows for sure whether there is life on Mars. It is possible that life existed there in the past. If scientists discover life there now, they will probably find it beneath the planet's surface. Future space missions will help scientists learn more about Mars. Someday, they will solve the fascinating mystery of whether we are alone in our solar system.

The writer shows where she found the information. She names each **source**.

The **conclusion** sums up the ideas. It reminds readers about the writer's **central idea**.

Student Model

Focus and Unity

What's It Like ?

Why is this a good photograph? Is it clear and sharp? What does it tell you about the Moon? Like a good photograph, your writing should be clear and focused, too. All you have to do is choose one main point and stick to it.

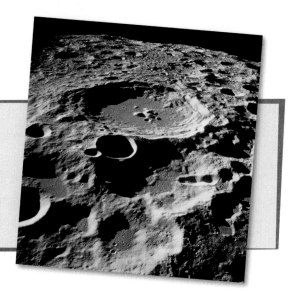

Why Focus Your Writing?

When your writing is focused and unified, it helps your readers follow and understand your ideas.

This writer wants readers to understand his central idea. He makes sure all the paragraphs and details work together to support that central idea.

> Astronauts Neil Armstrong and Buzz Aldrin took a "giant leap for mankind" when they became the first human beings to set foot on the Moon. At that time, the United States was involved in a "space race" with the Soviet Union. Each nation wanted to be the first to explore outer space.
>
> On July 16, 1969, the Apollo 11 mission was launched. It achieved a goal set by President Kennedy, who eight years earlier planned to have a man on the Moon before 1970 (Easton, 16).

The writer's main point, or **central idea**, is clear and specific.

Everything in the writing goes together and tells about that central idea.

Study the rubric on page 185W. What is the difference between a paper with a score of 2 and one with a score of 4?

Focus and Unity

	How clearly does the writing present a central idea, opinion, or thesis?	How well does everything go together?
4 Wow!	The writing expresses a clear central idea or opinion about the topic.	<u>Everything</u> in the writing goes together. • The main idea of each paragraph goes with the central idea of the paper. • The main idea and details within each paragraph are related. • The conclusion is about the central idea.
3 Ahh.	The writing expresses a <u>generally</u> clear central idea or opinion about the topic.	<u>Most</u> parts of the writing go together. • The main idea of most paragraphs goes with the central idea of the paper. • In most paragraphs, the main idea and details are related. • Most of the conclusion is about the central idea.
2 Hmm.	The writing includes a topic, but the central idea or opinion is not clear.	<u>Some</u> parts of the writing go together. • The main idea of some paragraphs goes with the central idea of the paper. • In some paragraphs, the main idea and details are related. • Some of the conclusion is about the central idea.
1 Huh?	The writing includes many topics and does not express one central idea or opinion.	The parts of the writing do not go together. • Few paragraphs have a main idea, or the main idea does not go with the central idea of the paper. • Few paragraphs contain a main idea and related details. • None of the conclusion is about the central idea.

Focus and Unity, continued

Compare Writing Samples

In a focused and unified report, everything in the writing goes together. Study these reports.

Focused and Unified

Picturing Our Galaxy—and Others!

In the past, our view of outer space was limited. But that all changed when the Hubble Space Telescope was launched into orbit in 1990. Thanks to the Hubble, we can now "see" what's really up there.

The Hubble works like a giant camera. It records images of stars, comets, and other objects. The images are then sent back to Earth.

This telescope is very powerful. It can "see" objects a hundred times clearer than from telescopes on Earth. It can picture entire galaxies. (Morrow, 21).

The Hubble is truly a breakthrough. It allows scientists to study outer space more closely than ever before. Using the Hubble's findings, we'll be able to unlock more and more secrets of the universe.

The report begins with a specific **central idea**.

Each paragraph has a **main idea** and **details** that develop the central idea.

Not Focused and Unified

Picturing Our Galaxy—and Others!

Our view of outer space changed in 1990. That's when the Hubble Space Telescope was launched.

The Hubble is like a giant camera. It records images of stars, comets, and other objects. Edwin Hubble discovered galaxies beyond the Milky Way (Smith, 9).

This telescope is very powerful. It can "see" objects a hundred times clearer than from telescopes on Earth. It can picture entire galaxies (Morrow, 21).

Astronomy is fascinating. Maybe someday astronomers will discover if there's life on Mars!

Without a **central idea**, the writer's point is not clear.

Some details don't stick to the topic.

The **conclusion** doesn't tie to the central idea.

Evaluate for Focus and Unity

Now read carefully the information report below.
Use the rubric on page 185W to score it.

Information Report

What is the central idea?

Does each paragraph and main idea tell about the topic? Are the details related?

Does the conclusion wrap up the ideas? What would you do to fix it?

The Death of a Star
by Jodi Tievsky

Could a star brighten our whole sky? If astronomers are right about Eta Carinae, maybe we will find out.

Eta Carinae is huge, about the size of our solar system, and located about 7,500 light-years away (Rizzo, 48). When first discovered, it did not seem very bright compared to other stars. But about 150 years later, the star became extremely bright and kept getting brighter for the next 15 years (Friel, 13).

Scientists believe an explosion caused the sudden brightness. When massive stars start to "die," their cores collapse and release a huge amount of energy. I wonder if a volcanic eruption is like that.

Sometimes stars form patterns, or constellations, that look like animals. Have you seen "Little Horse," "Great Dog," or "Scorpius"? Many constellations were named in ancient times.

Scientists are interested in Eta Carinae because it could explode again at any time. If it did, it would be amazing.

Scientists wonder when Eta Carinae might explode again. ▶

Raise the Score

These papers have been scored using the rubric on page 185W. Study each paper to see why it got the score it did.

Overall Score: 4

The title tells the **topic**. The writer introduces the **central idea**.

Distant Planets—With Diamonds?
Shauna Mullins

Imagine diamonds falling from the sky. This is what could be happening on some of the outer planets of our solar system. Scientists think that Uranus and Neptune might be producing diamonds that pile up deep within their cores.

The main idea of each paragraph goes with the central idea.

The atmospheres of Uranus and Neptune have enough heat and pressure to form diamonds. Diamonds form on Earth when carbon is exposed to a pressure of 14 pounds per square inch and heat above 752° Fahrenheit (Blum 32). The pressure on Uranus or Neptune is millions of times heavier. And, the temperatures can be as high as 12,000° Fahrenheit (Jones 56). Those are excellent conditions for making diamonds!

Researchers have performed experiments to test the theory that the planets produce diamonds. They created conditions like those in the planets' atmospheres and observed the chemical reactions (Porter 67). What were the results? Diamonds!

It is possible that Uranus and Neptune produce showers of diamonds. Lab experiments support the possibility. This is certainly something to think about the next time you gaze up into the night sky.

Neptune, the eighth planet from the sun, is about four times the size of Earth.

Each **detail** relates to the **main idea** of the paragraph.

The **conclusion** is also about the central idea.

The title tells the **topic**.

Distant Planets—With Diamonds?

Imagine diamonds falling from the sky. This is what could be happening on some of the outer planets of our solar system. Scientists have theories about certain planets.

The topic is clear, but the **central idea** is not specific.

The atmospheres of Uranus and Neptune have enough heat and pressure to form diamonds. Diamonds form on Earth when carbon is exposed to a pressure of 14 pounds per square inch and heat above 752° Fahrenheit (Blum 32). The pressure on Uranus or Neptune is millions of times heavier, and the temperatures are much hotter (Jones 56). Diamonds are measured in carats like other gems. The number of carats is how much the gem weighs.

The **main idea** of each paragraph goes with the **central idea**.

These **details** do not go with the **main idea** of the paragraph.

Researchers have performed experiments to test the theory that Uranus and Neptune can produce diamonds. They created conditions like those in the planets' atmospheres and observed the chemical reactions (Porter 67). What were the results? Diamonds!

It is possible that Uranus and Neptune produce showers of diamonds. Lab experiments support the possibility. This is certainly something to think about the next time you gaze up into the night sky.

The **conclusion** is about the **central idea**.

RAISING THE SCORE

The writer should make the central idea specific and take out details that don't fit. How else can she improve the focus?

Raise the Score, continued

Overall Score: 2

The title tells the topic, but there is no **central idea**.

This paragraph **has a main idea** but some details do not go with it.

Distant Planets—With Diamonds?

Have you ever seen a sparkling diamond? No wonder people love this gemstone.

On the planets Uranus and Neptune, there's enough heat and pressure to form diamonds. The planet Uranus is larger than Neptune and has more rings around it. It's also closer to Earth. The pressure on these planets is millions of times heavier than on Earth. The temperatures can be as hot as 12,000° Fahrenheit (Jones 56)!

Diamonds come in several different cuts and weights called carats. One of the largest is the Hope Diamond, which is more than 45 carats! You can see this diamond at the Smithsonian museum in Washington, D.C.

Researchers have tested the idea that planets could have diamonds. Maybe someday they'll experiment with producing showers of rubies, my favorite gem!

This paragraph is not about diamonds on distant planets, so it does not go with the **topic**.

The **conclusion** doesn't wrap up the **main ideas** in the paper.

RAISING THE SCORE

The writer needs to include a clear central idea and make sure each paragraph goes with it. What could she say?

Distant Planets—With Diamonds?

Is every planet's surface dusty, lifeless, and filled with craters? Some scientists think there may be showers of diamonds on some of the outer planets ! They don't know about other gemstones, though.

It's funny how planets get discovered. Neptune was discovered when astronomers noticed that the orbit of the planet Uranus was a little strange (Blum 21). This led them to discover Neptune.

The atmospheres of Uranus and Neptune are good for forming diamonds. It can be as hot as 12,000° Fahrenheit on those planets (Jones 56). How could it be so hot? After all, those planets are billions of miles away from the Sun.

Space travel has always fascinated people. Maybe someday we will travel to Uranus, Neptune, and any planets that lie beyond them.

The writing has too many **topics** and no **central idea**.

Main ideas in these paragraphs do not relate to the same **topic**.

This **detail** does not go with the main idea of the paragraph.

The **conclusion** doesn't wrap up the ideas.

RAISING THE SCORE

The writer should focus on one topic. If the topic is diamonds on distant planets, which sentences can be kept?

Plan Your Research

What will you do this weekend? Are you bored with the same old activities? Maybe you'll ask your friends, check the newspaper, or look online to discover something new to do. Planning research for a report is a lot like that. First you decide what you want to know about a topic, then you do research to find the answers.

Choose a Topic

When you write school reports, you might not be able to choose any topic you want. Your teacher will probably give you a general research area, such as "amazing discoveries." Once you know the general research area, here's what to do:

- Pick a specific topic within that area. Smaller, specific topics are easier to research and write about.

- Think of a topic that interests *you*. When you care about what you're writing, your research and writing will be better and more fun!

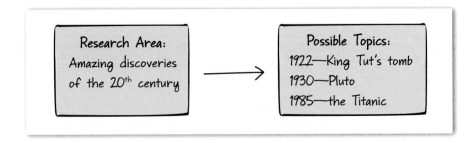

Research Area:
Amazing discoveries of the 20ᵗʰ century

Possible Topics:
1922—King Tut's tomb
1930—Pluto
1985—the Titanic

Brainstorm Questions

The next step is to ask yourself what you want to know about your topic. Asking questions helps you focus your research. Where could you find answers to the questions below?

The Orion Neb
1,500 light-yea

Research Questions

- How did astronomers first discover other planets?

- How do you become an astronaut?

- Is there life on Mars?

- Will human beings ever be able to visit other planets?

- What would it be like to live on Mercury?

Plan Your Research, continued

It takes a lot of thinking and planning to write a good information report. Before you begin your research, think carefully about your topic, audience, and purpose.

Focus Your Topic

The more specific your topic is, the easier it will be for you to research and write about it. Specific, or smaller, topics are also more interesting to read about in a report.

Outer Space

This topic is too general. Outer space has stars, planets, moons, and black holes. It would take forever to research all those topics!

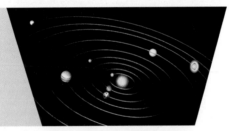

Planets

This topic is still too general. There are several planets in our solar system. You could do a report about Mars, but what do you want to know?

Life on Mars

This is a good topic because it's more specific than "Mars." Finding out if Mars has water, plants, animals, or other life forms could be very interesting.

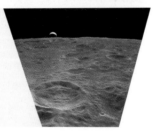

List Research Questions

What questions do you want your report to "answer"? Start out with your main research question, and then break it down into more specific questions.

Topic: Life on Mars
Main Question:
Is there life on Mars?
Smaller Questions:
1. Have scientists discovered any living things on Mars?
2. Is there water on Mars?
3. Is it warm enough on Mars for plants to grow?
4. Can human beings breathe on Mars?

Think About Sources of Information

Read your research questions. Think about the kind of information you're looking for:

- Do you need to look up facts or scientific data?

- Do you want to know about something that happened recently?

- Are you interested in someone's opinion, experience, or expert knowledge?

- Do you want to see pictures or video?

These questions will help you decide which sources of information to use.

Locate Sources of Information

Now that you know what you're looking for, start your research! Different sources will have different information about your topic. Here are just a few kinds of sources you might use:

- nonfiction books, such as biographies and textbooks

- reference books, such as encyclopedias, dictionaries, and atlases

- newspapers and magazines

- the Internet

- people who know a lot about your topic

Talking to an expert is a great way to get eyewitness or first-hand information about a topic. Here are some helpful tips:

Interviewing an Expert

1. Make an appointment. Explain to the person why you want to interview him or her.

2. Find out as much as you can about the topic before the interview. Make a list of questions to ask.

3. Use a tape recorder. Be sure to let the person know you're recording the interview. Write down the important points.

4. Ask all of the questions on your list. If your discussion makes you think of more questions, ask those questions, too!

5. Always be polite to the person you are interviewing. Afterward, write a note thanking the person for talking with you.

Locate Sources in the Library

The library has both print and electronic sources. Research your topic using more than one source and more than one kind of source. That way, you'll find the most useful and up-to-date information.

Most libraries have these sections:

- **Nonfiction books**—The books' call numbers stand for subject areas from the Dewey Decimal System.

- **Fiction books**—Remember, untrue stories are not good research sources.

- **Periodicals**—This section has magazines and newspapers. Use periodicals to find the most current information.

- **Biographies**—Biographies are usually grouped with nonfiction by the last name of the person the book is about.

- **Reference section**—This section has special resources you cannot check out, such as encyclopedias. But, you can photocopy information from them.

- **Computers**—Try the library's computerized card catalog to find sources or look up information on the Internet.

- **Juvenile and Young Adult sections**—Look here for books written just for kids (Juvenile) and teens (Young Adult).

- **Information desk**—Visit the information desk if you need help from a librarian.

Dewey Decimal System

Number Range	Subject Area
000–099	General Books
100–199	Philosophy
200–299	Religion
300–399	Social Sciences
400–499	Language
500–599	Pure Sciences
600–699	Technology
700–799	The Arts
800–899	Literature
900–999	History and Geography

Locate Sources of Information, continued

Using the Online Catalog

Computerized catalogs let you search for books by title, author, or subject. Just type in your keywords, and the computer will show you what's available in that library. For example:

1. Type in the word or phrase that names your subject. Hit the Return key or use your mouse to click "Search."

2. Look at the related subjects that come up. They will usually be more specific than the subject you typed in.

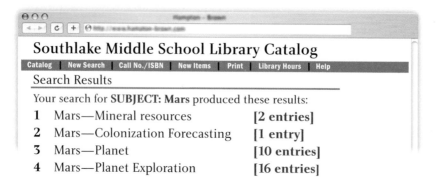

Southlake Middle School Library Catalog

| Catalog | New Search | Call No./ISBN | New Items | Print | Library Hours | Help |

Search Results

Your search for **SUBJECT: Mars** produced these results:

1   Mars—Mineral resources   **[2 entries]**
2   Mars—Colonization Forecasting **[1 entry]**
3   Mars—Planet   **[10 entries]**
4   Mars—Planet Exploration   **[16 entries]**

3. Read the entries and decide which sources seem the most useful. If you click on "Mars—Planet," this screen appears, and you see several books and videos on the planet Mars.

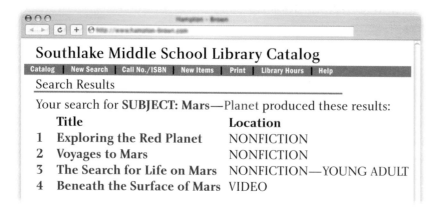

Southlake Middle School Library Catalog

| Catalog | New Search | Call No./ISBN | New Items | Print | Library Hours | Help |

Search Results

Your search for **SUBJECT: Mars**—Planet produced these results:

	Title	Location
1	**Exploring the Red Planet**	NONFICTION
2	**Voyages to Mars**	NONFICTION
3	**The Search for Life on Mars**	NONFICTION—YOUNG ADULT
4	**Beneath the Surface of Mars**	VIDEO

4. If you click on the book *The Search for Life on Mars*, you will see this screen. It gives you more information about the book. Read the summary to help you decide if the book will be useful. You can use the location and call number to find the book.

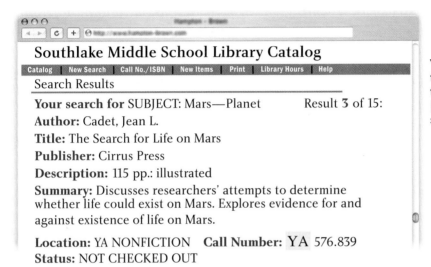

Southlake Middle School Library Catalog

Catalog | New Search | Call No./ISBN | New Items | Print | Library Hours | Help

Search Results

Your search for SUBJECT: Mars—Planet   Result 3 of 15:

Author: Cadet, Jean L.

Title: The Search for Life on Mars

Publisher: Cirrus Press

Description: 115 pp.: illustrated

Summary: Discusses researchers' attempts to determine whether life could exist on Mars. Explores evidence for and against existence of life on Mars.

Location: YA NONFICTION   **Call Number:** YA 576.839

Status: NOT CHECKED OUT

You can find this book in the **Young Adult** section.

Using Alphabetical Order

To look up a topic in an encyclopedia or an index, you'll need to use **alphabetical order**.

Mars

planet

space

Often you can find what you're looking for by using just the first letter of the word.

Mars

mission

moon

If all the words begin with the same letter, look at the second letter to find the entry.

magnetism

Mars

mass

If all the words begin with the same first two letters, look at the third letter.

Evaluate Sources

In your report, you will be presenting facts and don't want to mislead your reader. So, you'll want to use the most accurate and reliable sources—sources you can trust.

How to Evaluate Print Sources

To evaluate print sources like books and periodicals, ask yourself these questions:

1 Is it up to date?

People are always making new discoveries, especially in science, medicine, and technology. Check when your source was published. Use up-to-date sources to make sure you've got the latest facts.

2 Who wrote it?

You'd probably interview an expert about your topic instead of someone who knew nothing about it. The same is true for print sources. Look for information about the author and decide if she or he could be an "expert." Would you trust the information in this article? Why or why not?

> Certain features on Mars appear to have been shaped by water. However, liquid water no longer exists on the surface of Mars. The only water that remains on Mars is frozen underground at its north and south poles.
> –BY KENDRA PRESTON
>
> *Dr. Kendra Preston is the Director of the Museum of Space Exploration in Baltimore, MD.*

3 What's the purpose of the publication?

A story about Martians invading Earth might be very entertaining to read. However, when you're looking for facts about a topic, always use sources that are written to give information or explain an idea.

How to Evaluate Web Sites

Many experts and organizations carefully check the facts on their Web sites. However, some do not. So, you'll need to watch carefully for false information if you research online.

http://www.juliesspacepage.com

ALL ABOUT MARS!

Hi! Welcome to Julie's Space Page. This sectionn is dedicated to mars. Did you know Mars is just like earth in most ways. Click on the photo tofind out cool facts about the amazing "Red planet."
Site last updated: March 11, 2003

Mars, the third planet from the sun.

What clues show that this Web site is not a good source of information?

To evaluate Web sites, ask yourself questions:

1 Did the writer put some time and care into the Web site?

If the site has a lot of spelling and grammar mistakes, it may have other mistakes, too.

2 When did the writer last update the site?

The home page often says when the site was last updated. If it hasn't been updated since 1999, the facts may be out of date!

3 What kind of site is it?

Some kinds of sites are more carefully checked than others. You can usually trust Web sites created by the government, by colleges and universities, or by professional organizations.

4 Do the facts match what I found on other sites?

The facts should be the same from source to source if each source is reliable. Always double-check your facts.

TechTIP

Use the bookmark feature of your browser to keep track of Web resources. Organize your bookmarks into folders to make resources easy to find.

Locate Relevant Information

How do you decide which of the many sources you've gathered are worth reading? **Skim** and **scan** the text, or look at it quickly to see if it has the information you need. If it does, read the text more carefully. If it doesn't, go on to another source.

Skim and Scan an Article

- Skim the **title**, **beginning sentences**, and **headings** to see if they tell about your topic. Skim the **ending**, too. It often sums up all the ideas.

- Scan for **keywords** or details in bold or italic type. If they go with your topic, you'll probably want to read the article.

LOOKING FOR LIFE ELSEWHERE IN THE UNIVERSE

For years scientists have been trying to discover if there is life on other planets in our solar system or life elsewhere in the universe. Some scientists have been looking for evidence based on what is necessary for life on Earth—basics like water and proper temperature.

Beginning sentences

WHAT SCIENTISTS HAVE LEARNED SO FAR

Mars and Jupiter. In 1996, two teams of scientists examined two meteorites that may have come from Mars and found evidence that some form of life may have existed on Mars billions of years ago.

AND THE SEARCH CONTINUES

NASA (the National Aeronautics and Space Administration) has a program to look for life on Mars. Several spacecraft have been sent to Mars over the past ten years. Some have flown around Mars taking pictures, while others have studied the soil and rocks and looked for living things. The first two, Mars Pathfinder and Mars Global Surveyor, were launched in 1996. Pathfinder reached Mars in 1997.

Ending

Another program that searches for life on other worlds is called SETI. SETI (an acronym for Search for Extraterrestrial Intelligences) uses powerful radio telescopes to look for life elsewhere in the universe.

Question: Is there life elsewhere in the universe? Answer: No one knows yet.

Skim and Scan a Book

For books, skim the book jacket, the introduction, the first few pages, and the last few pages. You can try a few other tricks as well:

- Carefully read the summary in the library catalog. Does the book seem to have useful information for your report? If so, take a look at it. If not, keep looking for more useful sources.

- Look in the front of the book for the table of contents. Read the table of contents to see what topics it covers.

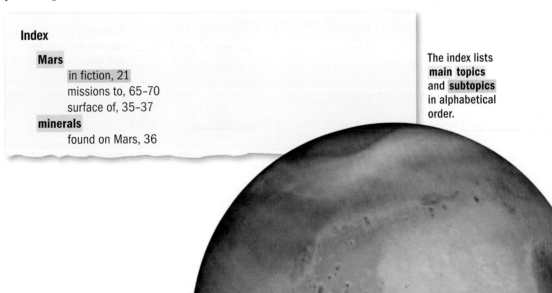

Contents

The **chapter titles** tell you what main topics the book covers.

- Look in the index in the back of a book to see if your specific topic is listed. Use alphabetical order to look up the topic. You can also scan the index for keywords about your topic.

Index

The index lists **main topics** and **subtopics** in alphabetical order.

How to Take Notes

You've found a lot of useful sources. Now you're ready to research your topic. But, how are you going to remember and organize all those facts and details for your report? By taking good notes! Here's how.

Use Note Cards

As you come across important facts and ideas, write them on index cards or in a computer file.

- Use a heading for each card. That'll be one of your main or smaller research questions.

- Write down the important details and facts that answer your research question.

- Identify the source, or where you got the information. Include the source's title or the author's name and the page number where the information appears.

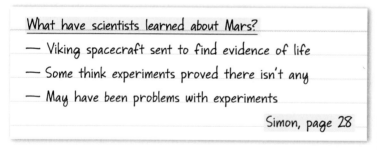

> What have scientists learned about Mars?
> — Viking spacecraft sent to find evidence of life
> — Some think experiments proved there isn't any
> — May have been problems with experiments
>   Simon, page 28

The **heading** will be useful when you get ready to organize your notes.

Recording the **source** will help you remember where you found the facts.

As you take notes be sure to

- write notes in your own words, or **paraphrase** the ideas

- use quotation marks for **direct quotes**, or words you copy exactly from the text.

TechTIP
Take notes on your computer. You can use a database or save them as documents.

Paraphrasing

When you paraphrase, you put the author's ideas into your own words. Using your own words is a good way to make sure you understand those ideas! Follow these steps when you paraphrase:

1 **Read the source carefully before you take notes.**

Mars Exploration Rovers performed impossible tasks. ▼

Source Information

What a Mineral on Mars Could Mean

By Chuck Petro

On the surface of Mars, scientists found evidence of hematite, a mineral. Scientists know hematite forms when water is present—and water is very important for supporting life on Earth. After this discovery, missions to Mars focused on finding liquid water. The mission of the Mars Exploration Rovers of 2004 was to find evidence that there once was liquid water on Mars's surface in the planet's ancient past.

2 **Think about the main ideas and details. Try to put them in your own words. Your paraphrase should be about as long as the original.**

Too close to the source

Was there ever liquid on Mars?
—On surface, scientists found evidence of a mineral called hematite
—forms when water is present
—After discovery, some missions to Mars focused on finding liquid water
        Petro, page 49

The student's own words

Was there ever liquid on Mars?
—hematite—mineral found where there is water
—scientists think hematite is on Mars
—scientists hope to find liquid water on Mars
        Petro, page 49

How to Take Notes, continued

Using Direct Quotes

Sometimes you will want to use the same, exact words that you read in the source. Follow these steps when you use a direct quote.

1 **Read the source carefully. Make sure you copy the words exactly.**

> It's no secret that scientists have wondered for a long time whether there is life on Mars. After all, the planet is next to Earth in the solar system. It is also like Earth in many ways. What would life on Mars look like? Would there be slimy green beings or tiny bacteria that you can't even see?

2 **Use quotation marks around any words you copy exactly from the source.**

Incorrect

Life on Mars
Would there be slimy
green aliens or bacteria that
you can't even see?
                    Jordan, page 84

Correct

Life on Mars
"Would there be slimy green
beings or tiny bacteria that you
can't even see?"
                    Jordan, page 84

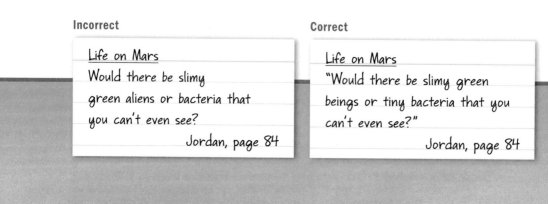

Why Taking Good Notes Is Important

When you take notes, you should always

- paraphrase ideas, or use your own words

- use quotation marks to show any direct quotations copied exactly from the source

- write down the source on each note card.

It's important to take notes carefully because when you write a report, you depend on other writers' ideas. You use their work to help you write your own paper. Not giving them credit is like borrowing your friend's favorite sweater without thanking her.

Using other people's ideas without giving them credit is called **plagiarism**. Sometimes writers do it by accident because they didn't take notes carefully. Sometimes writers do it on purpose. That's like *stealing* your friend's favorite sweater! Not only is it wrong, it can also get writers in a lot of trouble.

The surface of Mars is now a lifeless, frozen desert.

How to Decide on a Central Idea

How will you turn your pile of notes into a good report? Before you start writing, step back and think about the important things you've learned from your research.

1 **Think about your research questions.**

You may have answered most of your research questions during your research—or you may have come up with some new ones along the way.

2 **Decide if you need to do more research.**

Look carefully at your notes to help you figure out what to do next. Ask yourself: *Do I have all the facts I need to answer my research questions?* Be honest. If you need to do more research, it's best to do it now. Study this writer's notes.

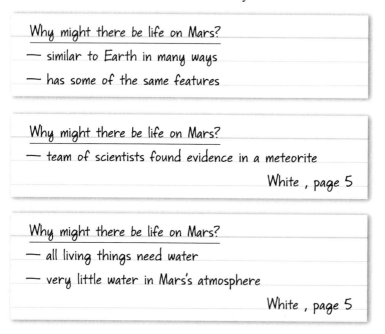

Why might there be life on Mars?
— similar to Earth in many ways
— has some of the same features

Why might there be life on Mars?
— team of scientists found evidence in a meteorite
         White , page 5

Why might there be life on Mars?
— all living things need water
— very little water in Mars's atmosphere
        White , page 5

This writer still has some questions to answer, such as: How is Mars similar to Earth? What have scientists learned about whether Mars has water? What did the scientists find in the meteorite?

3 **Turn your research question into your central idea.**

Once you're sure your research is complete, review your note cards again. Look to see how all of the facts and details fit together. Which cards have similar facts that can go together? Which ideas and facts come up again and again?

Why might there be life on Mars?
— has many of the features Earth has
— volcanoes, canyons, polar ice caps

Jordan, page 84

Why might there be life on Mars?
— all living things need water
— very little water in Mars's atmosphere but there might be water underground
— may have been water in past

White, page 5

▲ Evidence in a meteorite like this one led some scientists to think there once was life on Mars.

Why might there be life on Mars?
— team of scientists found evidence in a meteorite
— fossils of Martian bacteria

White, page 5

Research Question
Could life exist on Mars?
Why or why not?

→

Central Idea
There is no sign of life on Mars now, but life may have existed there once, and may still exist underground.

How to Make an Outline

You've organized all your information, so now you're ready to turn your research notes into an outline. Here's how:

1 Start with a title for your outline.

Your title should help your readers know what your report is about.

| **Discovering Life on Mars** |

2 Decide on your introduction.

Your opening paragraph should introduce your topic and state your central idea.

> **I. Introduction**
> A. Is there life on other planets?
> B. Possible life on Mars in the past—may still exist under surface

3 Turn your notes into the rest of the outline.

Put note cards with the same research question together. Then turn the questions into main ideas. Find supporting details in your notes, and add them to your outline.

What do we know about life on Mars?

What do we know about life on Mars?
—Mars has some features like Earth
—"It has volcanoes and giant canyons."
—hard to prove life, but maybe space
 missions like Pathfinder can find something

> **II. Searching for life on Mars**
> A. Lines on surface thought to be canals
> B. Missions to Mars proved this wrong
> C. How Mars is like Earth

Discovering Life on Mars

The **title** tells what your outline is about. Use it again for your report.

I. Introduction
A. Is there life on other planets?
B. Possible life on Mars in the past—may still exist under surface

Your **introduction** presents the **central idea** of your paper.

Each **main idea** follows a Roman numeral.

II. Searching for life on Mars
A. Lines on surface thought to be canals
B. Missions to Mars proved this wrong
C. How Mars is like Earth
   1. Volcanoes, canyons, ice caps
   2. Might have water

You present ideas and facts from research in the **body**.

III. David McKay's discovery
A. Meteorite in Antarctica
B. Had grooves resembling bacteria fossils
   1. Deep in center of meteorite
   2. Chemicals and minerals
   3. From a time when Mars probably had water
C. Other scientists disagree
   1. Grooves too small to be from living things
   2. Chemicals and minerals found in other places too

Each **detail** follows a capital letter. Each **related detail** follows a number.

IV. Continued search for life on Mars
A. No one knows
B. May have existed in past
C. Any life there now is probably underground
D. Learn more from future missions

You sum up your ideas in the **conclusion**.

Write an Information Report

WRITING PROMPT Now you will write an information report to inform your classmates about your topic. Once you've gathered all your notes and your outline, you're ready to get started!

Prewrite

You've picked a cool topic, decided what questions you wanted to find out about, and thought about your audience and purpose. Then you found your sources, took careful notes, and turned your notes into an outline. Now it's time to turn your outline into a draft.

Draft

Your plan is all set, so now you can turn your ideas into sentences and paragraphs.

1 Draft the introduction.

If you already thought of a great title for your outline, use it here for your paper. Then, think about how to get the reader's attention right away. Here are a few tricks you can use:

- Help readers see how the topic connects to their own experiences.

Discovering Life on Mars

Have you ever looked up at the stars wondering if there's life out there in space? So have many scientists.

- Ask the question you plan to answer in your paper.

Discovering Life on Mars

Could there be life on Mars, Earth's nearest neighbor? Many scientists believe it is possible.

- Start off with a surprising fact, an interesting quote, or a brief story.

Discovering Life on Mars

Did you know that over 50% of Americans believe we will one day discover life on other planets? What's more, scientists agree.

Once you've got your readers' attention, let them know what your paper will be about. Give some background about your topic, and state your central idea.

Discovering Life on Mars

Do aliens exist only in movies and on TV—or is there life in outer space? Some scientists believe that life could exist on Mars. People have always wondered if scientists will ever discover life on another planet. Scientists are especially curious about Mars, the planet closest to Earth.

The writer starts with a **question** to get readers' attention.

The writer establishes the **central idea** near the beginning of the paragraph.

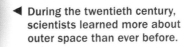

◄ During the twentieth century, scientists learned more about outer space than ever before.

Draft, continued

❷ **Write the body.**

Each paragraph in the body of your report will be about an important point you learned from your research. Here's how to write the body.

- Start with the main ideas from your outline. Turn each main idea into a topic sentence for a paragraph.

Outline

> **II. Searching for life on Mars**

Draft

> Scientists began to seriously consider the possibility of life on Mars over 100 years ago.

- Turn the facts and details next to the letters and numbers in your outline into sentences. Add them to the paragraph. Sometimes you may find a detail in your outline that doesn't go with your topic sentence, or main idea. If so, leave it out.

Outline

> **II. Searching for life on Mars**
> A. Lines on surface thought to be canals
> B. Missions to Mars proved this wrong

> Scientists began to seriously consider the possibility of life on Mars over 100 years ago. In the late 1800s, some astronomers noticed complicated patterns of lines on the planet's surface (Simon, 28). Astronomers included these lines on their maps of Mars's surface. They believed the lines were canals that intelligent living creatures had built (Simon, 29).

Draft

❸ Write the conclusion.

For the conclusion, sum up the most important information about your topic. Be sure to tie back to your <mark>central idea</mark>.

Outline

> IV. **Continued search for life on Mars**
>   A. No one knows
>   B. May have existed in past
>   C. Any life there now is probably underground
>   D. Learn more from future missions

> No one knows for sure whether there is life on Mars. It is possible that life existed there in the past. If scientists discover life there now, they will probably find it beneath the planet's surface. Future space missions will help scientists learn more about the Red Planet. Someday, they will solve the fascinating mystery of whether we are alone in our solar system.

Draft of the Conclusion

◀ Researchers are testing this "Hoop-Column antenna" for possible use on future missions to Mars.

Reflect

- Read your draft. Does it have a clear central idea?

- Does it have an introduction, a body, and a conclusion?

Draft, continued

Cite Your Sources

Where did the facts and details for your report come from? The information came from a variety of sources you used during your research.

Remember that whenever you use someone else's words or ideas, you need to give the person credit. To do this, you should always **cite your sources**, or tell where you found the information. It'll be easy to show all the sources you used for your final report if you record the sources when you do the research.

Citing Sources on Note Cards

For each note card you created during your research, you included the title or author of a source and a page number for the information. It is also a good idea to make a separate card that gives specific information *about* the source. What information is on each source card below?

Book

Source #1
Title: Mars
Author: Seymour Simon
Publisher: Canton Press
City: Philadelphia
Year: 2006

Web Site

Source #2
Article or Page Title: What Do
    We Know About Mars?
Author: Joanne Eng
Web Site Title: Planets 4 Kids
Web Address: www.planets4kids.gov

Magazine Article

Source #3
Article Title: "What a Mineral on
    Mars Could Mean"
Author: Chuck Petro
Magazine: Kids' Science
Issue Date: Nov. 2007
Pages: 48–51

Newspaper Article

Source #4
Article Title: "Brothers Battle Over
Question of Life on Mars"
Author: Amy White
Newspaper: Towson Tribune
Issue Date: Nov. 25, 2007
Page: H4

Citing Sources Within Your Paper

Each time you use an idea from a source, you must show where
the idea came from. As you edit your first draft, check that you
have cited your sources correctly.

- If you took words directly from a source, they should be
  in **quotation marks**. You use **your own words** to tell
  where the quote came from:

Space probe
Viking 2 explored
the surface
of Mars in 1977. ▼

> In his book *Mars*, Seymour Simon says that "Mars may
> look dry as dust, but water once flowed over the surface."

- If you paraphrased a source, you should list the author and
  page number in **parentheses** at the end of the sentence.

> The Viking spacecraft is supposed to find out if there's
> life on Mars (Simon, 28).

Citing Sources in a Bibliography

Do you need to include a list of sources, or a **bibliography**,
at the end of your paper? If so, just list all of the sources
you quoted or paraphrased from in alphabetical order.
List them by the author's last name.

Eng, Joanne. "What Do We Know About Mars?" Planets 4
    Kids. <www.planets4kids.gov>.

Petro, Chuck. "What a Mineral on Mars Could Mean." Kids'
    Science. Nov. 2007: 48–51.

Simon, Seymour. Mars. Philadelphia: Canton Press, 2006.

White, Amy. "Brothers Battle Over Question of Life on
    Mars." Towson Tribune. 25 Nov. 2007: H4.

Revise

① Evaluate Your Work

Other students can give you feedback during a peer conference. Here are a few questions you might ask:

What to Ask During a Peer Conference

- Is my introduction interesting?
- Does my paper have a clear central idea?
- Does everything in the writing go together?
- Are there any parts that are confusing or don't belong?

> *Revision in Action*

Draft

One student's response:

Every day scientists are discovering more about the Red Planet. We already know a lot, thanks to the *Viking* and *Pathfinder* missions.

During the 1970s, two *Viking* missions (Williams, 96) landed there. The pictures gathered by the *Viking 2* lander showed a desert of rocks. Other images showed volcanoes, canyons, moon-like craters, and winding valleys that looked like dried-up riverbeds. Perhaps there are live Martians after all!

" The first sentence is boring. Can it be more interesting?"

" There's a lot of information about Mars. Will you tell about it all in your paper?"

" I love reading about Martians, but this doesn't belong—it doesn't tell about the topic."

2 Mark Your Changes

Add Text You may need to add

- a question or interesting fact to your introduction
- details to make your central idea specific
- source information you left out.

Rearrange Text Are all your source references in the right place? Use ⤶ to show the text you want to move.

Delete Text Take out text that doesn't go with your central idea or tell more about a paragraph's main idea.

Reflect

- Does your final draft have a clear central idea?
- Does everything in your report tell about that idea?

Revising Marks

MARK	∧	⤶	⌐	⤸	⁋
WHAT IT MEANS	Insert something.	Move to here.	Replace with this.	Take out.	Make a new paragraph.

Revised Draft

Are you curious about Mars? Many people are.
∧Every day scientists are discovering more about the
Red Planet. We already know a lot, thanks to the *Viking* 〈*about Mars's surface*〉
and *Pathfinder* missions.

During the 1970s, two *Viking* missions (Williams, 96)
landed there. The pictures gathered by the *Viking 2*
lander showed a desert of rocks. Other images showed
volcanoes, canyons, moon-like craters, and winding
valleys that looked like dried-up riverbeds. Perhaps⤸ (Muirden, 181)
~~there are live Martians after all!~~⤸

The writer added a question to get his readers' attention.

The writer added a detail to make his central idea clear and specific.

The writer took out this detail because it didn't relate to the central idea.

Edit and Proofread

After you're satisfied with the content of your information report, read your paper again to fix language errors. This is what you do when you edit and proofread your work.

- **Check the Grammar** Make sure that you have used correct and conventional grammar throughout. In particular, check for correct use of irregular past tense verbs. (See page 221W.)

- **Check the Spelling** You may want to have a dictionary on hand to help you check for errors in your past tense verbs! Look carefully to see if you've changed the spelling of some past tense verbs when you added *-ed*. (See page 222W.)

- **Check the Mechanics** Errors in punctuation and capitalization can make your work hard to understand. In particular, check that you've used capital letters and quotation marks correctly for titles and direct quotes. (See page 223W.)

TechTIP

Save your report with a new file name every time you revise it.

Use these marks to edit and proofread your information report.

Editing and Proofreading Marks

MARK	WHAT IT MEANS	MARK	WHAT IT MEANS
∧	Insert something.	╱	Make lowercase.
⋏	Add a comma.	℘	Delete, take something out.
⋏	Add a semicolon.	⁋	Make new paragraph.
⊙	Add a period.	◯	Spell out.
⊙	Add a colon.	⌒	Replace with this.
⌄ ⌄	Add quotation marks.	∼	Change order of letters or words.
⌄	Add an apostrophe.	#	Insert space.
≡	Capitalize.	◡	Close up, no space here.

Reflect

- What kinds of errors did you find? What can you do to keep from making them?

GrammarWorkout

Check Irregular Verbs

When you write about an event that already happened, you use verbs in the past tense.

- For many verbs, you add **-ed** to show action in the past.

- For other verbs, you use a special form to show action in the past. Those are called **irregular verbs**.

Here are just a few irregular verbs that change their form to tell about the past.

Present	Past	Example in the Past
do	did	I **did** research for my paper last week.
bring	brought	Sarah **brought** extra paper to class.
find	found	Terry **found** a good book yesterday.
give	gave	Ms. Russ **gave** us more time for our reports.
go	went	Mark **went** to the library an hour ago.
run	ran	After school, I **ran** home.
tell	told	The scientist **told** us about comets.
think	thought	I **thought** about outer space all day.
write	wrote	Tess **wrote** a poem about the stars.

Find the Trouble Spots

      Last week I ~~finded~~ *found* a good book in the library about the Moon. I thinked about the 1969 *Apollo* mission to the Moon. Astronauts from that mission bringed back samples of Moon rocks. That ~~gived~~ *gave* me a good idea for my report.

Check the past tense verbs. Which verbs are not formed correctly?

Edit and Proofread, continued

SpellingWorkout

Check Past Tense Verbs with -ed

- For many verbs, you can just add **-ed** to tell about the past.

    work + -ed = worked   Last night, I worked on my report.

- When a verb ends with a silent *e*, drop the *e* before adding **-ed**.

    bake + -ed = baked   At 7 p.m., Sis baked cookies.

- If a verb ends with a vowel and then a consonant, double the consonant before adding **-ed**.

    plan + n + -ed = planned   She planned to give me some.

- If a verb ends with a consonant and then a *y*, change the *y* to *i*, and add **-ed**.

    cry + -ed = cried   I cried when I saw the burnt cookies!

Find the Trouble Spots

studied
I studyed very hard last night. That must be why
explored
I explord space in my dreams. In my dream, I watched food hover over my head. I grabbed for a hot dog, but it floated away. I tryed to get a soda, but tiped it over. All the liquid poured up instead of down!

Are all the other past tense verbs spelled correctly? Which ones do you need to fix?

> ## MechanicsWorkout

Check Titles and Quotes

For titles of books and articles:

- Capitalize the important words. Don't capitalize words like *a, the, to,* or *in* unless they are the first word of the title.

  EXAMPLE *Are We Moving to Mars?*

- Use quotation marks for titles of magazine, newspaper, or Internet articles.

  EXAMPLE "Mars: Is Anyone Up There?"

- If you are writing a paper by hand, underline book titles and the names of newspapers and magazines.

  EXAMPLES <u>Mars: The Basics</u>   <u>Kids' Science Weekly</u>

  If you are word processing, show the titles in italics.

  EXAMPLES *Mars: The Basics*   *Kids' Science Weekly*

For direct quotes, use quotation marks around the exact words you copy.

  EXAMPLE "There is much to explore on Mars," says Rivera.

Find the Trouble Spots

> In his article Martians on the planet Mars? Rivera says, "I can't wait to see if the latest mission discovers any signs of life!"
>
> The authors of the book New frontiers in Space are less hopeful. As one author says, Life on Mars? That's pure fantasy.

Can you find the other capitalization and punctuation errors in the passage?

Publish, Share, and Reflect

Now that your research is done and you've written a report that focuses on an interesting topic, you're ready to share the information with your readers.

1 **Publish and Share Your Work**

If you want to give your report a little more pizzazz, add some visuals.

- Include photographs, clip art, and illustrations about your topic. You may wish to include smaller pictures within your report, and save larger pictures to use if you present your work in front of your class.

- Add graphs, charts, diagrams, or maps. You can make your own or copy one you found in a source. Just be sure to cite the source if you copy an image from it.

- Make a model. Models are great ways to make your presentation more interesting. Is there a model or diorama you could make to help your audience better understand your topic?

- Post your report online. Do you remember what you learned about finding accurate sources online? Your research paper can be a source for others!

2 **Reflect on Your Work**

After you publish and present your report, take some time to think about it. What went well? What do you think you could do differently for your next research report?

Tech*TIP*

Be sure to post or share work on student-safe Web sites and never share your personal information. Review your school's Acceptable Use Policy.

Reflect

- What did I learn about myself while writing?

- How did following the research process help me tell about my topic?

How to Use Presentation Software

Multimedia presentations are great because they allow you to combine visuals, sound, and computer technology to enhance your presentation.

Many programs use a slideshow format. You create each of the screens, or slides, and then show them in order during the presentation. Here are some kinds of slides you may wish to make:

1. **Text slides:** Text slides contain mostly words, but the words are separated into key points with bullets or numbers. Limit the amount of text on the slide and make the type large so that people will be able to read it.

2. **Picture slides:** Import pictures that you have scanned into your computer or downloaded from the Internet.

3. **Charts and graphs:** Computer programs can help you create and display different kinds of charts and graphs to support your topic. You can also import charts and graphs that you have scanned into your computer or that you have downloaded from the Internet.

Text Slide

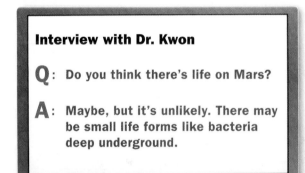

Picture Slide

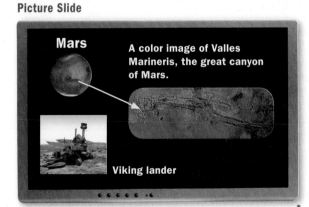

Research RESOURCES

Resource Books

Parts of a Book

When you hear the word *print,* what do you think of? Books!
There are many different kinds of books. All books share some
features that make it easier for readers to find what they need.
Let's look at the parts of a book.

Title Page

The **title page** is usually
the first page in a book.

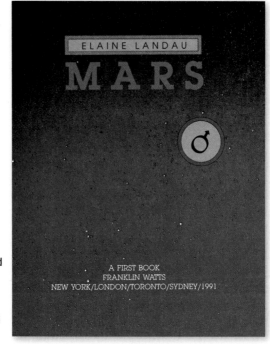

It gives the **title**
of the book and
the **author.**

It tells the
publisher and
often names
the cities
where the
publisher has
offices.

Copyright Page

The **copyright (©) page**
gives the year when the
book was published.

Check the
copyright
to see how
current the
information is.

Landau, Elaine
    Mars / by Elaine Landau
      p.cm. — (First book)
    Includes bibliographical references and index.
    Summary: Uses photographs and other recent findings to
      describe the atmosphere and geographic features of Mars.
    ISBN 0-531-20012-4 (lib. bdg)—ISBN 0-531-15773-3 (pbk)
    I. Mars (Planet)—Juvenile Literature. [1. Mars (Planet)]
1. Title.   II. Series.
QB641.L36 1991
523.4'3—dc20   90-13097 CIP AC

Table of Contents

The **table of contents** is in the front of a book. It shows how many chapters, or parts, are in a book. It tells the page numbers where those chapters begin. Look at the chapter names to see which ones might be useful to you.

A table of contents can be much more detailed than the one shown here. For example, it might list sections within chapters, important visuals, or special sections found in the book.

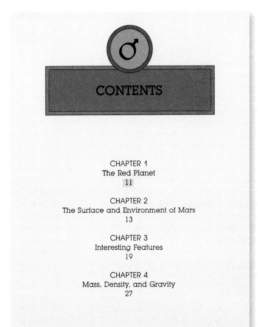

CONTENTS

A **chapter title** tells what the chapter is mostly about.

The **page number** tells where the chapter begins.

Chapter Headings

Once you have found a chapter you are interested in using from the table of contents, you will turn to the chapter. The first page in the chapter will contain a heading describing what you will find in the chapter. Often, chapters are numbered.

THE RED PLANET

CHAPTER ONE

The planet Mars appears as a rusty red ball in the nighttime sky. Because of its reddish color, the ancient Romans named the planet after their god of war—Mars. In fact, the fighting god's shield and spear are still used as the planet's symbol.

Mars is one of the nine planets that make up the *solar system*. The solar system consists of the sun and the planets, moons, and other objects that revolve around it. Mars is the fourth planet from the sun. Earth, Mars's neighbor, is the third planet from the sun.

Mars is not a very large planet. Its diameter is about 4,200 miles (6,790 kilometers). That makes Mars a little more than half the size of Earth. The only planets smaller than Mars are Mercury and

Parts of a Book, continued

Index

The **index** is usually found at the back of a book. It lists all the important subjects that are discussed in the book in alphabetical order. Use the index to see if the information you seek can be found in the book. After you read a book, the index can also be helpful when you want to locate a particular piece of information again.

Names of people are listed in alphabetical order by their last names.

Related details are often listed for a subject.

Sometimes page numbers are in *italics* to show that there is an illustration or photograph on that page.

Some indexes have words in parentheses that explain more about the subject. For example, these pages tell about the moons of Mars.

INDEX

Jet Propulsion Laboratory, 51
Jupiter, 53

Lowell, Percival, 30-33, *31*, 37
Lowell Observatory, 30-33
Lunar base, 43-45

Maria, 15-17
Mariner missions, 35-37, *36*, 38
Mars, *10*
  atmosphere of, 13-15, *16*
  density of, 27
  distance from Earth, 54
  distance from sun, 53
  fact sheet on, 53-54
  gravity on, 28
  length of year on, 12, 53
  manned mission to, 43-47, *48*, 50, 51
  mass of, 27
  moons of, 24, 25, *38*, *50*, 54
  naming of, 11
  orbit of, 11, 12, 53-54

possibility of life on, 13, 29-34, 37, 41-42, 43
  probes to, 35-42, *36*, *38*, *39*, 43, 47, *49*, 51
  reddish color of, 11, 41
  rotation of, 12, 53
  seasons and weather changes on, 12, 15-17
  size of, 11, 53
  surface of, 13, *14*, 15-25, *16*, 18, 21-23, 29-33, 34, 35, 37-42, *40*
  symbol for, 11, 53
  temperature on, 13
  water on, 13, 15, 17, 23, 25, 33
  wind storms on, 17, 41
Mass, 27
Mercury, 11
Moon (Earth), *36*
  base on, 43-45
Moons (Mars), 24, 25, *38*, 50, 54

62

Glossary

A **glossary** lists important words used in the book and their meanings. It is found at the back of the book. Use the glossary to help understand specific vocabulary in a book.

GLOSSARY

Words are listed in alphabetical order.

Astronomer– a scientist who studies the stars, planets, and all of outer space

Atmosphere– the various gases that surround a planet or other body in space

Axis– the invisible line through a planet's center around which it spins, or rotates

Crater– an irregular oval-shaped hole created through a collision with another object

Density– the compactness of materials

Equator– an imaginary circle around the center of the Earth, another planet, or the sun

Erosion– the process of being worn away by the action of wind, water, or other factors

The **definition** defines, or gives the meaning of, a word.

55

Types of Resource Books

Atlas

An **atlas** is a book of maps. There are several types of atlases, which are used for different purposes.

A **road atlas** is designed for drivers to use in deciding how to get from one place to another. The maps in a road atlas feature highways, streets, and other driving routes. Places such as cities, towns, and bodies of water are also shown on the road maps. The content of a road atlas might be limited to a small area such as one state, but a road atlas can also cover a huge area like a continent.

A **reference atlas** includes maps and information about every country in the world. Usually, a map of a country is shown on one page, and a second page shows facts and visuals about the country.

Historical atlases are filled with maps that show how people have explored and changed the world through time. These atlases also include interesting facts about history and often have timelines and other related visuals.

▼ historical atlas

▼ road atlas

▼ reference atlas

Since there are several types of atlases, it makes sense that you can find different types of maps inside them, doesn't it? You can use the different maps for different purposes. Let's see what some of them look like.

Physical Maps

A **physical map** shows the geographical features of a place, such as bodies of water and landforms.

Mapmakers often use techniques that make mountains look like they are rising off the page.

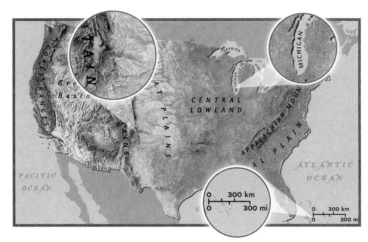

Landforms, like mountains or lakes, are often labeled.

The **scale** shows that this distance on the map is equal to 300 miles on land.

Product Maps

A **product map** uses pictures and symbols to show where products come from or where natural resources are found.

The **compass rose** shows the directions north, south, east, and west.

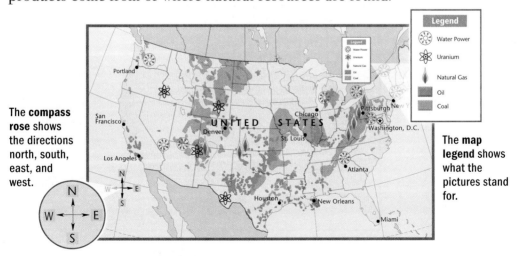

The **map legend** shows what the pictures stand for.

Types of Resource Books, continued

Political Maps

A **political map** shows the boundaries between countries, states, and other areas. It also shows capitals and other major cities. **Road maps** are usually set up like political maps.

A **grid system** is used on these maps to make it easy to find a particular place. Look up the place name in the index to find the right map and a code to the exact location on the map. For example, L-6 for this map is the square at which the row L and the column 6 intersect. Can you find Orlando somewhere in the square?

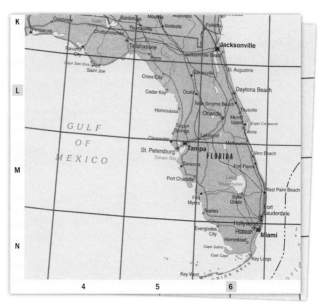

Historical Maps

A **historical map** shows when and where certain events happened.

Almanac

An **almanac** is an up-to-date book filled with facts about interesting topics such as inventions, awards, trends, weather, movies, and television. A new almanac is published each year, which is why the information is so current. You can use an almanac to find quick facts about a topic. Because almanacs tend to present information on a vast number of topics, you will find the **index** particularly useful in locating what you need.

INDEX

Solar cars, 60
Solar eclipses, 204
Solar power, 63
Solar system
    exploration of, 203
    facts about, 200–202
Solomon Islands, 162–163
    map, 131; flag, 145

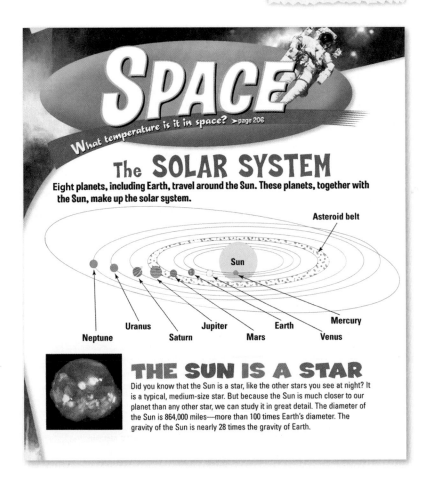

SPACE

What temperature is it in space? ➤page 206

The SOLAR SYSTEM

Eight planets, including Earth, travel around the Sun. These planets, together with the Sun, make up the solar system.

Asteroid belt

Sun

Neptune Uranus Saturn Jupiter Mars Earth Venus Mercury

THE SUN IS A STAR

Did you know that the Sun is a star, like the other stars you see at night? It is a typical, medium-size star. But because the Sun is much closer to our planet than any other star, we can study it in great detail. The diameter of the Sun is 864,000 miles—more than 100 times Earth's diameter. The gravity of the Sun is nearly 28 times the gravity of Earth.

Dictionary

Think of the **dictionary** as a tool you can use to learn everything you need to know about a word. Dictionaries tell you how to spell, say, and use words. From a dictionary you can learn how to divide a word into syllables, what part of speech a word is, and how to write different forms of a word. You can also learn the history of a word. Look for examples of all of these types of information on these dictionary pages.

 southwards ▶ space shuttle

ward slope of the mountain. Adjective.
south·ward (south′wərd) *adverb; adjective.*
southwards Another spelling of the adverb southward: *They drove southwards.* **south·wards** (south′wərdz) *adverb.*
southwest 1. The direction halfway between south and west. 2. The point of the compass showing this direction. 3. A region or place in this direction. 4. **the Southwest.** The region in the south and west of the United States. *Noun.*
○ 1. Toward or in the southwest: *the southwest corner of the street.* 2. Coming from the southwest: *a southwest wind. Adjective.*
○ Toward the southwest: *The ship sailed southwest. Adverb.*
south·west (south′west′) *noun; adjective; adverb.*
souvenir Something kept because it reminds one of a person, place, or event: *I bought a pennant as a souvenir of the baseball game.* **sou·ve·nir** (sü′və nîr′ *or* sü′və nîr′) *noun, plural* **souvenirs.**
sovereign A king or queen. *Noun.*
○ 1. Having the greatest power or highest rank or authority: *The king and queen were the sovereign rulers of the country.* 2. Not controlled by others; independent: *Mexico is a sovereign nation. Adjective.*
sov·er·eign (sov′ər ən *or* sov′rən) *noun, plural* **sovereigns;** *adjective.*
Soviet Union Formerly, a large country in eastern Europe and northern Asia. It was composed of 15 republics and was also called the U.S.S.R. The

largest and most important of the 15 republics was Russia.
sow¹ 1. To scatter seeds over the ground; plant: *The farmer will sow corn in this field.* 2. To spread or scatter: *The clown sowed happiness among the children.*
Other words that sound like this are **sew** and **so.**
sow (sō) *verb,* **sowed, sown** *or* **sowed, sowing.**
sow² An adult female pig. **sow** (sou) *noun, plural* **sows.**
soybean A seed rich in oil and protein and used as food. Soybeans grow in pods on bushy plants. **soy·bean** (soi′bēn′) *noun, plural* **soybeans.**
space 1. The area in which the whole universe exists. It has no limits. The planet earth is in space. 2. The region beyond the earth's atmosphere; outer space: *The rocket was launched into space.* 3. A distance or area between things: *There is not much space between our house and theirs.* 4. An area reserved or available for some purpose: *a parking space.* 5. A period of time: *Both jets landed in the space of ten minutes. Noun.*
○ To put space in between: *The architect spaced the houses far apart. Verb.*
space (spās) *noun, plural* **spaces;** *verb,* **spaced, spacing.**
spacecraft A vehicle used for flight in outer space. This is also called a spaceship. **space·craft** (spās′kraft′) *noun, plural* **spacecraft.**
space shuttle A spacecraft that carries a crew into space and returns to land on earth. The same

space shuttle

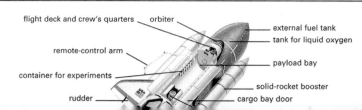

flight deck and crew's quarters — orbiter
external fuel tank
tank for liquid oxygen
remote-control arm
payload bay
container for experiments
solid-rocket booster
rudder
cargo bay door

space station ▸ Spanish Ⓢ

space shuttle can be used again. A space shuttle is also called a shuttle.

space station A spaceship that orbits around the earth like a satellite and on which a crew can live for long periods of time.

spacesuit Special clothing worn by an astronaut in space. A spacesuit covers an astronaut's entire body and has equipment to help the astronaut breathe. **space·suit** (spās'süt') *noun, plural* **spacesuits.**

Astronauts take spacewalks to repair satellites and vehicles.

spacewalk A period of activity during which an astronaut in space is outside a spacecraft. **space·walk** (spās'wôk') *noun, plural* **spacewalks.**

spacious Having a lot of space or room; roomy; large. —**spa·cious** *adjective* —**spaciousness** *noun.*

spade¹ A tool used for digging. It has a long handle and a flat blade that can be pressed into the ground with the foot. *Noun.*
○ To dig with a spade: *We spaded the garden and then raked it. Verb.*
spade (spād) *noun, plural* **spades;** *verb,* **spaded, spading.**

spade² 1. A playing card marked with one or more figures shaped like this. 2. **spades.** The suit

thin strings. It is made of a mixture of flour and water. **spa·ghet·ti** (spə get'ē) *noun.*

WORD HISTORY

The word spaghetti comes from an Italian word meaning "strings" or "little cords." Spaghetti looks a bit like strings.

Spain A country in southwest Europe. **Spain** (spān) *noun.*

spamming The sending of the same message to large numbers of e-mail addresses or to many newsgroups at the same time. Spamming is often thought of as impolite behavior on the Internet. **spam·ming** (spa'ming) *noun.*

span 1. The distance or part between two supports: *The span of that bridge is very long.* 2. The full reach or length of anything: *Some people accomplish a great deal in the span of their lives. Noun.*
○ To extend over or across. *Verb.*
span (span) *noun, plural* **spans;** *verb,* **spanned, spanning.**

This bridge spans a wide river.

spaniel Any of various dogs of small to medium size with long, drooping ears, a silky, wavy coat, and short legs. The larger types are used in hunting. **span·iel** (span'yəl) *noun, plural* **spaniels.**

Spanish 1. The people of Spain. The word *Spanish* in this sense is used with a plural verb. 2. The language spoken in Spain. It is also spoken in many countries south of the United States as well as in parts of the U.S. *Noun.*

Use the **guide words** at the top of each page to help you find the entry word you are looking up. The guide words are the first and last words on the page.

The **entry word** *spacesuit* falls between *space station* and *Spanish* in alphabetical order.

In this dictionary, words in **blue** have corresponding visuals. Special notes about how to use words also appear in blue.

237W

Types of Resource Books, continued

Thesaurus

A **thesaurus** is similar to a dictionary, but instead of giving word meanings, it lists synonyms and antonyms. A thesaurus can be especially useful when you are looking for just the right word to use. For example, you might want to describe how *good* of an experience NASA's Space Camp® is for kids—but without using that tired, overworked adjective. You could look up *good* in a thesaurus and find an entry that looks like this:

Synonyms are words with almost the same meanings.

Antonyms are words with opposite meanings.

fine

good adjective **1** *a good product* FINE, superior, quality; excellent, superb, outstanding, magnificent, exceptional, marvelous, wonderful, first-rate, first-class, sterling; satisfactory, acceptable, not bad, all right; *informal* great, OK, A1, jake, hunky-dory, ace, terrific, fantastic, fabulous, fab, top-notch, blue-chip, blue-ribbon, bang-up, killer, class, awesome, wicked; smashing, brilliant. ANTONYM bad.

2 *a good person* VIRTUOUS, righteous, upright, [bad] inding, moral, ethical, high-minded, principled; e......lary,

from Oxford American Writer's Thesaurus. Christine A. Lundberg. By permission of Oxford University Press, Inc.

Which synonym would you decide to use?

A thesaurus can also be helpful when you are trying to decide how to express your thoughts about a big idea or topic. If you can't seem to come up with the right words, look up the subject—for example, *universe*—and see what you find.

universe noun **1** *a collection of stars* COSMOS, creation, nature, heavens, luminaries, constellations, celestial, stellar.

These are only a few of the words listed in one thesaurus for that subject. Just think about how helpful these words might be.

A thesaurus might give more information than simple lists of words.

This thesaurus looks very similar to a dictionary. It includes a definition for each **entry word**. The definition is followed by a **sample sentence** featuring the word. This thesaurus also includes **guide words** at the top of the page.

baby

beautiful

baby *n.* a very young child or animal: The *baby* is only ten months old.
Synonyms
infant a child too young to walk or talk: You need to carry an *infant*.
newborn a baby that has just been born: The *newborn* and her mother go home from the hospital.

beat *n.* a repeated sound, usually with a regular occurrence: Tap your foot to the *beat*.
Synonyms
pounding I could feel the *pounding* of my own heart.
rhythm The *rhythm* of the rain put me to sleep last night.

This thesaurus does not include definitions, only sample sentences.

wakeful adjective **1** *he had been wakeful all night* AWAKE restless, restive, tossing and turning. ANTONYM asleep.
2 *I was suddenly wakeful* ALERT, watchful, vigilant, on the lookout, on one's guard, attentive, heedful, wary. ANTONYM inattentive.

walk verb **1** *they walked along the road* STROLL, saunter, amble, trudge, plod, dawdle, hike, tramp, tromp, slog, stomp, trek, march, stride, sashay, glide, troop, patrol, wander, ramble, tread, prowl, promenade, roam, traipse; stretch one's legs; *informal* mosey, hoof it; *formal* peram-

Types of Resource Books, continued

Encyclopedia

An **encyclopedia** is a series of books with articles that give facts about many different topics. Each book is called a **volume**. The volumes and articles are arranged in alphabetical order. You can use an encyclopedia for a broad overview of a subject.

An article about Mars would be in this volume.

This is where you would find information about space travel.

Most encyclopedias have a volume called an **index**. The index lists other related subjects to look up.

Some encyclopedias are on a computer disk. You can read the information from the disk on your computer screen.

Guide words are used on encyclopedia pages to make it easy to flip through and find the specific article you want to read.

Hale Observatories

NASA

Mars's surface features are visible in a photograph taken from the earth, *left*. The earth's atmosphere makes the picture blurry. A series of canyons called the Valles Marineris (Mariner Valleys) make up the diagonal landform in the photo at the right, taken by the U.S. Viking 1 space probe. This landform is more than 2,500 miles (4,000 kilometers) long.

The **entry word** of an article is its title.

Mars is the only planet whose surface can be seen in detail from the earth. It is reddish in color, and was named Mars after the bloody-red god of war of the ancient Romans. Mars is the only planet other than the earth to produce evidence suggesting that it was once the home of living creatures. However, there is no evidence that life now exists on Mars.

Mars is the fourth closest planet to the sun, and the next planet beyond the earth. Its mean distance from the sun is 141,600,000 miles (227,900,000 kilometers), compared with about 93,000,000 miles (150,000,000 kilometers) for the earth. At its closest approach to the earth, Mars is 34,600,000 miles (55,700,000 kilometers) away. Venus is the only planet in the solar system that comes closer to the earth.

The diameter of Mars is 4,223 miles (6,796 kilometers), a little over half that of the earth. Pluto and Mercury are the only planets smaller than Mars.

Headings tell what each section in an article is about.

Orbit and rotation

Mars travels around the sun in an *elliptical* (oval-shaped) orbit. Its distance from the sun varies from about 154,800,000 miles (249,200,000 kilometers) at its farthest point, to about 128,400,000 miles (206,600,000 kilometers) at its closest point. Mars takes about 687 earth-days to go around the sun.

As Mars orbits the sun, it spins on its *axis,* an imaginary line through its center. Mars's axis is not *perpendicular* (at an angle of 90°) to its path around the sun. The axis tilts at an angle of about 24° from the perpendicular position. For an illustration of the tilt of an axis, see **Planet** (The axes of the planets). Mars rotates once every 24 hours and 37 minutes. The earth rotates once every 23 hours and 56 minutes.

The **author** of each encyclopedia article is chosen because he or she is an expert on the topic.

The contributor of this article is Hyron Spinrad, Professor of Astronomy at the University of California, Berkeley.

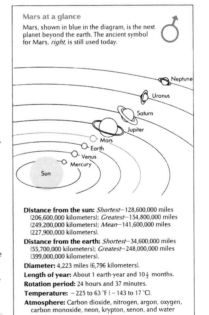

Mars at a glance

Mars, shown in blue in the diagram, is the next planet beyond the earth. The ancient symbol for Mars, *right*, is still used today.

Neptune
Uranus
Saturn
Jupiter
Mars
Earth
Venus
Mercury
Sun

Distance from the sun: *Shortest*—128,600,000 miles (206,600,000 kilometers); *Greatest*—154,800,000 miles (249,200,000 kilometers); *Mean*—141,600,000 miles (227,900,000 kilometers).

Distance from the earth: *Shortest*—34,600,000 miles (55,700,000 kilometers); *Greatest*—248,000,000 miles (399,000,000 kilometers).

Diameter: 4,223 miles (6,796 kilometers).

Length of year: About 1 earth-year and 10½ months.

Rotation period: 24 hours and 37 minutes.

Temperature: −225 to 63 °F (−143 to 17 °C).

Atmosphere: Carbon dioxide, nitrogen, argon, oxygen, carbon monoxide, neon, krypton, xenon, and water vapor.

Number of satellites: 2.

Other Print Resources

Newspapers

A **newspaper** is a daily or weekly series of publications that presents news of interest on the local, state, national, and world levels. People read newspapers to get information. You can use newspapers to find information about current events. You can look at old newspapers to help you write about something that happened in the past.

▲ Yang Liwei, Astronaut of China's First Manned Spaceflight

News Articles

Newspapers contain **news articles**. These are factual accounts of current events. As you read a news article you should find the answers to five key questions (sometimes referred to as the "Five Ws") about the event it describes: *Who? What? When? Where? Why?*

The **lead paragraph** gives a summary of the story.

The **headline** grabs readers' attention and gives a quick idea of the story content.

News stories often quote experts, eyewitnesses, and other voices of authority.

China's Big Plans for Space

Beijing, China By 2020, if all goes as planned, China will have put a human on the moon, a space station in orbit around Earth, and a joint China-Russia explorer ship on its way to Mars. For years China has been steadily but quietly building a space program the likes of which we have not seen since the 1960s space race.

In October 2007, China launched a lunar orbiter. China now has a spacecraft orbiting the moon and mapping its surface. China is looking for resources—things like helium-3, a fuel source that might make nuclear power a much safer, cleaner energy source on Earth. By 2017, China hopes to send robots to the moon to collect samples of resources and bring them back to Earth.

China also has big plans for manned space missions. In 2008, China hopes to broadcast a live spacewalk by three taikonauts (the Chinese version of astronauts). China also reportedly has thought about placing people on the moon to work at retrieving the valuable resources it hopes to find there.

Right now, United States officials still believe we are ahead of the Chinese technologically. Yet, as NASA head Michael Griffin has stated, "China will be back on the moon before we are . . . I think when that happens Americans will not like it."

Editorials

Most newspapers also usually include **editorials**. These are opinion-based pieces of writing on topics of interest to readers. Editorials often appear in their own section of a newspaper and look different from news stories. This is so that readers will know that editorials present opinions in addition to facts. You can use editorials to give you ideas to write a persuasive essay or to present the opinions of other people.

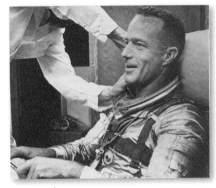

▲ American Astronaut Scott Carpenter

We Need to Make Astronauts Superstars Again

Americans seem to have become bored with manned space flight. We no longer remain glued to our screens when space shuttles launch, dock at the space station, and land back on Earth. Photos of astronauts floating around in space don't even make the front page of this newspaper! We need to appreciate the incredible accomplishments of our space travelers.

> The author's **opinion** is clearly stated.

Back in 1962, *Aurora 7*, the capsule of one of the Mercury rockets, almost didn't make its return to Earth. All kinds of problems occurred during reentry. If there had not been a human on board to correct the problems and make a landing, the capsule and all of its data would have been lost.

> **Facts** are used to support the opinion.

Do we truly believe complex space missions are best accomplished without trained humans? More and more I hear about robotics and unmanned probes as the future of U.S. space missions. Why is that happening? Simply put, astronauts are no longer the popular figures they once were, so NASA figures it's easier to do without them.

Only we can give astronauts back the star status they deserve. We can do that by caring about their work. Tune in, read all about it. Send some fan mail. Do whatever you can to tell these heroic men and women—and the people for whom they work—that they really do matter.

> Editorials often end with a specific **call to action**.

Magazines

A magazine is a special collection of articles. Some magazines are written about one interest or hobby, such as sports or music. Others are targeted for one group of people—teens or children, for example. Still other magazines, including news and entertainment magazines, are published to appeal to a wide variety of readers.

Magazines are published on a schedule such as monthly or weekly. For example, a monthly magazine publishes a new issue every month. Magazines are sometimes called periodicals. A period is a span of time. You can use magazines for a variety of writing purposes. Past issues of magazines are also helpful in writing about events that happened in the past.

A MASSIVE AIR AND SPACE MUSEUM...

Right by Dulles Airport!

On your next trip to our nation's capital, be sure to set aside some time to visit the Steven F. Udvar-Hazy Center. Located on land that is part of Washington Dulles International Airport, this companion site to the National Air and Space Museum could represent a stellar beginning to your trip or a wonderful grand finale.

The Udvar-Hazy Center originally opened in December 2003, and within six months the Center welcomed its one millionth visitor. Then, in November 2004, the James S. McDonnell Space Hangar opened at the Center. A third structure at the Center, the Donald D. Engen Observation Tower, allows visitors to view air traffic coming in and out of Dulles.

WHAT CAN YOU SEE?

Both the original Center complex and the McDonnell Space Hangar are remarkable for their size. Given that the goal of the Udvar-Hazy Center was to place actual

The headline and lead paragraph of a magazine article are designed to draw readers' attention.

Headings help to break up the text of magazine articles, which can be several pages long. The headings also tell what the sections are about.

aircraft and space vehicles on display, the hugeness of the spaces involved is no surprise. The original Center is 2½ football fields long and 10 stories high. Visitors walk among many aircraft and view others suspended from the ceiling. Helicopters, the world's fastest jet, and one-of-a-kind experimental planes are just some of the flying machines you can see.

Inside the 53,000 square-foot McDonnell Hangar, hundreds of space vehicles are displayed. The centerpiece is the space shuttle *Enterprise*, but rockets, satellites, space capsules, telescopes, and more are housed here as well.

Visitors can also experience IMAX® movies and flight simulators. Daily tours and activities are offered, and diners and shoppers will be pleased to find facilities to suit them as well. An especially interesting feature of the Udvar-Hazy Center is the Wall of Honor. As you enter the Center, you walk along this memorial to our great aviators and space explorers.

WHAT ABOUT THOSE NAMES?

Steven F. Udvar-Hazy is an American billionaire who made his fortune in the aviation industry. Born in Hungary, Steven fled with his family in 1958 to escape the Soviet occupation. Then 12 years old, Steven went on to attend UCLA. He began his own business in 1973. That fabulously successful business leases planes to airlines so that they do not have to buy and sell them on their own.

In 1999, Udvar-Hazy donated $60 million to the National Air and Space

Most magazines use color and plenty of visuals to make the pages more attractive and interesting to readers.

Museum, making him the biggest donor in the history of the Smithsonian. When asked why he gave so much, Udvar-Hazy commented, "I know this new museum will impart to millions of children the same love for aviation that I have, and it will inspire future generations."

Like Udvar-Hazy, James S. McDonnell was an industry leader. As a pioneer in the aerospace industry, McDonnell was a big player in the first American spaceflights. His company built the *Mercury* and *Gemini* rockets which carried the first American astronauts into space.

Donald D. Engen, for whom the observation tower is named, gave to the museum in a different way. Before he was killed in a glider accident in 1999, Admiral Engen worked tirelessly to get the plans for the Center underway. His efforts have been called "legendary" by fellow museum staffers. Without a doubt, Engen would be pleased with how the Center turned out. As for you… you will not want to miss the Center's "out of this world" experience!

10 | *Write to* Summarize

Model Study

Summary Paragraph

When you summarize something, you include only the most important ideas. You might write a summary

- while you read or after reading to help you remember

- when you do research for a project to keep track of information

- when you study for a test to help you remember.

To summarize a paragraph or short passage, write a **summary statement** of just one sentence. For longer works, such as an article or part of a book, write a **summary paragraph**.

When you write a summary, you have to read closely, figure out the most important ideas, and determine which details are not so important. That can be a challenge! Learning to summarize can help you become a better reader *and* writer.

SUMMARY PARAGRAPH

A good summary

☑ names the title and author of the work you are summarizing

☑ states the original writer's ideas in your own words

☑ includes the main ideas

☑ leaves out details that are not important.

Feature Checklist

CHAPTER 1: THE ROAD TO FREEDOM | Dee Wallis

How did people who escaped slavery travel North? They often used the Underground Railroad. It had no tracks or train cars. But it had safe houses where runaways could stay, and people willing to help even if it meant breaking the law.

Harriet Tubman was one of the heroes of the Underground Railroad. She was born into slavery in Maryland around the year 1820. In 1849, she left slavery and followed the North Star to freedom. A year later, Tubman started to rescue others seeking freedom.

In ten years, Harriet Tubman made nineteen trips. She helped more than 300 people reach freedom. At the end, she proudly said she "never lost a single passenger."

▼ During the 1850s, Harriet Tubman helped hundreds of people escape slavery.

Good Summary

In Chapter 1 of The Road to Freedom, Dee Wallis describes the Underground Railroad, a network of brave people who helped those escaping slavery. Harriet Tubman was part of this network, helping hundreds find freedom in the North.

The writer focuses only on the main ideas.

Poor Summary

Dee Wallis explains in The Road to Freedom that the Underground Railroad was not a real railroad. Harriet Tubman was one of the guides. She was born into slavery in Maryland around the year 1820. She went north. She followed the north star. Then she helped others. She made 19 trips.

The writer uses **unoriginal wording** and includes **unimportant details**.

Write a Summary Paragraph

WRITING PROMPT When you read, summarizing helps you determine what is important. Writing a summary paragraph helps you remember the main ideas.

Read the passage from Daniel Schulman's "Escaping to Freedom." Then, write a summary paragraph that

* names the title and author of the work you are summarizing
* restates the main ideas in your own words
* includes only the details that are important

Prewrite

The first part of summarizing is finding the most important ideas in what you read. Try these tricks for keeping track:

* Underline or highlight important ideas as you read.

   In 1830, Josiah Henson was 41 years old. A life of slavery was all he had ever known. Born in Maryland, Henson was taken from his family as a child. He was bought and sold many times. Henson lived on a plantation, or large farm, in Kentucky. He tried to buy his way out of slavery, but his owner, Amos Riley, tricked him. Riley kept the money that Henson paid for his freedom, but he did not let Henson go.

Escaping to Freedom
by Daniel Schulman

Stop the Runaway!

$100 Reward!

Runaway from the subscriber, living in Clay county, Mo., 3 miles south of Haynesville and 15 miles north of Liberty, a negro boy named SANDY, about 35 years of age, about 5 feet 6 inches high, rather copper color, whiskers on when he left, brown when spoken to, had black plush cap, and coarse jeans pants and coat, quick in his brown janes pants and coat, hended a reward of $25 will be given if taken in Clay county; $50 if out of the county, and $100 if taken out of the State, and delivered to me or confined in jail so that I can get him.

April 3, 1860.   ROBT. THOMPSON.

People who escaped slavery were pursued by their owners. ▶

- Mark paragraphs with sticky notes as you read. Write related ideas on each note. Later, you can turn the ideas on each note into one sentence that uses your own words.

Bad News

One day Henson learned some troubling news. He learned that Riley planned to sell him. Henson would have to move to Louisiana, and he might never see his wife and children again! Henson could not accept this, so he made a plan for his family to escape.

Path to Freedom

One dark night, Henson and his family left their home. He carried his two youngest children in a backpack. The family boarded a small boat and crossed the Ohio River into Indiana. Once in Indiana, the family had to move slowly. They had to be careful not to be seen. Some slave owners offered rewards for the capture of escaped slaves. If the family was found, they might be returned to Riley.

Bad News
—Riley was going to sell Henson.
—Henson would have to leave his family.

—Henson planned to escape.

Path to Freedom
—Henson and his family left their home.
—They crossed into Indiana.

—They had to lay low and avoid being seen.

- Use a summary planner to begin writing.

Summary Planner

Title: Escaping to Freedom
Topic: Slavery

Paragraph 1:
Josiah Henson was bought and sold many times as a slave and tried unsuccessfully to buy his own freedom.

+

Paragraph 2:

+
(to end of selection)

=

Summary of Selection: _____

Reflect

- Which method for finding the most important information do you like best?

- How can you begin to express the main ideas in your own words?

Draft

Use your prewriting notes to draft a summary paragraph. Remember that your draft does not need to be perfect. You just want to get the important ideas down on paper, using your own words and a logical flow.

- **Use Your Organizer** Follow your writing plan. That way you will include the important ideas in your summary.

> Josiah Henson was bought and sold many times as a slave. He tried unsuccessfully to buy his own freedom.

Anita used her Summary Planner to write sentences.

- **Use Your Own Words** Don't copy sentences from the original. Instead, try to restate the main points in fewer words.

Now read these summaries. There are lots of ways to say the same thing! Notice the different ways these writers did it.

Good Summary

> Daniel Schulman's "Escaping to Freedom" tells about Josiah Henson and his family, slaves on a Kentucky plantation.

Good Summary

> Josiah Henson and his family were slaves in Kentucky. Their lives are described in Daniel Schulman's "Escaping to Freedom."

Good Summary

> As Daniel Schulman explains in "Escaping to Freedom," the Hensons were slaves in Kentucky.

Reflect

- Did you state all of the important ideas in your own words?

- Should you take out any extra details?

TechManual

Take Command of Your Word Processor

There are several ways you can make, save, create, or format documents. Get to know what's above the page on your screen. Most programs have a command bar and a tool bar.

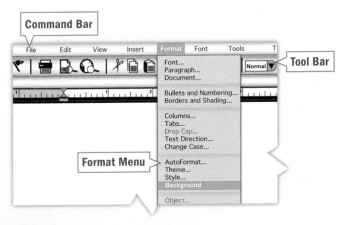

Keyboard Shortcuts

For some commands, you don't need to use a menu. You can just use keyboard shortcuts by selecting the text you want to change and hitting the **Control** or **Command** key and another key at the same time. Here are a few shortcuts:

Control or Command	Functions
A	Selects all of your text
C	Copies selected text
X	Cuts selected text
V	Pastes copied or cut text where your cursor is
Z	Undoes your last action
N	Creates a new document
S	Saves your document
B	Changes text to bold type
I	Changes text to italic type

Revise

As you consider how to revise your work, keep your audience and purpose in mind. Does your writing help you remember and communicate the key ideas?

❶ Evaluate Your Work

Read your summary aloud one sentence at a time and see what can be improved. As you read, ask yourself:

- **About the Form** Do I have all the important ideas in my own words?

- **About Focus and Unity** Does everything relate to the central idea?

This narrow tunnel was one route on the Underground Railroad. ▼

> ### Revision in Action

Anita's Draft

Escaping to Freedom

Daniel Schulman's "Escaping to Freedom" tells how the Henson family escaped from slavery in 1830. The Hensons were slaves on a plantation in Kentucky. Josiah Henson paid for his freedom. However, his owner, Amos Riley, wouldn't let him go. Riley was going to sell Josiah and break up the family. In 1830, they ran away. The family followed the Underground Railroad, as many other escaped slaves had. In Indiana, they stayed out of sight. They didn't want slave catchers to find them and return them to Riley.

Anita thinks:

"I could combine these two sentences."

"Parts of the paragraph are too wordy. I need to decide which details to cut."

❷ Mark Your Changes

Consolidate To make your summary shorter, you may need to consolidate ideas. When you consolidate, you add, delete, and rearrange to make things shorter. You can consolidate by

- joining sentences that discuss related ideas and details
- deleting unnecessary words, and information that your reader can figure out without your stating it directly.

Reflect

- Have you included all the important ideas?

- Are there details you could still leave out?

Revising Marks **MARK**	∧	↶	⌐	◡	⁋
WHAT IT MEANS	Insert something.	Move to here.	Replace with this.	Take out.	Make a new paragraph.

Revised Draft

Escaping to Freedom

Daniel Schulman's "Escaping to Freedom" tells how the Henson family escaped from ~~slavery in 1830. The Hensons were slaves on~~ a plantation in Kentucky. Josiah Henson's paid for his freedom. However, his owner, Amos Riley, *tricked him and* ~~wouldn't let him go. Riley~~ was going to sell Josiah and break up the family. In 1830, they ran away. The family followed the Underground Railroad, as many other escaped slaves had. In Indiana, they *hid to avoid being captured and returned.* ~~stayed out of sight. They didn't want slave catchers to find them and return them to Riley.~~

Anita took out extra words and unnecessary details.

Anita made her summary shorter by combining two sentences.

Anita cut out some of the details to focus on the central idea.

Edit and Proofread

After you're satisfied with the content of your summary paragraph, read it again to fix language errors. This is what you do when you edit and proofread your work:

- **Check the Grammar** Make sure that you have used correct and conventional grammar throughout. In particular, check for correct use of subject and object pronouns. (See page 255W.)

- **Check the Spelling** Spell-check can help, but it isn't always enough. Read your work carefully, and use a dictionary if you need to. Pay special attention to words ending in -y. (See page 256W.)

- **Check the Mechanics** Errors in punctuation and capitalization can make your work hard to understand. Check that you have capitalized the names of organizations and historical periods correctly. (See page 257W.)

Use these marks to edit and proofread your paragraph.

Editing and Proofreading Marks

MARK	WHAT IT MEANS	MARK	WHAT IT MEANS
∧	Insert something.	⁄	Make lowercase.
∧	Add a comma.	℮	Delete, take something out.
∧	Add a semicolon.	¶	Make new paragraph.
⊙	Add a period.	◯	Spell out.
⊙	Add a colon.	∧	Replace with this.
∨ ∨	Add quotation marks.	∼	Change order of letters or words.
∨	Add an apostrophe.	#	Insert space.
≡	Capitalize.	◡	Close up, no space here.

Reflect
- What kind of errors did you find? What can you do to keep from making them?

Grammar Workout

Check Subject and Object Pronouns

- Pronouns, like nouns, can be the subject of a sentence or the object of a verb in the predicate.

  EXAMPLE   Joe wanted freedom.
              subject   object

                    He dreamed of it.
              subject   object
              pronoun   pronoun

- Subject and object pronouns often have different forms.

Subject Pronouns	I	you	he	she	it	we	they
Object Pronouns	me	you	him	her	it	us	them

  EXAMPLE   They worked hard. Sarah helped them.

- When a pronoun is used together with a noun or with another pronoun, it must still be in the correct form.

  INCORRECT   Ana and me escaped. Joe met Ana and I later.

  CORRECT   Ana and I escaped. Joe met Ana and me later.

Find the Trouble Spots

>   Josiah Henson wasn't free. Amos Riley owned ~~he~~ *him*.
> Amos planned to sell Josiah, which meant that she
> would be separated from his family.
>   *He* ~~Him~~ couldn't leave they! So the family escaped from
> the plantation. Them fled north from Kentucky.

Find and fix three more pronoun errors.

Edit and Proofread, continued

> ## SpellingWorkout

Check Words Ending in y

Sometimes, you change a word by adding **-s, -ed,** or **-ing** at the end. For words that end in *y*, follow these spelling rules:

- If the word ends in a vowel followed by *y*, just add the ending.

EXAMPLES	stay + -s	⟶	stays
	play + -ed	⟶	played
	stray + -ing	⟶	straying

- If the word ends in a consonant followed by *y*, change the *y* to *i*, then add **-es** or **-ed.** You do not need to make this change if you're adding **-ing.**

EXAMPLES	pity + -s	⟶	pities
	cry + -ed	⟶	cried
	fly + -ing	⟶	flying

Find the Trouble Spots

Henson and his family hurr*i*ed to escape. They feared that they might encounter enem*ies*. As runawa*y*es, they worried that slave catchers might turn them in. Fortunately, they found helpful familys as they followed the Underground Railroad. Their journey was just one of many journies to freedom.

Find and fix three more spelling errors.

Mechanics Workout

Check Capitalization of Proper Nouns

When you write, always capitalize proper nouns. If a proper noun includes more than one word, capitalize every important word.

- The names of **organizations** are proper nouns.

  EXAMPLES   The **American Anti-Slavery Society** was founded by William Lloyd Garrison.

  The **New York Committee of Vigilance** protected fugitive slaves.

- The names of **historical periods** are proper nouns.

  EXAMPLES   During the **Age of Exploration,** slaves were brought to the New World.

  The period just after slavery ended is called **Reconstruction.**

Find the Trouble Spots

Many slaves were helped by the underground railroad. After slavery ended, the government set up the freedman's bureau. Its full name was the bureau of refugees, freedmen, and abandoned lands. Its job was to help protect former slaves. It provided money for medical care and education. It also reunited many families. It was an important organization in the civil war era.

Find and fix additional errors in capitalization.

"To figure out why something happened, like a historical event, I can write about it."
—David

Model Study

Cause-and-Effect Essay

When you write a **cause-and-effect essay,** you tell what happened, why it happened, and what happened because of it.

1. Introduction

◀ State your **central idea.**

2. Body

◀ Explain the causes and effects.

3. Conclusion

◀ Write a conclusion that ties back to your central idea.

CAUSE-AND-EFFECT ESSAY

A good cause-and-effect essay

☑ has an introduction with a clear central idea

☑ has a body that explains the causes and effects in detail

☑ has a conclusion that connects to the central idea and leaves you with something to think about.

Anne Frank's Diary
by Reesa Villinen

Introduction:

The **main idea** is stated in the introduction.

People have lost their freedom because of their religion, ideas, and skin color. Anne Frank was born in 1929 to a German Jewish family. During World War II, she lost her freedom because she was Jewish.

Body:

The writer explains causes and effects related to the central idea.

In the 1930s, the German Nazi government restricted Jewish people's freedoms. Jews could not have certain jobs or attend certain schools. Soon, the Nazis began to deport Jews to concentration camps. For these reasons, Anne Frank's family moved to the Netherlands. At first they were safe. But in 1940, Germany occupied the Netherlands. Anne's sister was called to report to a labor camp in 1942. The family hid in two rooms in a warehouse. Because Anne could not go to school, she kept a diary to pass time. Anne and her family lived in the warehouse for two years. In 1944, the police arrested Anne's family. Anne died in a concentration camp in 1945.

The writer uses **signal words** to identify causes and effects.

Conclusion:

The conclusion sums up the main idea of the essay and leaves the reader with something to think about— freedom today.

Anne's father was the only family member to survive. Years later, he published his daughter's diary. It was read all over the world. Thanks to the diary, people know what it means to lose your freedom. The diary helps us remember how important it is to support freedom for all people around the world.

Student Model

Use Graphic Organizers

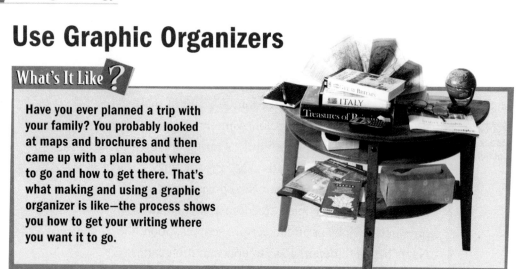

What's It Like ❓

Have you ever planned a trip with your family? You probably looked at maps and brochures and then came up with a plan about where to go and how to get there. That's what making and using a graphic organizer is like—the process shows you how to get your writing where you want it to go.

Cause-and-Effect Organizers

Use these graphic organizers to organize ideas for your cause-and-effect essay.

Sometimes, a cause leads to a single effect. You might want to show each cause and its effect in a chart.

Cause-and-Effect Chart

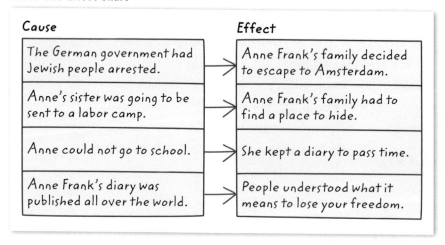

Cause	Effect
The German government had Jewish people arrested.	Anne Frank's family decided to escape to Amsterdam.
Anne's sister was going to be sent to a labor camp.	Anne Frank's family had to find a place to hide.
Anne could not go to school.	She kept a diary to pass time.
Anne Frank's diary was published all over the world.	People understood what it means to lose your freedom.

Sometimes, causes and effects form a chain of linked events. Each event causes another event to happen.

Use a cause-and-effect chain when you need to write about effects that become the causes of additional effects.

Cause-and-Effect Chain

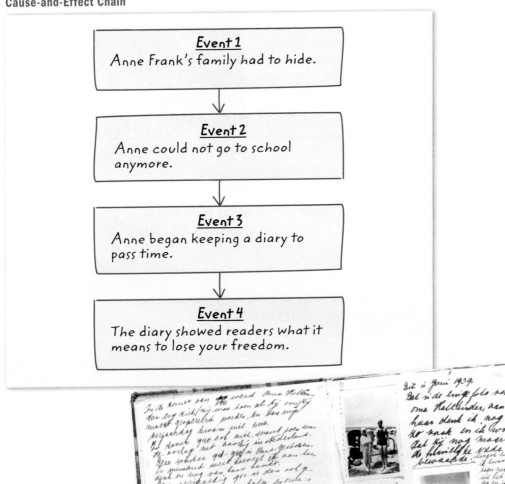

Event 1
Anne Frank's family had to hide.

Event 2
Anne could not go to school anymore.

Event 3
Anne began keeping a diary to pass time.

Event 4
The diary showed readers what it means to lose your freedom.

Anne put photos of herself and her sister, Margot, in her diary. ▶

How to Write a Good Introduction

What's It Like

How do you introduce yourself? Do you say, "Let me tell you the story of my life"? Or do you say, "My name is Dave. I am a student at your school"? You stay organized by focusing on one piece of information. You also include information that will interest your listener. To write an introduction, follow the same rule: focus on providing important information that will capture your reader's interest.

State a Central Idea

When you write an essay, you state the **central idea** in the introduction. The central idea helps you decide which details fit in your essay. It keeps your writing focused.

You can state your central idea in a **topic sentence** that tells your purpose for writing. To create a topic sentence, narrow your main idea. Here's how one writer did it.

Central Idea

> I want to write about women refugees around the world.

Sample Topic Sentences

> Many people live in countries with no freedom.

< Too broad

> In 2004, Amnesty International found out how tough life was for women refugees from Darfur.

< Too narrow

> Many women in the world flee their countries for freedom.

< Just right

The Ongoing Fight for Women's Rights
by Stella Graham

Women in the United States have the same rights as men. This doesn't happen everywhere in the world. In fact, many women around the world must leave their home countries to find freedom. In many places, women do not have many rights. Their lives are very difficult. Some of them cannot vote. Others cannot choose their jobs or get an education.

The introduction includes the writer's **central idea**.

Without a clear central idea expressed in a topic sentence, the introduction would sound dull and unfocused. The reader would be confused about the main topic of the essay.

▼ The crisis in Darfur, in western Sudan, has caused many women to flee to safety.

How to Write a Good Introduction, continued

There are a million ways to start an essay. How does a writer invite readers in and make them want to stay? The best writers do it in the introduction. A strong introduction catches the readers' attention and leaves them wanting to read more.

Use these techniques to catch readers' attention:

- Start with a question or statistic.

Question

> How can women with no freedom change their lives?

Statistic

> In the past, Afghan women had more freedom. At one time, 70% of school teachers in Afghanistan were women.

▼ This Afghan teacher is helping women learn to read.

- Start with a simile or metaphor.

Similes use *like* or *as* to compare two things. Often they compare things that seem different but have hidden similarities. Similes add color to your writing.

Simile

> A book is like a good friend. It keeps you company.

Metaphors make comparisons, but without using *like* or *as*.

Metaphor

> A book is a journey through someone else's world.

- Start by discussing an experience that your readers will understand.

Personal Connection

> Nobody likes to feel useless. Well, many women in Afghanistan felt just like that. They could not study, or work, or dress as they liked. They felt like they could not help people they cared about.

Study the following introduction.

Women in Afghanistan
by Terrence Bell

What would you do if suddenly you were robbed of your freedom? In Afghanistan, women lived through this. When their government changed, women could no longer do what they wanted.

Which technique does the writer use to catch the reader's attention?

How would you rewrite this introduction to use a simile or metaphor?

How to Link Causes and Effects

You are about to join in a game and your shoelace snaps. What do you do? You tie the broken piece to the old one. Transitions work just like that. They tie different sentences together so they work better.

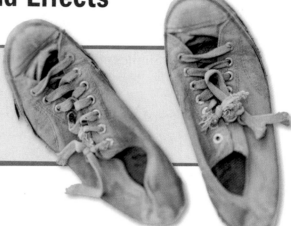

Use Transition Words

As you write the body of your essay, you can use certain transitions that are especially helpful in signaling causes and effects.

> **Because** there are more than 2 million refugees, people are creating organizations to help them. **As a result,** refugees are able to start their lives again. This is progress.

Notice how some words make causes and effects clear.

Confusing

Women in Afghanistan could not get an education. Many Afghan women left their country. It was a difficult choice. These women must be very brave.

Clear

Women in Afghanistan could not get an education. This is why many Afghan women left their country. Since it was a difficult choice, these women must be very brave.

The words below are used to signal one event leading to another, and to show how causes and effects are linked. Read the words and study the passage.

because	**therefore**	**so**
as a result	**since**	**due to**

Building New Lives
by Ali Saghal

In past years, the situation of Afghan women had been very difficult. So, many of them fled their own country. Now these women are getting help. For example, because Afghan women were not allowed to work in their country, they often have no skills. Therefore, some organizations are offering them classes. Often, the women learn a new language. Then they are able to apply for jobs. As a result, these women are becoming more independent.

What words does the writer use to show how causes and effects are linked?

Many Afghan women are now furthering their education. ▼

How to Finish Strong

Imagine your best friend is about to move away. Wouldn't you give your friend a gift to remember you by? The gift should be something that tells about your friendship and that shows the connection between you and your friend. A good conclusion is like that. It reminds your readers of the main idea of your essay. It also makes a connection with your readers and leaves them with something to think about.

Create a Strong Conclusion

You've worked hard to write a good introduction. You carefully organized the body of your essay. Now you need to write a conclusion that readers will remember.

A good conclusion should sum up your central idea. A good conclusion will help the reader remember your topic. Use these techniques to write a good conclusion:

- Link the ideas in the conclusion to your central idea.

> People today are more aware of the situation of Afghan women. Afghan women are fighting to get their freedom back. There is still a lot to change. But many people around the world are willing to help.

- Summarize the central idea.

> Afghan women are still struggling to find freedom. Many now live abroad. Others are still at home, waiting for change.

- Pose a question based on what you have written that gives the reader something to think about.

> How can Afghan women get their old lifestyle back? They certainly need help from other countries. They also need a lot of courage.

- Conclude with a personal example that inspires the reader to think about the issue or topic.

> Researching the situation of Afghan women taught me one thing. Freedom is the most important value. In our country, we speak freely and choose for ourselves. We cannot take freedom for granted, though. We must fight for our freedom, and that of others, every day.

Study the following conclusion.

> What is happening to Afghan women today? Many Afghan women began a new life in a different country. Of course, they miss their culture and their traditions. But they know they cannot go back to Afghanistan just yet.

Which technique does the writer use to connect with the reader?

How would you rewrite the conclusion to revisit the central idea of the essay?

Write a Cause-and-Effect Essay

WRITING PROMPT Freedom is very important to people. People such as George Washington, Eleanor Roosevelt, and Dr. Martin Luther King, Jr., fought so that everybody could enjoy the same freedoms.

Think about a person who defended or defends freedom. Then write a cause-and-effect essay that tells

- what caused this person to fight for freedom
- the effects of this person's fight for freedom.

Prewrite

Here are some tips for planning your essay before you write.

1 **Choose a Topic**

Brainstorm names of people who fought for freedom. Think about what caused them to do that.

Mohandas Gandhi	He preached nonviolence.
Rosa Parks	She defended equality for African Americans.
Nelson Mandela	He worked to stop apartheid.

Choose the person you know the most about or who interests you the most. You may need to do some research.

2 **Write Your Central Idea**

The central idea is the most important thing you want to write about. All the details must go with the central idea.

Rosa Parks was a brave African American woman who helped start the Civil Rights Movement.

③ Organize Ideas

Use a cause-and-effect chain to put your ideas in order. In the first box, put the first event. Then, list the first effect from that event. In the next box, list the next effect, and so on.

Sierra's Cause-and-Effect Chain

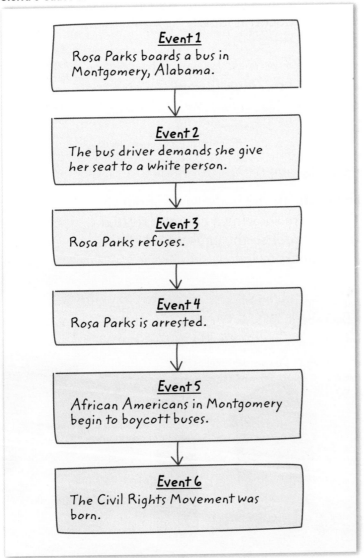

Event 1
Rosa Parks boards a bus in Montgomery, Alabama.

↓

Event 2
The bus driver demands she give her seat to a white person.

↓

Event 3
Rosa Parks refuses.

↓

Event 4
Rosa Parks is arrested.

↓

Event 5
African Americans in Montgomery begin to boycott buses.

↓

Event 6
The Civil Rights Movement was born.

TechTIP

Use the Internet for inspiration and research. Select your search words carefully so you don't get too many results. Remember to check that the information you find is accurate and reliable!

Reflect

• Do you have a clear central idea in your introduction?

• Are your causes and effects clearly organized?

Draft

Now that you have a central idea and your causes and effects, it's time to draft! Follow these steps:

1 **Begin by Drafting Your Introduction**

Make sure your opening sentence catches your readers' attention. Then, state your central idea.

> Who are the leaders who have fought for people's freedom? Rosa Parks was one person who made a difference. She was an important part of the Civil Rights Movement. Her courage inspired many others.

Sierra uses a question to catch her readers' attention. Then she states her central idea.

2 **Draft the Body Paragraphs**

Include Causes and Effects In the body, write about the causes and effects. If you're showing a chain of related events, present them in order so the causes and effects will be easy for your readers to follow.

From Sierra's Draft

> It all began on December 1, 1955, in Montgomery, Alabama. Rosa Parks boarded a bus and took a seat. The driver asked her to give up her seat to a white person. She refused.

After the year-long bus boycott ended, Parks and others could ride integrated buses. ▼

Use Signal Words Make sure you use signal words to show the reader how causes are linked to effects.

because	since	for	so
therefore	as a result	for this reason	

From Sierra's Draft

> Parks was arrested. In Montgomery, African Americans had to give up their bus seat if asked. Civil rights activists called for a one-day bus boycott. Hundreds of African Americans stayed off the buses. As a result, the bus company lost business. Activists realized they had the power to cause change. So they decided to continue the boycott.

3 **Draft Your Conclusion**

Your conclusion restates the central idea of your cause-and-effect essay. It also gives readers something more to think about.

From Sierra's Draft

> The boycott lasted for over a year. It resulted in a complicated legal battle. It also received lots of media attention. The boycott ultimately caused the Supreme Court to change the law. Bus segregation was ruled unconstitutional. African Americans were free to sit where they wanted. Rosa Parks's courage led to a movement—and a victory. She continues to inspire people today.

TechTIP

If you find yourself repeating the same words too often, use the _Thesaurus_ feature on your computer to find replacement words.

Reflect

• Do you have an introduction, body, and conclusion?

• Are your causes and effects clearly linked?

Revise

As you consider how to revise your work, keep your audience and purpose in mind. Does your writing do what you want it to do? Will it connect with your readers?

1 Evaluate Your Work

Read your essay aloud to a partner. To get ideas for improvement, ask your partner questions:

- **About the Form** Did you understand the central idea of my essay? Did my writing make you think?

- **About the Organization** Are the causes and effects clear? Are there parts that you can explain better?

Rosa Parks boarded the bus here, Dec. 1, 1955.

> ## Revision in Action

From Sierra's Draft

Who are the leaders who have fought for people's freedom? Rosa Parks was one person who made a difference. She was an important part of the Civil Rights Movement. Her courage inspired many others.

It all began on December 1, 1955, in Montgomery, Alabama. Rosa Parks boarded a bus and took a seat. The driver asked her to give up her seat to a white person. She refused. Parks was arrested.

In Montgomery, African Americans had to give up their bus seat if asked. Civil rights activists called for a one-day bus boycott. Hundreds of African Americans didn't ride the buses that day.

Sierra's partner says:

" It is not clear what your essay is about. "

" This is confusing. Move some details and combine paragraphs. "

" Adding some cause-and-effect words would make things flow. "

2 Mark Your Changes

Consolidate Text Consolidate means to bring together. When you consolidate text, you may use many different editing marks to

- remove text that is unnecessary

- remove details that are not important

- combine paragraphs that discuss related ideas

- add transitions to connect sentences or signal causes and effects.

Reflect

- Is your main idea interesting and meaningful?

- Do causes and effects flow smoothly?

Revising Marks	MARK	∧	↶	⌐	⌐	⊕
	WHAT IT MEANS	Insert something.	Move to here.	Replace with this.	Take out.	Make a new paragraph.

Revised Draft

Sometimes one person's choices can change history.
~~Who are the leaders who have fought for people's~~
                                          is one example
~~freedom?~~ Rosa Parks ∧ ~~was one person who made a~~
~~difference.~~ She was an important part of the Civil
Rights Movement. Her courage inspired many others.
   It ~~all~~ began on December 1, 1955, in Montgomery,
                        an African American woman,
Alabama. Rosa Parks ∧ boarded a bus and took a seat.
The driver asked her to give up her seat to a white
        Defying Montgomery's laws,   and
person. ∧ She refused. Parks was arrested ∧ ←
   ~~In Montgomery, African Americans had to give up~~
~~their bus seat if asked. Civil rights~~ activists called for
                        As a result
a one-day bus boycott. Hundreds of African Americans
didn't ride the buses that day.

Sierra deleted unnecessary text and added a general statement to clarify the point of her essay.

Sierra deleted unimportant details and combined paragraphs.

Sierra added a transition to make a cause and effect clearer.

Edit and Proofread

After you're satisfied with the content of your cause-and-effect essay, read your paper again to fix language errors. This is what you do when you edit and proofread your work:

- **Check the Grammar** Make sure that you have used correct and conventional grammar throughout. In particular, check places where you used possessive adjectives. (See page 277W.)

- **Check the Spelling** Spell-check can help, but it isn't always enough. Read your work carefully, especially any multisyllabic words. Say each one aloud, count the syllables, and then spell the word. You can use a dictionary for a final check. (See page 278W.)

- **Check the Mechanics** Errors in punctuation and capitalization can make your work hard to understand. In particular, check that you've used apostrophes in possessive nouns correctly. (See page 279W.)

Use these marks to edit and proofread your cause-and-effect essay.

Editing and Proofreading Marks

MARK	WHAT IT MEANS	MARK	WHAT IT MEANS
∧	Insert something.	/	Make lowercase.
∧	Add a comma.	ℰ	Delete, take something out.
∧	Add a semicolon.	¶	Make new paragraph.
⊙	Add a period.	◯	Spell out.
⊙	Add a colon.	⌒	Replace with this.
⌄ ⌄	Add quotation marks.	∿	Change order of letters or words.
⌄	Add an apostrophe.	#	Insert space.
≡	Capitalize.	‿	Close up, no space here.

Reflect

- What kinds of errors did you find? What can you do to keep from making them?

Grammar Workout

Check Possessive Adjectives

A **possessive adjective** is used before a noun to show ownership.
Notice that possessive adjectives do not use apostrophes.

Possessive adjectives	Example sentences
my	That is **my** topic.
your	I like **your** idea.
her	Did you see **her** essay?
his	**His** paper is about Rosa Parks.
its	**Its** introduction is interesting!
our	I am glad we finished **our** assignments.
their	Our classmates finished **their** work, too.

Use the correct possessive adjective and spell it properly to avoid
confusing your reader.

INCORRECT   Rosa Parks would not give up **their** seat.

CORRECT   Rosa Parks would not give up **her** seat.

INCORRECT   We owe her **our's** thanks for being so brave.

CORRECT   We owe her **our** thanks for being so brave.

Find the Trouble Spots

Rosa Parks died in 2005. She was 92 years old. ~~Her's~~ Her
casket was placed in the United States Capitol. People
came from all over ours nation to pay ~~his~~ their respects. I
read that people waited for hours. Their's appreciation
for Rosa Parks's work was moving.

Find two more
pronoun errors
to fix.

Edit and Proofread, continued

> ## Spelling Workout

Check Multisyllabic Words

Many English words follow a pattern, or a regular form. Learning these patterns can help you spell words correctly.

- When the first syllable contains a short vowel, it is often followed by a double consonant. This pattern is referred to as **VCCV** (**v**owel, **c**onsonant, **c**onsonant, **v**owel).

  EXAMPLE   matter   ⟶   mat | ter

                 ribbon   ⟶   rib | bon

- When the first syllable contains a long vowel, it is often followed by a single consonant. This pattern is referred to as **VCV** (**v**owel, **c**onsonant, **v**owel).

  EXAMPLE   shaken   ⟶   sha | ken

                 rotate   ⟶   ro | tate

When you are unsure of how many consonants to put in a two-syllable word, follow these rules. Circle each word, too, and check it in the dictionary to be sure your spelling is correct!

Find the Trouble Spots

When we study Rosa Parks, we foccus on how her arrest started the Montgomery Bus Boycott. But Parks worked to beter the lives of African Americans long before she reffused to give up her seat on the bus. Parks was active in the Montgomery NAACP and went to meetings where the boycott was discussed. Many boycotts folowed during her trial.

Fix the misspelled words.

> # Mechanics Workout

Check Apostrophes in Possessives

Use a **possessive noun** to show that someone owns, or possesses, something.

	Action	Examples
One Owner	Add **'s**.	Jeff**'s** book is in his backpack.
More Than One Owner	Add **'** if the noun ends in **-s**.	The workers**'** strike got results.
	Add **'s** if the noun does not end in **-s**.	I'm reading a lot about the women**'s** movement.

Writers often mix up the **possessive adjective** *its* with *it's*. Remember that possessive adjectives never use apostrophes.

- **Its** is the possessive form of **it**.

    EXAMPLE   The eagle spread **its** wings.

- **It's** is a contraction for **it is**.

    EXAMPLE   **It's** a shame that the team lost. I think **it's** true.

Find the Trouble Spots

Martin Luther King˅s famous "I Have a Dream" speech still means a lot in the 21st century. It˅s studied in schools across the entire country. King gave the speech in 1963. He expressed many peoples hope for freedom and equality. The speech was a landmark moment in Americas history. It's legacy still lives on.

Find three more errors with possessives to fix.

Publish, Share, and Reflect

You've worked hard to write a cause-and-effect essay that is clear and correct. Now it's time to share it!

1 Publish and Share Your Work

When you publish your writing, you put it in final form. Then, you share it with others. The way you publish will depend on your audience.

If you want to share your work with a lot of people, you might publish your cause-and-effect essay in

- your blog or Web site
- your school or town newspaper
- your school newsletter.

If you only want to share with family or friends, you can try one of the following:

- Type your essay on the computer and print copies to hand out (see page 281W).
- Arrange a private reading, where you can read your essay aloud.

2 Reflect on Your Work

After you publish your work, keep thinking about what you've written. Reflect on your work by asking questions.

Reflect

- Did I show why the person I wrote about was important?
- How can I work on improving organization?

How to Format Your Essay

When you write using a computer, you can set the **document margins** to make your essay look better on the page. You can also use the **ruler** at the top of your computer screen. Remember, you can use the command bar, tool bar, and your keyboard. Here are a few techniques to start with.

To change the paragraph margins:

1. Select the text of your essay.

2. Go to the **File** menu and click **Page Setup**.

3. Use the up and down arrows to change the measurements of the margins.

4. Click **OK**.

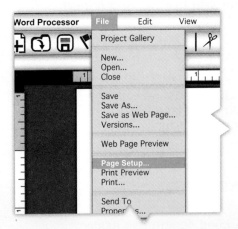

To use the ruler:

1. Select the text of your essay.

2. Move your cursor to the ruler at the top of your computer screen.

3. Click on the left arrow to change the left margin, or the right arrow to change the right margin.

4. Move the arrow to make the margin wider or narrower.

Model Study

Descriptive Essay

To record what something or someone is like, you can write a description. You give descriptions of people, places, and things every day. You might describe your favorite shirt, the street you live on, or a friend.

A **descriptive essay** gives a clear picture of a person, place, or thing. A good descriptive essay includes plenty of **sensory details**. Sensory details help the reader know what something looks, sounds, feels, tastes, or smells like.

The student model on page 283W shows the features of a good descriptive essay.

DESCRIPTIVE ESSAY

A good descriptive essay

☑ clearly describes a real person, place, or thing

☑ uses vivid words

☑ includes specific details, especially sensory details.

Feature Checklist

Pictures in the Sky

by Milo Michaelopoulos

The writer describes **something in the real world**.

Look up at the sky on a clear night. What do you see? You probably notice stars twinkling like bits of broken glass. But if you were one of my Greek ancestors, you would see animals and people.

When the ancient Greeks looked at the night sky, they saw bright stars that stood out from fainter stars. As their eyes moved from star to star, they saw outlines, like a connect-the-dots puzzle. Those stars made pictures called constellations. Some constellations looked like animals. The ancient Greeks imagined lions, oxen, bulls, and scorpions. They also saw images of their heroes.

On hot summer nights, I like to lie in my yard and look at the stars, too. I listen to crickets chirp and stare into endless space. It makes me feel connected to my Greek ancestors. Some day, I want to sail around the Mediterranean Sea. At night, I'll look up at the glowing sky. I'll look for animals and heroes.

The writer uses **specific details** and **vivid words** to help readers picture the night sky.

Student Model

The Big Dipper is part of a larger constellation called Ursa Major, meaning "the Great Bear."

Development of Ideas

What's It Like?

A good descriptive essay is like a deep-dish pizza with lots of tasty toppings. If you develop your ideas as deeply as a deep-dish pizza and pile it high with details, you will have an essay that readers will enjoy. Applause for the chef!

Why Is It Important to Develop Ideas?

A good descriptive essay has ideas that attract the reader's interest. The writer explains and supports the ideas, which makes the reader feel satisfied.

Writers develop their ideas in a way that fits their purpose for writing. This writer wants her readers to really picture what she is describing. So she uses sensory details to explain and support her ideas.

> When I stepped outside my house at dawn, I experienced a magical world. There was silence all around, except for the chirping of birds in the distant trees. The air smelled clean and pure. I looked up and saw the sky. The stars were fading, and the moon looked like a pale coin above the trees. The chilly air made me shiver, so I wrapped myself tighter in my fuzzy red blanket. It was special to be outside at the dawn of the day!

The writer develops her ideas with **sensory details**.

Study the rubric on page 285W. What is the difference between a paper with a score of 2 and one with a score of 4?

Development of Ideas

	How thoughtful and interesting is the writing?	How well are the ideas explained and supported?
4 Wow!	The writing engages the reader with worthwhile ideas and an interesting presentation.	The ideas are fully explained and supported. • The ideas are well developed with important details and examples. • The writing feels complete, and the reader is satisfied.
3 Ahh.	<u>Most</u> of the writing engages the reader with worthwhile ideas and an interesting presentation.	<u>Most</u> of the ideas are explained and supported. • Most of the ideas are developed with important details and examples. • The writing feels mostly complete, but the reader is left with some questions.
2 Hmm.	<u>Some</u> of the writing engages the reader with worthwhile ideas and an interesting presentation.	<u>Some</u> of the ideas are explained and supported. • Only some of the ideas are developed. Details and examples are limited. • The writing leaves the reader with many questions.
1 Huh?	The writing does <u>not</u> engage the reader.	The ideas are <u>not</u> explained or supported. The ideas lack details and examples, and the writing feels incomplete.

Development of Ideas, continued

Compare Writing Samples

A good descriptive essay has interesting, well-developed ideas.
Study the two examples of a descriptive essay on this page.

Well-Developed

Comets

Comets are one of the greatest marvels of the sky. They
appear as long streaks of light. They are also rare.

Comets start as lumps of hard rock and ice. Scientists
sometimes call them " dirty snowballs ." Comets move
around the sun in a long oval path . When a comet gets
close to the sun, it creates a wide tail of vapor and dust .
Sometimes you can see a comet's tail with the naked eye. A
comet's tail can be up to 6,000 miles long! A comet's tail can
be many different colors. It can be silver, bluish, and purple .

I saw many pictures of comets on the Internet. They don't
look like dirty snowballs to me. They look like beautiful
flashes of color and light.

The ideas are
interesting.
**Sensory
details**
support the
ideas.

The writing
makes you feel
like you were
there.

Not So Well-Developed

Comets

Comets are one of the greatest marvels of the sky. They
are also very rare.

Comets are made of hard rock and ice . Scientists
sometimes call them " dirty snowballs ." Comets move
around the sun. When they get close to the sun, they create
a tail of vapor and dust . Sometimes you can see a comet's
tail with the naked eye. A comet's tail can be very long, and
it can be many different colors.

I saw many pictures of comets on the Internet.

Only a few
**sensory
details**
support the
ideas.

You don't get
the sense
that you were
there.

Evaluate for Development of Ideas

Now read carefully the descriptive essay below. Use the rubric on page 285W to score it.

Solar Eclipse
by Paula Cooper

A solar eclipse is an amazing thing to see. It happens when the moon passes between Earth and the sun.

Total solar eclipses are very rare. What you usually see is a partial eclipse. This happens when the moon doesn't cover the sun completely.

A few years ago, I saw a total solar eclipse. First, I saw the moon moving across the sun. It covered only a part of the sun at first. After a few hours, it covered the sun completely. When the sun disappeared, there was a purple light all around. All the birds got quiet because they thought it was time to sleep.

After a minute or so, the moon started to move away. A sunbeam appeared, and things went slowly back to normal.

Are the ideas interesting? What else would you like to know?

Are the ideas well developed? What kinds of details might help?

What could the writer add to give the reader the sense of being there?

During a total solar eclipse, the sun's corona, or outer atmosphere, may become visible.

Raise the Score

These papers have been scored using the **Development of Ideas Rubric** on page 285W. Study each paper to see why it got the score it did.

Overall Score: 4

The Wonder of Thunderstorms

Anna Perlman

These **ideas** engage the reader's interest.

Some people are afraid of thunder and lightning. But I don't find them scary. As long as I'm inside and away from windows, I'm perfectly safe. And thunderstorms are fascinating events.

A thunderstorm usually starts with wind and rain. As the wind howls outside, gray-green clouds gather and the sky darkens. Soon the rain is falling heavily. I hear it drumming on the roof.

The writer includes many **sensory details** and **vivid words** to develop the ideas.

First comes the lightning. It might be a bright flash that lights up the whole sky. Or it might look like a jagged, white-hot fork.

Then there are the sounds of thunder. It might be a loud crash that shakes the house and sets dishes rattling. Or sometimes it's a low, threatening rumble.

A storm might cause the neighborhood to lose electric power. Our appliances all shut off at once. Suddenly, my house feels quiet and empty.

Many specific details give the reader the sense of being in a thunderstorm.

Thunderstorms can last from a few minutes to a few hours. But they always give a spectacular show of nature's power! That's why I find them so exciting.

The Wonder of Thunderstorms

These **ideas** will probably interest the reader.

Some people are afraid of thunder and lightning. But I think they are interesting, not scary. As long as I'm inside and away from windows, I'm safe.

A thunderstorm usually starts with wind and rain. Clouds gather and the sky darkens. Then the rain starts to fall, lightly at first. Soon the rain is falling heavily, and I hear it drumming on the roof.

First comes the lightning. It might be a bright flash that lights up the sky. Or it might look like a jagged fork.

Then comes the thunder. It might be a loud crash that shakes the whole house. Or sometimes it's a low, threatening rumble.

A storm might cause the neighborhood to lose electric power, too. Then I see the lights and appliances turn off. Suddenly, my house feels quiet.

Thunderstorms can last from a few minutes to a few hours. But they always give a show of nature's power.

The writer uses some **sensory details** and **vivid words** to support the ideas.

There are fewer specific details to allow the reader to imagine being in a thunderstorm.

RAISING *THE SCORE*

The writer needs to add more sensory details and vivid words. Where could she add them?

Raise the Score, continued

Overall Score: 2

The Wonder of Thunderstorms

The writer does not develop the **ideas** in the introduction.

Thunderstorms can happen anywhere. There are many different types of storms. Some thunderstorms are very strong. I think powerful thunderstorms are interesting.

During a storm, it is best to stay away from phones and electronics. A thunderstorm usually starts with wind and rain. The sky gets dark and the rain starts to fall heavily. Soon I can hear the rain on my roof.

First, there is lightning. It might be a bright flash or more like a fork. Either way, it is pretty cool.

The sounds of thunder are exciting, too. It might be a loud crash or something much quieter.

A storm might cause the neighborhood to lose power. Then the lights go out. My house feels quiet.

Thunderstorms can last from a few minutes to a few hours.

The writer uses a few **details** to develop her ideas, but the details aren't very interesting or vivid.

It's hard for the reader to feel what a thunderstorm is like.

▲ RAISING THE SCORE

The writer needs to elaborate on her ideas using specific examples and interesting details. What details would you add?

The Wonder of Thunderstorms

Thunderstorms can happen anywhere. I like many different types of storms. Some thunderstorms are very strong.

During a storm, it is best to stay away from phones and electronics. A thunderstorm usually starts with wind and rain. Then the rain starts to fall heavily. It can be pretty loud sometimes.

I like the sound of thunder, whether it is loud thunder or the very quiet kind you can barely hear.

There are different kinds of lightning, too. I like to watch lightning strikes.

A storm might cause the neighborhood to lose power, too. Then the lights go out.

RAISING THE SCORE

The writer needs to choose one or two interesting ideas and then develop them with examples and sensory details.

Elaborate

Have you ever been in a room that hasn't been decorated yet? It has walls, a ceiling, and maybe even some furniture, but it seems empty and boring. A room only comes to life when it has posters, curtains, photographs—and some personal touches, of course. In the same way, writing needs details to bring it to life. Add details and examples to make your descriptive essay lively and interesting.

Build on Your Ideas

If your readers aren't clear about what your essay is saying, try **elaborating**. When you elaborate, you add details, facts, and examples to support an idea. It's like adding flesh and muscle to bare bones! Try these techniques.

Add Sensory Details

Record what you saw, heard, felt, smelled, or tasted.

Just OK

> Falling stars are not stars. They are pieces of rock that burn in the air as they fall.

Better with Details

> Falling stars are not stars. They are pieces of rock that burn in the
> They make a quick, bright streak of light.
> air as they fall. ∧

Add Quotations

Adding quotations gives readers a clearer picture of what you are describing.

Just OK

> Falling stars are not stars. They are pieces of rock that burn in the air as they fall.

Better with a Quotation

> Falling stars are not stars. They are pieces of rock that burn in the air as they fall. Astronomer Kay Steinfeld ∧ explains, "Falling stars are actually meteoroids. Meteoroids are small pieces of rock."

Add Examples, Facts, and Statistics

These details help bring your description to life.

Just OK

> Falling stars are not stars. They are pieces of rock that burn in the air as they fall.

Better with An Example

> Falling stars are not stars. They are pieces of rock that burn in the air as they fall. If they reach the ground, ∧ they can create a crater. The biggest crater in the world was formed almost 50,000 years ago in Arizona.

Show How You Know

It's not enough to just give an example or add a detail. Part of elaborating is to *show how* you know what you're saying. You can back up your ideas with your own memories and experiences, or information from people you know. You can also use what you've learned from books, the media, or the Internet.

Better with Added Support

> Falling stars are not stars. They are pieces of rock that burn in the air as they fall. Last year's meteor shower brought many falling stars. Our teacher ∧ said they came from a comet's tail.

Choose an Organization

If you were going to reorganize your bedroom, what would you do? You might draw a sketch to show what you want in your room and where each object will go. Organizing a description is like that. Before you write, make a plan to show what you will write about and how you want to arrange all the parts.

Use Spatial Order

For a description, try using spatial order to tell what you see—from left to right, from near to far, or from top to bottom, for example.

Picture Diagram

Try labeling a picture to show how you'll organize details for a description.

> A shuttle orbiter has a pointed nose. That is where the crew works. The orbiter has a long cylindrical body that ends in two flat side wings. At the bottom, there are the main engines. They are especially big, to propel the shuttle into space.
>
> — nose
>
> — body
>
> — side wing
>
> — engine

Circle Diagram

Whether you want to describe an area from the inside to the outside or the other way around, try using a circle diagram to show your plan.

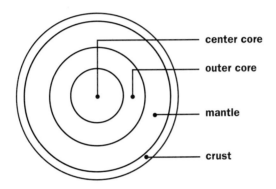

- center core
- outer core
- mantle
- crust

TechTIP

List details as phrases or sentences. Then use **cut** and **paste** from the Edit menu to move details around as you need to.

The Layers of Earth

Planet Earth is kind of like a ball of candy with many layers inside. A piece of candy might have a cherry or a blob of jam in the center, but Earth is different, of course. It has a solid center core made of metal. Around the inner core is an outer core. It is made of hot, liquid metal. The mantle surrounds the outer core. Above the mantle is the crust, which is like the hard shell on a piece of candy. The crust is where we live.

▼ Mountains and deserts are part of Earth's crust.

Write a Descriptive Essay

WRITING PROMPT What experiences have you had that relate to the moon, the stars, and the sky? Maybe you've seen a meteor shower or looked through a friend's telescope. Or perhaps you've visited a planetarium or a space camp.

Think of an experience or event that you'd like to share with the class. Then write a descriptive essay about it that includes

- ideas that capture the reader's attention
- examples and explanations that support and develop the ideas
- sensory details that give the reader the sense of being there.

Prewrite

After you choose a topic, follow these tips for planning and preparing your writing.

① Collect Descriptive Details

Try to remember as many details as you can about your topic. If you have photos or journal entries that relate to the topic, be sure to look at them. Use a **five-senses diagram** to jot down sensory details.

Five-Senses Diagram

I saw . . .	• stars and planets in the planetarium • the biggest projector I have ever seen
I heard . . .	• the voice of our tour guide • the buzzing sound of the projector
I smelled . . .	• the clean smell of the museum
I tasted . . .	• the food in the cafeteria
I touched or felt . . .	• the soft, comfortable chair of the planetarium • the cold surface of the telescope

② Plan How Your Ideas Will Flow

Think about the best way to organize your description. What spatial order could you use? You might want to list objects from bottom to top, as Isabella did.

How Isabella Organized Her Ideas

the hall

—hundreds of dark blue chairs around a huge projector

—The chairs are soft and comfortable.

the projector

—The projector is placed on a tall platform and rises above the chairs. It ends in a big ball that casts the images.

—It makes a buzzing sound when it moves around.

the screen

—It is like a dome that covers the entire room.

—It is round and smooth.

—It changes colors and brightness.

◀ A planetarium projector creates images of objects in the sky.

Reflect

- Does your plan include details related to some or all of the senses?

- Do you know how you will organize your ideas?

Draft

Now that you have a plan, it's time to draft! Engage your readers' attention in the first sentence of your essay so that they'll want to continue reading.

To hook your readers, you might:

- start with a thought-provoking question or statement

> Would you like to feel like an astronaut for a day?

- start with an especially vivid, meaningful, or unusual detail

> Entering a planetarium is a thrilling experience. It's like stepping into an alien movie theater. The chairs look like they belong in a spaceship. They face up toward a huge round screen.

Use your plan to stay organized as you keep writing. Include lots of sensory details and vivid words to support and develop your ideas.

From Isabella's Draft

> I sat down in my seat and could not believe how comfortable I was. I was almost lying down! The chairs were dark blue with a red stripe across them. They looked very modern.
>
> In the middle of the chairs, rising above them, was the projector. It looked like a spacecraft. It was white and ended in a huge ball covered in small lenses. The images of stars and planets come through those lenses.

Reflect

- Does your introduction engage the reader right away?

- Do you have enough details to support your ideas?

DRAFTING TIPS

Trait: **Development of Ideas**

If You Have Trouble Developing Your Ideas . . .

Sometimes, you cannot come up with enough details to develop your ideas. You keep trying, but you can't focus on the details you need.

Try Adding a Ba-Da-Bing

When you need to add more details,

- think BA and add where you were and what you were doing

- think DA and tell what you saw, or what you experienced through one of your other senses

- think BING and write what you thought about it all.

Here's a bare-bones description: I saw images of stars and planets on the screen.

Now here's how you can enrich it with Ba-Da-Bing.

Where You Were
:

I was sitting comfortably in my chair. Slowly, the lights in the planetarium went off.

What You Saw
:

The screen turned deep blue and twinkling stars appeared all over it. Slow music started to play.

What You Thought
:

I thought about how it must feel to travel in space. I imagined that I was an astronaut in the starry sky.

Ba-Da-Bing in Action

Revise

As you consider how to revise your work, keep your audience and purpose in mind. Does your writing do what you want it to do? Will it connect with your audience?

1 Evaluate Your Work

Read your draft aloud to a partner, who will sketch what you've described. Look at the sketch and ask yourself:

- **About the Form** Does the sketch match my own mental image? Did I leave out any important ideas or details?

- **About the Development of Ideas** Are my ideas interesting? Are they supported with enough details and examples?

Revision in Action

Isabella's Draft

Isabella thinks:

> Would you like to feel like an astronaut for a day? Then visit a planetarium. It's like stepping into an alien movie theater. The chairs look like they belong in a spaceship. They are very comfortable, like some chairs we have at home. They face up toward a huge rounded screen.

" The part about our chairs at home is not necessary."

> Rising above the chairs is the projector. It looks like a spacecraft. It is white and ends in a huge ball covered in small lenses. Above it, there is a rounded screen. On the screen appear images of stars, planets, and constellations. The tour guide explains everything in detail.

" I only said what things looked like. What other sensory details can I include?"

> Whenever I visit a planetarium, I imagine being an astronaut. It must be great to be surrounded by stars.

" I need to let the reader know how I felt, too."

2 **Mark Your Changes**

Add Text To help your readers see what you are describing, you may need to add more details and vivid words. Use this mark: ∧ .

Delete Text To improve your description, you might need to cut unnecessary words and sentences. Use this mark ⌒ to take out

- unimportant details that don't develop your ideas

- ideas that you repeat.

Consolidate Text To make sure your description gets right to the point, you might consolidate ideas by adding, deleting, or rearranging text.

Revising Marks MARK	∧	⌒	⌃	⌒	⁋
WHAT IT MEANS	Insert something.	Move to here.	Replace with this.	Take out.	Make a new paragraph.

Revised Draft

    Would you like to feel like an astronaut for a day? Then visit a planetarium. It's like stepping into an alien movie theater. The ∧ chairs look like they belong
soft, comfortable
in a spaceship. ~~They are very comfortable, like some chairs we have at home~~. They face up toward a huge rounded screen.
    Rising above the chairs is the projector. It looks
and swings around with a buzzing sound
like a spacecraft. It is white and ends in a huge ball
black
covered in small ∧ lenses. Above it, there is a rounded
that hangs over the entire room
screen. On the screen appear images of stars,
It really feels like you're floating in space.
planets, and constellations. ∧ The tour guide explains everything in detail.
    Whenever I visit a planetarium, I imagine being an
incredible   and experience the vastness of space
astronaut. It must be ~~great~~ to be surrounded by stars. ∧

Isabella took out unnecessary details and consolidated ideas.

Isabella added more sensory details.

Isabella used vivid words to describe how she felt.

Edit and Proofread

After you're satisfied with the content of your descriptive essay, read your paper again to fix language errors. This is what you do when you edit and proofread your work:

- **Check the Grammar** Make sure you have used correct and conventional grammar throughout. In particular, check that you've used prepositional phrases effectively and correctly. (See page 303W.)

- **Check the Spelling** Spell-check can help, but it isn't always enough. To catch errors with sound-alike words, you'll have to read your work carefully. You might need to check the words in a dictionary. (See page 304W.)

- **Check the Mechanics** Errors in punctuation and capitalization can make your work hard to understand. In particular, check parentheses and commas. (See page 305W.)

Use these marks to edit and proofread your description.

Editing and Proofreading Marks

MARK	WHAT IT MEANS	MARK	WHAT IT MEANS
∧	Insert something.	╱	Make lowercase.
∧	Add a comma.	℘	Delete, take something out.
∧	Add a semicolon.	⁋	Make new paragraph.
⊙	Add a period.	◯	Spell out.
⊙	Add a colon.	⌃	Replace with this.
∀ ∀	Add quotation marks.	∼	Change order of letters or words.
∨	Add an apostrophe.	#	Insert space.
≡	Capitalize.	◡	Close up, no space here.

Reflect

- Is your work now ready to share with others?

- What kinds of errors did you find? What can you do to keep from making them?

GrammarWorkout

Check Prepositional Phrases

A **prepositional phrase** starts with a **preposition** and ends with a noun or a pronoun. It includes all the words in between.

Prepositional phrases give more information. Using them is a great way to add details to your writing.

Without Prepositional Phrases	With Prepositional Phrases
Please get me the book.	Please get me the book **about** stars.
The shuttle flew.	The shuttle flew **above** the city.
The astronauts were ready.	The astronauts were ready **for the landing**.

Here are some common prepositions you can use:

about	above	below	behind	during
in	inside	outside	for	of
on	to	toward	by	at
over	under	beside	between	near

For more about prepositions, see page 455W.

Find the Opportunities

> The guide talked about the constellations. Lines were
> *on the screen*
> drawn ᴧ to make each constellation clear. We read the
> *between the stars*
> names. Before the compass was invented, constellations
> were very useful. They helped ships find the right
> direction.

Add two more prepositional phrases to this paragraph.

Edit and Proofread, continued

> ### Spelling Workout
>
> # Check Sound-Alike Words
>
> If you hear the following sentences read aloud, you'll have no trouble understanding them:
>
> > The sun is two bright to look at directly. I looked through a special viewer with a tiny whole in it.
>
> But if you see them written, it's likely that you'll be confused. The reason is that there are problems with sound-alike words.
>
> | Word | Meaning |
> |------|---------|
> | two
too
to | number between one and three
to a greater degree than is wanted
a preposition showing direction or purpose |
> | whole
hole | complete, entire
hollow place or opening |
>
> To find and fix problems with sound-alike words, you have to know which words are the troublemakers. Study the list of common sound-alike words on page 464W.
>
> ### Find the Trouble Spots
>
> My favorite thing about the planetarium was the part about black ~~wholes~~ *holes*. There were ~~sum~~ *some* things I didn't know about them. For example, they are dying stars. I also enjoyed learning all the differences between the planets of the solar system. I think everybody should go (too) a planetarium. I can promise you won't get (board)!

Check the circled words. Are they spelled correctly?

Mechanics Workout

Check Parentheses and Commas

You can use **parentheses** to give extra information. Always use parentheses in pairs.

> EXAMPLE   I finally met Sonia (when our class went to the planetarium).

- When the information in parentheses is part of a sentence, end punctuation goes outside the parentheses.

> EXAMPLE   Did you see the movie (the one with the car chase)?

- When the entire sentence is in parentheses, end punctuation goes inside the parentheses.

> EXAMPLE   Latreese and I went to the game by ouselves. (We asked Tara, but she couldn't come.)

Use a **comma** to separate the items in a list of three or more items. This is called the **serial comma**. Use a comma between the next-to-last item in the list and the word *and*.

> EXAMPLE   I looked up at the clouds, the moon, and the stars.

Find the Trouble Spots

At the planetarium I saw satellites, asteroids∧and meteors. However, the galaxies were more impressive. The screen was white with light. ⸤It looked like daytime!⸥ A galaxy is a system of stars. It includes stars planets and other celestial bodies. The Milky Way galaxy (which includes the solar system looks like a spiral.

Fix the problems with parentheses and commas.

Publish, Share, and Reflect

You've worked hard to craft a descriptive essay that is filled with sensory details to make your writing interesting. Don't keep it to yourself—share it!

❶ Publish and Share Your Work

There are lots of creative ways to publish a descriptive essay. You've used words to create a memorable picture for your readers. You might also want to add visuals to your writing to make it come alive.

How you'll publish it depends on the people you want to share it with. If you want to share it with only a few people, you can

- add a photograph or drawing, make copies, and share it. (See page 307W for how to add a picture to a computer document.)

- place your description in a family photo album or scrapbook

- hold a reading for family or friends.

If you want more people to read it, publish it by

- posting it on your blog (with a photograph included)

- submitting it to the school newspaper

- entering it into a writing contest for students.

❷ Reflect on Your Work

Publishing and sharing your work doesn't mean that you've stopped thinking about it. Think back on your essay. What are its strongest points? What are some ways you'd like to make your writing even better?

Reflect

- Does my description capture what the topic means to me?

- What was hard about writing this essay? What came easily?

How to Insert a Picture in a Document

Do you want your readers to see the exact person, place, or thing you are describing? Use your computer to add a picture to your essay. You can use a photograph taken with a digital camera, or scan a printed photograph or a drawing. Follow these steps:

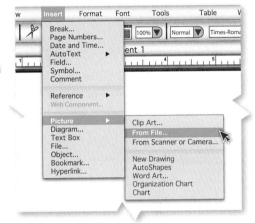

1. Save the picture file on your desktop.

2. Click on the place in your essay where you want to insert the picture.

3. Go to the **Insert** menu and click **Picture**.

4. Click on the words **From File**.

5. Double click on the name of the picture file you want to insert. The picture will appear where your cursor is.

6. To resize the image, click on its lower right-hand corner. Move it up and to the left to make it smaller, or down and to the right to make it larger.

7. To move the picture, just hold the cursor over the picture until the cursor turns into a small hand. Click and drag the picture to the place you want it.

A Heavenly Place
by Isabella Martineau

Would you like to feel like an astronaut for a day? Then visit a planetarium. It's like stepping into an alien movie theater. The soft comfortable chairs look like they belong in a spaceship. They face up toward a huge rounded screen.

Rising above the chairs is the projector. It looks like a spacecraft and swings around with a buzzing sound. It is white and ends in a huge ball covered in small black lenses.

Write to Persuade

"If I want to bring about change, I write to someone who can make it happen."

—Cynthia

Model Study

Persuasive Business Letter

To convince people to agree with you, you use **persuasion**. You tell them what you want or believe. Then you give reasons for your position.

You might use persuasion in a **business letter**. A business letter is a formal letter you write to an adult, such as the mayor of your town. You might write a **persuasive business letter** to get the reader to take action on an important issue.

The student model on page 309W shows the features of a good persuasive business letter.

PERSUASIVE BUSINESS LETTER

A good persuasive business letter

☑ includes the date, a greeting and closing, and the writer's and reader's addresses

☑ clearly states what you want the reader to do

☑ gives two to four supporting reasons

☑ backs up reasons with facts and evidence

☑ uses a formal, respectful tone.

Feature Checklist

4242 Cloud Dr.
Sunnyville, TN 34271
February 16, 2009

Principal Coretta Simmons
Midvale Middle School
214 Main St.
Sunnyville, TN 34271

Dear Principal Simmons:

    I am writing to suggest a change that will help the environment. Our school keeps outside lights on all night. I think we should turn them off at 9 p.m.

    Keeping the lights on leads to light pollution. That makes it hard to see stars at night. Also, migrating birds could get lost because of it.

    By turning the lights off, our school will set a good example. We will also save money. We could use that money to buy new books or for a class trip.

    Please consider turning the lights off after 9 p.m. Thank you for your time and attention.

Sincerely,

Jerome Martin
Jerome Martin

Jerome includes his own address and the address of the person he's writing to.

The greeting is followed by a colon.

The first paragraph states what Jerome wants the reader to do.

Jerome gives reasons to persuade the reader.

Jerome restates his request.

Jerome uses a formal closing, followed by his signature.

Student Model

Write a Persuasive Business Letter

WRITING PROMPT Have you ever wanted to persuade people to do something differently? Maybe you'd like people to stop littering so your town is cleaner, or to be more careful about safety rules at the local swimming pool. Or maybe you just want them to understand an issue that's important to you.

Think of an issue you feel strongly about. What could people do to make a difference? Write a persuasive business letter that

- includes the elements of a standard business letter and uses a polite, respectful tone
- states your position clearly in the first paragraph
- supports your position with reasons and evidence
- uses logical and/or emotional appeals
- closes by asking your reader to take action.

Prewrite

After you choose a topic, follow these tips for planning and preparing your writing.

1 Think About Your Audience and Purpose

Knowing who your audience is and why you're writing will help you choose effective arguments and evidence for your persuasive letter. Luis came up with this **FATP chart**.

> **FATP Chart**
>
> **F**orm: *persuasive business letter*
>
> **A**udience: *museum officials*
>
> **T**opic: *the Space Museum*
>
> **P**urpose: *to persuade museum officials to keep the Space Museum open*

2 Plan to Appeal to Your Reader's Logic

To appeal to your reader's thinking, you need to give reasons for your position and support them with evidence.

Reasons Back up your point of view with two or three solid reasons. Present them in order—from strongest to weakest (as shown below) or from weakest to strongest.

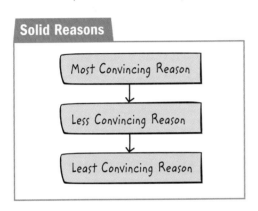

Solid Reasons

Most Convincing Reason

↓

Less Convincing Reason

↓

Least Convincing Reason

▲ This unusual fountain is at the MacMillan Space Centre in Canada.

Evidence Support your reasons with evidence, such as facts, statistics, and examples. Luis used the chart below to help organize his arguments and evidence. The chart also helps him check that he has enough evidence.

Argument	Evidence
Our community loves the Space Museum.	Hundreds of people in the community go there every day.
If the museum closes, our community will lose an important educational institution.	The Space Museum is the only big museum in our city.

Prewrite, continued

❸ Plan to Appeal to Your Reader's Emotions

Emotional appeals can help get your reader to take action. To appeal to your reader's feelings, it helps to use persuasive language and to present personal examples.

Persuasive Language Use language that shows you believe strongly in your position. Don't overdo it, though. Using harsh words and exclamation marks is like shouting on paper. Try to sound reasonable, but committed to what you believe.

How Luis's Emotional Appeals Might Sound

Boring—No Emotion

People here like the Space Museum. They like it a lot.

Effective Appeal to Emotions

Our community loves the Space Museum. They are proud of it and visit it often.

Overly Emotional

People in this community just love the Space Museum! It's so mean to shut it down!

TechTIP

On the computer, you can save different versions of your writing. Use the **Save As** command from the **File** menu and add a number to the document name. Then you can look back and choose the version you like best.

Use Personal Examples You can appeal to your reader's emotions by talking about the people who are affected by an issue. These examples don't take the place of facts and statistics, but they help get the reader to care more about what you are saying.

Personal Examples That Luis Might Use

- My niece wants to be an astronaut. It's her dream. "I learn so much at the Space Museum," she says. "It's really important to me and my future goals."

- Mr. Jackson works in the gift shop at the Space Museum. "I've worked here for twenty-three years," he says. "I'll lose my job if the museum closes."

- The science teachers at my school are upset. They hope the Space Museum doesn't close. "We take our classes there sometimes for lessons," one of them told me. "It is really helpful to the students."

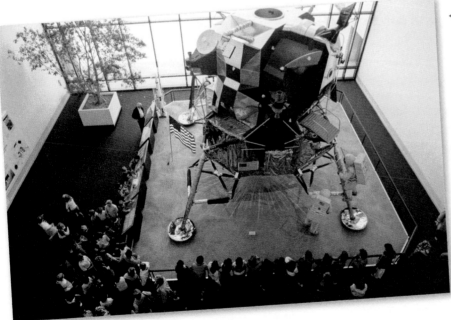

◀ Many tourists visit the National Air and Space Museum in Washington, DC.

Reflect

- Do you need to find more evidence to support your position?

- Does your plan have a good balance of logic and emotion?

Draft

Now it's time to start your letter. Your draft doesn't have to be perfect. There will be time later to make changes.

Before you begin, research to whom you should send your letter, and at what address. Then draft the body of your letter.

- **State Your Position** Start by introducing your reader to the situation and your argument.

  > I read that the Space Museum will close next year. Apparently, the exhibits are becoming too expensive. Also, there are not enough tourists coming in the summer. Our community should do everything possible to keep the museum open.

  Luis makes his position clear early in the letter.

- **Prove Your Point** Add your supporting arguments and evidence.

  > The Space Museum is a great resource for students. It is the only major museum in our city. People living in our community are proud of it and visit often. I am among those people. My community wants the chance to keep the Space Museum open.

  Luis gives reasons to support his position.

- **Ask Your Reader to Take Action** In your final paragraph, restate your position. Then tell what you want your reader to do. Be clear and specific.

  > The Space Museum deserves another chance. We could raise the admission price by one dollar. We could also consider a special property tax. Please write to the city council and let them know that you're willing to support any reasonable effort to keep the museum open.

Reflect

- Is your position clearly stated?
- How can you refine your language so that it's more persuasive?

DRAFTING TIPS

Trait: **Development of Ideas**

If You Can't Write Enough . . .

Writing persuasively can be hard. You believe in your ideas, but sometimes you can't think of enough good reasons to support them.

No way!

Prove it!

You made that up!

It's hot!

Try Getting into an Argument . . . with Yourself!

Think about how you would respond to someone who's arguing with you. If someone challenges you to prove your ideas, there's a lot more to say!

To argue with confidence, though, you have to know *how* you know things.

Ways You Know Things

	1. You go places and experience things.		5. You read things in newspapers.
	2. You have feelings and thoughts.		6. People tell you things.
	3. You see things on television.		7. You hear things on the radio.
	4. You read things in books.		8. You learn things online.

In a real argument, you can reveal your sources to prove your ideas. In an imaginary argument to help you write persuasively, you can do the same. Use your proof to add details that support your ideas.

Revise

As you revise your work, think about your audience and purpose. Will your letter persuade your reader?

1 Evaluate Your Work

After a partner reads your draft, have a debate. What does your partner think of your arguments and ideas? Then ask yourself questions:

- **About the Form** Did I include all the parts of a business letter?

- **About the Development of Ideas** Did I state my ideas clearly and completely? Is my letter convincing?

▲ This model of the solar system can be found at the American Museum of Natural History in New York City.

> ## Revision in Action

Draft

> Our community loves the Space Museum. Hundreds of people in the area visit the museum every day. I go there almost every month with some of my friends. We have a lot of fun!
>
> The Space Museum is also the only big museum in our city. If the museum closes, we will lose an important educational institution.
>
> Let's find a solution to keep the Space Museum. We need to collect more money to keep the museum open.

The partner says:

" **You need to put more feeling into this.** "

" **You could make this argument stronger by adding some evidence.** "

" **The part about collecting money is unclear. You need to be more specific.** "

2 Mark Your Changes

Add or Replace Text To improve your persuasive writing, you may need to add or replace text to make your arguments clearer. Use these marks ∧, ⌃ to add:

- facts, examples, and other evidence to support your beliefs and arguments

- sources that show where you got your evidence

- emotional appeals to your reader

- clearer, more specific arguments.

Reflect

- What other evidence could you add to back up your arguments?

- Is your letter too angry or emotional? How can you tone it down?

Revising Marks

MARK	∧	↶	⌃	⎯ꝭ	¶
WHAT IT MEANS	Insert something.	Move to here.	Replace with this.	Take out.	Make a new paragraph.

Revised Draft

Our community loves the Space Museum.
Hundreds of people in the area visit the museum
For many of us, one of our earliest memories is going
every day. ~~I go there almost every month with some~~
there with our moms as young children.
~~of my friends. We have a lot of fun!~~

The Space Museum is also the only big museum
in our city. If the museum closes, we will lose an
Many science teachers use the museum's resources to inspire
important educational institution. and motivate their students.
Please let the city council know that you will support
~~Let's find a solution to keep the Space Museum.~~
higher admission or a special tax. Let's keep our museum alive!
~~We need to collect more money to keep the Museum~~
~~open.~~

The writer added an emotional appeal.

The writer added evidence to support his argument.

The writer added a specific suggestion for helping to solve the problem.

Edit and Proofread

After you are satisfied with your writing, read your paper again to correct language errors. This is what you do when you edit and proofread your work:

- **Check the Grammar** Make sure that you have used correct grammar throughout. In particular, check for correct use of object pronouns. (See page 319W.)

- **Check the Spelling** Spell-check on a computer can be helpful, but it may not catch every spelling mistake. It is important to read your work carefully and use a dictionary to double-check tricky spellings. (See page 320W.)

- **Check the Mechanics** Mistakes in punctuation and capitalization can make your work hard to understand. In particular, pay attention to how you've used commas with participial phrases and appositives. (See page 321W.)

Use these marks to edit and proofread your letter.

TechTIP

Use the **Find** feature to look for commas that set off participial phrases and appositives. If the computer skips these phrases, you'll know you've left commas out.

Editing and Proofreading Marks

MARK	WHAT IT MEANS	MARK	WHAT IT MEANS
∧	Insert something.	╱	Make lowercase.
∧	Add a comma.	℘	Delete, take something out.
∧	Add a semicolon.	¶	Make new paragraph.
⊙	Add a period.	◯	Spell out.
⊙	Add a colon.	⌃	Replace with this.
∨ ∨	Add quotation marks.	∼	Change order of letters or words.
∨	Add an apostrophe.	#	Insert space.
≡	Capitalize.	◡	Close up, no space here.

Reflect

- **What kinds of errors did you find? What can you do to keep from making them?**

GrammarWorkout

Check Object Pronouns

Object pronouns have special forms.

Singular	Plural
me	us
you	you
him, her, it	them

- You can use an **object pronoun** as the object of the **verb**.

    EXAMPLES I see a bright star. I **see** **it**.
    Lights confuse the birds. Lights **confuse** **them**.

- You can also use an **object pronoun** after a **preposition**.

    EXAMPLES Lights glow near the house. Lights glow **near** **it**.
    The sky **above** **me** is dark.

Find the Trouble Spots

> I didn't know that our Space Museum was about
> to close. Then I read about ~~them~~ *it* in a news magazine.
> The article said the museum is too costly. It also said
> that there are fewer and fewer tourists every year. The
> museum doesn't attract ~~her~~ *them*. The article upset I a lot. I
> heard that city officials are interested in the issue. I will
> write a proposal to us.

Find two other object pronoun errors to fix.

Edit and Proofread, continued

> ## SpellingWorkout
>
> # Check Words with *q* or *ei*
>
> There are some spelling rules in the English language that are
> pretty reliable. Learn some basic rules like the ones below, and
> you'll be right most of the time.
>
> - The letter *q* nearly always has the letter *u* right after it.
>   Some proper nouns are exceptions.
>
> | | |
> |---|---|
> | **EXAMPLES** | queen, quick, quench |
> | **EXCEPTIONS** | Iraq, Qatar |
>
> - When the letters *i* and *e* appear together, *i* usually comes
>   before *e*. However, this changes when the letters come
>   after the letter *c* or sound like long *a*.
>
> | | |
> |---|---|
> | **EXAMPLES** | field, friend, thief |
> | **EXCEPTIONS** for *c* | ceiling, receive, receipt |
> | **EXCEPTIONS** for long *a* | weigh, neighborhood |
>
> ### Find the Trouble Spots
>
> > *Believe*
> > ~~Beleive~~ it or not, the Space Museum will close next
> >   *question*
> > year. I would have to ~~qestion~~ this decision. I know the
> > Space Museum never recieved enough funding. Let's work
> > together to bring tourism back. Let's collect funds qickly!
> > Help save the museum for yourself, your friends, and your
> > nieghbors.
>
> Find three other
> spelling errors
> to fix.

Mechanics Workout

Check Commas

- A **participle** is a verb form that often ends with **-ed** or **-ing**. A **participial phrase** is a group of words that includes a participle.

  Put a comma after a participial phrase when it comes at the beginning of a sentence.

  EXAMPLES **Confused** by the light, the birds lost their way. **Landing** near the campfire, they surprised the campers.

- An **appositive** is a noun or noun phrase that immediately follows another noun or noun phrase and tells more about it.

  Set off appositives with commas unless leaving the appositive out would make the meaning unclear.

  EXAMPLES **Mars, the red planet,** has been known since antiquity. I would love to travel to the planet **Mars.**

Find the Trouble Spots

I spoke with Dr. Turner the director of the Space Museum. I learned many interesting things. Opened in 1981 the Space Museum should have had a planetarium. The mayor at that time Colleen O'Reilly opposed this. Thinking the planetarium wasn't important city officials invested the money elsewhere. I think that wasn't very smart.

Find two more places to add commas.

Model Study

Invitation

When you communicate with friends and family, you use an **informal tone.** When you communicate with adults or someone you don't know, you use a more **formal tone.**

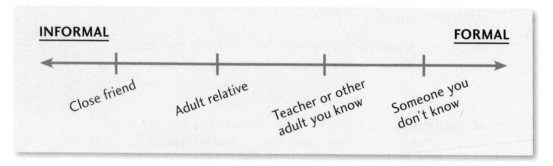

An invitation is one form of informal communication. It should make an event sound exciting and fun. After all, the point is to make the reader want to come! An invitation also provides all the information the reader needs to know about the event.

The model on page 323W shows the features of an invitation.

INVITATION

A good invitation includes

☑ details about the event—who, what, when, why, and where

☑ a tone that is appropriate for the audience

☑ information about how to contact the writer.

Feature Checklist

The writer describes the event in a way that appeals to readers.

The writer tells **when** and **where** the event will take place.

Come to the

Valentine's Day Talent Show!

I'm going to be competing in a talent show on Valentine's Day. I get to invite ten people. I hope you will come!

For: my friends and family members

Date: February 14, 2009

Time: 2–5 P.M.

Place: Sandy Lane Middle School, 1357 Clydesdale Lane

R.S.V.P. Elena Jackson, 555-8763

Student Model

The writer is inviting friends and family. Her tone is informal.

The writer uses **R.S.V.P.** to ask readers to contact her. R.S.V.P. stands for "Please respond" in French.

Thank-You Note

A thank-you note is a good way to let people know that you appreciate something nice they have done for you. You can use thank-you notes to thank someone for giving you a gift, coming to your special event, or anything else you feel grateful for.

A good thank-you note is polite, but not stiff and formal. Adjust your tone so that it is appropriate to your audience. Include specifics about why you are expressing thanks. That will make the reader feel good. Be warm and enthusiastic. Finally, don't forget to include the words *thank you*!

The student model on page 325W shows the features of a good thank-you note.

THANK-YOU NOTE

A good thank-you note

☑ includes the date and a greeting

☑ is written in a polite tone

☑ says "thank you" and names the gift or act for which you are grateful

☑ tells specifically why you like the gift or appreciate the act

☑ includes a closing and your signature.

Feature Checklist

February 20, 2009

Elena includes the **date** and a **greeting**.

Dear Aunt Ellen,

Elena gives specific details about why she is grateful.

Thank you so much for coming to see me play my guitar in the talent show on Valentine's Day. It really made me feel proud to know you were there watching!

I'd also like to thank you for the flowers you brought me. They are very pretty. I'm keeping them in a vase on my desk.

I hope that the next time I am in a competition, you will be able to come again.

Elena is writing to a relative. She uses a polite, somewhat formal tone.

Love,
Elena

Elena includes a **closing** and her **signature**.

Student Model

Write an
Invitation or a Thank-You Note

WRITING PROMPT Write an invitation or a thank-you note—or both!
Your invitation can be for any event you plan to host or would like to
host. Your thank-you note can be for anything someone did for you
that you feel grateful for.

Be sure to include

* the key elements listed on the Feature Checklists on pages 322W
  and 324W

* language that is appropriate for your audience.

Plan and Draft

Once you have some ideas, you can draft your invitation or
thank-you note.

Invitation

* **Give Information** Start with a a few sentences about the
  event. Then give readers all the information they need if
  they want to attend: what, when, where, who, why.

* **Use Appropriate Language** Think about who you are
  communicating with—your audience. Imagine you are
  talking to your audience. What words would you use?
  Write those words into your draft.

*Tech*TIP

Use the paragraph
feature to make
your text double-
or triple-spaced.
The extra space
will give you room
to mark your
changes later on.

Come to the
Riverside Winter Holiday Recital

My brother Chen will be playing several piano pieces at this year's recital. Come with me to hear him! (Don't tell him you are coming. It will make him nervous.)

For: Chen's best friends
Date: December 19, 2009   **Time:** 7–9 P.M.
Place: Riverside Community Center, 9735 Glendale Court
R.S.V.P. Ken Wong, 555-1337

Ken describes the event and gives important information.

Thank-You Note

- **Be Specific** Remind the reader what he or she did for you or gave you. Then tell why you are grateful or what you are doing with the gift.

- **Express Your Feelings** Write in a personal, friendly way. Explain to the reader how his or her kindness or generosity made you feel.

December 22, 2009

Dear Becca,

I would like to thank you for coming to the Winter Holiday Recital. I know Chen was shocked to see his friends there. The look on his face was priceless. He is shy about asking people to come hear him play. But I know he was happy. His best friends were there!

I truly appreciate your coming.

Your friend,
Ken

Ken tells why he is thanking the reader and expresses his feelings.

Reflect

- Did you include all the important information?

- Is your tone appropriate?

Revise

As you consider how to revise your work, keep in mind your audience and your purpose for writing. Does your writing do what you want it to do? Will it connect with your readers?

1 **Evaluate Your Work**

Ask a family member to help you evaluate your work. Have the person read it, or read it aloud. Then, ask questions:

- **About the Form** Did I include all the information the reader needs?

- **About the Voice** Is my writing lively and interesting? Are there any places where the tone doesn't sound quite right?

Revision in Action

From Ken's Invitation Draft

Come to the
Riverside Winter Holiday Recital

My brother Chen will be playing several piano pieces at this year's recital. Come with me to hear him! (Don't tell him you are coming. It will make him nervous.)

Ken's relative says:

" Your tone doesn't sound right. You sound bossy. Your sentences are a little choppy. "

From Ken's Thank-You Note Draft

I would like to thank you for coming to the Winter Holiday Recital. I know Chen was shocked to see his friends there. The look on his face was priceless. He is shy about asking people to come hear him play. But I know he was happy. His best friends were there!
I truly appreciate your coming.

" You sound too stiff and formal in some sentences. You can be more casual with your friend. "

" You have too many short sentences. "

2 Mark Your Changes

- **Replace Text** You may want to change some words to improve the sound or style of your writing. Use this mark: .

- **Consolidate Text** You might need to make other changes to make your sentences flow better. Use the "take out," "insert," and "move" marks to show your changes.

Reflect

- Does your writing sound too formal? too informal?

- What can you change to make your sentences flow together better?

Revising Marks

MARK	∧	↶	⌐	ℓ	¶
WHAT IT MEANS	Insert something.	Move to here.	Replace with this.	Take out.	Make a new paragraph.

Revised Drafts

From Ken's Invitation Draft

> **Come to the**
> ## Riverside Winter Holiday Recital
>
> My brother Chen will be playing several piano pieces at this year's recital. ~~Come with me~~ *Let's go together* to hear him! (Don't *Please* tell him you are coming^*because* ̶I̶t̶ will make him nervous.)

Ken changed or added words to soften the tone. He combined sentences to improve the flow.

From Ken's Thank-You Note Draft

> *Thanks so much*
> ^~~I would like to thank you~~ for coming to the Winter Holiday Recital. I know Chen was shocked to see his friends there. The look on his face was priceless. He is shy about asking people to come hear him play. But I know he was happy^*that* ̶H̶is best friends were there!
> *Thanks again for*
> ^~~I truly appreciate your~~ coming.

Ken changed the first and last sentences to make them more casual.

Ken combined sentences to make the text smoother.

Edit and Proofread

Now that your invitation or thank-you note says everything you want it to, all that's left is to fix language errors. This is what you do when you edit and proofread your work:

- **Check the Grammar** Make sure you have used correct and conventional grammar throughout. In particular, make sure each sentence has a subject and a predicate. (See page 331W.)

- **Check the Spelling** For words with tricky consonants, like the **w** in **write**, you may need to check a dictionary. (See page 332W.)

- **Check the Mechanics** Errors in punctuation or capitalization can make your work hard to read. Make sure the names of all works of art, musical compositions, TV shows, movies, plays, and holidays are capitalized. (See page 333W.)

Use these marks to edit and proofread your invitation or thank-you note.

Editing and Proofreading Marks

MARK	WHAT IT MEANS	MARK	WHAT IT MEANS
∧	Insert something.	/	Make lowercase.
∧	Add a comma.	℘	Delete, take something out.
∧	Add a semicolon.	¶	Make new paragraph.
⊙	Add a period.	◯	Spell out.
⊙	Add a colon.	⌃	Replace with this.
⌄ ⌄	Add quotation marks.	∼	Change order of letters or words.
⌄	Add an apostrophe.	#	Insert space.
≡	Capitalize.	◡	Close up, no space here.

Reflect

- What kinds of errors did you find? What can you do to keep from making them?

Grammar Workout

Check for Complete Sentences

- A complete sentence has two parts: the **subject** and the **predicate**.

    EXAMPLE   The kids thanked their uncle for the gift.

- Make sure each sentence is complete. If a sentence is missing the subject or the predicate, add the missing part to make a complete sentence.

    MISSING SUBJECT   Received a nice thank-you note.
    COMPLETE   Jeda received a nice thank-you note.

    MISSING PREDICATE   My cousins
    COMPLETE   My cousins gave a birthday party.

- You can often fix an incomplete sentence by making it part of a nearby sentence.

    INCORRECT   I'll see you soon. At the concert
    CORRECT   I'll see you soon at the concert.

Find the Trouble Spots

I can't believe the recital is over. ^I Had a great time seeing my brother play. Chen did a wonderful job. ^He is Such a talented musician! Thank you so much for being there. Hope we can get together again soon. At my house. My brother's birthday

Find and fix all the sentence errors.

Edit and Proofread, continued

> ## SpellingWorkout

Check for Tricky Consonant Sounds

- The hard **c** sound can be spelled with **c, k,** or **ck**.

  EXAMPLES   camera   kiss   speak   pick

  At the beginning of a word, this sound is most often spelled with a **c** before **a, o,** and **u.** It is most often spelled with a **k** before **e** and **i.** At the end of a word, use **k** after a long vowel sound and **ck** after a short vowel sound.

- The **j** sound can be spelled with **j, g, ge,** or **dge**.

  EXAMPLES   jump   genius   cage   fudge

  At the beginning of a word, this sound is always spelled with a **j** before **a, o,** and **u.** Before **e** and **i,** sometimes it's spelled with **g** and sometimes with **j**—use a dictionary or spell-check. At the end of a word, the sound is always spelled with **ge** or **dge**.

- Many words start with the sound for **n** or **r.** Some of the words are spelled with a pair of consonants, even though the first consonant is silent.

  EXAMPLES   not   right
                  know   wrong

You have to memorize the spelling of words with silent consonants.

Find the Trouble Spots

I wanted to ~~rite~~ *write* to thank you for coming to the *concert* ~~konsert~~. I new Chen would give a great performance! He just has a knak for the piano. The juge was definitely impressed with Chen's skills. Chen said his rists ache from so much practice!

Find and fix four more spelling errors.

MechanicsWorkout

Check Capitalization and Style

Of course, all proper nouns in your writing should be capitalized. Proper nouns name a particular person, place, thing, or idea. Some proper nouns have other style conventions as well:

Type of Proper Noun	How to Treat It	Example
painting or sculpture	Use *italics*.	Leonardo da Vinci painted the ***Mona Lisa***.
short song or poem	Use quotation marks.	My music teacher played **"The Star-Spangled Banner"** for us.
long musical composition with lyrics	Use *italics*.	Gershwin's ***Porgy and Bess*** was the first American opera.
published music CDs	Use *italics*.	I played ***Jazz Express*** over and over again last summer.
movies, plays, and TV shows	Use *italics*.	We watched a classic movie called ***It's a Wonderful Life***.
names of holidays	Just capitalize.	What did you do on **Labor Day**?

Find the Trouble Spots

Chen started piano lessons just after new year's day two years ago. He is really good. He played the song "Heart and Soul" for the Valentine's day concert last year. He is trying to get on the TV show American Player, for their fourth of July show. He could make a lot of money!

Find and fix three more errors.

"Writing about a book is fun. It helps you figure out what you really think about it."
—Brett

Model Study

Literary Response

Imagine that your friend has given you his favorite book to read. You read it, and it turns out you don't like it. Your friend wants to know why. How will you support your opinion?

When you respond to literature, you tell what you think and feel about something you have read. You need to go beyond "I like it" or "I don't like it," though. You must give reasons to support your ideas.

The student model on page 335W shows the features of a good literary response.

LITERARY RESPONSE

A good literary response tells

☑ the name of the work and the author

☑ what the work is mostly about

☑ how you feel about the work and why

☑ something important you learned from the work.

Feature Checklist

Joseph Bruchac's *The Warriors*
by Elizabeth Clarke

The writer tells the **title of the work** and the **name of the author** in the first paragraph.

In *The Warriors*, Joseph Bruchac tells the story of Jake, an Iroquois boy. He has to move from his reservation to Washington, D.C. Jake is a lacrosse player. To the Iroquois, lacrosse is the Creator's game. It was given to them as a gift. It united them and made them strong. But in his new school, the other kids don't understand.

The writer tells what the story is mostly about, how she feels about it, and why.

I really like this story because Jake is like a real kid. I felt close to him and understood his problems and his life. Jake learns many important lessons from Grampa Sky. These lessons help you understand Jake's heritage. They make the Iroquois culture come alive. Bruchac includes vivid details of Jake's lacrosse games. They make you feel like you are right there with him. You can picture the field and his teammates clearly.

The writer tells something important she learned from the story.

This book teaches a lot about the Iroquois, too. Until I read it, I did not know that lacrosse has its roots in Native American culture. It was interesting to learn about this history and the importance of lacrosse to the Iroquois.

▼ Native Americans playing lacrosse

Find Out What You Think

Many of today's reality TV shows have judges. These judges usually have strong opinions about why they do or do not like a contestant. The judges must watch a performance, judge it, and give reasons for their opinions. In the same way, when you write a response to literature, you support your opinions about the work.

Choose a Book You Feel Strongly About

The first step in writing a good literary response is to write about a book that you have strong opinions about. Maybe you have read some books that you still think about because they really sparked a reaction in you.

If you can't remember any books like that, ask your teacher to suggest a book that you could read. Read the entire book. Get to know it well so that you can form opinions about it.

Keep Track of Your Feelings

As you read (or reread) a literary work, keep track of your thoughts and feelings. Answer questions like the ones below, and use a chart to keep track of your responses.

- What is my overall opinion of the book? How did I generally react to it?

- What's good about this book? What's not so good?

- Would I ask my friends to read this book? Why or why not?

Literature

Fly Like a Bird by Darren Knowles

Opinions and Reactions

I can completely understand how the main character, Raymond, feels at his school. Other kids can be cruel to someone who is different from them.

What's good about it?	What could be better?
— real-life dialogue — sensitive description of feelings — gets inside the head of a kid who is not like everyone else	The "other kids" are all exactly alike. In real life, kids have a variety of feelings. They're not all the same.

Would I recommend this to other people? Why or why not?

yes, because many kids could relate to the events and to Raymond's feelings

---

Support Your Statements with Specifics

Gather Evidence

Once you really know your opinions about a book, think about how to back them up. Look back through the story carefully. Choose passages that best support your opinions. Aim for at least two supporting examples for each of your opinions.

Use a chart like this to help you organize your thoughts.

> Opinion
> The author really shows what it's like to be a kid who is different or odd.
>
> Supporting Examples
> —the description of Raymond when he tells his classmates that he can speak with birds, and the kids tease him
> —the happiness Raymond feels because one kid is nice to him

Tech TIP

Save your ideas, drafts, and other resources in a single file folder on your computer. That will make it easier to find everything when you need it.

Get Down to Specifics

Once you have your basic opinions and supporting examples in place, dig deeper. Look in the text for specific details and exact quotes or dialogue that back up your evidence.

Supporting Example

—the happiness Raymond feels because one kid is nice to him

Specific Text Detail

Raymond sits in a corner of the schoolyard. He watches from a distance as the other kids laugh and play games. His face brightens when Olga speaks to him.

Exact Quote

"Hi, can I join you?" says Olga.
"That'd be great, Olga," Raymond answers.

In the examples below, notice how specific details and quoted dialogue add depth and power to the writing.

Weak—No Text Support

At lunch, Raymond sat alone. But when Olga came up and said hello, Raymond smiled.

Strong—With Text Support

At lunch, Raymond sat by himself in a corner of the schoolyard. He watched the other kids laugh and play games. But then Olga came up and said, "Hi, can I join you?" and Raymond's face brightened.
"That'd be great, Olga," he said.

Give Your Opinion

At the Olympics, judges evaluate an athlete's performance based on what's expected in the sport and on what's been accomplished in the past. When you write a literary response, you also evaluate someone's performance—but you have to come up with a lot more than just a number!

Include Your Evidence

Use the evidence you have gathered to give your opinion. Try these techniques:

- **Solid Reasons** Include two or three solid reasons to support your opinions. Present them from strongest to weakest or weakest to strongest.

- **Examples** Notice how an example can help support what the writer thinks about the book *Fly Like a Bird*.

Unconvincing—No Examples

> I really like this story. It shows that you shouldn't be mean to people who are different. When you get to know them, you discover that they are a lot like you.

Convincing—With an Example

> I really like this story. It shows that you shouldn't be mean to people who are different. When you get to know them, you discover that they are a lot like you. When Raymond told Olga that he could talk to birds, she didn't laugh. She thought of the special way she communicated with her dog, Toby.

Share Your Emotions

Your literary response includes emotions, or feelings. Here are some ways to share your emotions in your literary response:

- **Persuasive Language** Use words that show the strength of your feelings. Don't be harsh or extreme. You want your opinions to sound reasonable.

  Boring—No Emotion

  > You should read Fly Like a Bird. It's a good book.

  Good Appeal to Emotions

  > Fly Like a Bird is a wonderful book. You will come to really like Raymond, a boy who is different. I think many teens today can relate to Raymond and his situation.

  Too Emotional

  > It would be really silly not to read Fly Like a Bird. The problems of the main character will make you cry! It's terrible and sad. You have to read about him!

- **Personal Connections** Everyone likes to feel part of something! You can appeal to your readers' emotions— and help them understand your feelings—by connecting them to the story. For example:

  Without a Personal Connection

  > Reading about other people is interesting.

  With a Personal Connection

  > Have you ever felt out of place in your own environment? Then you'll enjoy reading about Raymond.

Build Your Layers

Now that you have all the ingredients of a literary response, you need to put them together. A good literary response is built in layers—like a cake! Each layer contains one of the ingredients you have learned about.

- The top layer identifies the book (title and author) and presents your opinion. How do you feel about the story? Tell the reader why you do or do not like it.

- The middle layer is the thickest. Here is where you put the most important details of the story, such as the setting, characters, and plot. Include enough details to support your opinion and to give the reader a good idea of what the book or story is about.

- The bottom layer is about you. Here is where you explain what life lesson you learned from the story or how it affected you personally.

Layers of a Good Literary Response

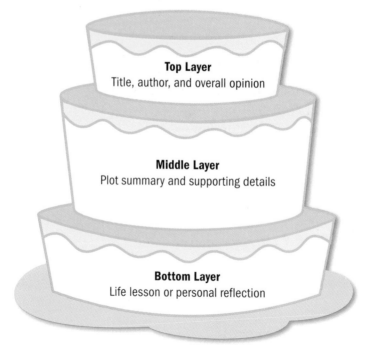

Top Layer
Title, author, and overall opinion

Middle Layer
Plot summary and supporting details

Bottom Layer
Life lesson or personal reflection

TechTIP

List details from the book as phrases or sentences. Then use cut and paste from the Edit menu to move details around as you need to.

As you write a literary response, keep these layers in mind. Layering will make your paper more interesting and effective.

Compare the two writing samples below to see what a difference layering can make.

Fly Like a Bird is about a kid who is different because he likes to talk to birds. The other kids at school usually laugh at him. The book was interesting to read. I learned a lot about people.

There are few details to help the reader get a good sense of what the book is about.

Fly Like a Bird, by Darren Knowles, is a very interesting book with very interesting characters. The author makes you feel that the characters are real people, and you get to know them as if they were friends. It is a book that teens will enjoy reading.

The book tells the story of a boy named Raymond. He is "different," because he likes to talk to birds. Of course, the other kids at school laugh at him for this. The only one who doesn't laugh is Olga. She gets to know Raymond well. She becomes his friend.

The book really shows how hard things can be for someone who is different. Raymond always sits alone at lunch, watching the other kids eat together and play. Things don't change until Olga comes up to him one day. "Hi," she says. "Can I eat with you?"

Olga gets to know Raymond really well—and so did I! Through his friendship with Olga, Raymond learns to "fly like a bird" emotionally and socially.

Fly Like a Bird taught me the importance of getting to know people, not just judging them. I also learned that people do better when other people support them.

The introduction names the book and author. It gives the writer's overall opinion.

The writer provides enough detail to support her opinion. The reader gets a good sense of the book.

The writer ends with a personal reflection.

Write a Literary Response

WRITING PROMPT Have you ever read a book that you couldn't put down? What was it that made you want to keep reading? Did you identify with the characters, or did you just have to know what would happen next?

Think of a favorite book that you would like to recommend to your classmates. Then write a literary response that includes

- the title of the work and name of the author
- your opinion of the book
- what the book is mostly about, with evidence to back up your opinions
- something important that you learned from the book.

Prewrite

Here are some tips for planning your literary response.

1 Choose a Book

Don't choose a so-so book to write about. Choose a book or story that sparked strong feelings in you and that you really want your classmates to read.

Make a list of possible books, as Nathan did. Consider each book. Then choose the one you want to write about.

Island of Blue Dolphins by Scott O'Dell
The Talking Earth by Jean Craighead George
The Bonesetter's Daughter by Amy Tan

Cypress trees grow in the Everglades, where *The Talking Earth* takes place. ▼

② Organize Your Ideas

Reread the book. What are your opinions and ideas? Nathan jotted down his thoughts.

Nathan's Notes

> **Book**
> Jean Craighead George's <u>The Talking Earth</u>
>
> **Opinions and Reactions**
> I could really relate to the main character, Billie. She has a mind of her own. She doesn't just accept what people tell her, and she stands up for her beliefs.

③ Plan Your Layers

Think about the overall structure of your response. Jot down what you plan to cover in each layer. You can use a **"Cake" Diagram** like the one below.

Nathan's "Cake" Diagram for *The Talking Earth*

> **Title:** The Talking Earth
> **Author:** Jean Craighead George
> **Opinion:** Great book. I like how Billie Wind stands up for her beliefs. The "talking" animals are cool.

> **Summary and supporting details**
> —Billie Wind, Seminole tribe
> —doesn't agree with tribal beliefs
> —goes into Everglades, connects with nature

> **Life lesson or personal reflection**
> You can be yourself and still learn from your culture.

Reflect

- Do you need to gather more evidence to support your opinions?

- Is your personal reflection personal enough?

Draft

You know what you think. Now it's time to get it all on paper.
Use your notes and diagram as you draft.

- **Review Your Notes** Look at the opinions and reactions
  to your book that you jotted down. Remember, you will
  communicate and explain these ideas in your paper.

- **Use Your Diagram** As you write the first paragraph, use
  the information in the top layer of your diagram as
  a guide.

From Nathan's Draft

> One of my favorite books of all time is Jean Craighead
> George's The Talking Earth. Mostly I like it because I can
> relate to the main character. Her name is Billie Wind, and she
> knows how to really stand up for her beliefs. The book also
> uses "talking animals" that lend the story a magical air.

- **Support Your Opinions** Use specific examples to support
  your ideas. Keep the book nearby as you write. Check
  details or examples if you need to.

From Nathan's Draft

> Billie Wind is a member of the Seminole tribe. The Seminole
> elders believe in nature spirits. Their beliefs seem silly to Billie.
> She can't hide how she feels, and so she gets into a conflict
> with the elders.

Reflect

- Are your opinions
  supported with
  specific details?

- What can you add
  to give readers a
  better sense of
  the book?

DRAFTING TIPS
Trait: **Development of Ideas**

If Your Writing Sounds Like a List . . .

Listy writing goes from one thing to the next too quickly, without explaining or developing anything. It is like a skeleton—bare bones.

Try Adding Meat to the Bones

When you add concrete details, you add meat to the bones and fix listy writing. Concrete details that develop and support your ideas can include

- direct quotations from the story
- key details from the plot
- "thoughtshots," or what you were thinking as you read the story.

Here are some examples of how you can use these devices to add meat to the bones of your writing:

Direct Quotation

> Billie gets into trouble. No one understands her. The elders ask, "What do you think would be a suitable punishment for you, Billie Wind?"

Key Detail

> Billie thinks the tribal beliefs are silly. They don't have much to do with the modern world.

"Thoughtshot"

> I was really impressed with Billie when she decided to do something totally crazy, like going into the wilderness by herself. I was also worried that she might get hurt.

Revise

As you revise, keep in mind your audience and your purpose for writing. Will your literary response give your readers a good sense of the book and what you think of it?

1 **Evaluate Your Work**

Share your draft with different people, such as family members or friends. Afterward, ask questions:

- **About the Form** Do I have a clear beginning, middle, and end? Do you understand what the book is about?

- **About the Development of Ideas** Did I include enough details to back up my opinion?

> ## Revision in Action

Nathan's Draft

> Billie Wind is a member of the Seminole tribe. The Seminole elders believe in nature spirits. Billie does not agree with tribal beliefs. She says she believes only in what she sees. No one really understands her, not even her sister. Her sister is named Mary.
>
> Later, Billie's beliefs change. She goes out into the Everglades and stays there by herself. Over time, she sees that the Seminole elders were right, in a way. She starts feeling more connected to nature and animals.
>
> I like this book because I can relate to Billie. She stands up for her beliefs. I respect that.

Nathan's friend says:

" There is too much about Billie's sister."

" You should include more detail about why her beliefs change."

" This part is great, but you need to explain better what you learned."

② Mark Your Changes

Add Text To support your opinions and develop your ideas, you may need to add more details, examples, or quotes from the book. Use this mark: ∧ . To add a paragraph, use this symbol: ¶.

Delete and Consolidate Text You might want to take out unnecessary details that do not relate directly to the point you're trying to make. Use this mark: ⟶ℓ.

Reflect

- Do you need to work on your "layers"?

- What can you change to make your writing more interesting?

Revising Marks	MARK	∧	⟲	⌐	⟶ℓ	¶
	WHAT IT MEANS	Insert something.	Move to here.	Replace with this.	Take out.	Make a new paragraph.

Revised Draft

Billie Wind is a member of the Seminole tribe. The Seminole elders believe in nature spirits. Billie does not agree with tribal beliefs. She says she believes only in what she sees. No one really understands her, not even her sister. ~~Her sister is named~~ Mary.

Later, Billie's beliefs change. She goes out into the Everglades and stays there by herself. *She starts talking to animals, and they help her.* ∧ Over time, she sees that the Seminole elders were right, in a way. She starts feeling more connected to nature and animals. ∧ *She feels as if they are almost a family.*

I like this book because I can relate to Billie. She stands up for her beliefs. I respect that.

¶ *Billie also learns to respect her culture's beliefs, though. From this book, I learned that you can be yourself but still learn from your culture.*

Nathan deleted an unimportant detail and consolidated.

Nathan added specific details from the book.

Nathan added a truth about life that he learned from the book.

Edit and Proofread

After you're satisfied with the content of your literary response, read your paper again to fix language errors. This is what you do when you edit and proofread your work:

- **Check the Grammar** Make sure that you have used correct and conventional grammar throughout. In particular, check for correct formation of compound sentences. (See page 351W.)

- **Check the Spelling** Spell-check doesn't catch every mistake. For words with prefixes and suffixes, you'll need to read your work carefully and perhaps use a dictionary. (See page 352W.)

- **Check the Mechanics** Errors in punctuation and capitalization can make your work hard to understand. In particular, check that you've written titles and quotations correctly. (See page 353W.)

Use these marks to edit and proofread your literary response.

Editing and Proofreading Marks

MARK	WHAT IT MEANS	MARK	WHAT IT MEANS
∧	Insert something.	╱	Make lowercase.
∧	Add a comma.	℘	Delete, take something out.
∧	Add a semicolon.	⁋	Make new paragraph.
⊙	Add a period.	◯	Spell out.
⊙	Add a colon.	⌒	Replace with this.
⌄ ⌄	Add quotation marks.	∼	Change order of letters or words.
⌄	Add an apostrophe.	#	Insert space.
≡	Capitalize.	⌒	Close up, no space here.

Reflect

- What kinds of errors did you find? What can you do to keep from making them?

> ## GrammarWorkout

Check Compound Sentences

When your writing has too many short sentences, it can sound choppy and boring.

EXAMPLE   I like to read. Amy likes to sing.

To make your writing smoother, you can combine short sentences using **and, but,** or **or**. The resulting longer sentence is a **compound sentence**.

- Use a comma (,) plus **and** to join similar or related ideas.

  EXAMPLE   I like to read, **and** Amy likes to sing.

- Use a comma (,) plus **but** to join different or opposite ideas.

  EXAMPLE   I like to read, **but** Amy hates books.

- Use a comma (,) plus **or** to show a choice.

  EXAMPLE   I can read this book, **or** I can practice this song.

Find the Opportunities

  Billie is sent into the woods, ^but^ She only has to stay a short time. She does not know what to do. She could lie ^or^ She could try something else. She doesn't really want to stay in the forest. She wants to understand her tribe's beliefs. She doesn't like talking to animals. Soon she feels as if they understand her.

How can you combine sentences to make two more compound sentences?

Edit and Proofread, continued

SpellingWorkout

Check Suffixes

Suffix	Meaning
-able	able, likely, or fit to be
-er	one who does something
-ful	full of
-ly	in a certain way
-ous	having or like
-y	having the quality of

When you add a suffix to a base word, most of the time the spelling of the base word doesn't change—but sometimes it does! Pay special attention to these cases:

- If the base word ends in *e* and the suffix starts with a vowel, drop the final *e* before adding the suffix.

  EXAMPLE   dance ⟶ dancer

- If the base word ends in a consonant plus *y*, change the *y* to an *i* before adding the suffix. Do **not** change the *y* to *i* if the base word ends in a vowel plus *y*.

  EXAMPLE   silly ⟶ silliness   joy ⟶ joyful

- If the base word ends in a short vowel plus a consonant, double the consonant before adding the suffix *-y* or another suffix starting with a vowel.

  EXAMPLE   snap ⟶ snappy

Find the Trouble Spots

>   At first, Billie is ~~furyous~~ *furious* about her punishment. She tries to think of a way out of it. However, she finds peace in the wilderness. It is unexpectedly ~~beautyful~~ *beautiful*. Billie learns that she is resourceful and adventureous. Alone in the swampy, mudy Everglades, she finds true happyness.

Find and fix three more misspelled words with a suffix.

MechanicsWorkout

Check Titles and Quotes

Follow these rules for titles and exact quotes from texts:

- Capitalize the first word of the title and all other important words.

    EXAMPLE   Have you read the book *Julie of the Wolves*?

- Use quotation marks around the title of a short story or poem.

    EXAMPLE   I enjoyed Christopher Myers's story "Wings."

- Put book titles in italics (or underline them if you're writing by hand).

    EXAMPLE   In our classroom, there's a copy of the book *Greek Mythology*.

- Use quotation marks around any words you quote from a text. Show exactly where the quoted words begin and end, and use the exact words in the original source.

    EXAMPLE   Myers describes the kids' "staring eyes and wagging tongues."

Find the Trouble Spots

My favorite book is <u>The talking Earth</u>, by Jean Craighead George. It describes the struggle of a girl named Billie who is considered too scientific. Billie tells her sister, What I don't see, I don't believe. That is my favorite quote. Another book by the same author is My side of the mountain. I will read that next.

Find and fix more problems with titles and quotes.

Publish, Share, and Reflect

You've worked hard to create a literary response that is well developed and full of supporting details—and that gets your feelings across. Why not share your opinions with others?

1 Publish and Share Your Work

Publishing your writing means putting it into a final form and sharing it with others. There are several different ways you can publish a response to literature.

If you prefer to share your response with just a few friends, you might

- read it aloud in a book group (see page 355W)
- make copies and e-mail them to friends.

To make your response more public, you can

- send it to a Web site that publishes teens' writing
- post it on a blog
- put it on a bulletin board at your local or school library
- submit it to your school literary magazine.

2 Reflect on Your Work

After you've shared your work, keep thinking about it. Reflect on what went well, and think about the areas you need to work on. You might also think of other books you'd like to write about!

Tech*TIP*

"Dress up" your final paper! Use special fonts for your title and body text.

Reflect

- What did I learn about myself through writing about this book?

- What can I do to make my writing more interesting to others?

How to Conduct a Book-Club Meeting

To share your writing with a few classmates or friends, you might arrange a book-club discussion. Members of a book club decide in advance what books they want to read. They all read the same book on their own. Then, they come together to share their thoughts about it.

To conduct a book-club meeting:

1. Work with your group to decide on a book, as well as a date, time, and place to meet. (You might have it at your house, or ask a teacher if you can reserve a classroom after school.)

2. Schedule the meeting at least two weeks in advance. That way, everyone will have time to read.

3. Be prepared! Read the book (or reread it) beforehand. Write down your thoughts and responses.

4. Plan a relaxed, fun gathering. If it's at your house, you might provide snacks and arrange chairs in a circle.

5. Begin the discussion by asking a question about the book. You might ask about people's overall reactions or about a particular point you found interesting.

6. Be courteous. Allow time for everyone to share their responses. Don't interrupt, even if you disagree.

7. Share your own response. Don't be shy about expressing your opinions!

" My favorite scene from this book is when Billie first realizes that the animals are understanding her, and she's understanding the animals."

Writing
FORMS

Advertisements	Letters
Autobiography	Literary Response
Biography	Myth
Book Review	Newspaper
Character Sketch	Personal Narrative
Description	Play
Directions	Poetry
E-mail	Procedure
Envelope	Story
Essay	Tall Tale
Fable	Thank-You Note
Folk Tales and Fairy Tales	Web site
Greetings	Workplace and Consumer Resources
Interview	
Invitation	
Job Application	

Advertisements

Print Ad

Advertisements are a powerful form of persuasion. They can be used to "sell" almost anything—food, clothes, vacation spots, even political candidates. Print ads appeal to readers by combining text with eye-catching visual images.

"Whistle" was a soft drink popular in the 1920s. ▼

Attracts readers' attention with images

Uses descriptive words to appeal to consumers

TV Ad Script

Advertisements on television get viewers' attention and present a brief, persuasive message, often with catchy phrases and vivid images. Some ads try to sell a product. Others, like the public-service announcement (PSA) below, try to persuade viewers to take action on a community concern.

Crushed aluminum cans ready for recycling ▶

"Recycling" PSA

Scene: A living room with doorway to the kitchen visible in background. JAMAL is taking a nap on the couch in the living room.

KEVIN begins wrestling a heavy garbage bag from the trash can in the kitchen. JAMAL wakes up.

JAMAL (*annoyed*): Why does taking out the trash have to make so much noise?

KEVIN: It's all these soda cans.

JAMAL: What are those doing in the garbage?

KEVIN: Making noise, I guess.

KEVIN puts the heavy bag down. It drops loudly.

JAMAL: No, I mean, why are they in the trash when they aren't garbage? Those cans could be melted down and reused. Recycling metal cans saves energy and resources.

Cut to a recycling bin full of cans.

VOICE-OVER: If it clinks, it's not garbage. Recycle.

Cut to CCFEA logo and URL.

VOICE-OVER: For more information about recycling in your neighborhood, visit www.ccfea.org. Paid for by Concerned Citizens for Environmental Activism.

Stage directions tell what happens on-screen.

Dialogue defines what the actors will say.

A clear persuasive message often uses brief, memorable language.

Autobiography

An autobiography is the story of someone's own life. When you write an autobiography, you tell about the experiences that made you who you are today.

At age 7, Firoozeh Dumas moved to the U.S. from Iran. ▶

Often includes background about family history and childhood experiences

Moving to America was both exciting and frightening, but we found great comfort in knowing that my father spoke English. Having spent years regaling us with stories about his graduate years in America, he had left us with the distinct impression that America was his second home. My mother and I planned to stick close to him, letting him guide us through the exotic American landscape that he knew so well. We counted on him not only to translate the language but also to translate the culture, to be a link to this most foreign of lands.

Uses first-person pronouns.

Once we reached America, we wondered whether perhaps my father had confused his life in America with someone else's. Judging from the bewildered looks of store cashiers, gas station attendants, and waiters, my father spoke a version of English not yet shared with the rest of America. His attempts to find a "vater closet" in a department store would usually lead us to the drinking fountain or the home furnishings section.

Tells about specific memorable events.

Asking my father to ask the waitress the definition of "sloppy Joe" or "Tater Tots" was no problem. His translations, however, were highly suspect. Waitresses would spend several minutes responding to my father's questions, and these responses, in turn, would be translated as "She doesn't know." Thanks to my father's translations, we stayed away from hot dogs, catfish, and hush puppies, and no amount of caviar in the sea would have convinced us to try mud pie.

Biography

A biography tells the story of someone else's life. Long biographies can appear in books. Shorter ones may appear in magazines, encyclopedias, or Web sites.

▲ This engraving shows pioneers traveling West in the 1800s.

Laura Ingalls Wilder
born Feb. 7, 1867,
Lake Pepin, Wis., U.S.;
died Feb. 10, 1957,
Mansfield, Mo.

Laura Ingalls Wilder

Laura Ingalls grew up in a family that moved frequently from one part of the American frontier to another. Her father took the family by covered wagon to Minnesota, Iowa, Missouri, Kansas, Indian Territory, and Dakota Territory. At age 15 she began teaching in rural schools. In 1885 she married Almanzo J. Wilder, with whom she lived from 1894 on a farm near Mansfield, Missouri. Some years later she began writing for various periodicals.

Prompted by her daughter, Wilder began writing down her childhood experiences. In 1932 she published *Little House in the Big Woods*, which was set in Wisconsin. After writing *Farmer Boy* (1933), a book about her husband's childhood, she published *Little House on the Prairie* (1935), a reminiscence of her family's stay in Indian Territory. The "Little House" books were well received by the reading public and critics alike.

Wilder continued the story of her life in *On the Banks of Plum Creek* (1937), *By the Shores of Silver Lake* (1939), *The Long Winter* (1940), *Little Town on the Prairie* (1941), and *These Happy Golden Years* (1943). Her books remain in print.

Often describes the subject's life and work, using chronological order

Time words and dates cue the order of events.

450

Book Review

Sometimes you read a book that you just have to tell others about. You can tell about it by writing a book review.

The *Circuit*
by Francisco Jiménez

Reviewed by Vicente P.

The first paragraph tells what the book is mostly about, or its main idea.

The Circuit is about a boy, Panchito, from a family of poor migrant farmworkers. He loves school. But Panchito works in the fields, and his family moves from town to town, so he can't go to school very often. When he does go to school, sometimes he has to start in the middle of the school year. It's hard for him because he is a stranger in the class and he doesn't speak or understand English well.

The next section tells how you feel about the book and why.

I like this book. My dad is in the army, so my family moves a lot. I know how Panchito feels being the new kid in class. I feel sorry for him because just when he starts to like a place and he makes friends there, he has to leave. I know how that feels, too.

The final paragraph tells the most important idea you learned from the book.

This book makes me thankful that I don't have to work hard like Panchito. And, even though my family moves a lot, I'm thankful that I always have a home and enough to eat. I also realize that I'm lucky because I speak English and I get to go to school.

Character Sketch

A character sketch may appear in fiction or nonfiction writing. It's like a quick word portrait of another person. A character sketch may portray a real person or a fictional character.

THIS BOY'S LIFE | Tobias Wolff   15

Dwight was a short man with curly brown hair and sad, restless brown eyes. He smelled of gasoline. His legs were small for his thick-chested body, but what they lacked in length they made up for in spring; he had an abrupt, surprising way of springing to his feet. He dressed like no one I'd ever met before—two-tone shoes, hand-painted tie, monogrammed blazer with a monogrammed handkerchief in the breast pocket. Dwight kept coming back, which made him chief among the suitors. My mother said he was a good dancer—he could really make those shoes of his get up and go. Also he was very nice, very considerate.

I didn't worry about him. He was too short. He was a mechanic. His clothes were wrong. I didn't know why they were wrong, but they were. We hadn't come all the way out here to end up with him. He didn't even live in Seattle; he lived in a place called Chinook, a tiny village three hours north of Seattle, up in the Cascade Mountains. Besides, he'd already been married. He had three kids of his own living with him, all teenagers. I knew my mother would never let herself get tangled up in a mess like that.

Includes **descriptive details** about appearance, actions, and personality

The writer tells his opinion of the character.

Description

A description uses specific details to help readers picture whatever is being described. Use words that appeal to the reader's senses.

Includes vivid sensory details

It was one of those super-duper cold Saturdays. One of those days that when you breathed out your breath kind of hung frozen in the air like a hunk of smoke and you could walk along and look exactly like a train blowing out big, fat, white puffs of smoke.

It was so cold that if you were stupid enough to go outside your eyes would automatically blink a thousand times all by themselves, probably so the juice inside of them wouldn't freeze up. It was so cold that if you spit, the slob would be an ice cube before it hit the ground. It was about a zillion degrees below zero.

Word pictures create a memorable image of this very cold day.

It was even cold inside our house. We put sweaters and hats and scarves and three pairs of socks on and still were cold. The thermostat was turned all the way up and the furnace was banging and sounding like it was about to blow up but it still felt like Jack Frost had moved in with us.

Directions

Directions tell how to play a game, how to get somewhere, or how to make something. When you write directions, the most important thing to do is to put the steps in order.

Game Directions

The **beginning** tells how many people can play.

The **middle** tells how to play the game.

The **end** tells how to win the game.

Order words show the steps.

Rock, Paper, Scissors

Number of players: 2

How to Play: First make a fist with one hand. Next, shake your fist three times as you say *rock, paper, scissors*. Then do one of these:
  –Keep a fist for *rock*
  –Put two fingers out for *scissors*
  –Put your palm down for *paper*
Finally, look at your hands to see who wins.

Who Wins: Rock beats scissors, scissors beats paper, and paper beats rock. Play again if both players have the same hand position.

Directions to a Place

Direction words tell people which way to go.

Describing words help someone find the correct place.

To get to the theater, turn left out of the parking lot. Go four blocks past the school, to Citrus Street. Turn Right. The theater is on the left. It's a yellow building with a big, white sign.

E-mail

People write e-mail messages for many different reasons—to chat with friends and family, communicate with coworkers, sometimes even to apply for a job. Therefore, they can be as informal as a note left on the fridge or as formal as a business letter—make sure you get the tone right!

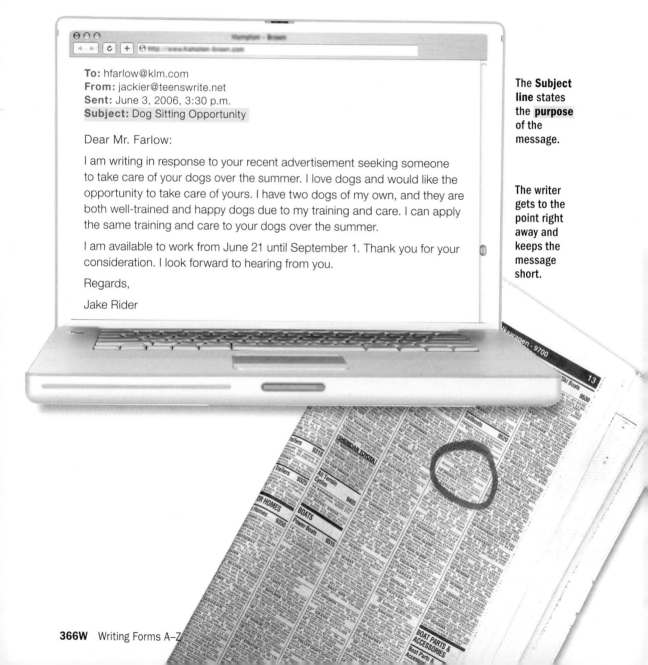

To: hfarlow@klm.com
From: jackier@teenswrite.net
Sent: June 3, 2006, 3:30 p.m.
Subject: Dog Sitting Opportunity

Dear Mr. Farlow:

I am writing in response to your recent advertisement seeking someone to take care of your dogs over the summer. I love dogs and would like the opportunity to take care of yours. I have two dogs of my own, and they are both well-trained and happy dogs due to my training and care. I can apply the same training and care to your dogs over the summer.

I am available to work from June 21 until September 1. Thank you for your consideration. I look forward to hearing from you.

Regards,

Jake Rider

The **Subject line** states the **purpose** of the message.

The writer gets to the point right away and keeps the message short.

Envelope

To send a letter, put it in an **envelope**.

Use **abbreviations** for the names of states.

The **return address** is at the top. That's your address.

The **mailing address** is the address of the person you are writing to.

Ann Gardneer
2397 Casanova Street
Neptune Shores, FL 34744

Electronic Games, Inc.
57821 Sutter Blvd.
New York, NY 10017

Essays

Cause-and-Effect

A cause-and-effect essay tells why something happened.
When you write a cause-and-effect essay, you may focus mainly
on causes or mainly on effects, or you may discuss both.

THE CAR WASH

The introduction in column 1 introduces the topic.

The first section of the body explains the effects the car wash had on the team.

I'm on the Stingrays Softball team. We're a club team made up of girls from different schools in this area.

Last spring our team hoped to go to the club team tournament up in Pleasanton. But there was a big entry fee, plus we needed money for travel and a weekend hotel stay.

Someone suggested we have a car wash to make money. Someone else suggested a bake sale. We decided to do both at the same time, on two weekends.

Family members, coaches, and volunteers helped organize the event and prepare food for it. But we girls did all of the car washing!

WHAT WE GOT, BESIDES MONEY

We had the car wash/bake sale at the side of the grocery store in town. Lots of cars came, so we really had to work hard—and it was hot! It was good exercise, though. It actually made us stronger and fitter.

We worked together and took turns doing different

tasks. This made us feel more like a team, which helped us play better later.

We sacrificed our free time for the car wash, but even before that we hardly ever went out to shop, eat, or see movies. We needed to save up for our trip. This experience made us realize what time and money are really worth.

We all love softball. After all we had to go through, we really appreciated that we got the chance to play it.

The Community Impact

People were generous. Some even paid extra, more than the price of the car wash or the food.

Because of the car wash, more people found out about our team and started coming to our games to support us. The stands were usually packed with fans!

It made us realize how much people care. We wanted to do well for all the fans who supported us, so we tried even harder to win.

I almost forgot. The "event" was a huge success. We made more than enough money for the trip, so we were able to buy some new equipment we badly needed.

We didn't win the tournament, but we came in second, which was amazing for a team just starting out. We had a great season. Now we can't wait for this season to begin. And it all started with a car wash!

The second section explains other effects of the car wash, including the effect on the community.

The conclusion leaves the reader with something to think about.

Comparison-Contrast

A comparison-contrast essay describes how two things are alike and different. You may choose to describe one item completely before you move on the next. Or, you might organize your essay according to the specific points you're comparing.

The introduction names the **two things** being compared.

The body has section heads and point-by-point organization.

Each section covers the main similarities and differences.

RECREATION

TWO CHOICES, NO EXCUSES

We all know we need to exercise. What can we do when school's out? Of course, if the weather's nice, you can always walk your dog, or play tennis or basketball on the outdoor courts at school. In our town, we can go to the Community Center or Teen Center, too. What's the difference, you ask?

INSIDE AND OUT

The Community Center has a large multi-purpose room, which serves as a gym, a dance hall, theater, and banquet room. You can play basketball or table tennis, or take karate, dance, and other classes there. There's another room with a pool table. Outside, there's a playground for younger kids, but older kids can exercise on the equipment, too.

The Teen Center has a music room, and a pool table and table-tennis table in separate rooms.

Outdoors, there's one basketball hoop, a sand volleyball court, and the main feature: a huge skate park.

ATMOSPHERE

All ages are welcome at the community Center, so you never know who you might run into there. Special classes and activities are offered for kids ages 5–12 and senior citizens ages 55 and up.

The Community Center gym

Depending on the activity in the main room, it may be "quiet time" for kids or seniors, there may be music playing for a dance or singing class, or there may be a basketball game or table tennis tournament going on.

In contrast, all the posters, bulletin-board information, games, and activities at the Teen Center are for kids ages 13–18. Music isn't permitted out in the skate park, but teens can share their music in the music room.

WHERE YOU SHOULD GO

The Community Center offers lots of activities, but not all at the same time. If you want to play a game on a wood court, check the schedule for basketball hours, or join the Youth Basketball League.

However, if you're a teen, and you just want to shoot baskets and hang out with kids your age, go to the Teen Center. It is always open after school and on weekends. If you want to skate, it's the *only* place to go.

These **transition words** show a contrast.

The conclusion sums up the major differences to help the reader make a decision.

The skate park is open to all ages.

Persuasive Essay

Writing as a citizen often involves writing to persuade. In a persuasive essay, you try to convince others to agree with your position on an important issue—and to take action.

What position does Mike take in his essay? What arguments does he use to try to convince his readers?

End the Curfew Now

Mike Bozarth

The opening provides background on the issue. States the writer's **position**.

The city officials in San Antonio believe that imposing a curfew on teenagers makes our city a better place. I disagree. Lifting the curfew would help local businesses by encouraging people to visit downtown stores at night. Furthermore, it would help make our city safer and reduce crime. It would also reward the city's hard-working students by allowing them to hang out with their friends at more comfortable times of day. Ending the curfew would improve life in San Antonio.

The body gives **reasons** for the writer's position and provides supporting evidence.

Ending the curfew would benefit our city's economy. Right now, our town is nearly empty at night because there aren't any teenagers around. But if the curfew were lifted, more people would spend time shopping downtown at night. That would help local businesses to grow and encourage stores to stay open longer. Longer store hours, in turn, would lead to better wages and more jobs available for retail workers.

Furthermore, although many people think the curfew reduces crime, it actually doesn't. In fact, since the curfew began last year, vandalism and theft have been on the

A view of San Antonio, Texas, at sunset ▶

rise. Officer Cheryl Williams of the San Antonio Police Department says that most of these crimes occur in quiet areas when no one's around. So, if more people were outside during the evenings, our town would be safer. People would think twice about committing a crime, since more potential witnesses, including teenagers, would be around to report it.

Finally, dropping the curfew would benefit the city's students. Right now, by the time they finish their homework and want to see their friends, it's too late to do anything. Some people say, "Why can't teenagers hang out downtown after school?" The problem with that suggestion is that it's really hot here in Texas. In the daytime, when it's 100 degrees outside and super sunny, people just want to stay in. At night, it's cooler, and the sun isn't hurting your skin. Students should be allowed to enjoy a nighttime social life.

Persuasive essays often include a response to an anticipated objection.

The curfew law penalizes good kids and does nothing to benefit local businesses or to make our city safer. People should write to the mayor and urge her to lift the curfew on teens. It's the right thing to do.

The conclusion Includes a **summary** of the writer's ideas and a **call to action**.

Fable

A fable is a story written to teach a lesson. It often ends with a moral that states the lesson.

The **beginning** tells what the story is about.

The **middle** tells about the event and what the characters do.

The **end** tells what finally happens.

The Wolf and the Lamb

by Aesop

A wolf met a little lamb who had wandered away from his flock. He made up his mind to eat the lamb. But first he decided he would explain to the lamb why he must eat him.

"Lamb," he said, "last year you insulted me by calling me a bad name." "No, I couldn't have," replied the lamb. "I was not even born then." Then the wolf said, "You eat the grass in my pasture." "No, sir," said the lamb. "I haven't yet tasted grass." Then the wolf said, "You drink out of my well." "No," exclaimed the lamb. "I have never drunk water, because my mother's milk is still my only food. It is all I drink."

"Well, I won't go without supper, even though you deny everything I say," said the wolf. And with that, he ate up the lamb.

Moral: Those who are bad will always find a reason to do bad things.

A fable often has **talking animals**.

A fable has a **moral** that tells what you can learn from the story.

Folk Tales and Fairy Tales

Folk Tale

A **folk tale** is a story that people have been telling one another for many years.

Stone Soup

The **characters** in a folk tale often have a problem to solve.

Three hungry men walked into a tiny village one day. Everyone told these travelers that there was no food. Really, the villagers were greedy and didn't want to share with the men.

"Oh well, there is nothing more delicious than a bowl of stone soup," one traveler said.

The **setting** is often a made-up place, long ago.

The villagers thought this was odd but agreed to lend the men a huge soup pot. The men lit a fire, put three stones in the pot with some water, and waited.

A villager looked at the soup and thought, "Ridiculous! No soup is complete without some carrots." He went home, got a bunch of carrots, and put them in the pot.

Another villager looked at the soup and thought, "What that really needs is onions!" So she took a few onions and added them to the soup.

Soon, lots of people brought beef, cabbage, celery, potatoes—a little of everything that makes a soup good.

The **ending** is usually a happy one.

When the stone soup was done and everyone tasted it, they all agreed that they hadn't ever had anything so delicious! And imagine, a soup from stones!

Fairy Tale

A **fairy tale** is a special kind of folk tale. It often has royal characters like princes and princesses, and magical creatures like elves and fairies.

Cinderella

A fairy tale often begins with *Once upon a time.*

Once upon a time, there was a sweet, gentle girl named Cinderella, who wanted to go to the royal ball. Her mean stepmother told her to stay home and scrub the floor while she and her daughters went to the ball. Cinderella wept.

Suddenly, Cinderella's fairy godmother appeared. She waved her magic wand and turned Cinderella's ragged clothes into a sparkling gown and her shoes into glass slippers. She also turned a pumpkin into a coach and mice into horses. Now Cinderella could go to the ball! However, the fairy godmother warned Cinderella that if she wasn't home by midnight, her clothes would change into rags again.

When the prince saw Cinderella, he was overwhelmed by her beauty. All night, he refused to dance with anyone but her. At the stroke of midnight, Cinderella ran away so quickly that she lost a glass slipper, and her clothes turned back into rags. The broken-hearted prince chased her but found only the slipper.

It usually has a happy ending

The next day, the prince asked every woman to try on the tiny slipper. No one could squeeze into it except Cinderella. Then the prince knew that he had found the woman of his dreams. Cinderella and the prince were soon married, and they lived happily ever after.

Greetings

Cards

Is your cousin having a birthday? Is your aunt in the hospital? Do you want to send Kwanzaa greetings to your friend? All of these are reasons to send a **greeting card**.

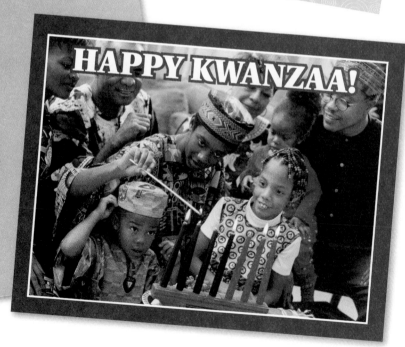

Jeffrey Dibrell
1836 Hamlin Road
Washington, D.C. 20017

Postcards

When you go on a trip, you can send greetings
to a friend. Just write a **postcard**!

June 10, 2003

Dear Marc,

Chicago is amazing! O'Hare
airport is huge—even bigger than
the one in Los Angeles. Can you
believe that the Sears Tower is 110
stories tall? I walked along Lake
Michigan yesterday and found out
why Chicago's nickname is "The
Windy City."

I'm having a great time. I can't
wait to show you my pictures when
I get back.

Your friend,
Felipe

Marc Rountree
347 Driscol Street
Los Angeles, CA 90064

Interview

An interview presents a conversation in question-and-answer format. When you write an interview, prepare your questions beforehand and record carefully the answers of the person you are interviewing.

Molding Troubled Kids into Future Chefs
An Interview with Neil Kleinberg
by Kathy Blake

Neil Kleinberg is the culinary-arts training manager at a tiny, 12-seat, takeout cafe operated by Covenant House, a shelter for runaway teenagers in New York City. Kleinberg says his job at Ezekiel's Cafe involves being father, mother, brother, counselor, teacher, and adviser, as well as a tough boss to the 17- to 21-year-old trainees who work with him.

Starts with background information about the person interviewed

How do you work as executive chef and culinary-arts trainer?

A place this small doesn't need an executive chef. My real job is teaching. Ezekiel's Cafe exists to give kids who live at Covenant House hands-on training in food service so they can get good jobs. Of course, when you say Covenant House, you know that these are kids with troubled pasts who need a lot of training in life skills, not just job skills. We screen the kids to try to get the ones who really have the desire to work in the industry, because to work this hard takes a lot of commitment.

When did you know you wanted to cook?

I always wanted to be a chef, and this was before it was trendy. When I was a kid growing up in Brooklyn, I'd go to Lundy's, which was the largest restaurant in the world at one time, and I'd think, "I want to be the chef here someday." That's why I tell the kids to be careful what they wish for! I got my wish, and it was really hard work. We did 1,500 dinners on Saturday nights. I essentially gave up my life for two years.

Was that immediately before you went to Ezekiel's?

Yes. I'd worked really hard my whole career; and when I left Lundy's, I needed some soul-searching time. So I took about a month and a half off and traveled to Australia, Thailand and Europe. When I got back, I wanted to teach but I still wanted to cook. I knew I'd always been good at directing people.

Lists the interviewer's questions and the interviewee's responses

Invitation

To invite people to come to a party or other special event, send them an invitation!

Tells **what** the event is all about.

COME TO A PARTY!

Shhh!
It's a Surprise Birthday Party!

Tells **when** and **where** the event will take place.

For: Alma

Date: Saturday, March 19

Time: 3 p.m. (Don't be late, please.)

Place: 263 Newland Street

R.S.V.P: 555-8301 (Ask for Casandra, not Alma.)

Job Application

Many companies ask job candidates to fill out applications before they can be considered for a position. When you fill out a job application, make sure that the information is clear, accurate, and easy to read.

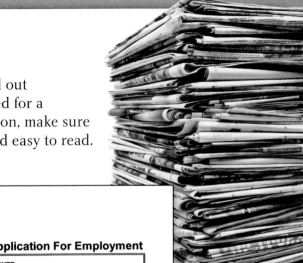

Application For Employment

WE ARE AN EQUAL OPPORTUNITY EMPLOYER

We consider applicants for all positions without regard to race, color, religion, sex, national origin, age, marital or veteran status, the presence of a non-job related medical condition or handicap, or any other legally protected status.

(PLEASE PRINT)

Date of Application: 5/15/07

Position(s) Applied For: Newspaper Delivery Person

Name: Torres | Maria | A.
Last Name | First Name | Middle Name

Address: 17 Redwood Rd. | Baxter | IA | 50028
Number and Street | City | State | Zip Code

Phone Numbers: (641)555-8384 | Social Security Number: 200/00/0000
Home | Cell | Other

Provides personal information

If you are under 18, can you provide required proof of your eligibility to work? — ☑ Yes ○ No

Have you ever filed an application with us before? — ○ Yes ☑ No
If yes, give date

Have you ever been employed with us before? — ○ Yes ☑ No
If yes, give date

Are you currently employed? — ☑ Yes ○ No

May we contact your present employer? — ☑ Yes ○ No

Are you prevented from lawfully becoming employed in this country because of Visa or Immigration Status? — ○ Yes ☑ No
(Proof of citizenship or immigration status will be required upon employment.)

On what date would you be available for work? 6/21/07

Are you available to work: ☑ Full Time ○ Part Time ○ Shift Work ○ Temporary

Have you been convicted of a crime? *(Conviction will not necessarily disqualify an applicant from employment.)* — ○ Yes ☑ No
If yes, please explain:

EDUCATION:

	Elementary	High School	College/University	Graduate
School Name and Location	Baxter Elementary	Baxter High School	N/A	
Years Completed	K-8	9-11		
Diploma/Degree	N/A	N/A		

Writes "N/A" in any section that does not apply

EMPLOYMENT EXPERIENCE: Start with your present or last job. Include job-related military service assignments and volunteer activities. You may exclude organizations which indicate race, color, religion, gender, national origin, handicap or other protected status.

Employer: Baxter Tutoring Center | Phone Number (641)555-1240

Address/City/State/Zip: 2 W. Klondike Ave., Baxter, IA 50028

Job Title: Tutor | Supervisor: Robin Hedding

Duties: Tutor elementary-school students in math and science

Dates of Employment: 9/05—present | Hourly Rate/Salary: $6/hr

Reason for Leaving: Tutoring center is closed from June through September.

Tells about past work experience

Letters

Friendly

In a friendly letter, you write to someone you know, using an informal tone. A friendly letter often tells about recent events in the writer's life.

August 31, 2007

Dear Amber,

How are you? My family and I just got back from our vacation late last night. We had such a great time out west. It was like nothing I had ever seen before.

We traveled all over Colorado and Arizona. First we went to a National Park near the Rocky Mountains in Colorado. We hiked all day until I thought my legs were going to fall off. I was really surprised by how many deer we saw along the trails. The mountains themselves were incredibly beautiful. Some of them are over 12,000 feet high!

Believe it or not, Arizona was even more amazing. We went to see the Grand Canyon. I'd seen pictures of it before, but looking at pictures is nothing like seeing it in person. The pictures don't show all the different colors in the rocks and soil, and they definitely don't show how huge the canyon really is. It's truly an awesome sight.

Write to me and tell me about your summer. Hopefully we can get together sometime before school starts.

Your "best pal,"
Kelsey

Include the date. It is not necessary to include your address.

Tell your news in an informal tone.

Use an affectionate closing.

Inquiry/Request

When you write a letter of inquiry or request, you ask for specific favors, materials, or information. Use business-letter format.

242 Crescent Ln.
Oceanside, CA 91147
July 14, 2008

Mr. Nelson Tatupu
Recreation Dept.
Fallbrook City Hall
27 Leatherneck St.
Fallbrook, CA 92648

Dear Mr. Tatupu:

    I am writing to request information about your city's Youth Football team, the Rebels. I will be moving to Fallbrook soon, and I have heard that your community has an excellent Youth Football program. I would like to learn more about it.

    Please send me more information about the program, including age and weight requirements for players. Please also send me an application to join the team.

    Thank you very much for your time. I look forward to hearing from you.

Sincerely,

Robert Truitt

Robert Truitt

Includes your address as well as the date

States the reason for writing

Requests specific information or materials

Closes formally with full signature

Praise

A letter of praise expresses appreciation for the actions of a person. When you write to offer praise, be specific about why you are pleased.

37 Scotson Road
Parkville, OR 97086
October 6, 2007

Mr. Fred Simms
Parkville Youth Athletic League
1100 Carey Lane
Parkville, OR 97086

Dear Coach Simms:

Thank you so much for your patience, caring, and hard work this summer. Your efforts have made my teammates and me into better players and made this year's baseball season one to remember.

When the season started, most of us didn't know each other and we didn't work together very well. In only a few weeks, you brought us together and taught us how to play as a team. Under your coaching, my skills greatly improved. Even when I made a bad play in the field, you didn't get upset. Instead, you taught me how I could learn from my mistakes and do better next time.

Thanks again for making this baseball season so memorable. I can't wait to play on your team again next year!

Sincerely,
Tony Lopez
Tony Lopez

Tells why the person mattered to the writer

Provides specific details

Problem-Solving

Consumers write problem-solving letters to inform a company or organization about a problem. State your complaint and explain how the problem can be solved.

714 Almond Road
Fresno, CA 93707
August 1, 2007

Mr. Gary Zimmer, Chairman
Green Grass Teen Craft Fair Committee
43 Howard Avenue
Fresno, CA 93707

Dear Mr. Zimmer:

On June 23, 2006, I paid to reserve a table to sell my handmade jewelry at the upcoming Green Grass Teen Craft Fair. However, I recently read on your website that the date of the fair has been moved forward a week. Unfortunately, I will be out of town during the festival's new date, and I will not be able to attend.

I am enclosing a copy of my approved reservation application and my receipt. I would like you to send me a refund for the price of my reservation.

Thank you for your time and attention. Please feel free to call me at 555-6784 with any questions.

Sincerely,

Beth Vaden
Beth Vaden

Politely states the complaint

Tells how the writer wants the problem resolved

Often includes contact information

Literary Response

A response to literature is similar to a literary critique, but it focuses more on the writer's personal, individual reactions to the work. You still need to support your response with concrete details from the text.

When I Was Puerto Rican

by Esmeralda Santiago

Reviewed by Jennifer K.

States opinion and summarizes the book

This is a delightfully woven story of immense passion and unconquerable spirit. In this extraordinary autobiography, Santiago, an immigrant to New York from rural Puerto Rico, tells the story of her trials and triumphs, defeats and heartaches, in vivid detail.

Santiago grew up in what her *mami* calls "savage" conditions, dutifully obeying her parents as they constantly moved. Her greatest relocation occurred when a "metal bird" flew her, her mother, and two of her siblings to the rough city of New York. . . .

Using words as her medium, Santiago paints a beautiful picture of her life. I smelled the spices and herbs emanating from the special Puerto Rican dishes her *mami* prepared. Mesmerized, I watched as her *abuela* delicately stitched her needlework. . . . Santiago writes with such clarity and fierceness that it is impossible for any person not to see, feel, and understand what she went through in her remarkable journey.

Santiago's unique style is easy to follow. When I read the book, I was immediately hooked and could not stop until I read the last word. The stories are interesting and full of insight. Santiago addresses fears and trials of all people. I especially related to her conflicts with her cultural identity. Anyone who has lived in between two cultures can relate to her story. Santiago wrote, "When I returned to Puerto Rico after living in New York for seven years, I was told I was no longer Puerto Rican. . . . In writing the book I wanted to get back to that feeling of Puertoricanness I had before I came here. Its title reflects who I was then, and asks, who am I today?"

Santiago's book provides a sense of hope. The narrator is transformed from a confused and frightened child into a spirited woman full of courage and hope. Her success in life—acceptance into New York City's High School of Performing Arts and graduating from Harvard with highest honors—proves she is capable of achieving her dreams.

Santiago's strong will and courage are evident throughout her story. *When I Was Puerto Rican* describes the remarkable journey that her life has been.

Describes the writer's emotional response to the book

Myth

A **myth** is a very old story. It usually explains something about the world or teaches a lesson. Most myths are about gods or other super-human characters, or about people who try to act like gods.

DAEDALUS and ICARUS

Most cultures have myths. Many myths come from Greek culture.

A long time ago in Greece, there lived an inventor named Daedalus. An angry king had imprisoned Daedalus and his young son, Icarus, on an island.

Daedalus planned to escape by flying away. He used melted wax and bird feathers to make bird wings. Daedalus practiced flying and then taught Icarus how to fly.

Before they took off, Daedalus warned Icarus, "No one has ever done what we are about to do. But do not feel too proud as you soar. If you fly too high, the sun will melt your wings."

This myth is about humans who give themselves god-like powers.

Finally, father and son took off. They flew over the island. People thought they were gods. Icarus became so excited and proud that he headed up into the brilliant sun.

"No, Icarus!" his father cried. But Icarus was too far away. The feathers on his wings melted off, and he plunged into the dark ocean. Daedalus couldn't save him. Later, Daedalus buried his son and called the place Icaria in his memory.

A myth can tell how a place got its name.

Newspaper

Editorial

An editorial is a newspaper or magazine article that is written to persuade people to believe the same way you do. When you write an editorial, tell how you feel about something. That's your opinion. Give facts to support your opinion.

February 6, 2008

Save the Gentle Manatees

Opinions about the subject are in the first paragraph.

Next, facts expand on the opinion.

Our manatees need protection from speeding boats. If we don't keep boat speeds slow, more and more of these gentle beasts will die.

A few members of the City Council want to pass a law that will increase boat speeds in some waterways where manatees live. When boats go too fast, the manatees can't get out of the way of the dangerous boat propellers in time.

We need to tell the City Council that saving the manatees is important to us. Increasing boat speeds is not. You can take action no matter where you live. Call, write, fax, or e-mail City Council members. Ask them to support protection for manatees and their home, and to *keep existing slow speed zones in our waters*! Any type of letter or call helps!

The end tells what people can do to help, and states your opinion again.

News Article

A news article tells about a recent event. It covers the "5 Ws": who, what, where, when, and why. A news article uses an "inverted pyramid" structure: it states the main points in the beginning, and then provides less important details in later paragraphs.

States the main point

Tells what happened and when

Tells where and who might be affected

Often connects the story to a broader subject

May include photos and captions

Tropical Storm Florence Forms in Atlantic

Weather system intensifies but poses no immediate threat to land

MIAMI, FL—Tropical Storm Florence formed today in the open Atlantic, becoming the sixth named storm of the 2006 hurricane season.

Florence had top sustained winds near 40 mph, 1 mph over the 39 mph threshold for a tropical storm, and it was expected to slowly intensify over the next few days, according to the National Hurricane Center.

Its tropical storm force winds extended 115 miles from its center, but posed no immediate threat to land.

At 11 a.m., the storm was centered 935 miles east of the Lesser Antilles and was moving west at about 12 mph, forecasters said.

Florence follows Tropical Storm Ernesto, which was briefly the season's first hurricane before hitting Florida and North Caro-lina last week as a tropical storm.

At least nine deaths have been attributed to Ernesto, and the aftereffects were still being felt early today. About 75,000 people remained without power in New York's Westchester County.

Last year's Atlantic storm season set a record with 28 named storms and 15 hurricanes, including Katrina, which devastated the Louisiana and Mississippi coasts.

Radar image of hurricane approaching west coast of Florida

Personal Narrative

When you write a personal narrative, you tell a story about something that happened to you. Because the story is about you, you'll use the words *I*, *me*, and *my* a lot.

Urff

The **beginning** tells what the event was.

One afternoon, two summers ago, I was walking on the beach. I was looking out at the bay, daydreaming.

Suddenly, something pushed me on my chest, and I fell back a step. A big, hairy dog had just put wet paw prints on my shirt! "Urff!" he barked playfully. Dogs are always romping on the beach. I figured his owner was nearby. I petted the dog. Then I started to walk again.

The writer tells her **feelings** about the event.

The **middle** gives details about the event.

After a few steps, I noticed the dog was walking beside me. "Go on, now," I said. I tried to gently shoo him away with my hand. I looked around for his owner, but no one seemed to be calling for him.

This happened a couple more times, but he kept following me. He followed me as I left the beach and walked home. He followed me into my house and room, where he slept that night by my bed.

The writer gives **details** that describe what happens.

The **end** tells what finally happened.

The next day, my mom made me take him to the shelter. I checked on him after a month. No one had claimed him. So I took him home. (Mom said, "OK," after much begging by me.) And Urff has been my best friend ever since.

Play

A play is a story that is acted on stage. Real people, or actors, pretend to be characters in the story.

The actors perform the play *Annie* **on stage**.

The **audience** watches the play in a **theater**.

The author of a play is called a **playwright**. The playwright writes the script.

The actor's part in a play is called a **role**.
The girl is performing the role of Annie.

The actors wear different **costumes** to look like their characters. **Props**, or objects on stage, help the action seem more real.

This **scene**, or part of the play, takes place in the city. The **scenery** shows what this place looks like. The scenery can change between scenes.

Play, continued

You can turn any story into a play. Follow these steps.

1. Start with a story. Make one up or choose one from a book.

THE LEGEND
OF THE
CHINESE ZODIAC

In ancient times, the Jade Emperor wanted to name each year in the twelve-year cycle after an animal. He couldn't decide which animals to honor, however. He invited all the animals on earth to participate in a race. The first twelve to finish the race would each have a year named for them. The rat won the race; the ox was second. The tiger, rabbit, dragon, snake, horse, sheep, monkey, rooster, dog, and boar were the next ten animals to cross the finish line. The Jade Emperor named a year for the animals in the order they finished.

2. Turn the story into a script. The script names the characters and the setting. It describes what the characters say and do.

Write a title and act number.

ACT TWO

The Race

List all the characters.

CHARACTERS: *the Jade Emperor, rat, ox, tiger, rabbit, dragon, snake, horse, sheep, monkey, rooster, dog, boar*

Tell about the setting.

SETTING: Long ago, in front of the Jade Emperor's palace. There is a starting line on the ground. The Jade Emperor is telling all the animals the rules of the race.

JADE EMPEROR *(loudly, to get everyone's attention):* Listen! Listen! We are going to start the race soon. First, I want to explain the course and the rules.

BOAR *(raising his hand):* Will we be allowed to stop for water along the way?

JADE EMPEROR: *Please let me tell you the rules of the whole race before you ask questions. (pointing at the line on the ground)* This is the starting line. You must have all of your toes behind this line.

SNAKE *(raising his tail):* What if you don't have toes?

JADE EMPEROR *(Surprised):* Good point.

Name each character and write the dialogue, or the words the characters say.

Use stage directions to tell how the characters should say lines or move around.

3. Perform the play. Choose people to play the characters. Have them use script to practice. Then put on the play.

Poetry

Rhymed Verse

Rhymed verse follows a set rhyme scheme
and often uses a regular rhythm as well.

Stopping By Woods on a Snowy Evening

by Robert Frost

Whose woods these are I think I know.	*a*
His house is in the village, though;	*a*
He will not see me stopping here	*b*
To watch his woods fill up with snow.	*a*
My little horse must think it queer	*b*
To stop without a farmhouse near	*b*
Between the woods and frozen lake	*c*
The darkest evening of the year.	*b*
He gives his harness bells a shake	*c*
To ask if there is some mistake.	*c*
The only other sound's the sweep	*d*
Of easy wind and downy flake.	*c*
The woods are lovely, dark, and deep,	*d*
But I have promises to keep,	*d*
And miles to go before I sleep,	*d*
And miles to go before I sleep.	*d*

This poem has an interesting rhyme pattern, shown by the letters.

Free Verse

Free verse has no fixed rhythm and uses irregular rhyme or no rhyme at all. However, free verse often includes other poetic devices, such as repetition, imagery, or figurative language.

MOTHER

by Maya Angelou

During the years when you knew nothing
And I knew everything, I loved you still.
Condescendingly of course,
From my high perch
Of teenage wisdom.
I grew older and
Was stunned to find
How much knowledge you had gleaned
And so quickly.

Haiku

A haiku is a brief poem that focuses on a single image or emotion. The haiku form originated in Japan and often describes images found in nature. The form traditionally uses three lines with five, seven, and five syllables, respectively.

> by the noonflower
> a rice-pounder cools himself:
> a sight so moving
>
> —*Bashō*

> the cathedral bell
> is shaking a few snowflakes
> from the morning air
>
> —*Nicholas Virgilio*

> heat before the storm:
> a fly disturbs the quiet
> of the empty store
>
> —*Nicholas Virgilio*

> A bitter morning:
> sparrows sitting together
> without any necks.
>
> —*James Hackett*

Concrete Poem

A concrete poem is written so the words make a picture of what they are describing.

(a poem to be read from the bottom up)

this great oak

into the coming night

its capillary ends

its garbled limbs

against the hazy light

now stretches

to stand winter and the wind

from wells far underground

with strength

girthed itself

upon a trunk

upon a branch

upon a sprig

upon a leaf

spring by spring

a century ago

from under land

this tree unrolled

Simple as a flower

–Dawn L. Watkins

Procedure

A procedure is a list of steps that must be followed to complete a task. When you write a procedure, clearly describe, in order, what needs to be done.

Headings help organize the instructions.

Gives clear, specific, step-by-step instructions

PROCEDURE FOR HOUSE SITTER

When Entering

Open door and close it quickly. Rufus will try to escape if the door is left open!

In the Morning

1. Give Rufus fresh water and dry kibble.
2. Play with Rufus and let him outside for $\frac{1}{2}$ hour.
3. Water plants on kitchen windowsill.
4. Feed fish with flakes next to tank.
5. Bring in the morning's newspaper and leave on kitchen table.

In the Afternoon

1. Bring in the day's mail and leave on kitchen table.
2. Feed Rufus $\frac{1}{2}$ can of dog food.
3. Play with Rufus and walk him for at least 20 minutes.
4. Check the tomato plants and place any ripe tomatoes on the kitchen table.

When Leaving

1. Close windows.
2. Turn off lights and fans.
3. Don't forget to lock the door and deadbolt.

Emergency Phone Numbers

Mr. & Mrs. Rhoades (cell): (212) 555-7834

Dr. Sternberg (vet): (212) 555-4700
Annandale Police Dept.: (212) 555-2299

Story

Writers use their imaginations and make up different types of stories to entertain their readers. They decide where a story will happen, who will be in it, and what will happen.

Parts of a Story

Every story happens in a place at some time. That place and time are called the **setting**.

The people or animals in a story are called the **characters**. In most stories, the characters speak. Their words are called **dialogue**.

Saturday morning in our apartment

Come by this afternoon to see if you have won.

woman from the bike store

Anything is possible, but don't count on winning the bike, Alex.

Alex and his mom

The things that happen in a story are the events. The order, or **sequence of events**, is called the **plot**.

1. Mom filled out a form for the bike drawing.

BIKES

OPEN

2. We went to the bike store.

MOUNTAIN BIKE WINNER
Alex Sanchez

3. I saw a huge sign that said I won!

Realistic Fiction

Some stories have characters that seem like people you know. They happen in a place that seems real. These stories are called realistic fiction because they tell about something that could happen in real life.

Another Saturday Morning

The **characters** are like people you know.

Mom and I were eating breakfast Saturday morning when a woman knocked on the door to our apartment.

The **setting** is in a time and a place you know.

"Hello," she said. "I'm from Bikes and Stuff. We're having a drawing for a mountain bike. Would you be interested in signing up?" Mom agreed and filled out a form for me.

The events in the **plot** could really happen.

"Come by this afternoon to see if you have won," the woman said.

"Anything is possible, but don't count on winning the bike, Alex," Mom said when the woman left.

The **dialogue** sounds real.

So I forgot all about the bike and started reading my new book. Before I knew it, Mom came in the room and said it was time to go to the bike store.

When I walked in, the first thing I saw was a huge sign that said: *Mountain bike winner: Alex Sanchez!* I couldn't believe it!

They put my name and photograph in the newspaper in an ad for Bikes and Stuff. That was the day I learned anything is possible on a Saturday morning.

Historical Fiction

Historical Fiction is a story that takes place in the past during a certain time in history. Some of the characters may be real people, and some of the events really happened. Even so, the story is fiction because the writer made it up.

January 13, 1778

The characters act and talk like the people in that time did.

Today when we returned the laundry to the army headquarters, I was astounded to see only General Washington in the parlor, no other officers. I know not where Bill Lee was. The General was sharpening his quill with his penknife. He looked up at us and smiled.

"Thank you, Abigail. Thank you, Elisabeth," he said.

I curtsied, unable to speak. How did he know our names?

He looked at us with kind eyes—they're gray-blue—then he returned to his pen and paper. Mrs. Hewes says Mr. Washington writes at least fifteen letters a day, mostly to Congress. He is pleading for food, clothing, and other supplies for the soldiers, she told us.

It can have **real people** and **made up characters** who lived during that time.

Fantasy

A fantasy is a story that tells about events that couldn't possibly happen in real life. Here is part of a fantasy about some children playing a very unusual board game.

JUMANJI | Chris Van Allsburg   15

At home, the children spread the game out on a card table. It looked very much like the games they already had.

"Here," said Judy, handing her brother the dice, "you go first."

Peter casually dropped the dice from his hand.

"Seven," said Judy.

Peter moved his piece to the seventh square.

"'Lion attacks, move back two spaces,'" read Judy.

"Gosh, how exciting," said Peter, in a very unexcited voice. As he reached for his piece he looked up at his sister. She had a look of absolute horror on her face.

"Peter," she whispered, "turn around very, very slowly."

The boy turned in his chair. He couldn't believe his eyes. Lying on the piano was a lion, staring at Peter and licking his lips. The lion roared so loud it knocked Peter right off his chair. The big cat jumped to the floor. Peter was up on his feet, running through the house with the lion a whisker's length behind. He ran upstairs and dove under a bed. The lion tried to squeeze under, but got his head stuck. Peter scrambled out, ran from the bedroom, and slammed the door behind him. He stood in the hall with Judy, gasping for breath.

"I don't think," said Peter in between gasps of air, "that I want . . . to play . . . this game . . . anymore."

"But we have to," said Judy as she helped Peter back downstairs. "I'm sure that's what the instructions mean. The lion won't go away until one of us wins the game."

The **characters** can be like real people.

Some of the **events** could never happen in real life.

Tall Tale

A **tall tale** is a story told just for fun. It has lots of exaggerated details. When the details are exaggerated, they make the story impossible to believe.

From *Paul Bunyan* by Steven Kellogg

The main character has special powers or great strength and solves a problem in an unusual or exaggerated way.

Paul's next job was to clear the heavily forested Midwest. He hired armies of extra woodsmen and built enormous new bunkhouses. The men sailed up to bed in balloons and parachuted down to breakfast in the mornings.

Unfortunately the cooks couldn't flip flapjacks fast enough to satisfy all of the newcomers.

To solve the muddle, Paul built a colossal flapjack griddle.

The surface was greased by kitchen helpers with slabs of bacon laced to their feet.

Every time the hot griddle was flooded with batter, it blasted a delicious flapjack high about the clouds. Usually the flapjacks landed neatly beside the griddle, but sometimes they were a bit off target.

Paul took a few days off to dig the St. Lawrence River and the Great Lakes so that barges of Vermont maple syrup could be brought to camp.

Fueled by the powerful mixture of flapjacks and syrup, the men leveled the Great Plains and shaved the slopes of the Rocky Mountains.

Thank-you Note

A **thank-you** note thanks someone for doing something or for giving you a gift. It's a lot like a friendly letter.

The **date** is at the top.

The **greeting** comes next.

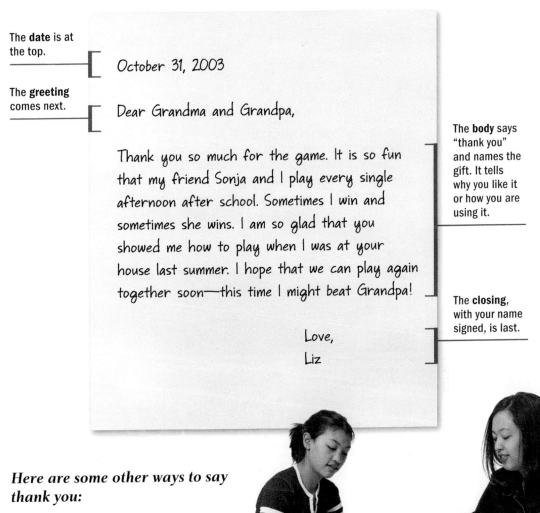

October 31, 2003

Dear Grandma and Grandpa,

Thank you so much for the game. It is so fun that my friend Sonja and I play every single afternoon after school. Sometimes I win and sometimes she wins. I am so glad that you showed me how to play when I was at your house last summer. I hope that we can play again together soon—this time I might beat Grandpa!

Love,
Liz

The **body** says "thank you" and names the gift. It tells why you like it or how you are using it.

The **closing**, with your name signed, is last.

Here are some other ways to say thank you:

Many thanks...

I really appreciate...

Thanks a million...

You are so thoughtful...

I'm so grateful...

Web Site

A Web site can be personal or professional and can be about any subject. Web sites often include images, sound files, video, and links to related pages or sites.

As a Web-site "writer" you have to think "in time."
What happens when you click a link?
How do you get back "home" after listening to a song?

Workplace and Consumer Resources

Instruction Manual

Most products come with directions, often in the form of an **instruction manual**, or booklet. The instruction manual usually describes the product's parts and features and tells how to use the product.

Some products, especially more complicated ones, come with two sets of instructions. A short **quick-start guide** may give you the most essential information, so you can start using the product and its basic features right away. The quick-start guide may be as short as a single page (sometimes a big page!).

The complete instruction manual is sometimes called a **user manual**. A good instruction manual covers everything you might want to know about the product, both right away and later on.

CONTENTS

1: LightningStar 3 Parts and Features
3: Setting Up Your LightningStar 3
4: Loading and Playing Games
7: Using the Controller: Basics
9: Using the Controller: Advanced Play
11: Multiplayer Games
13: Online Play
15: Wireless Play (requires accessories sold separately)
16: Troubleshooting
18: Important Warnings and Safeguards
Back Cover: Customer Support

LIGHTNING STAR
GAME SYSTEM
③

QUICK-START GUIDE

Set-Up

IIn order to start the LightningStar game system, first insert the accompanying cd-rom into your computer. The program will automatically install the necessary software onto your computer. Follow the steps in the Installation Wizard. Your system may need some additional support software to effectively run your LightningStar game system. If this is the case, the system will automatically link you to the site to download the appropriate software for free, as long as you have an active internet connection.

Once you have completed the steps, you will be ready to calibrate, or set up, your LightningStar joystick. Directions on how to calibrate your joystick will follow installation.

Basic Play

LightningStar is a game in which you will explore various solar systems to hunt for life on other planets. Once life is located, you will help the civilizations move forward by helping them develop new tools and methods. For example, in the solar system for Star X587, the planet Zevob has a population that has not yet discovered farming. Your task is to teach the Zevobians about farming, as well as to help the population develop tools to stop the invading Nostrarians who are from a nearby planet.

Play continues until populations from all of the planets under your supervision have developed useful tools and are no longer at war with others.

Tips

The following tips will help you have the most successful journey through your stars and planets:
- Use the tutorial to walk you through your first planet encounter.
- You can always ask the planet guide to walk you through a difficult task.
- You must solve the problems of the planet you are on before you can travel to another planet or solar system.

- Multiple planets in a solar system may have life. Be sure to check all of the planets before moving to the next solar system.

Troubleshooting Checklist

LightningStar game system is a quick-installation game system. If you are unable to start or control your game system, check the following:
- Make sure that the joystick is plugged into an active USB port and is turned on.
- Check that the system successfully installed missing software components during the installation process. To ensure this has been done properly, re-install the CD-ROM and go through the installation process once more. If the system sends you an error message for any necessary software, check if your computer has the correct operating system needed to play LightningStar.
- Be sure to calibrate your joystick and set the various controls so that you know what each button does. Improperly calibrated joysticks can have control problems during a game.
- For more troubleshooting help, please visit our Web site at www.lightningstargame.com or call us at 1-800-555-3939.

Workplace and Consumer Resources, continued

Warranty

When you buy a product, you hope it will keep working the way it's supposed to. But what if it doesn't? Most products come with a written **warranty** that states what the manufacturer will do if something goes wrong. It's a good idea to check out the warranty before you buy the product, so you'll know what kind of protection you're getting.

A warranty will usually spell out the following:

• What is (and is not) covered

• How long the warranty period lasts

• What the consumer needs to do to take advantage of the warranty.

USER MANUAL

LIMITED WARRANTY FOR THE LIGHTNINGSTAR GAME SYSTEM

LightningStar warrants to the original purchaser that the LightningStar 3 game system shall be free of defects in material and workmanship for a period of one (1) year from the original date of purchase (the "Warranty Period"). LightningStar will, at its sole discretion, repair or replace a defective system returned during the warranty period in accordance with the instructions below. No other warranty is expressed or implied.

Tells what the warranty covers and how long the warranty period lasts

This warranty shall not apply if the game system has been damaged, misused, or altered after purchase. This warranty does not cover accessories purchased separately.

Tells what is *not* covered

To arrange for service under this warranty, visit the Customer Service section of our website or call the toll-free number listed in the User Manual. You will need to have the product serial number available when you contact us. You will also need a copy of your original purchase receipt when you send the system in for repair. You are responsible for shipping charges to our repair facility. LightningStar is not responsible for units lost or damaged in transit to or from our repair facility.

Tells what to do if you need to use the warranty

Employment Advertisements

When it's time to get your first job, an important source of information for you will be the **Classified** section of your local newspaper. Employers place advertisements for workers they need to hire in this section. By reading an **employment advertisement** carefully, you can find out details about the job, including: hours, tasks, qualifications, and how to apply. Look for each of these pieces of information in the ad below.

Retail Sales

Out of This World gift shop seeks (P/T) person (eves and weekends) to assist customers as they browse and buy. Our one-of-a kind shop offers a wide range of space-oriented items, and we seek someone who is enthusiastic about our products. Good math skills, friendly personality, and dependability required. Min. wage with attractive sales bonus. Apply in person at City Mall, Saturdays (9:00 a.m.–noon).

Most advertisers use standard abbreviations. *P/T* stands for *part-time*.

Employment Contract

Once you are hired for a job, you might be asked to sign an **employment contract**. This is a legal document, so you will want to read it very carefully before you sign it. The purpose of an employment contract is to ensure that you and your employer agree on the terms of your employment. It usually states when your employment begins, what the expectations are for you on the job, what your starting pay will be, and what special benefits (such as paid vacation) you will receive. A sample is provided below.

EMPLOYMENT AGREEMENT

This Employment Agreement (hereinafter "Agreement") is entered into on December 5, 2008, by and between The Daily Herald (The "Employer") and Starry Jackson (The "Employee")

Employer and Employee each agree with the other as follows:

1. **EMPLOYMENT** Employer has agreed to employ Employee for the position of Newspaper Delivery Person, and Employee has agreed to accept such employment. Employee's duties shall include: collating and delivering papers and collecting payment from customers.

2. **TERM** The term of this Agreement shall begin December 6, 2008, and shall continue until terminated in accordance with the terms set forth below.

3. **COMPENSATION** For services provided, Employer shall employ Employee at a rate of $6.55/hour. The Employee shall be paid weekly. The remuneration is subject to all required withholdings, paid in accordance with Employer's regular payroll policies and procedures.

4. **PROBATION** The probationary period is 3 months.

5. **VACATION** Vacation time can be taken at the employee's discretion, with notice to The Daily Herald.

6. **HOURS OF WORK** The Employee agrees that the working hours are flexible with a minimum of 15 hours per week.

7. **CONDUCT**   Employee agrees that during the time of employment with Employer, the Employee shall adhere to all rules, regulations, and policies established by the Employer for the conduct of its employees. Employee agrees to devote his/her full time, attention, and energies to the business of the Employer.

8. **TERMINATION**   The employment of the Employee by the Employer may be terminated by either the Employer or the Employee upon the giving of 14 days prior written notice to the other party. The employment of the Employee by the Employer may be immediately terminated upon the occurrence of any of the following events:

   a. In the event the Employee shall willfully and continuously fail or refuse to comply with the standards, rules, regulations, and policies established by the Employer.

   b. In the event the Employee shall be guilty of fraud, dishonesty, or any other misconduct in the performance of the Employee's duties on behalf of the Employer.

   c. In the event the Employee shall fail to perform any provision of this Agreement to be performed by the Employee.

9. **GOVERNANCE**   This Agreement shall be governed by the Laws of the State of Florida. The parties hereby indicate by their signatures below that they have read and agree with the terms and conditions of this Agreement in its entirety.

Employer:

_____
Signature

_____
Name/Title

_____
Date

Employee:

_____
Signature

_____
Printed Name

_____
Date

ONE OF THE HARDEST PARTS of writing is organizing your ideas. You can use graphic organizers and idea organizers to plan and organize what you are going to write. Idea organizers can help you plan how to present your ideas. They help the reader (and the writer—you!) follow your thinking process. You can use graphic organizers to narrow your writing topic or to remember the sequence of your ideas before writing.

Find out more about the different kinds of graphic organizers and idea organizers.

Writing ORGANIZERS

Logical Order

Chronological Order

Spatial Order

Showing Causes and Effects

Showing Comparisons

Showing Goals and Outcomes

Showing Problems and Solutions

Showing Your Position

Idea Organizers

Writing Organizers

Logical Order

Logical order makes the most sense when you want to group ideas that have something in common, or you want to organize them by importance.

Topic and Main Idea Diagram

A diagram like this can help you plan the focus for each paragraph in an essay.

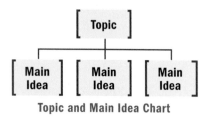

Topic and Main Idea Chart

Main Idea and Detail Diagrams

For each paragraph in the essay, try one of these diagrams to plan the details you'll include.

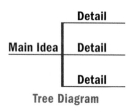

Tree Diagram

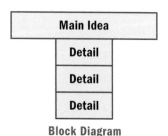

Block Diagram

Category Chart

Try sorting information into groups or categories.

Carlos and Me

Category

Helped me	Caused me problems
helped me pass math class	was rude to my parents
convinced me to try out for the football team	never shows up on time
lent me money to buy concert tickets	went to the concert with someone else

Example

Category Chart

Hypothesis-and-Results Chart

You could use a chart like this to explain the results of a survey.

Question:	Hypothesis:
What percentage of teens at Washington High School sometimes lie to their best friends?	Most teenagers at Washington High lie to their best friends occasionally.
	Data:
	50 teens surveyed 30 have lied about minor things (60%) 5 have lied about something important (10%) 15 always tell their best friends the truth (30%)
Conclusions:	**Observations:**
70% of teens sometimes lie to their best friends.	Most teens will not lie to their best friends about something important.

Hypothesis-and-Results Chart

Outline

You can also use an outline to help you organize your ideas logically. List the main ideas and supporting details using roman numerals, letters, and numbers.

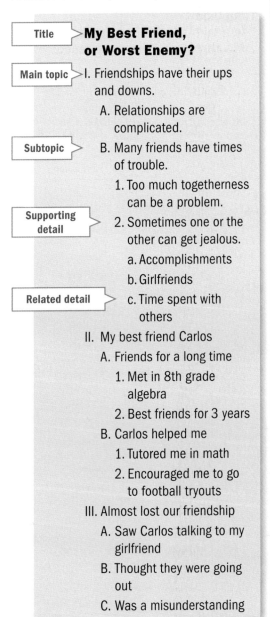

Title > **My Best Friend, or Worst Enemy?**

Main topic > I. Friendships have their ups and downs.

   A. Relationships are complicated.

Subtopic > B. Many friends have times of trouble.

     1. Too much togetherness can be a problem.

Supporting detail >   2. Sometimes one or the other can get jealous.

       a. Accomplishments

       b. Girlfriends

Related detail >   c. Time spent with others

II. My best friend Carlos

   A. Friends for a long time

     1. Met in 8th grade algebra

     2. Best friends for 3 years

   B. Carlos helped me

     1. Tutored me in math

     2. Encouraged me to go to football tryouts

III. Almost lost our friendship

   A. Saw Carlos talking to my girlfriend

   B. Thought they were going out

   C. Was a misunderstanding

Outline

Order-of-Importance Diagrams

Sometimes you'll want to organize your ideas by how important they are.

1. You can organize from most important to least important.

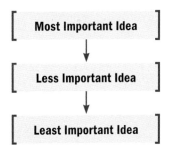

2. Or, you can organize from least important to most important.

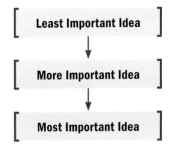

A Chronological Order

To tell about events in the order in which they happen or to explain the steps in a process, use chronological order.

Sequence Chain

A diagram like this one can help you plan plot events for stories.

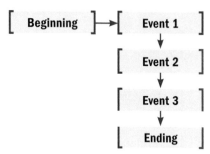

Sequence Chain

Flow Chart

Use a flow chart to explain how to do something or how something works.

Making a 3-D Theatrical Mask

Step 1
A cast of the actor's face is made.

↓

Step 2
The cast is then used to shape the features of the mask.

↓

Step 3
This new character's "face" is then used to make a mold for the final mask.

↓

Step 4
Latex rubber is poured into the mold to create the mask.

↓

Step 5
The mask is then painted and attached to the actor with a special glue.

Flow Chart

Time Line

Use a time line to help you keep track of when important events happened.

Evolution of The Wizard of Oz

1900 — L. Frank Baum publishes The Wonderful Wizard of Oz.
First event

1925 — The full-length silent film version of the book opens.

1939 — MGM releases the classic film version of The Wizard of Oz.

1956 — The Wizard of Oz is shown on network television for the first time.
Date

1975 — The Wiz, an African American stage musical based on the story, opens.

1978 — A film version of The Wiz is released.

1995 — Wicked, based on the Oz story, is published by Gregory Maguire.

2003 — The musical Wicked opens on Broadway.

Time Line

Spatial Order

For a description, try using spatial order to tell what you see—from left to right, from near to far, or from top to bottom, for example.

Picture Diagram

Try labeling a picture—or drawing one— to show how you'll organize details for a description.

Picture Diagram

beat-up hat

plaster nose

rope belt

hay stuffing

busted shoes

Circle Diagram

Whether you want to describe an area from the inside to the outside or vice versa, try using a circle diagram to show your plan.

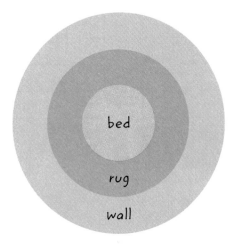

bed

rug

wall

Circle Diagram

Showing Causes and Effects

When you write about causes and effects, you explain what happens and why.

Cause-and-Effect Chart

Sometimes a cause leads to a single effect. You might want to show each cause and its effect in a chart.

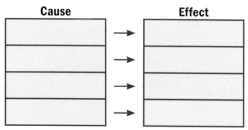

Cause-and-Effect Chart

Cause-and-Effect Diagrams

Maybe what you want to explain has a single cause and multiple effects, or a single effect and multiple causes.

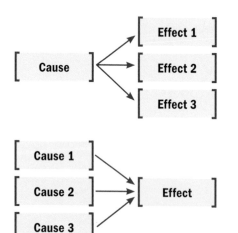

Cause-and-Effect Diagrams

Cause-and-Effect Chain

Sometimes causes and effects form a chain of linked events. One event causes the next event to happen.

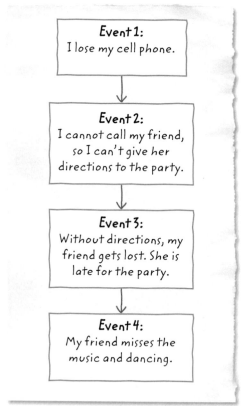

Event 1:
I lose my cell phone.

Event 2:
I cannot call my friend, so I can't give her directions to the party.

Event 3:
Without directions, my friend gets lost. She is late for the party.

Event 4:
My friend misses the music and dancing.

Cause-and-Effect Chain

Showing Comparisons

Plan what you'll say about how people, places, or things are alike or different. It'll be easy to see the comparisons if you show your ideas side by side.

T-chart
Use a T-chart to help you compare and contrast specific characteristics of a topic.

What you compare

Buying a Costume	Making a Costume
limits your choices	gives you many choices
requires little work or skill	may require skills, such as sewing or painting
can be done quickly	takes a long time

T-chart

Characteristics

Venn Diagram
A Venn diagram uses overlapping circles to compare and contrast.

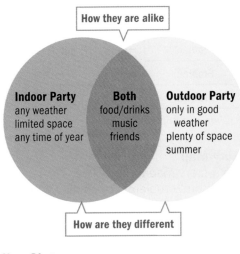

How they are alike

Indoor Party
any weather
limited space
any time of year

Both
food/drinks
music
friends

Outdoor Party
only in good
weather
plenty of space
summer

How are they different

Venn Diagram

Showing Goals and Outcomes

Whether you want to share your own personal accomplishments or create a story about a fictional character, try organizing your ideas by goal and outcome.

Goal	Actions	Obstacles	Outcome
I wanted to get the lead role in the school play.	I found out the date and time of the audition. I prepared a monologue. I attended the audition and performed the monologue.	I had a cold on the day of the audition. I kept coughing during my monologue. My best friend tried out for the lead, too.	My friend got the lead role. I got a minor part.

Goal-and-Outcome Chart

What stands in the way?

Showing Problems and Solutions

Both fiction and nonfiction often present problems and solutions.
In your writing, organize the ideas by first telling why something is a
problem and then how the problem is or can be solved.

Problem-and-Solution Chart

A chart like this one works best for
nonfiction in which there are several
problems, each with its own solution.

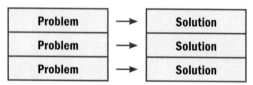

Problem	→	Solution
Problem	→	Solution
Problem	→	Solution

Problem-and-Solution Chart

Story Map

Use a story map to show your
characters' problems, or conflicts, and
how they work to solve the problems.

Title: Finding a Place
Author: Jasmine Porter

Characters: Cathy, Cathy's German host
family, Anke, other students
Setting: Munich, Germany

Problem: Cathy feels lonely.

Event 1: Cathy signs up for a study-abroad
program and goes to Germany.
Event 2: She has trouble fitting in because she
doesn't speak German.
Event 3: She meets and befriends a German
student named Anke.

Solution: Anke helps Cathy improve her
German and meet more people.

Story Map

Essay Map

For an essay, complete a map to help
you organize and explain your ideas.

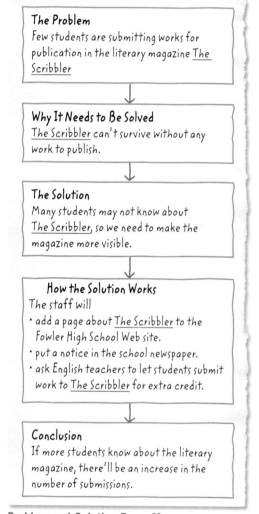

The Problem
Few students are submitting works for
publication in the literary magazine The
Scribbler

Why It Needs to Be Solved
The Scribbler can't survive without any
work to publish.

The Solution
Many students may not know about
The Scribbler, so we need to make the
magazine more visible.

How the Solution Works
The staff will
• add a page about The Scribbler to the
Fowler High School Web site.
• put a notice in the school newspaper.
• ask English teachers to let students submit
work to The Scribbler for extra credit.

Conclusion
If more students know about the literary
magazine, there'll be an increase in the
number of submissions.

Problem-and-Solution Essay Map

Showing Your Position

When you write to persuade, you want to convince people to agree with you. So, to be sure you've included all the important and persuasive details, use a chart or a diagram to plan what you'll say.

Opinion Chart

You can use an opinion chart to organize the reasons and supporting evidence for your opinion.

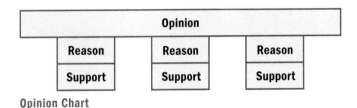

Opinion Chart

Position-and-Support Diagram

Sometimes people will disagree with you. When this happens, you need to plan how to respond to their objections with rebuttals.

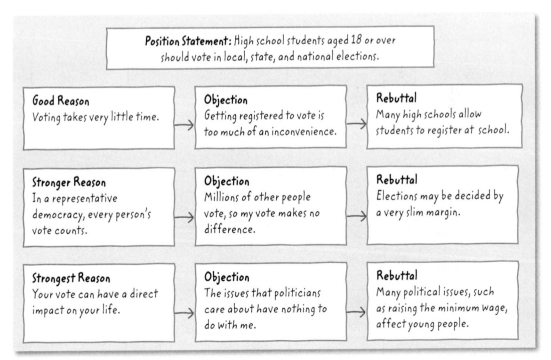

Position-and-Support Diagram

Idea Organizers

Choose an Organizer

Idea organizers can help you plan how to present your ideas. They help the reader (and the writer—you!) follow your thinking process.

The Story of My Thinking

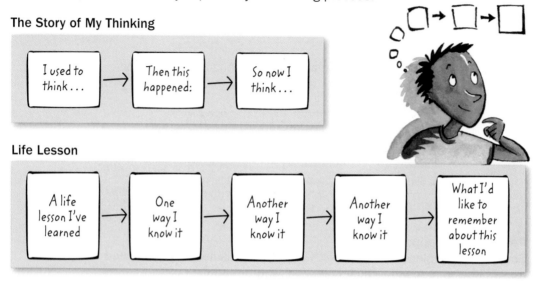

I used to think . . . → Then this happened: → So now I think . . .

Life Lesson

A life lesson I've learned → One way I know it → Another way I know it → Another way I know it → What I'd like to remember about this lesson

Comparing Notes

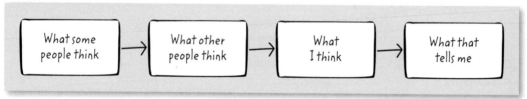

What some people think → What other people think → What I think → What that tells me

Memory Reflections

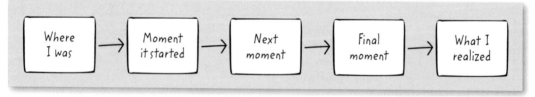

Where I was → Moment it started → Next moment → Final moment → What I realized

Wrong Assumption

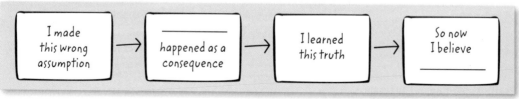

I made this wrong assumption → _____ happened as a consequence → I learned this truth → So now I believe _____

Sensory Associations

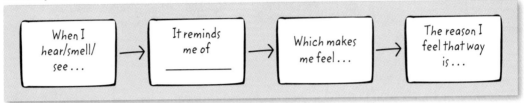

When I hear/smell/ see... → It reminds me of _____ → Which makes me feel... → The reason I feel that way is...

Something Big

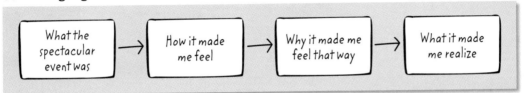

What the spectacular event was → How it made me feel → Why it made me feel that way → What it made me realize

Finding Out for Sure

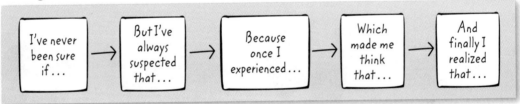

I've never been sure if... → But I've always suspected that... → Because once I experienced... → Which made me think that... → And finally I realized that...

Making a Change

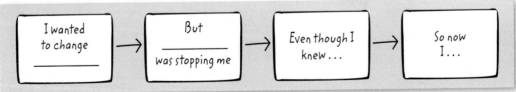

I wanted to change _____ → But _____ was stopping me → Even though I knew... → So now I...

Learning From Mistakes

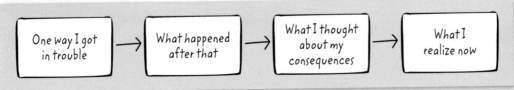

One way I got in trouble → What happened after that → What I thought about my consequences → What I realize now

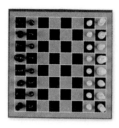

Grammar, Usage, Handwriting, AND Spelling

Sentences

A **sentence** is a group of words that tells a complete thought. Every sentence has a **subject** (a main idea) and a **predicate** that describes what the main idea is, has, or does.

A sentence must have both of these parts in order to be a **complete sentence**. If one part of a sentence is missing, a **fragment** is the result. Sentences can be classified according to their function and structure.

Sentences and Fragments	Examples
Begin a complete sentence with a capital letter, and end it with a period or other end mark.	<u>These parks</u> / <u>have many tourist attractions.</u> 　　subject　　　　　　predicate
A **fragment** is a sentence part that is incorrectly used as a complete sentence. For example, the fragment may be missing a subject. Add a subject to correct the problem.	**Incorrect:** Fun to visit because they have many attractions. **Correct:** Parks are fun to visit because they have many attractions.
Writers sometimes use fragments on purpose to emphasize an idea or for special effect.	I did not camp in bear country. **No way. Too dangerous**.

Sentence Functions

Sentence Types	Examples
A **statement** ends with a period.	The football game was on Friday. The coach made an important announcement.
A **question** ends with a question mark.	Who heard the announcement? What did the coach say?
A **exclamation** shows surprise or strong emotion. It ends with an exclamation mark.	That's fantastic news! I can't believe it!
In a command, the subject **you** is understood. It is not stated.	Give the team my congratulations.
• An imperative sentence usually begins with a verb and ends with a period.	**Be** on time.
• If an imperative sentence shows strong emotion, it ends with an exclamation mark.	Beat the opponent!

Sentence Structures

Clauses	Examples
A **clause** is a group of words that has both a **subject** and a **predicate**.	<u>California's population</u> / <u>grew during the 1840s</u>. *subject* *predicate*
An **independent clause** can stand alone as a complete sentence.	<u>California's population</u> / <u>increased</u>. *subject* *predicate*
A **dependent clause** cannot stand alone as a complete sentence because it begins with a subordinating conjunction. A dependent clause can be combined with an independent clause to form a complete sentence.	**because** gold / was found there during that time California's population grew because gold was found. *independent clause* *dependent clause*
An **adjective clause** gives more details about the noun or pronoun that it describes.	The news **that gold had been found** spread fast.
An **adverb clause** gives more details about the verb, adjective, or adverb that it describes.	**When someone found gold**, people celebrated.

Simple Sentences	Examples
A **simple sentence** is one independent clause with a subject and a predicate. It has no dependent clauses.	Supplies / were scarce. The miners / needed goods and services.

Compound Sentences	Examples
When you join two independent clauses, you make a **compound sentence**. • Use a comma and a **coordinating conjunction** to join independent clauses. • Use a semicolon to join independent clauses that are short and closely related.	People opened stores, **but** supplies were scarce. People went hungry; there was no food.
Joining independent clauses without a conjunction or proper punctuation creates a **run-on sentence**.	**Incorrect:** The miners were hungry supplies were scarce. **Correct:** The miners were hungry, <u>and</u> supplies were scarce.

Sentence Structures, continued

Complex Sentences	Examples
To make a **complex sentence**, join an independent clause with one or more dependent clauses.	Many writers visited camps **where miners worked**. *independent* *dependent*
If the dependent clause comes first, put a **comma** after it.	**While the writers were there**, they wrote stories about the miners.

Compound-Complex Sentences	Examples
You can make a **compound-complex sentence** by joining two or more independent clauses and one or more dependent clauses.	Many miners never found gold, **but** they stayed in California **because they found other jobs there**. *dependent*

Phrases	Examples
A **phrase** is a group of related words that does not have both a subject and a verb. Phrases add details to sentences.	The team won the game **in overtime**. **With only seconds left**, the quarterback scored.
A **prepositional phrase** starts with a preposition and ends with a noun or a pronoun. (See page 481W for a list of prepositions.) It includes all the words in between. The noun or pronoun is the **object of the preposition**.	I live **near the Chávez Community Center**. *preposition* *object of preposition* Tom wants to walk there **with you and me**. *preposition* *objects of preposition*
Prepositional phrases can function either as **adjectives** or as **adverbs**. • They function as adjectives when they modify a noun or pronoun. • They function as **adverbs** when they modify a verb, an adjective, or another adverb.	The **guy in the yellow shirt and khaki pants** is my friend Joel. He is **excited about the new Chávez Center**. He wants to **come with us**.
A **participial phrase** begins with a participle. A **participle** is a word made from a verb but used as an adjective (**sizzling** burgers, **burned** hot dogs) Most participles end in **-ing** or **-ed**. A participle phrase includes the participle and its modifiers. Place the phrase next to the noun it describes.	**Correct: Standing by the grill**, he soon had the hamburgers cooked to perfection. **Incorrect**: He soon had the hamburgers cooked to perfection standing by the grill.

Parenthetical Phrases and Appositives	Examples
A **parenthetical phrase** adds nonessential information to a sentence. You can leave out a nonessential phrase without changing the meaning of the sentence. Use commas to set off a nonessential phrase.	Most miners did not, **in fact**, find gold. Gold, **every miner's dream**, lay deeply buried.
An **appositive phrase** renames the noun next to it. An appositive phrase usually comes after the noun or pronoun it refers to.	James Marshall, **a mill worker**, started the Gold Rush when he found gold nuggets in 1848.

Combining Sentences

Good writers use many different types of sentences. You can combine short, related sentences in different ways.

Combined Sentences	Examples
You can use **appositives**.	Samuel Brannan was a newspaper publisher. He told everyone about the discovery of gold. Samuel Brannan, **a newspaper publisher**, told everyone about the discovery of gold.
You can use **participial phrases**.	The search for gold was dangerous. The miners stood in rushing streams. The search for gold was dangerous for miners **standing in rushing streams**.
You can use **prepositional phrases**.	The trip to California was difficult. People traveled in covered wagons. The trip to California **by covered wagon** was difficult.
You can join clauses. Use **coordination** to join clauses of equal weight, or importance.	Gold was often found next to streams, **and** it was also found deep beneath the earth.
Use **subordination** to join clauses of unequal weight, or importance. Put the main idea in the main clause and the less important detail in the dependent clause.	The miners were called '49ers. *main idea* Many miners arrived in 1849. *less important detail* The miners were called '49ers because they arrived in 1849.

Subjects and Predicates

A **subject** tells who or what the sentence is about. A **predicate** tells something about the subject.

Complete and Simple Subjects and Predicates	Examples
The **complete subject** includes all the words in the subject.	**Many people** visit our national parks. **My favorite parks** are in the West.
The **simple subject** is the most important noun or pronoun in the complete subject.	Many <u>people</u> visit our national parks. My favorite <u>parks</u> are in the West.
The **complete predicate** includes all the words in the predicate.	Visitors **explore caves in Yellowstone Park**. Some people **climb the unusual rock formations**.
The **simple predicate** is the **verb**. It is the most important word in the predicate.	Visitors **<u>explore</u> caves in Yellowstone Park**. Some people **<u>climb</u> the unusual rock formations**.

Compound Subject and Compound Predicate	Examples
A **compound subject** is two or more simple subjects joined by **and** or **or**.	<u>Yosemite</u> and <u>Yellowstone</u> are both in the West. Either **spring or fall** is a good time to visit.
A **compound predicate** has two or more verbs joined by **and** or **or**.	At Yosemite, some people **fish and swim**. My family **hikes** to the river **or stays** in a cabin.

Subject-Verb Agreement

The subject and verb of a sentence or clause must agree in number.

Subject-Verb Agreement	Examples
Use a **singular subject** with a **singular verb**.	Another popular **park is** the Grand Canyon.
Use a **plural subject** with a **plural verb**.	We **were amazed** by the colors of its cliffs.
If the simple subjects in a **compound subject** are connected by **and**, use a plural verb. If they are connected by **or**, look at the last simple subject. If it is singular, use a **singular verb**. If it is plural, use a **plural verb**.	**<u>Rafts</u>** and a **<u>boat</u> are** available for a trip down the canyon. These **rafts** or this **<u>boat</u> is** the best way to go. This **boat** or these **<u>rafts</u> are** the best way to go .
The **subject** and **verb** must agree, even when other words come between them.	The **bikers** in the park **are looking** for animals.

Parts of Speech

All the words in the English language can be put into one of eight groups. These groups are the eight **parts of speech**. You can tell a word's part of speech by looking at how it functions, or the way it is used, in a sentence. Knowing about the functions of words can help you become a better writer.

The Eight Parts of Speech	Examples
A **noun** names a person, place, thing, or idea.	**Erik Weihenmayer** climbed the highest **mountain** in the **world**. The **journey** up **Mount Everest** took **courage**.
A **pronoun** takes the place of a noun.	**He** made the journey even though **it** was dangerous.
An **adjective** describes a noun or a pronoun.	Erik is a **confident** climber. He is **strong**, too.
A **verb** can tell what the subject of a sentence does or has. A **verb** can also link a noun or an adjective in the predicate to the subject.	Erik also **skis** and **rides** a bike. He **has** many hobbies. Erik **is** an athlete. He **is** also blind.
An **adverb** describes a verb, an adjective, or another adverb.	Illness **slowly** took his eyesight, but it **never** affected his spirit. His accomplishments have made him **very** famous. He has been interviewed **quite** often.
A **preposition** shows how two things or ideas are related. It introduces a prepositional phrase.	Erik speaks **to** people **around** the world. **In** his speeches, he talks **about** his life.
A **conjunction** connects words or groups of words.	Courage **and** skill have carried him far. He has one disability, **but** he has many abilities.
An **interjection** expresses strong feeling.	**Wow**! What an amazing person he is! **Hurray**! He reached the mountaintop.

Nouns

A **noun** names a person, place, thing, or idea. There are different kinds of nouns.

Common and Proper Nouns	Examples
A **common noun** names a general person, place, thing, or idea.	A **teenager** sat by the **ocean** and read a **magazine**.
Capitalize a common noun only when it begins a sentence.	**Magazines** are the perfect thing to read at the beach.
A **proper noun** names a specific person, place, thing, or idea. Always capitalize a proper noun.	**Jessica** sat by the **Pacific Ocean** and read *Teen Talk* magazine.

Regular Plural Nouns	Examples
Plural nouns name more than one person, place, thing, or idea. Add –**s** to most nouns to make them plural.	My favorite **guitar** was made in Spain, but I also like my two American **guitars**.

Other nouns follow different rules to form the plural.

Forming Noun Plurals

When a Noun Ends in:	Form the Plural by:	Examples
ch, **sh**, **s**, **x**, or **z**	adding -**es**	box—box**es** brush—brush**es**
a consonant + **y**	changing the **y** to **i** and adding -**es**	story—stor**ies**
a vowel + **y**	just adding -**s**	boy—boy**s**
f or **fe**	changing the **f** to **v** and adding -**es**, in most cases for some nouns that end in **f** or **fe**, just add -**s**	leaf—lea**ves** knife—kni**ves** cliff—cliff**s** safe—safe**s**
a vowel + **o**	adding -**s**	radio—radio**s** kangaroo—kangaroo**s**
a consonant + **o**	adding -**s**, in most cases; other times adding -**es**	ego—ego**s** potato—potato**es**

Irregular Plural Nouns	Examples
Some nouns are **irregular**. These nouns do not follow the rules to form the plural.	At first only one **person** came, but within an hour there were many **people**.

Forming Plurals of Irregular Nouns

For some irregular nouns, change the spelling to form the plural.	one child many **children** one foot many **feet**	one man several **men** one ox ten **oxen**	one mouse a few **mice** one woman most **women**
For other irregular nouns, keep the same form for the singular and the plural.	one deer two **deer**	one fish many **fish**	one sheep twelve **sheep**

Possessive Nouns	Examples
Possessive nouns show ownership or relationship of persons, places, or things.	**Ted's** daughter made the guitar. The **guitar's** tone is beautiful.
Follow these rules to make a noun possessive: • Add **'s** to a singular noun or a plural noun that does not end in **s**. • Add an apostrophe after the final **s** in a plural noun that ends in **s**.	When she plays the piano, it attracts **the children's** attention. Three **musicians'** instruments were left on the bus.

Noun Phrases	Examples
A **noun phrase** is made up of a noun and its modifiers. Modifiers are words that describe, such as adjectives.	**The flying frog** does not actually fly. It glides on **special skin flaps**. Thailand is a **frog-friendly habitat**.

Articles

An **article** is a word that helps identify a noun.

Articles	Examples
A, **an**, and **the** are **articles**.	It is **an** amazing event when **a** flying frog glides in **the** forest.
A and **an** are **indefinite articles**. Use **a** or **an** before a noun that names a nonspecific thing.	**A flying frog** stretched its webbed feet. **An owl** watched from a nearby tree.
• Use **a** before a word that starts with a consonant sound.	a **f**oot a **r**ainforest a **p**ool a **u**nion (*u* is pronounced like *y*, a **n**est a consonant)
• Use **an** before a word that starts with a vowel sound.	an **e**gg an **a**nimal an **a**dult an **i**dea an **o**cean an **h**our (The *h* is silent.)
The is a **definite article**. Use **the** before a noun that names a specific thing.	Leiopelmids are **the** oldest kind of frog in **the** world. They are survivors of **the** Jurassic period.

Pronouns

A **pronoun** is a word that takes the place of a noun. A pronoun often changes its form depending on how it is used in a sentence.

Subject Pronouns	Examples
Use a **subject pronoun** as the subject of a sentence.	**Antonio** is looking forward to the homecoming dance. **He** is trying to decide what to wear.

Singular	Plural
I	we
you	you
he, she, it	they

The pronoun **it** can be used as a **subject** to refer to a noun. **But**: The pronoun **it** can be the subject without referring to a specific noun.	The **dance** starts at 7:00. **It** ends at 10:00. **It** is important to arrive on time. **It** is fun to see your friends in formal clothes.

Object Pronouns	Examples
Use an **object pronoun** after an **action verb**.	Tickets are on sale, so buy **them** now.

Singular	Plural
me	us
you	you
him, her, it	them

Also use an **object pronoun** after a **preposition**.	Antonio invited Caryn. He ordered flowers for **her**.

Pronouns, continued

Possessive Pronouns	Examples
A **possessive pronoun** tells who or what owns something or belongs with something.	**His** photograph of a tree won an award. The digital camera is **mine**.
Some forms of possessive pronouns are always used before a noun.	Aleina's photographs are beautiful because of **her** eye for detail.

Forms Used with Nouns

Singular	Plural
my	our
your	your
his, her, its	their

Other forms of possessive pronouns are used alone, without a noun.	Which camera is Aleina's? The expensive camera is **hers**. **Mine** is a single-use, disposable camera.

Forms Used without a Noun

Singular	Plural
mine	ours
yours	yours
his, hers, its	theirs

Demonstrative Pronouns	Examples
A **demonstrative pronoun** points out a specific person, place, thing, or idea.	**That** phone takes great photographs. I've never seen **those** before.

Singular	Plural
this	these
that	those

Like possessive pronouns, demonstrative pronouns can be used with a noun or by themselves. The same form is used in both cases.	**These** photographs are of my grandparents as children. A life of hard work from morning till night—I can't even imagine **that**!

Indefinite Pronouns	Examples
Use an **indefinite pronoun** when you are not talking about a specific person, place, or thing.	**Someone** has to lose the game. **Nobody** knows who the winner will be.

Some Indefinite Pronouns

These **indefinite pronouns** are always singular and need a **singular verb**.				
anybody	either	neither	one	**Something is** happening on the playing field. We hope that **everything goes** well for our team.
anyone	everybody	nobody	somebody	
anything	everyone	no one	someone	
each	everything	nothing	nothing	

These **indefinite pronouns** are always plural and need a **plural verb**.				
both	few	many	several	**Many** of us **are** hopeful.

These **indefinite pronouns** can be singular or plural.				
all	any	most	none	some	**Most** of the players **are** tired. **Most** of the game **is** over.
Look at the phrase that follows the indefinite pronoun. If the noun or pronoun in the phrase is plural, use a **plural verb**. If it is singular, use a **singular verb**.					

Relative Pronouns	Examples
A **relative pronoun** introduces **a relative clause**. It connects, or relates, the clause to a word in the sentence.	**Relative Pronouns** who / what / which / whom / whoever / whatever / whose / whomever / whichever
Use **who**, **whom**, or **whose** for people. The pronouns **whoever** and **whomever**, also refer to people.	The student **who** was injured is Joe. We play **whomever** we are scheduled to play.
Use **which**, **whichever**, **what**, and **whatever** for things.	Joe's wrist, **which** is sprained, will heal.
Use **that** for people or things.	The trainer **that** examined Joe's wrist is sure. The injury **that** Joe received is minor.

Pronouns, continued

Reflexive and Intensive Pronouns	Examples
Reflexive and **intensive pronouns** refer to nouns or other pronouns in a sentence. These pronouns end with **–self** or **–selves**. 	**I** will go to the store by **myself**.

Singular	Plural
myself	ourselves
yourself	yourselves
himself, herself, itself	themselves

Use a **reflexive pronoun** when the object **refers back to the subject**.	To surprise her technology teacher, **Kim** taught **herself** how to create a Web site on the computer.
Use an **intensive pronoun** when you want **to emphasize a noun or a pronoun** in a sentence.	The technology **teacher himself** learned some interesting techniques from Kim.

Agreement and Reference	Examples
When nouns and pronouns **agree**, they both refer to the same person, place, or thing. The **noun** is the **antecedent**, and the **pronoun** refers to it.	**Rafael and Felicia** visited a local college. **They** toured the campus. antecedent pronoun
A pronoun must agree (match) in **number** with the noun it refers to. • **Singular pronouns** refer to one person. • **Plural pronouns** refer to more than one person.	**Rafael** plays violin. **He** enjoyed the music school. **The teenagers** were impressed. **They** liked this college.
Pronouns must agree in **gender** with the nouns they refer to. Use **she**, **her**, and **hers** to refer to females. Use **he**, **him**, and **his** to refer to males.	Felicia told **her** uncle about the college visit. **Her** uncle told **her** that **he** received **his** graduate degree from that school.

Adjectives

An **adjective** describes or modifies a noun or a pronoun. It can tell what kind, which one, how many, or how much.

Adjectives	Examples
Adjectives provide more detailed information about a noun. Usually, an adjective comes before the noun it describes.	Deserts have a **dry** climate.
But an adjective can also come after the noun.	The climate is also **hot**.
Number words are often used as adjectives.	While I was out in the desert I saw **one** road runner, **two** Gila monsters, and **six** cacti.
Sometimes the number word tells the **order** that things are in.	The **first** day, I just saw some lizards. The **third** day, I got to see a coyote!

Proper Adjectives	Examples
A proper adjective is formed from a proper noun. It always begins with a capital letter.	Major deserts are found in Africa, Asia, and the Americas. The largest **African** desert is the Sahara.

gigantic

huge

big

Adjectives, continued

Adjectives That Compare	Examples
Comparative adjectives help show the similarities or differences between two nouns.	Deserts are **more fun** to study than forests.
To form the comparative of most adjectives, add **-er**, and use **than**. Use **more ... than** if the adjective has three or more syllables.	The Sechura Desert in South America is small**er than** the Kalahari Desert in Africa. Is that desert **more <u>interesting</u> than** this one?
Superlative adjectives help show how three or more nouns are alike or different.	Of the Sechura, Kalahari, and Sahara, which is the **largest**?
To form the superlative of most adjectives, add **-est**. Use **most** if the adjective has three or more syllables.	Which of the three deserts is the **smallest**? I think the Sahara is the **most <u>beautiful</u>**.
Irregular adjectives form the comparative and superlative differently. good better best bad worse worst some more most little less least	I had the **best** time ever visiting the desert. But the desert heat is **worse** than city heat.
Some two-syllable adjectives form the comparative with either **-er** or **more** and the superlative with either **-est** or **most**.	Desert animals are usually **more lively** at night than during the day. Desert animals are usually **livelier** at night than during the day. **Incorrect:** Desert animals are usually **more livelier** at night than during the day.

Adjective Phrases and Clauses	Examples
An **adjective phrase** is a group of words that work together to modify a noun or a pronoun. A phrase has no verb.	Plants **in the desert** have developed adaptations.
An **adjective clause** also works to modify a noun or a pronoun. Unlike an adjective phrase, an adjective clause has a subject and a verb.	The saguaro, **whose flowers bloom at night**, soaks up surface water after it rains. Desert plants **that have long roots** tap into water deep in the earth.

Verbs

Every complete sentence has two parts: a subject and a predicate. The subject tells what or whom the sentence is about. The predicate tells something about the subject. For example:

The dancers / **performed** on stage.

       subject   predicate

The **verb** is the key word in the predicate because it tells what the subject does or has. Verbs can also link together words in the subject and the predicate.

Action Verbs	Examples
An **action verb** tells what the subject of a sentence does. Most verbs are action verbs.	Dancers **practice** for many hours. They **stretch** their muscles and **lift** weights.
Some **action verbs** tell about an action that you cannot see.	The dancers **recognize** the rewards that come from their hard work.

Linking Verbs	Examples
A **linking verb** connects, or links, the subject of a sentence to a word in the predicate. Forms of the verb *be* are most commonly used, but other verbs are used as well. **Forms of the Verb *Be*** am are were is was **Other Linking Verbs** appear seem become feel smell taste look	
The word in the predicate can describe the subject.	Their feet **are** calloused.
Or the word in the predicate can rename the subject.	These dancers **are** athletes.

Verbs, continued

Helping Verbs	Examples
Some verbs are made up of more than one word. They need help to show exactly what is happening.	Ballet **is considered** a dramatic art form. *helping verb* *main verb*
The action word is called the **main verb**. It shows what the subject does, has, or is.	This dance form **has been evolving** over the years. *helping verbs* *main verb*
Any verbs that come before the **main** verb are the **helping verbs**.	Ballet **must have been** very different in the 1500s. *helping verbs* *main verb*

Helping Verbs

Forms of the Verb *Be*	Forms of the Verb *Do*	Forms of the Verb *Have*
am are were is was	do did does	have had has

Other Helping Verbs	
To express ability: **can, could**	I **can** dance.
To express possibility: **may, might, could**	I **might** dance tonight.
To express necessity or desire: **must, would**	I **must** dance more often.
To express certainty: **will, shall**	I **will** dance more often.
To express obligation: **should, ought**	I **should** practice more often. I **ought** to practice more often.

Helping verbs agree with the subject.	Baryshnikov **has performed** around the world. Many people **have praised** this famous dancer.
When used, the adverb *not* always comes between the **helping verb** and the main verb.	If you **have** not **heard** of him, you can watch the film *Dancers* to see him perform.
In questions, the subject comes between the **helping verb** and the **main verb**.	**Have** you **heard** of Mikhail Baryshnikov?

Verb Tense: Past, Present, Future

The **tense** of a verb shows when an action happens.

Present Tense Verbs	Examples
The **present tense** of a verb tells about an action that is happening now.	Greg **checks** his watch to see if it is time to leave. He **starts** work at 5:00 today.

Habitual Present Tense Verbs	Examples
The **habitual present tense** of a verb tells about an action that happens regularly or all the time.	Greg **works** at a pizza shop. He **makes** pizzas and **washes** dishes.

Past Tense Verbs (Regular and Irregular)	Examples
The **past tense** of a verb tells about an action that happened earlier, or in the past.	Yesterday, Greg **worked** until the shop closed. He **made** 50 pizzas.
• The past tense form of **regular verbs** ends with **-ed**.	He **learned** how to make a stuffed-crust pizza. Then Greg **chopped** onions and peppers.
• **Irregular verbs** have **special forms** to show the past tense. See pages 480W–481W for a list. Here are some examples of irregular verbs:	Greg **cut** the pizza. It **was** delicious. We **ate** all of it!

Present Tense	Past Tense
cut	cut
is	was
eat	ate

Future Tense Verbs	Examples
The **future tense** of a verb tells about an action that will happen later, or in the future. To show future tense, use:	Greg **will ride** the bus home after work tonight.
• the helping verb **will** plus a main verb	Greg's mother **will drive** him to work tomorrow. On Friday, he **will get** his first paycheck.
• the phrase **am going to**, **is going to**, or **are going to** plus a verb.	He **is going to** take a pizza home to his family. They **are going to** eat the pizza for dinner.

Verb Tense: Perfect Tenses

All verbs in the **perfect tenses—present perfect**, **past perfect**, and **future perfect**—have a helping verb and a form of the main verb that is called the **past participle**.

Present Perfect Tense Verbs	Examples
The **present perfect tense** of a verb uses the helping verb **has** or **have** plus the past participle.	
Use the present perfect tense to tell about something that happened at an unknown time in the past.	I **have looked** things up on the Internet.
You can also use the present perfect tense to tell about something that happened in the past and may still be going on.	The public **has used** the Internet since the 1980s.
For **regular verbs**, the past participle ends in -**ed**. **Present Tense** like **Past Participle** liked	I like the Internet. I **have** always **liked** the Internet.
Irregular verbs have **special forms** for the past participle. See pages 478W–479W. **Present Tense** know **Past Participle** known	I know a lot about the Internet. I **have known** about it for a long time.

Past Perfect Tense Verbs	Examples
The **past perfect tense** of a verb tells about an action that was completed before some other action in the past. It uses the helping verb **had**.	My grandmother **had graduated** from high school before computers were even invented!

Future Perfect Tense Verbs	Examples
The **future perfect tense** of a verb tells about an action that will be completed at a specific time in the future. It uses the helping verbs **will have**.	By the end of next year, 100,000 people **will have visited** our Web site.

Verb Forms

The **form** a verb takes changes depending on how it is used in a sentence, phrase, or clause.

Progressive Verbs	Examples
The **progressive** verb forms tell about an action that occurs over a period of time.	
The **present progressive** form of a verb tells about an action as it is happening.	They **are expecting** a big crowd for the fireworks show this evening.
• It uses the helping verb **am**, **is**, or **are**. The main verb ends in -**ing**.	**Are** you **expecting** the rain to end before the show starts?
The **past progressive** form of a verb tells about an action that was happening over a period of time in the past.	They **were thinking** of canceling the fireworks.
• It uses the helping verb **was** or **were** and a main verb. The main verb ends in -**ing**.	A tornado **was heading** in this direction.
The **future progressive** form of a verb tells about an action that will be happening over a period of time in the future.	The weather forecasters **will be watching** for tornados.
• It uses the helping verbs **will be** plus a main verb. The main verb ends in -**ing**.	I hope that they **will** not **be canceling** the show.

Transitive and Intransitive Verbs	Examples
Action verbs can be transitive or intransitive. A **transitive verb** needs an **object** to complete its meaning and to receive the action of the verb.	**Not complete:** Many cities **use** **Complete:** Many cities **use** fireworks.
The object can be a **direct object**. A direct object answers the question *Whom?* or *What?*	**Whom:** The noise **surprises** the audience. **What:** The people in the audience **cover** their ears.
An **intransitive verb** does not need an object to complete its meaning.	**Complete:** The people in our neighborhood **clap**. They **shout**. They **laugh**.
An **intransitive verb** may end the sentence, or it may be followed by other words that tell how, where, or when. These words are not objects since they do not receive the action of the verb.	The fireworks **glow** brightly. Then, slowly, they **disappear** in the sky. The show **ends** by midnight.

Verb Forms, continued

Active and Passive Voice	Examples
A verb is in **active voice** if the **subject** is doing the action.	Many cities **hold** fireworks displays for the Fourth of July.
A verb is in **passive voice** if the **subject** is not doing the action.	Fireworks displays **are held** by many cities for the Fourth of July.

Two-Word Verbs

A **two-word verb** is a verb followed by a preposition. The meaning of the two-word verb is different from the meaning of the verb by itself.

Some Two-Word Verbs

Verb	Meaning	Example
break	to split into pieces	I didn't **break** the window with the ball.
break down	to stop working	Did the car **break down** again?
break up	to end	The party will **break up** before midnight.
	to come apart	The ice on the lake will **break up** in the spring.
check	to make sure you are right	We can **check** our answers at the back of the book.
check in	to stay in touch with someone	I **check in** with my mom at work.
check up	to see if everything is okay	The nurse **checks up** on the patient every hour.
check off	to mark off a list	Look at your list and **check off** the girls' names.
check out	to look at something carefully	Hey, Marisa, **check out** my new bike!
fill	to place as much as can be held	**Fill** the pail with water.
fill in	to color or shade in a space	Please **fill in** the circle.
fill out	to complete	Marcos **fills out** a form to order a book.
get	to receive	I often **get** letters from my pen pal.
get ahead	to go beyond what is expected	She worked hard to **get ahead** in math class.
get along	to be on good terms with	Do you **get along** with your sister?
get out	to leave	Let's **get out** of the kitchen.
get over	to feel better	I hope you'll **get over** the flu soon.
get through	to finish	I can **get through** this book tonight.

Verb	Meaning	Example
give	to hand something to someone	We **give** presents to the children.
give out	to stop working	If she runs ten miles, her energy will **give out**.
give up	to quit	I'm going to **give up** eating candy.
go	to move from place to place	Did you **go** to the mall on Saturday?
go on	to continue	Why do the boys **go on** playing after the bell rings?
go out	to go someplace special	Let's **go out** to lunch on Saturday.
look	to see or watch	Don't **look** directly at the sun.
look forward	to be excited about something	My brothers **look forward** to summer vacation.
look over	to review	She **looks over** her test before finishing.
look up	to hunt for and find	We **look up** information on the Internet.
pick	to choose	I'd **pick** Lin for class president.
pick on	to bother or tease	My older brothers always **pick on** me.
pick up	to increase	Business **picks up** in the summer.
	to gather or collect	**Pick up** your clothes!
run	to move quickly	Juan will **run** in a marathon.
run into	to unexpectedly see someone	Did you **run into** Chris at the store?
run out	to suddenly have nothing left	The cafeteria always **runs out** of nachos.
stand	to be on your feet	I have to **stand** in line to buy tickets.
stand for	to represent	A heart **stands for** love.
stand out	to be easier to see	You'll **stand out** with that orange cap.
turn	to change direction	We **turn** right at the next corner.
turn up	to appear	Clean your closet and your belt will **turn up**.
	to raise the volume	Please **turn up** the radio.
turn in	to go to bed	On school nights I **turn in** at 9:30.
	to present or submit	You didn't **turn in** the homework yesterday.
turn off	to make something stop	Please **turn off** the radio.

Verb Forms, continued

Forms of Irregular Verbs

Irregular verbs do not follow the same rules for changing form as the "regular" verbs do. These verb forms have to be memorized. Here are some irregular verbs.

Irregular Verb	Past Tense	Past Participle	Irregular Verb	Past Tense	Past Participle
be: am, is, are	was, were	been	eat	ate	eaten
beat	beat	beaten	fall	fell	fallen
become	became	become	feed	fed	fed
begin	began	begun	feel	felt	felt
bend	bent	bent	fight	fought	fought
bind	bound	bound	find	found	found
bite	bit	bitten	fly	flew	flown
blow	blew	blown	forget	forgot	forgotten
break	broke	broken	forgive	forgave	forgiven
bring	brought	brought	freeze	froze	frozen
build	built	built	get	got	gotten
burst	burst	burst	give	gave	given
buy	bought	bought	go	went	gone
catch	caught	caught	grow	grew	grown
choose	chose	chosen	have	had	had
come	came	come	hear	heard	heard
cost	cost	cost	hide	hid	hidden
creep	crept	crept	hit	hit	hit
cut	cut	cut	hold	held	held
dig	dug	dug	hurt	hurt	hurt
do	did	done	keep	kept	kept
draw	drew	drawn	know	knew	known
drink	drank	drunk	lead	led	led
drive	drove	driven	leave	left	left

Irregular Verb	Past Tense	Past Participle	Irregular Verb	Past Tense	Past Participle
let	let	let	sink	sank	sunk
light	lit	lit	sit	sat	sat
lose	lost	lost	sleep	slept	slept
make	made	made	slide	slid	slid
mean	meant	meant	speak	spoke	spoken
meet	met	met	spend	spent	spent
pay	paid	paid	stand	stood	stood
prove	proved	proved, proven	steal	stole	stolen
put	put	put	stick	stuck	stuck
read	read	read	sting	stung	stung
ride	rode	ridden	strike	struck	struck
ring	rang	rung	swear	swore	sworn
rise	rose	risen	swim	swam	swum
run	ran	run	swing	swung	swung
say	said	said	take	took	taken
see	saw	seen	teach	taught	taught
seek	sought	sought	tear	tore	torn
sell	sold	sold	tell	told	told
send	sent	sent	think	thought	thought
set	set	set	throw	threw	thrown
shake	shook	shaken	wake	woke, waked	woken, waked
show	showed	shown	wear	wore	worn
shrink	shrank	shrunk	win	won	won
sing	sang	sung	write	wrote	written

Contractions

A **contraction** is a shortened form of a verb plus the word *not*, or of a verb-and-pronoun combination.

Contractions	Examples
Use an **apostrophe** to show which letters have been left out of the contraction.	is not = isn't I would = I'd can not = can't They are = They're
In contractions made up of a verb and the word **not**, the word **not** is usually shortened to **n't**.	I **can't** stop eating these cookies!

Adverbs

An **adverb** describes a verb, an adjective, or another adverb.

Adverbs	Examples
Adverbs answer one of the following questions: • How? • Where? • When? • How much? or How often?	**Carefully** aim the ball. Kick the ball **here**. Try again **later** to make a goal. Cathy **usually** scores.
An adverb can come before or after a **verb**.	Our team **always wins**. The whole team **plays well**.
An adverb can modify the meaning of an **adjective** or another **adverb**.	Gina is **really good** at soccer. She plays **very well**.

Adverbs That Compare	Examples
Some **adverbs** compare actions. Add -**er** to compare the actions of two people. Add -**est** to compare the actions of three or more people.	Gina runs **fast**. Gina runs **faster** than Maria. Gina runs **the fastest** of all the players.
If the adverb ends in -**ly**, use **more** or **less** to compare two actions.	Gina aims **more carefully** than Jen. Jen aims **less carefully** than Gina.
Use **the most** or **the least** to compare three or more actions.	Gina aims **the most carefully** of all the players. Jen aims **the least carefully** of all the players.

Prepositions

A **preposition** comes at the beginning of a prepositional phrase. **Prepositional phrases** add details to sentences.

Uses of Prepositions				Examples
Some prepositions show **location**.				The Chávez Community Center is **by my house**.
behind	between	inside	outside	The pool is **behind the building**.
below	by	near	over	
beside	in	on	under	
Some prepositions show **time**.				The Teen Club's party will start **after lunch**.
after	before	during	until	
Some prepositions show **direction**.				Go **through the building** and **around the fountain** to get **to the pool**.
across	down	out of	toward	The snack bar is **down the hall**.
around	into	through	up	
Some prepositions have **multiple uses**.				We might see Joshua **at the party**.
about	among	for	to	Meet me **at my house**.
against	as	from	with	Come **at noon**.
along	at	of	without	

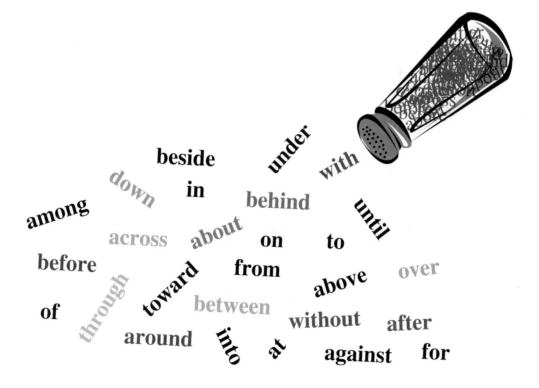

Conjunctions

A **conjunction** connects words or groups of words.

Conjunctions	Examples
A **coordinating conjunction** connects words, phrases, or clauses. To show similarity: **and** To show difference: **but**, **yet** To show choice: **or** To show cause/effect: **so**, **for** To put negative ideas together: **nor**	Irena **and** Irving are twins. I know Irena, **but** I do not know Irving. They will celebrate Friday **or** Saturday night. I have a cold, **so** I cannot go to the party. My mother will not let me go, **nor** will my father.
Correlative conjunctions are used in pairs. The pair connects phrases or words.	**Some Correlative Conjunctions** both ... and not only ... but also either ... or whether ... or
A **subordinating conjunction** introduces a **dependent clause** in a complex sentence. It connects the **dependent clause** to the main clause.	**Some Subordinating Conjunctions** after before till although if until
A **conjunctive adverb** joins two independent clauses. Use a semicolon before the conjunction and a comma after it.	**Some Conjunctive Adverbs** besides meanwhile then consequently moreover therefore

Interjections

An **interjection** expresses strong feeling or emotion.

Interjections	Examples
An **interjection** shows emotion. If an interjection stands alone, follow it with an exclamation point.	**Help!** **Oops!** **Oh boy!**
An interjection used in a sentence can be followed by a comma or an exclamation mark. Use a comma after a weak interjection. Use an exclamation mark after a strong interjection.	**Oh**, it's a baby panda! **Hooray**! The baby panda has survived!

Capitalization

Knowing when to use capital letters is an important part of clear writing.

First Word in a Sentence	Examples
Capitalize the first word in a sentence.	**W**e are studying the Lewis and Clark expedition.

In Direct Quotations	Examples
Capitalize the first word in a **direct quotation**.	Clark said, "**T**here is great joy in camp." "**W**e are in view of the ocean," he said. "**I**t's the Pacific Ocean," he added.

In Letters	Examples
Capitalize the first word used in the **greeting** or in the **closing** of a letter.	**D**ear Kim, **Y**our friend,

In Titles of Works	Examples
All important words in a **title** begin with a capital letter. Short words like *a, an, the, in, at, of,* and *for* are not capitalized unless they are the first or last word in the title.	**book:** *The Longest Journey* **poem:** "Leaves of Grass" **magazine:** *Flora and Fauna of Arizona* **newspaper:** *The Denver Post* **song:** "The Star-Spangled Banner" **game:** Exploration! **TV series:** "The Gilmore Girls" **movie:** *The Lion King* **play:** Fiddler on the Roof **work of art:** Mona Lisa

Pronoun *I*	Examples
Capitalize the pronoun *I* no matter where it is located in a sentence.	**I** was amazed when **I** learned that Lewis and Clark's expedition was over 8,000 miles.

Capitalization, continued

Proper Nouns and Adjectives	Examples
Common nouns name a general person, place, thing, or idea. Proper nouns name a particular person, place, thing, or idea. All the important words in a **proper noun** start with a capital letter.	**Common Noun:** team **Proper Noun:** Corps of Destiny
Proper nouns include the following: • names of people and their titles Do not capitalize a title if it is used without a name. • family titles like *Mom* and *Dad* when they are used as names. • names of organizations • names of languages and religions • months, days, special days, and holidays • names of academic cources • historical events and documents	Stephanie Eddins Captain Meriwether Lewis The **captain's** co-leader on the expedition was William Clark. "William Clark is one of our ancestors," **Mom** said. I asked my **mom** whose side of the family he was on, hers or my **dad's**. United Nations History Club Wildlife Society Spanish Christianity April Sunday Thanksgiving Algebra I World History Boston Tea Party Bill of Rights
Names of geographic places are proper nouns. Capitalize street, city, and state names in mailing addresses.	**Cities and States:** Dallas, Texas **Regions:** New England **Streets and Roads:** Main Avenue **Bodies of Water:** Pacific Ocean **Countries:** Ecuador **Landforms:** Sahara Desert **Continents:** North America **Public Spaces:** Muir Camp **Buildings, Ships, and Monuments:** *Titanic* **Planets and Heavenly Bodies:** Neptune
A **proper adjective** is formed from a **proper noun**. Capitalize proper adjectives.	Napoleon Bonaparte was from **Europe**. He was a **European** leader in the 1800s.

Abbreviations of geographic places are also capitalized.

Words Used in Addresses

Avenue	Ave.	Drive	Dr.	North	N.	Suite	Ste.
Apartment	Apt.	East	E.	Place	Pl.	West	W.
Boulevard	Blvd.	Highway	Hwy.	South	S.		
Court	Ct.	Lane	Ln.	Street	St.		

State Names

Alabama	AL	Indiana	IN	Nebraska	NE	South Carolina	SC
Alaska	AK	Iowa	IA	Nevada	NV	South Dakota	SD
Arizona	AZ	Kansas	KS	New Hampshire	NH	Tennessee	TN
Arkansas	AR	Kentucky	KY	New Jersey	NJ	Texas	TX
California	CA	Louisiana	LA	New Mexico	NM	Utah	UT
Colorado	CO	Maine	ME	New York	NY	Vermont	VT
Connecticut	CT	Maryland	MD	North Carolina	NC	Virginia	VA
Delaware	DE	Massachusetts	MA	North Dakota	ND	Washington	WA
Florida	FL	Michigan	MI	Ohio	OH	West Virginia	WV
Georgia	GA	Minnesota	MN	Oklahoma	OK	Wisconsin	WI
Hawaii	HI	Mississippi	MS	Oregon	OR	Wyoming	WY
Idaho	ID	Missouri	MO	Pennsylvania	PA		
Illinois	IL	Montana	MT	Rhode Island	RI		

Abbreviations of Personal Titles

Capitalize abbreviations for a personal title. Follow the same rules for capitalizing a personal title.

Mr. .... Mister	**Mrs.** ...... Missus	**Dr.** .... Doctor
Jr. .... Junior	**Capt.** ..... Captain	**Sen.** ...... Senator

Punctuation

Punctuation marks are used to emphasize or clarify meanings.

Apostrophe	Examples
Use an **apostrophe** to punctuate a **possessive noun**.	
If there is one owner, add **'s** to the owner's name, even if the owner's name ends in **s**.	Mrs. Ramos**'s** sons live in New Mexico.
If there is more than one owner, add **'** if the plural noun ends in **s**. Add **'s** if it does not end in **s**.	Her sons**'** birthdays are both in January. My children**'s** birthdays are in March.
Use an **apostrophe** to replace the letters left out of a contraction.	could ~~not~~ = couldn**'t** he ~~would~~ = he**'d**

End Marks	Examples
Use a **period** at the end of a statement or a polite command.	Georgia read the paper to her mom. Tell me if there are any interesting articles.
Or use a period after an indirect question. An indirect question tells about a question you asked.	She asked if there were any articles about the new restaurant on Stone Street near their house.
Use a **question mark** at the end of a question.	What kind of food do they serve?
Or use a question mark after a question that comes at the end of a statement.	The food is good, isn't it?
Use an **exclamation mark** after an interjection.	Wow!
Or use an exclamation mark at the end of a sentence to show you feel strongly about something.	The chicken parmesan is delicious!

Colon	Examples
Use a **colon**:	
• after the greeting in a business letter	Dear Sir or Madam:
• to separate hours and minutes	The restaurant is open until 11:30 p.m.
• to start a list	If you decide to hold your banquet here, we can: 1. Provide a private room 2. Offer a special menu 3. Supply free coffee and lemonade.

Comma	Examples
Use a comma:	
• before the **coordinating conjunction** in a compound sentence	Soccer is a relatively new sport in the United States, **but** it has been popular in England for a long time.
• to set off words that interrupt a sentence, such as an **appositive phrase** that is not needed to identify the word it describes	Mr. Okada, **the soccer coach,** had the team practice skills like passing, **for example,** for the first hour.
• to separate three or more items in a **series**	Shooting, passing, and dribbling are important skills.
• between two or more adjectives that tell about the same noun	The midfielder's quick, unpredictable passes made him the team's star player.
• after an **introductory phrase or clause**	**In the last game,** he made several goals.
• before someone's exact words and after them if the sentence continues	Mr. Okada said, "Meet the ball after it bounces," as we practiced our half-volleys.
• before and after a **clause** if the clause is not necessary for understanding the sentence	At the end of practice, **before anyone left,** Mr. Okada handed out revised game schedules.
• before a question at the end of a statement	You talked to Mr. Okada, **didn't you?**
• to set off the name of a person someone is talking to	Mr. Okada said, "That's not how you do it, **Jimmy.**"
Use a comma in these places in a letter:	
• between the city and the state	Milpas, AK
• between the date and the year	July 3, 2008
• after the greeting of a personal letter	Dear Mr. Okada,
• after the closing of a letter	Sincerely,

Dash	Examples
Use a **dash** to show a break in an idea or the tone in a sentence.	Water—a valuable resource—is often taken for granted.
Or use a dash to emphasize a word, a series of words, a phrase, or a clause.	It is easy to conserve water—wash full loads of laundry, use water-saving devices, fix leaky faucets.

Punctuation, continued

Ellipsis	Examples
Use an **ellipsis** to show that you have left out words.	A recent survey documented **...** water usage.
Or use an ellipsis to show an idea that trails off.	I don't know **...** so much waste **...**

Hyphen	Examples
Use a **hyphen** to:	
• connect words in a number and in a fraction	**One-third** of the people surveyed used at least **thirty-two** gallons of water every day.
• join some words to make a compound word	A **15-year-old** boy and his **great-grandmother** have started an awareness campaign.
• connect a letter to a word	They designed a **T-shirt** for their campaign.
• divide words at the end of a line. Always divide the word between two syllables.	Please join us today in our awareness **campaign**. It's for the good of the planet.

Italics and Underlining	Examples
When you are using a computer, use **italics** for the names of:	
• magazines and newspapers	I like to read *Time* magazine and the *Daily News*.
• books	They help me understand our history book, *The U.S. Story*.
• plays	Did you see the play *Abraham Lincoln in Illinois*?
• movies	It was made into the movie *Young Abe*.
• musicals	The musical *Oklahoma!* is about Southwest pioneers.
• music albums	*Greatest Hits from Musicals* is my favorite album.
• TV series	Do you like the singers on the TV show *American Idol*?
If you are using handwriting, underline.	

Parentheses	Examples
Use **parentheses** around extra information in a sentence.	The new story (in the evening paper) is very interesting.

Quotation Marks	Examples
Use **quotation marks** to show:	
• a speaker's exact words	"Listen to this!" Jim said.
• the exact words quoted from a book or other printed material	The announcement in the paper was: "The writer Josie Ramón will be at Milpas Library on Friday."
• the title of a song, poem, short story, magazine article, or newspaper article	Her famous poem "Speaking" appeared in the magazine article "How to Talk to Your Teen."
• the title of a chapter from a book	She'll be reading "Getting Along," a chapter from her new book.
• words used in a special way	We will be "all ears" at the reading.

Semicolon	Examples
Use a **semicolon**:	
• to separate two simple sentences used together without a conjunction	A group of Jim's classmates plan to attend the reading; he hopes to join them.
• before a conjunctive adverb that joins two simple sentences. Use a comma after the adverb.	Jim wanted to finish reading Josie Ramón's book this evening; however, he forgot it at school.
• to separate a group of words in a series if the words in the series already have commas	After school, Jim has to study French, health, and math; walk, feed, and brush the dog; and eat dinner.

Using Words Correctly

This section will help you to choose between words that are often confused or misused.

a lot • allot

A lot means "many" and is always written as two words, never as one word. *Allot* means "to assign" or "to give out."

> I have **a lot** of friends who like to eat.

> We **allot** one hour for lunch.

a while • awhile

The two-word form *a while* is often preceded by the prepositions *after*, *for*, or *in*. The one-word form *awhile* is used without a preposition.

> Let's stop here for **a while**.

> Let's stop here **awhile**.

accept • except

Accept is a verb that means "to receive." *Except* can be a verb meaning "to leave out" or a preposition meaning "excluding."

> I **accept** everything you say, **except** your point about music.

advice • advise

Advice is a noun that means "ideas about how to solve a problem." *Advise* is a verb and means "to give advice."

> I will give you **advice** about your problem today, but do not ask me to **advise** you again tomorrow.

affect • effect

Affect is a verb. It means "to cause a change in" or "to influence." *Effect* as a verb means "to bring about." As a noun, *effect* means "result."

> Sunshine will **affect** my plants positively.

> The governor is working to **effect** change.

> The rain had no **effect** on our spirits.

ain't

Ain't is not used in formal English. Use the correct form of the verb *be* with the word *not*: *is not, isn't; are not,* or *aren't.*

> We **are not going** to sing in front of you.

> I **am not going** to practice today.

all ready • already

Use the two-word form, *all ready*, to mean "completely finished." Use the one-word form, *already*, to mean "previously."

> We waited an hour for dinner to be **all ready**.

> It is a good thing I have **already** eaten today.

alright • all right

The expression *all right* means "OK" and should be written as two words. The one-word form, *alright*, is not used in formal writing.

> I hope it is **all right** that I am early.

all together • altogether

The two-word form, *all together*, means "in a group." The one-word form, *altogether*, means "completely."

> It is **altogether** wrong that we will not be **all together** this holiday.

among • between

Use *among* when comparing more than two people or things. Use *between* when comparing a person or thing with one other person, thing, or group.

> How can we share one piece of pizza **among** the four of us?

> We will split the money **between** Sal and Jess.

amount of • number of

Amount of is used with nouns that cannot be counted. *Number of* is used with nouns that can be counted.

> The **amount of** pollution in the air is increasing.

> A record **number of** people attended the game.

assure • ensure • insure

Assure means "to make certain." *Ensure* means "to guarantee." *Insure* means "to cover financially."

> I **assure** you that he is OK.

> I will personally **ensure** his safety.

> If the car is **insured**, the insurance company will pay to fix the damage.

being as • being that

Neither of these is used in formal English. Use *because* or *since* instead.

> I went home early **because** I was sick.

beside • besides

Beside means "next to." *Besides* means "plus" or "in addition to."

> Located **beside** the cafeteria is a vending machine.

> **Besides** being the fastest runner, she is also the nicest team member.

bring • take

Use *bring* to speak of transporting something to where you are now. Use *take* to speak of transporting something to a place where you're not now.

> **Bring** the snacks here to my house, and then we'll **take** them to the party at Ann's.

bust • busted

Neither of these is used in formal English. Use *broke* or *broken* instead.

> I **broke** the vase by accident.

> The **broken** vase cannot be fixed.

Using Words Correctly, continued

can't • hardly • scarcely

Do not use *can't* with *hardly* or
scarcely. That would be a double
negative. Use only *can't*, or use *can*
plus a negative word.

> I **can't** get my work done in time.

> I **can scarcely** get my work done in
> time.

capital • capitol

A *capital* is a place where a
government is located. A *capitol* is the
actual building the government meets
in.

> The **capital** of the U.S. is Washington,
> D.C.

> The senate met at the **capitol** to vote.

cite • site • sight

To *cite* means "to quote a source."
A *site* is "a place." *Sight* can mean
"the ability to see" or it can mean
"something that can be seen."

> Be sure to **cite** all your sources.

> My brother works on a construction
> **site**.

> Dan went to the eye doctor to have his
> **sight** checked.

> The sunset last night was a beautiful
> **sight**.

complement • compliment

Complement means "something
that completes" or "to complete."
Compliment means "something nice
someone says about another person"
or "to praise."

> The colors you picked really
> **complement** each other.

> I would like to **compliment** you on your
> new shoes.

**could have • should have • would
have • might have**

Be sure to use "have" not "of" with
words like *could*, *should*, *would*, and
might.

> I **would have** gone, but I didn't feel
> well last night.

council • counsel

A *council* is a group organized to study
and plan something. To *counsel* is to
give advice to someone.

> The city **council** met to discuss traffic
> issues.

> Mom, please **counsel** me on how to
> handle this situation.

different from • different than

Different from is preferred in formal
English and is used with nouns and
noun clauses and phrases. *Different
than*, when used, is used with
adverbial clauses.

> My interest in music is **different from**
> my friends.

> Movies today are **different than** they
> used to be in the 1950s.

farther • further

Farther refers to a physical distance. *Further* refers to time or amount.

> If you go down the road a little **farther**, you will see the sign.

> We will discuss this **further** at lunch.

fewer • less

Fewer refers to things that can be counted individually. *Less* refers to things that cannot be counted individually.

> The farm had **fewer** animals than the zoo, so it was **less** fun to visit.

good • well

The adjective *good* means "pleasing," "kind," or "healthy." The adverb *well* means: "ably."

> She is a **good** person.

> I am glad to see that you are **well** again after that illness.

> You have performed **well**.

immigrate to • emigrate from

Immigrate to means "to move to a country." *Emigrate from* means "to leave a country."

> I **immigrated to** America in 2001 from Panama.

> I **emigrated from** El Salvador because of the war.

it's • its

It's is a contraction of *it is*. *Its* is a possessive word meaning "belonging to it."

> **It's** going to be a hot day.

> The dog drank all of **its** water already.

kind of • sort of

These words mean "a type of." In formal English, do not use them to mean "partly." Use *somewhat* or *rather* instead.

> The peanut is actually a **kind of** bean.

> I feel **rather** silly in this outfit.

lay • lie

Lay means "to put in a place." It is used to describe what people do with objects. *Lie* means "to recline." People can *lie* down, but they *lay* down objects. Do not confuse this use of *lie* with the verb that means "to tell an untruth."

> I will **lay** the book on this desk for you.

> I'm tired and am going to **lie** on the couch.

> If you **lie** in court, you will be punished.

learn • teach

To *learn* is "to receive information." To *teach* is "to give information."

> If we want to **learn**, we have to listen.

> She will **teach** us how to drive.

leave • let

Leave means "to go away." *Let* means "to allow."

> **Leave** the keys on the kitchen table.

> I will **let** you borrow my pen.

Using Words Correctly, continued

like • as

Like can be used either as a preposition or as a verb meaning "to care about something." *As* is a conjunction and should be used to introduce a subordinate clause.

> She sometimes acts **like** a princess. But I still **like** her.

> She acts **as** if she owns the school.

loose • lose

Loose can be used as an adverb or adjective meaning "free" or "not securely attached." The verb *lose* means "to misplace" or "to be defeated."

> I let the dog **loose** and he is missing.

> Did you **lose** your homework?

> Did they **lose** the game by many points?

passed • past

Passed is a verb that means "to have moved ahead of." *Past* is a noun that means "the time before the present."

> I **passed** my English test.

> Poor grades are in the **past** now.

precede • proceed

Precede means "to come before." *Proceed* means "to go forward."

> Prewriting **precedes** drafting in the writing process.

> Turn left; then **proceed** down the next street.

principal • principle

A *principal* is "a person of authority." Principal can also mean "main." A *principle* is "a general truth or belief."

> The **principal** of our school makes an announcement every morning.

> The **principal** ingredient in baking is flour.

> The essay was based on the **principles** of effective persuasion.

raise • rise

The verb *raise* always takes an object. The verb *rise* does not take an object.

> **Raise** the curtain for the play.

> The curtain **rises**.

> I **rise** from bed every morning at six.

real • really

Real means "actual." It is an adjective used to describe nouns. *Really* means "actually" or "truly." It is an adverb used to describe verbs, adjectives, or other adverbs.

> The diamond was **real**.

> The diamond was **really** beautiful.

set • sit

The verb *set* usually means "to put something down." The verb *sit* means "to go into a seated position."

> I **set** the box on the ground.

> Please **sit** while we talk.

than • then

Than is used to compare things. *Then* means "next" and is used to tell when something took place.

> She likes fiction more **than** nonfiction.

> First, we will go to the bookstore; **then** we will go home.

they're • their • there

They're is the contraction of *they are*. *Their* is the possessive form of the pronoun *they*. *There* is used to indicate location.

> **They're** all on vacation this week.

> I want to use **their** office.

> The library is right over **there**.

> **There** are several books I want to read.

this • these • that • those

This indicates something specific that is near you. *These* is the plural form of *this*. *That* indicates something specific that is farther from you. *Those* is the plural form of *that*.

> **This** book in my hand belongs to me. **These** pens are also mine.

> **That** book over there is his. **Those** notes are his, too.

where

It is not necessary to use *at* or *to* with *where*.

> **Where** are you going?

> **Where** is Ernesto?

who • whom

Who is a subject. *Whom* is an object. If you can replace *who* or *whom* with *he*, *she*, *they*, or *it*, use *who*. If you can replace the word with *him*, *her*, or *them*, use *whom*.

> **Who** is going to finish first?

> My grandmother is a woman to **whom** I owe many thanks.

who's • whose

Who's is a contraction of *who is*. *Whose* is the possessive form of *who*.

> **Who's** coming to our dinner party?

> **Whose** car is parked in the garage?

you're • your

You're is a contraction of *you are*. *Your* is a possessive pronoun meaning "belonging to you."

> **You're** going to be late if you don't hurry.

> Is **your** backpack too heavy?

Handwriting Handbook

It's important to use your best **penmanship**, or handwriting. That way your audience will be able to read what your write.

Handwriting Hints

You can **print** your words or write in **cursive**. Printing is sometimes called **manuscript**.

Manuscript

Manuscript is less formal than cursive and is usually easier to read at a glance. That makes manuscript good to use for filling out forms and for writing things like posters, ads, and short notes. When you write in manuscript, hold the pencil and paper this way.

Left-handed

Right-handed

Cursive

Cursive is good to use for longer pieces, such as letters or stories, because you can write faster. You don't have to lift your pencil between letters. Also, cursive writing gives your finished pieces a polished look. When you write in cursive, hold the pencil and paper this way.

Left-handed

Right-handed

Manuscript Alphabet

Capital Letters

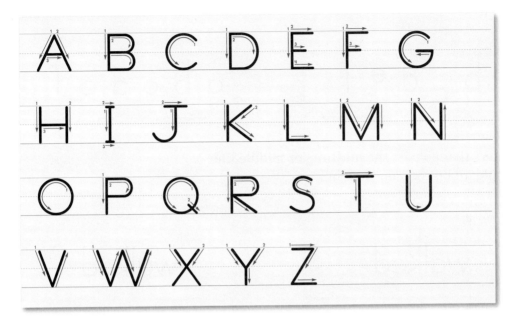

Lowercase Letters, Numbers, and Punctuation

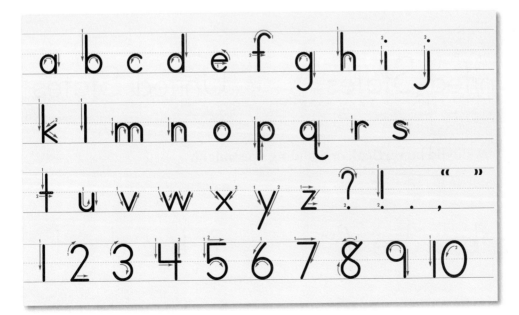

Writing Manuscript Letters

- Make letters sit on the **baseline**, or bottom line. Make letters the same size.

NOT OK

a b c d e f

OK

a b c d e f

- Letters that go past the **midline**, or middle line, should all be the same height.

NOT OK

walked

OK

walked

- Make your capital letters touch the **headline**, or top line. Make half-size letters touch the midline.

NOT OK

United States

OK

United States

- Letters should be **vertical**, or standing up straight.

NOT OK

a b c d e f

OK

a b c d e f

Writing Words and Sentences

- Put the same amount of space between each word.

NOT OK

Votefor Juji for ClassPresident!

OK

Vote for Juji for Class President!

- Put the right amount of space between each letter.

NOT OK

She wil l work hard for our school.

OK

She will work hard for our school.

- Write smoothly. Do not press too hard or too light.
  Make your lines the same thickness.

NOT OK

Who will you **vo**te **for**?

OK

Who will you vote for?

Writing a Paragraph in Manuscript

Indent, or leave a space at the beginning of each paragraph. Leave blank spaces, or **margins**, around the top, bottom, left, and right sides of your writing.

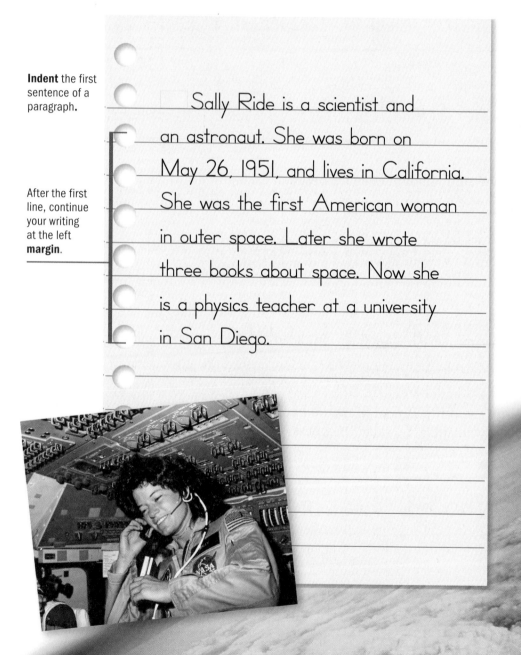

Indent the first sentence of a paragraph.

After the first line, continue your writing at the left **margin**.

Sally Ride is a scientist and an astronaut. She was born on May 26, 1951, and lives in California. She was the first American woman in outer space. Later she wrote three books about space. Now she is a physics teacher at a university in San Diego.

Cursive Alphabet

Capital Letters

Lowercase Letters

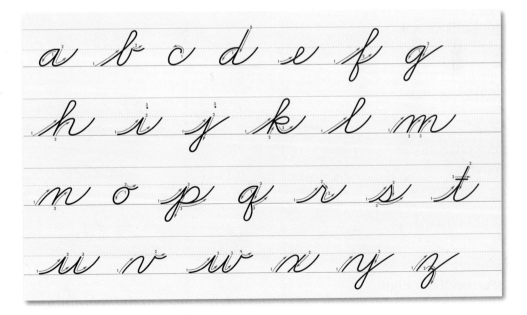

Writing Cursive Letters

Be careful not to make these common mistakes when you
write in **cursive**.

MISTAKE	NOT OK	OK	IN A WORD
The **a** looks like a **u**.	*u*	*a*	*again*
The **d** looks like a **c** and an **l**.	*d*	*d*	*dad*
The **e** is too narrow.	*e*	*e*	*eagle*
The **h** looks like an **l** and an **i**.	*h*	*h*	*high*
The **i** has no dot.	*i*	*i*	*inside*
The **n** looks like a **w**.	*w*	*n*	*none*
The **o** looks like an **a**.	*a*	*o*	*onion*
The **r** looks like an **i** with no dot.	*i*	*r*	*roar*
The **t** is not crossed.	*l*	*t*	*title*
The **t** is crossed too high.	*t*	*t*	*that*

Writing Words and Sentences

- Slant your letters all the same way.

NOT OK

My Chinese-language class today was interesting.

OK

My Chinese-language class today was interesting.

- Put the right amount of space between words.

NOT OK

I learned how togreet adults.

OK

I learned how to greet adults.

- Write smoothly. Do not press too hard or too lightly.

NOT OK

*I practiced on my teacher.
He was impressed.*

OK

*I practiced on my teacher.
He was impressed.*

Writing a Paragraph in Cursive

Indent, or leave a space, at the beginning of each paragraph. Leave blank spaces, or margins, around the top, bottom, left, and right sides of your writing.

Day *Wednesday, May 7, 2003*

Indent the first sentence of a paragraph.

A couple of days ago I was thinking, I really hope to go into one of the Chinese classes during my years in college. I want to learn Chinese since that's my original background and the language of my ancestors and also of my parents and relatives. (Most of my relatives do not speak English at all.) I think that it's really

After the first line, continue your writing at the left margin.

Leave a margin at the bottom page.

important that I keep
the communication going.
   Also, when we travel, I
think it would be hard
to communicate if I didn't
know any Chinese.
   I am an American
citizen now, but I still have
that feeling, that strong
feeling, that I want to
know about my background.

Stop before
the right margin.

Spelling Handbook

Spelling. It's one of those subjects that seem to make a lot of people anxious. You now—like going to the dentist or taking a pop quiz. It's time to take control of spelling and turn worries into word work!

The truth is that spelling can be fun, especially when you see yourself getting better and better at it. It's also true that once you learn the spelling basics, you will know how to spell six out of seven words. That's right! Most words follow spelling patterns. Most words obey spelling rules. Tricky words are definitely in the minority.

Don't just read this guide. Apply it! Think like a speller. Here are some ideas:

- Start your own lists of related words.

- Make other lists of unusual words.

- Become a pattern finder. As you figure out a pattern, write the rule down in your own words.

- Create your own dictionary for words that are tricky for you.

- Make up your own ways to remember a tough word.

Write it all down, and watch your personal spelling guide grow right along with your spelling skills!

Don't forget every speller's best friend—the dictionary! ▶

Learning New Words

Follow six steps when you are learning how to spell a new word.

STEP 1: Look at the word carefully.

STEP 2: Say the word aloud. Look at the word as you say it, and listen to yourself saying it.

STEP 3: Picture the whole word in your mind.

STEP 4: Spell the word aloud, letter by letter.

STEP 5: Write the word. Use your memory.

STEP 6: Check the word. You can use a dictionary, a computer spell checker, or a word list.

If you find errors in **STEP 6**, circle them. Write the word correctly. Then repeat the steps again for the word.

Use all Your Senses

Good spellers remember how words look and how they sound. When you are learning how to spell a new word, you should also get the rest of your senses involved. Try these ideas to use all of your senses together:

Ideas for Learning New Words

See it.	Really study the word. Look at every letter.
Hear it.	As you study the word, say it aloud. Say each sound and notice how it matches the letters.
Work it.	As you say each sound, tap your finger or foot. As you look at each letter, write it in the air.
Feel it.	Write the word slowly. Shape the letters carefully. Imagine writing the word in sand to really feel it!

Making Words Your Own

Every person has trouble spelling some words. The secret is to help yourself remember these troublesome words. You can make up your own memory tools that fit your way of thinking. Here are some examples.

Rhymes

Here's a famous rhyme to use when deciding whether to use *ie* (brief) or *ei* (receive).

> "*i* before *e*
> except after *c*
> or when sounded *a*
> as in *neighbor* and *weigh* . . .
> and *weird* is just weird!"

Acronyms

Think of a word that begins with each letter. The words in the correct order should be easy for you to remember.

EXAMPLES	**because**
	big elephants can always understand small elephants
	rhythm
	rhythm helps your two hips move
	ocean
	only cats' eyes are narrow

Explanations

Think of a clever way to remember *why* letters appear or not in a word.

EXAMPLES	**argument**
	"I lost an *e* in an argument."
	dessert
	"It has two *s*'s for sweet stuff!"
	necessary
	"It is *necessary* for a shirt to have one collar (one *c*) and two sleeves (two *s*'s)."

Stories

Make up a story that will help you remember how to spell a word.

> **EXAMPLES** **cemetery**
> I got scared walking through the cemetery and yelled, "e-e-e!" as I ran away. (The word *cemetery* has three e's.)
>
> **separate**
> A lady was married to a man named Sep. One day she saw a rat. She yelled, "Sep! A rat! E!"

The best memory tools are the ones you make up. Here are examples from students' personal spelling guides.

from Grace's Memory Tricks

When I get a bargain, I feel like I gain money.

from Alphonso's Explanations

The desert is too dry to grow more than one s.

from Anna's Amazing Acronyms

said: Sailor Al is daring.

from Julian's Spelling Stories

My aunt always says that I have "cute scarlet cheeks." (Scarlet is another word for red.) When I am embarrassed, my two scarlet cheeks turn really red. The word embarrassed takes two r's and two s's, to match my two red or scarlet cheeks.

Reflect

- Which memory tool looks most fun?

- Which memory tool would probably work best for me because of how I am able to remember things?

Finding and Fixing Errors

Spelling and the Writing Process

You focus on spelling during the editing and proofreading stage of writing. But what should you do while drafting? When you are drafting, let your ideas flow. Keep writing even if you are unsure of how to spell a word. When you want to write a word and are unsure of the spelling, follow these steps:

1. Recall spelling rules you know. Think about related words and how they are spelled.

2. Write the word down.

3. Circle the word so you remember to check the spelling.

Check Your Spelling

Read your paper carefully, word by word. Study each spelling. Think about the rules you know. Remember, six out of every seven words follow common spelling rules.

How do you know if a word is spelled wrong? Trust what you know. If you are not sure, circle it. Many of the words you circle and check may be spelled correctly! There are common errors that many writers make. Look out for these problems:

- Missing letters
- Missing syllables
- Flipped letters
- Words that sound alike
- Sounds that can be spelled many different ways

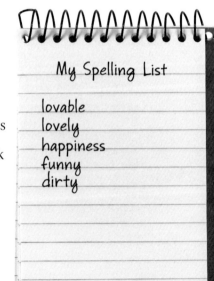

My Spelling List

lovable
lovely
happiness
funny
dirty

Whether you work along or with a partner, keep track of the words that you misspell. Create a personal spelling list. Review the words on a regular schedule and you will see your spelling improve.

Bryon used these spelling tips to find the errors in his personal narrative.

Byrons First Draft

I really enjoyed our famly reunion this summer. More than 20 of us got together at Clear Lake for the Fourth of July. There were some surprises. My Uncle Al hadn't seen me for two years, and he was amazed by my hieght. There were three new babys born since last year's reunion, including twin girls! Other things at the reunion were expected, includeing great food, lots of laughs, fun games, and warm feelings.

Byron thinks:

" This word follows the *i* before *e* rule, but it just doesn't look right."

" I need to think about how to make a word that ends in *y* plural."

You should always check your own spelling. It's also helpful to have a friend or classmate check your work. Remember we all have different words that challenge us. Ask your friend to circle words to check. Talk about the words. Work together to use a dictionary to find the correct spellings.

Byrons Edited Draft

I really enjoyed our famly reunion this summer. More than 20 of us got together at Clear Lake for the Fourth of July. There were some surprises. My Uncle Al hadn't seen me for two years, and he was amazed by my height. There were three new babies born since last year's reunion, including twin girls! Other things at the reunion were expected, includeing great food, lots of laughs, fun games, and warm feelings.

" I remember to really say the middle syllable to myself so I don't leave it out: *fam·i·ly.*"

" Remember to drop the e before adding an ending that starts with a vowel."

Making Sound-Spelling Connections

English words are made up of combinations of more than 40 different sounds. You can expect each sound to be spelled by certain letters. (Yes, there are exceptions!) Let's start with vowel sounds.

LONG VOWELS	
Spellings	**Example Words**
i ie igh i_e _y	item pie night fine cry
o oa ow o_e	open soap grow vote
u ew ue ui u_e oo	unit few blue fruit pure tooth

OTHER VOWELS	
Spellings	**Example Words**
au aw	author shawl
al all	also ball
ow ou	cow scout
oy oi	toy boil
oo u	foot bush
ar	yard
er ir ur	over bird curl
or	horn
a e i o u	about effect rabbit second circus

Now let's look at consonant sounds.

CONSONENT SOUNDS	
Spellings	Example Words
ch _tch	chin patch
d	did
f ph	first graph
g	gum
h	hen
j g _dge	jump giant fudge
k c ck	king camp luck
x	six
qu	quack
l	left
m mb	make lamb

CONSONENT SOUNDS	
Spellings	Example Words
n kn	name know
p	pond
r wr	red wrist
s c	safe pencil
sh	shell
t	time
th	thank
th	this
v	van
w	wash
wh	when
y	yell
z s	zebra news

Breaking Words Down

One great way to learn how to spell a word is to break it into parts. You can break words into **syllables**. Learn how to spell each syllable. Then put them together.

Syllable Rules (Look in the middle of the word. Look for the patterns named below. Say the word aloud.)	Examples
The VCV Rule: **A consonant between two vowels** If the first vowel is long, the break usually comes before the consonant. If the first vowel is short, the break usually comes after the consonant.	before: be·fore vacant: va·cant music: mu·sic cabin: cab·in wagon: wag·on linen: lin·en
The VCCV Rule: **Two consonants between vowels** The break comes between the consonants, unless the consonants work together to make one sound (as in *sh* and *th*).	blanket: blan·ket perhaps: per·haps picture: pic·ture fashion: fash·ion weather: weath·er
The VCCCV Rule: **Three consonants between vowels** The break comes between the two consonants that work together to make a sound and the third consonant.	pumpkin: pump·kin exchange: ex·change instead: in·stead although: al·though
Compound Words: Always divide a compound word between the two smaller words forming it.	afternoon: after·noon driveway: drive·way skateboard: skate·board

Look for these patterns in longer words, too. For example:

possible: pos•si•ble

controversy: con•tro•ver•sy

responsibility: re•spon•si•bil•i•ty

Making Words Plural

Once you learn how to spell a word, you also need to learn how to get it right in its different forms. For example, when you make nouns plural, you might need to make some spelling changes.

Rules	Examples
Make most nouns plural by adding –s to the end.	author ➡ authors crowd ➡ crowds principal ➡ principals niece ➡ nieces
If the word ends in *s, sh, ch, x, or z,* add –es.	business ➡ businesses brush ➡ brushes speech ➡ speeches fox ➡ foxes waltz ➡ waltzes
If the word ends in a consonant followed by *y,* change the *y* to *i* and add –es.	category ➡ categories puppy ➡ puppies library ➡ libraries fly ➡ flies
If the word ends in a vowel followed by *y,* just add –s.	birthday ➡ birthdays toy ➡ toys turkey ➡ turkeys key ➡ keys
If the word ends in a consonant followed by *o,* add –es.	hero ➡ heroes potato ➡ potatoes
If the word ends in a vowel followed by *o,* just add –s.	video ➡ videos radio ➡ radios
Words that end in *f* or *fe* are tricky. Sometimes you change the *f* to *v* and add –es. Sometimes you just add –s.	knife ➡ knives half ➡ halves roof ➡ roofs belief ➡ beliefs

Making Words Plural, continued

Some words have irregular plural forms. They do not follow the normal rules for creating plurals.

Singular	Plural	Singular	Plural
auto	autos	man	men
axis	axes	medium	media
basis	bases	mouse	mice
child	children	oasis	oases
crisis	crises	ox	oxen
criterion	criteria	parenthesis	parentheses
datum	data	piano	pianos
Eskimo	Eskimos	radius	radii
focus	foci	solo	solos
foot	feet	stimulus	stimuli
goose	geese	tooth	teeth
index	indices	woman	women

Some words are used for both the singular and the plural forms: deer, fish, moose, series, sheep, traffic, trout, wheat.

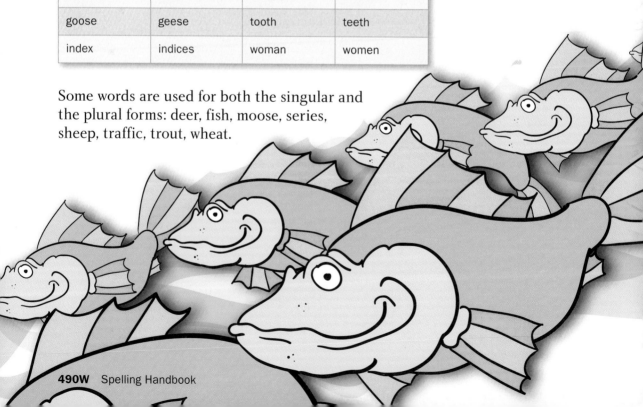

Knowing Your Roots

Many English words came from other languages. In many modern English words, you can see Greek and Latin roots. In some cases, you can find the same root in several words. So, if you learn how to spell these common roots, you will be on your way to knowing how to spell many words!

Root	Origin	Meaning	Examples
act	Latin	do	action, enactment
alter	Latin	other	alternate, alternative
anim	Latin	life	animated, inanimate
ann	Latin	year	annual, anniversary
aqua	Latin	water	aquarium, aquatic
ast	Greek	star	astronaut, astronomy
aud	Latin	hear	auditorium, audible
bio	Greek	life	biography, biology
cred	Latin	believe	credit, incredible
cycl	Greek	circle	bicycle, recycle
dic	Latin	speak	dictate, verdict
form	Latin	shape	uniform, transform
geo	Greek	earth	geologist, geography
gram	Greek	written	grammar, telegram
loc	Latin	place	location, local
meter	Greek	measure	thermometer, diameter
nat	Latin	born	native, national
phon	Greek	sound	phonics, telephone
poli	Greek	city	politics, cosmopolitan
port	Latin	carry	portable, import

Root	Origin	Meaning	Examples
rect	Latin	straight	rectangle, erect
rupt	Latin	break	erupt, interrupt
san	Latin	health	sane, sanitary
sci	Greek	know	science, conscious
sign	Latin	mark	signal, signature
spec	Latin	see	spectacles, inspect
struct	Latin	build	instruct, destruction
terr	Latin	land	terrace, territory
tract	Latin	pull	tractor, subtract
trib	Latin	give	contribution, attribute
vac	Latin	empty	vacant, evacuate
var	Latin	different	variety, variable

Adding Inflected Endings

Other word forms are made when certain endings, called **inflected endings**, are added. These endings include –*ed, -ing,* –*er,* and –*est.* Sometimes the spelling of a word changes when these endings are added.

Rules	Examples
If the word ends with one vowel and two consonants, just add the ending.	weigh ⟶ weighed, weighing grand ⟶ grander, grandest
If the word ends with two vowels and one consonant, just add the ending.	repair ⟶ repaired, repairing great ⟶ greater, greatest
If the word ends in silent e, drop the e before adding the ending.	acquire ⟶ acquired, acquiring safe ⟶ safer, safest

Rules, continued	Examples, continued
If the word ends in one vowel and one consonant (except x), double the consonant before adding the ending	trim ⟶ trim<u>med</u>, trim<u>ming</u> wet ⟶ wet<u>ter</u>, wet<u>test</u>
If the word ends in y, change the y to i before adding –ed, –er, or –est. However, keep the y if you are adding –ing.	study ⟶ stud<u>ied</u> easy ⟶ eas<u>ier</u>, eas<u>iest</u> study ⟶ stud<u>ying</u>
If the word ends in c, add a k before the ending.	panic ⟶ panic<u>ked</u>, panic<u>king</u>

Adding Suffixes and Prefixes

Other **suffixes** (the letters after the root word) can also change the spelling of a word.

Suffix Rules	Examples
If the word ends in silent e, drop the e before adding a suffix that starts with a vowel. However, if the suffix starts with a consonant, just add it to the word.	lie + -ar ⟶ li<u>ar</u> white + -en ⟶ whit<u>en</u> life + -less ⟶ life<u>less</u> confine + ment ⟶ confine<u>ment</u>
If the word ends in a consonant and y, change the y to i before adding the suffix.	pretty + -ly ⟶ prett<u>ily</u> silly + -ness ⟶ sill<u>iness</u>
If the word ends in a vowel and y, just add the suffix.	enjoy + -ment ⟶ enjoy<u>ment</u> play + -ful ⟶ play<u>ful</u>
If the word ends in le, drop the final le before adding the suffix –ly.	able + -ly ⟶ ab<u>ly</u> comfortable + -ly ⟶ comfortably
If the word ends in l, just add –ly to the end.	usual + -ly ⟶ usual<u>ly</u> annual + -ly ⟶ annual<u>ly</u>

When it comes to **prefixes** (the letters before the root word), you are lucky. You do not have to memorize any spelling rules to add prefixes! The spelling of a word does not change when you add a prefix.

Prefix Examples
<u>dis</u>agree, <u>im</u>possible, <u>re</u>heat, <u>un</u>able

Knowing the Long and Short of It

Compound Words

- A **compound word** is made up of two smaller words. The compound word has a new meaning.

Examples
sailboat
high school
well-known

- Most of the time, you just put the two short words together without changing their spellings. These are called **closed compounds**.

Examples
baseball
homework
raincoat

- Sometimes compound words are **open compounds**. They are spelled with a space between the two words.

Examples
potato chips
vacation home
health food

- **Hyphenated compounds** use a hyphen to join the two words.

Examples
ice-cold
brand-new
long-term

- When a compound word is used as an adjective or adverb, it is usually hyphenated, except when part of the compound is an adverb ending in *–ly*.

Examples
The track meet was an all-day event.

Exception
The badly injured woman was taken away in an ambulance.

Contractions

When two words are joined into one with a loss of one or more letters, the word is called a **contraction**. The missing letter is replaced by an apostrophe.

- Many contractions are formed with a pronoun and the verb forms *am, are, is, have,* or *will.*

EXAMPLE		
I + am	⟶	I'm
we + are	⟶	we're
he + is	⟶	he's
they + have	⟶	they've
she + will	⟶	she'll

- Many other contractions are formed with a verb and the word *not.* To make this kind of contraction, an apostrophe replaces the *o* in *not.*

EXAMPLES

could + not ⟶ couldn't

does + not ⟶ doesn't

EXCEPTIONS

can + not ⟶ can't (just one n)

will + not ⟶ won't (a different word)

Making Spelling Generalizations

You can memorize certain rules about spelling patterns within words. These rules are nearly always true, so they are known as **generalizations**.

Generalizations	Examples	Exceptions
ie or *ei* for the long e sound: Write *i* before *e* except right after *c*.	chief, relief, shield, receive	weird, seize, either, leisure, neither
words ending with a syllable pronounced "shent": This ending is spelled *cient*.	efficient sufficient ancient	
the letter *q*: Always follow the letter *q* with *u*.	quantity, quiet, request, inquiry, antique	Iraq, Iraqi, Qatar
the schwa sound followed by /l/ at the end of a word: These two sounds combined at the end of the word will be spelled –*le*, -*el*, or –*al*.	staple, jewel, dental	
c: the /k/ or /s/ sound? When *c* is followed by *e*, *i*, or *y*, it makes the sound /s/. When *c* is followed by *a*, *o*, or *u*, it makes the sound /k/.	celery, city, fancy camera, copy, cushion	
words ending with a short vowel followed by /k/: The /k/ sound is spelled ck.	pack, check, sick, lock, buck	
words ending with a short vowel followed by /j/: The /j/ sound is spelled *dge*.	badge, ledge, ridge, dodge, fudge	
words ending with /v/: Final /v/ is spelled *ve*.	brave, dive, cove	names like Tel Aviv and Isaac Asimov
words with endings pronounced /shon/: This final syllable is spelled *cion*, *sion*, or *tion*. If the base word has a *t*, the spelling is –*tion*. If the base word has a *d* or an *s*, the spelling is –*sion*.	suspicion, tension creation delete, deletion decide, decision confuse, confusion	attend, attention

Learning to Spell Tricky Words

Some words are tricky because they just don't follow the rules or sound-spelling connections. Other words are confusing because they sound alike but are spelled differently and have different meanings. These words are called **homophones**. Still other words are easily confused because they sound similar.

Lists of homophones and easily confused words are started here. On the next page, see more lists of common words that don't follow the rules. Add your own words to these lists as you come across them. Remember to make the words your own by coming up with good ways to connect their meanings to their spellings.

Homophones and Meanings	Example Sentences
all together (in a group) altogether (completely)	It is **altogether** wrong that we will not be **all together** this holiday.
capital (a place where a government is located) capitol (the actual building the government meets in)	We saw the senate vote in their chambers at the **capitol** during our tour of the **capital**.
cite (to quote a source) site (a place) sight (the ability to see or something that can be seen)	Be sure to **cite** your sources. My brother works on a construction **site**. The sunset last night was a beautiful **sight**.
council (a group organized to study and plan something) counsel (to give advice to someone)	The city **council** asked a lawyer to come and **counsel** them about civil rights.
it's (a contraction of *it is*) its (a possessive word meaning "belonging to it")	**It's** true that the dog drank all of **its** water already.
passed (to have moved ahead of) past (the time before the present)	In the **past** my brother drove too fast and often **passed** cars when he shouldn't.
principal (a person of authority or main) principle (a general truth or belief)	Our school **principal** makes announcements every morning. The **principal** ingredient in baking is flour. The essay was based on the **principles** of effective persuasion.
they're (contraction of *they are*) their (possessive form of the pronoun *they*) there (used to indicate location)	**They're** all on vacation this week. I want to use **their** office. The library is right over **there**.

Homophones and Meanings	Example Sentences
who's (contraction of *who is*) whose (possessive from of *who*)	**Who's** coming to our dinner party? **Whose** car is parked in the garage?
you're (contraction of *you are*) your (possessive pronoun meaning "belong to you")	**You're** going to be late if you don't hurry. Is **your** backpack too heavy? **from Grace's Memory Tricks** My principal is my PAL. A ruLE can be called a principLE.

Easily Confused Words and Meanings	Example Sentences
accept (to receive) except (to leave out or excluding)	I **accept** everything you say **except** your point about music.
advice (ideas about how to solve a problem) advise (to give advice)	I will give you **advice** about your problem today, but do not ask me to **advise** you again tomorrow.
affect (to cause a change in or to influence) effect (to bring about or the result)	Sunshine will **affect** my plants in a positive way. The rain will have a good **effect** on my plants, too.
assure (to make certain) ensure (to guarantee) insure (to cover financially)	I **assure** you that he is OK. I will personally **ensure** his safety. If the car is **insured**, the insurance company will pay to fix the damage.
beside (next to) besides (in addition to)	A parking lot is right **beside** the store. **Besides** being the fastest runner, she is also the nicest team member.
farther (refers to a physical distance) further (refers to time or amount)	If you go down the road a little **farther**, you will see the sign. We will discuss this **further** at lunch.
loose (free or not securely attached) lose (to misplace or to be defeated)	The dog got **loose** and now he is missing. First I **lose** my homework, and then we **lose** the game!
precede (to come before) proceed (to go forward)	Prewriting **precedes** drafting in the writing process. Please **proceed** carefully on the icy sidewalk.
than (used to compare things) then (next)	She likes to read fiction more **than** nonfiction. First, we will go to the bookstore; **then** we will go home.

Learning to Spell Tricky Words continued

Some of the most common words in the English language do not follow spelling rules. Check out these examples from the 25 most frequently used words:

are   have   of   on   to   they   you   was

You see these words so often that you tend to learn them by sight. You memorize what they look like. For this reason, these common words are sometimes called *sight* words.

A list is started here of other tricky words that just don't follow the ususal rules and patterns. These words come from the 1,000 most common words in the English language and from lists of words that students your age often misspell. You will probably have more words that are tricky for you to spell for one reason or another. Add those words to this list.

A	C	F	K	O
above	century	father	knowledge	ocean
accurate	certain	favorite		often
ache	chocolate	February	**L**	once
again	city	foreign	language	one
aisle	clothes	four	laughed	only
although	color	friend	listen	opposite
among	come	from		other
ancient	conquer		**M**	
answer	conscience	**G**	many	**P**
anxious	control	give	marriage	people
any	cough	gone	material	persuade
	country	great	meant	picture
B		group	measure	piece
balloon	**D**	guard	minute	put
bargain	design	guess	money	
beautiful	determine		mother	**Q**
become	discipline	**H**	mountain	quarterly
been	does	heard	move	quarter
both	done	height		
bought			**N**	**R**
brilliant	**E**	**I**	necessary	receipt
brought	earth	iron	none	restaurant
building	early	island	notice	rhythm
bury	engine			route
busy	enough	**J**		
buy	evening	jealousy		
	experience			

S	T	V	XYZ
said	though	vacuum	yacht
says	thought	valley	young
several	through	various	youth
shoes	toward	very	
should	trouble	villian	
sign			
soldier	**U**	**W**	
some	usually	want	
southern		watch	
special		water	
sugar		Wednesday	
sure		were	
surface		what	
		where	
		whose	
		woman	
		work	
		would	

My Word List

mansion

gorgeous

daughter

fruit

chalk

Index of Skills and Strategies

At-A-Glance Index

Acknowledgments

Bill Smith Studios: Design and artwork of "Space" from THE WORLD ALMANAC FOR KIDS 2003. Copyright © Bill Smith Studios. Used by permission.

Encyclopædia Britannica: Reprinted with permission from Encyclopædia Britannica, © 2008 by Encyclopædia Britannica, Inc.

Grove/Atlantic, Inc.: *This Boy's Life* © 1989 by Tobias Wolff. Used by permission of Grove/Atlantic, Inc.

James W. Hackett: "A bitter morning" by James W. Hackett from hacketthaiku.com. Reprinted by permission.

HarperCollins Publishers: Excerpt and one illustration from PAUL BUNYAN by Steven Kellogg. Text copyright © 1984 Steven Kellogg. Illustrations copyright © 1984 Steven Kellogg. Used by permission of HarperCollins Publishers.

Henry Holt and Company: "Stopping by Woods on a Snowy Evening" from THE POETRY OF ROBERT FROST edited by Edward Connery Lathem. Copyright 1923, 1969 by Henry Holt and Company. Copyright 1951 by Robert Frost. Reprinted by permission of Henry Holt and Company, LLC.

Highlights for Children: "Oak" by Dawn Watkins. Copyright © 1997 by Highlights for Children, Inc., Columbus, Ohio. Reprinted by permission.

Houghton Mifflin Harcourt Publishing Company: Excerpt from JUMANJI by Chris Van Allsburg. Copyright © 1981 by Chris Van Allsburg. Reprinted by permission of Houghton Mifflin Harcourt Publishing Company. All rights reserved.

McGraw-Hill: "southward" through "Spanish" is from the MACMILLAN DICTIONARY FOR CHILDREN Copyright © 1997 by Simon & Schuster and was originally published in the MCGRAW-HILL SCHOOL DICTIONARY.

MOSI: Job Application from Museum of Science and Industry website (www.mosi.org) copyright © 2006 MOSI. All rights reserved.

NASA: Background image on title page of *Mars* by Elaine Landau is from NASA.

National Geographic Society: Cover of FAMILY REFERENCE ATLAS OF THE WORLD, Second Edition. Copyright © 2007 National Geographic Society. All rights reserved. Cover of NATIONAL GEOGRAPHIC HISTORICAL ATLAS OF THE UNITED STATES. Copyright © 2004 National Geographic Society. All rights reserved. Cover of NATIONAL GEOGRAPHIC ROAD ATLAS, ADVENTURE EDITION. Published by National Geographic Maps in association with MapQuest, Inc. Copyright © 2007 by MapQuest, Inc. and Adventure section copyright © 2007 National Geographic Society. Cover photo by Steve Casimiro. All rights reserved.

Overseas Compatriot Affairs Commission: "The Birds Learn How to Build a Nest" from CHINESE FABLES by Tung Chung-ssu. Copyright © 1985 by Overseas Chinese Affairs Commission. All rights reserved.

Oxford University Press: "good" from OXFORD AMERICAN WRITER'S THESAURUS. Copyright © 2004 by Oxford University Press. Used by permission of Oxford University Press, Inc.

Random House, Inc.: From MOTHER by Maya Angelou, copyright © 2006 by Maya Angelou. Used by permission of Random House, Inc. From THE WATSONS GO TO BIRMINGHAM—1963 copyright © 1995 by Christopher Paul Curtis. "Funny in Farsi" excerpt was originally titled "Hot Dogs and Wild Geese", from FUNNY IN FARSI by Firoozeh Dumas, copyright © 2003 by Firoozeh Dumas. Used by permission of Villard Books, a division of Random House, Inc.

Scholastic Library Publishing, Inc.: *Mars* by Elaine Landau. All rights reserved. Reprinted by permission of Franklin Watts an imprint of Scholastic Library Publishing, Inc.

Scholastic, Inc.: Adapted from DEAR AMERICA: THE WINTER OF RED SNOW—THE REVOLUTIONARY WAR DIARY OF ABIGAIL JANE STEWART by Kristiana Gregory. Copyright © 1996 by Kristiana Gregory. Reprinted by permission of Scholastic Inc. Cover design of DEAR AMERICA: THE WINTER OF RED SNOW—THE REVOLUTIONARY WAR DIARY OF ABIGAIL JANE STEWART by Kristiana Gregory and the DEAR AMERICA logo was reprinted by permission of Scholastic Inc.

SUNY Press: Reprinted by permission from BASHO'S HAIKU: SELECTED POEMS OF MATSUO BASHO by Matsuo Basho, translated by David Landis Barnhill, the State University of New York Press © 2004, State University of New York. All rights reserved.

Teen Ink Magazine: "Book Review of When I Was Puerto Rican by Esmeralda Santiago" by Jennifer K. Reprinted with permission of Teen Ink Magazine and teenink.com.

Anthony Virgilio: "heat before the storm" and "the cathedral bell" by Nicholas Virgilio. From SELECTED HAIKU (Second Edition) by Nicholas Virgilio co-published by Burnt Lake Press and Black Moss Press, copyright © 1988 Nicholas A. Virgilio. Reprinted by permission by Anthony Virgilio.

World Almanac Education Group: "Space" from THE WORLD ALMANAC FOR KIDS 2003. Copyright © 2002 World Almanac Education Group. All rights reserved. Used by permission.

World Book, Inc.: For images of 1998 The World Book Encyclopedia and CD-ROM: Images of *The World Book Encyclopedia* and *The World Book Multimedia Encyclopedia* on CD-ROM courtesy of World Book, Inc. By permission of the publisher. www.worldbookonline.com. For Screenshot of first page of the "Mars" article: Spinard, Hyron. "Mars." *The World Book Encyclopedia.* © 1998. World Book, Inc. By permission of the publisher. http://www.worldbookonline.com.

The YGS Group: "Molding Troubled Kids into Future Chefs" by Kathy Blake. Used with permission of Nation's Restaurant News © 2008 All Rights Reserved. "Tropical Storm Florence Forms in Atlantic" by The Associated Press, September 5, 2006. Used with permission of The Associated Press © 2008 All Rights Reserved.

Photographs

xiii (l) Gisela Grob/zefa/Corbis. (m) PhotoDisc. (r) PhotoDisc. **2W** Corbis Premium RF/Alamy. **3W** UpperCut Images/Alamy. **4W** Foodfolio/Alamy. **5W** Denis Sinyakov/Reuters/Corbis. **8W** Frances Roberts/Alamy. **12W** Jim Craigmyle/Corbis. **14W** Peter Dazeley/Photographer's Choice/Getty Images. **15W** Digital Vision/Alamy. **16W** Corbis. **17W** (r) Richard Cummins/Corbis. (l) Joe Drivas/ Photographer's Choice Getty Images. **19W** Steve Skjold/Alamy. **22W** Mike Kemp/Rubberball Productions/Getty Images. **23W** (t) Lew Robertson/ FoodPix/Jupiterimages. (b) Renee Comet/StockFood Creative/Getty Images. **24W** Steven Mark Needham/ Envision/Corbis. **25W** Photo Resource Hawaii/Alamy. **26W** David Jay Zimmerman/Corbis. **29W** Steven Widoff/Alamy. **32W** Royalty-Free Corbis/Jupiterimages. **33W** Bruce Heinemann/Photodisc/Getty Images. **34W** ImagineThat/Alamy. **35W** Sèbastien Baussais/Alamy. **39W** claudio h. artman/Alamy. **41W** (l) Stefan Sollfors/Alamy. (c) Bettmann/ Corbis. (r) Phil Degginger/Alamy. **46W** (t) Geoff du Feu/Alamy. (r) Life Boat/ Stockbyte/Getty Images. **48W** Scott B. Rosen/Bill Smith Studio. **49W** Image Source Black/Alamy. **50W** Tom & Dee Ann McCarthy/Corbis. **51W** (tr) Walter Bibikow/Corbis. (tl) Ariel Skelley/Corbis. (br) Lee Page/Stone/ Getty Images. (bl) Corbis. **52W** (t) P. Wilson/zefa/Corbis. (c) Simon Harris/ IFA Bilderteam/Jupiterimages. (b) Steve Hamblin/Alamy. **54W** Jim Richardson/Corbis. **55W** PhotoAlto/ Alamy. **56W–57W** L. Nicoloso/ PhotoCuisine/Corbis. **58W–59W** George Steinmetz/Corbis. **60W** (t) James W. Porter/Corbis. (b) Ron Chapple/Corbis. **63W** (t) LWA-Stephen Welstead/Corbis. (ml) Allana Wesley White/Corbis. (mr) ImageState Royalty Free/Alamy. (b) Ron Chapple Stock/Alamy. **64W** Chris Howes/Wild Places Photography/Alamy. **65W** (t) Caroline Schiff/Blend Images/Getty Images. (ml) Stockbyte/Getty Images. (mr) Image Source-Hola/Alamy. (b) Digital Vision/Alamy. **67W** (t) Tom Grill/Corbis. (ml) Carl Glover/Image Source. (mr) Imagebroker/Alamy. (b) Ron Chapple Stock/Alamy. **69W** Travelshots.com/Alamy. **70W** Ariel Skelley/Corbis. **71W** Atlantide Phototravel/Corbis. **73W** Steve Skjold/Alamy. **78W** Photo taken by Craig Raine for This Old House magazine. **79W** Jon Arnold Images Ltd/Alamy. **82W** M Stock/Alamy. **83W** Image Source/Corbis. **90W** (fg) C Squared Studios/Photodisc/Getty Images. (bg) Paul Conrath/Digital Vision/Getty Images. **92W** Imagebroker/Alamy. **93W** Scott B. Rosen/Bill Smith Studio. **96W** IT Stock International/Jupiterimages. **97W** Imagebroker/Alamy. **99W** Andy Myatt/Alamy. **103W** Dea/C. Dani -I. Jenske/De Agostini Picture Library/ Getty Images. **108W** David Young-Wolff/PhotoEdit. **109W** Photo by Miami Herald/Getty Images. **110W** Romeo Gacad/AFP/Getty Images. **113W** Ralph Wetmore/Getty Images. **114W** Jamie Squire/Getty Images. **118W** (tl) Chicken Feed Photos/ Creatas Images/Jupiterimages. (tr) Photos.com/Jupiterimages. **118W– 119W** Jerry Grayson/Helifilms Australia PTY Ltd/ Getty Images. **121W** David J. Phillip/Pool/Reuters/ Corbis. **125W** Roger Ressmeyer/ Corbis. **127W** Reuters/Corbis. **137W** PhotoLink/Getty Images. **138W** Image Source Pink/Alamy. **139W** Mike McGill/Corbis. **144W** John Kobal Foundation/Hulton Archive/ Getty Images. **146W** John Kobal Foundation/Hulton Archive/Getty Images. **148W** Image Source Black/ Getty Images. **150W** Fabio Cardoso/ zefa/Corbis. **152W** Bill Bachman/ Alamy. **156W** Judith Collins/Alamy. **157W** Peter Mumford/Alamy. **158W** LWA-Sharie Kennedy/Corbis. **160W** Max Morse/Reuters/Corbis. **161W** Carsten Reisinger/Alamy. **162W** Photos 12/Alamy. **164W** Lisette Le Bon/SuperStock. **167W** Photos 12/ Alamy. **169W** Bettmann/Corbis. **172W** PhotoAlto/Odilon Dimier/Getty Images. **179W** Tony Freeman/ PhotoEdit. **180W** Comstock Images/ Jupiterimages. **181W** Jupiterimages/ Brand X/Alamy. **182W** NASA/JPS-Caltech/University of Arizona. **182W– 183W** Jupiterimages/Brand X/Alamy. **184W** NASA/Roger Ressmeyer/ Corbis. **187W** STScI/NASA/ASU/ Hester/Ressmeyer/Corbis. **188W** Trip/Alamy. **192W** Glowimages/Getty Images. **193W** Design Pics Inc./ Alamy. **194W** (t) Peter Arnold, Inc./ Alamy. (m) Elvele Images/Alamy. (b) ImageState-Pictor/Jupiterimages. **197W** Jupiterimages/Comstock Images/Alamy. **201W** Jupiterimages/ Brand X/Alamy. **203W** NASA Hubble Space Telescope/epa/Corbis. **205W** NASA/epa/Corbis. **206W–207W** Jupiterimages/Brand X/Alamy. **209W** NASA/JPL/Cornell/epa/Corbis. **211W** Design Pics Inc./Alamy. **212W–213W** Charles O'Rear/Corbis. **215W** Roger Ressmeyer/Corbis. **217W** MPI/ Stringer/Hulton Archive/Getty Images. **225W** (tl) NASA Hubble Space Telescope/epa/Corbis. (tr) NASA Viking Orbiter/U.S. Geological Survey. (bl) Handout/Reuters/Corbis. (bg) George Doyle/Stockbyte/Getty Images. **226W** (tl) Tupungato/Big Stock Photo. Time & Life Pictures/ Getty Images. (tml) Artville. (tmr) Spike Mafford/Getty Images. (tr) Visuals Unlimited/Corbis. (ctm) Dana Hoff/Brand X Pictures/Jupiterimages. (cbl) Artville. Stockbyte. (cbm) PhotoDisc. (cbr) Comstock Images/ Jupiterimages. **227W** PhotoDisc. **229W** NASA/JPL-Caltech-Mars Rover/Science Faction/Getty Images. **230W–231W** NASA/JPL-Caltech-Mars Pathfinder/Science Faction/ Getty Images. **235W** William Radcliffe/Science Faction/Getty Images. **237W** The Stocktrec Corp/ Brand X Pictures/Jupiterimages. **239W** Stockbyte. **242W** Xinhua/ Xinhua Photo/Corbis. **243W** Bettmann/Corbis. **244W** Herman Beals/Reuters/Corbis. **245W** David Sailors/Corbis. **246W** BananaStock/ Jupiterimages. **247W** North Wind Picture Archives/Alamy. **248W** (t) Janice Northcutt Huse. (b) American School/The Bridgeman Art Library/ Getty Images. **252W** Associated Press. **258W** Photodisc/Alamy. **260W** Fotoniche/Alamy. **261W** Anne Frank Fonds-Basel/Anne Frank House/ Hulton Archive/Getty Images. **262W** Steve Skjold/Alamy. **263W** Picture Contact/Alamy. **264W** Ahmad Masood/Reuters/Corbis. **266W** Gary S. Chapman/Photographer's Choice/ Getty Images. **267W** Paula Bronstein/ Getty Images. **268W** Zia Soleil/ Iconica/Getty Images. **269W** Paula Bronstein/Getty Images. **272W** Don Cravens/Time & Life Pictures/Getty Images. **274W** Associated Press. **280W** Simon Jarratt/Corbis. **282W**

Intl St. Clair/Digital Vision/Getty Images. **283W** Roger Ressmeyer/Corbis. **284W** Tim Hawley/FoodPix/Jupiterimages. **287W** Peter Arnold, Inc./Alamy. **288W** Kul Bhatia/zefa/Corbis. **292W** Janine Wiedel Photolibrary/Alamy. **294W** (t) Sindre Ellingsen/Alamy. (b) NASA/Corbis. **295W** Bryan Allen/Corbis. **297W** Jan-Peter Kasper/epa/Corbis. **299W** (l) Tim McGuire/Corbis. (r) Comstock/Superstock. **307W** Chris Hondros/Getty Images. **308W** Comstock Images/Jupiterimages. **308W–309W** Owaki/Kulla/Corbis. **311W** Rudy Sulgan/Corbis. **313W** Kenneth Garret/National Geographic/Getty Images. **315W** Photos.com. **316W** Geray Sweeney/Corbis. **322W** Ian Shaw/Alamy. **323W** Kayte M. Deioma/PhotoEdit. **325W** Photodisc/Alamy. **327W** David Young-Wolff/PhotoEdit. **334W** Bananastock/Jupiterimages. **335W** North Wind Picture Archives/Alamy. **336W** (t) Frank Micelotta/American Idol/Getty Images. (b) Andersen Ross/Blend Images/Getty Images. **338W** Jose Luis Pelaez, Inc./Corbis. **340W** Jamie Squire/Getty Images Sport. **344W** SuperStock, Inc./SuperStock. **346W** Tim Fitzharris/Minden Pictures/Getty Images. **348W** Image Source Black/SuperStock. **350W** Reg Charity/Corbis. **353W** DLILLC/Corbis. **355W** Stefanie Grewel/zefa/Corbis. **356W** (tl) PhotoDisc. (tml) PhotoDisc. (tmr) PhotoDisc. (tr) William Whitehurst/Corbis. (mlt) PhotoDisc. (mlb) siamimages/Big Stock Photo. (mr) PhotoDisc. (b) PhotoDisc. **357W** © PhotoDisc. **358W** (l) Anthony Nex/Newscom. (r) Image courtesy of Advertising Archives. **359W** Damien Lovegrove/Science Photo Library. **360W** Aicha Nystrom. **361W** The Granger Collection, New York. **362W** University of New Mexico Press. **363W** Russell Monk/Masterfile. **364W** Todd Gipstein/Corbis. **365W** PhotoAlto/Alamy. **366W** Corbis/Jupiterimages. **367W** (t) Forever Stamp Design © 2007 United States Postal Service. All Rights Reserved. Used with Permission. John Morrison/PhotoEdit. (b) Creative Studio Heinemann/Westend61/Getty Images. **368W** Jupiterimages/Creatas/Alamy. **369W** Moodboard/Corbis. **370W** Digital Vision/Alamy. **371W** (t)

Fernando Bengoechea/Beateworks/Corbis. (b) Leah Warkentin/Design Pics/Corbis. **373W** Donovan Reese/Getty images. **374W** Dover Publications Inc., New York. **377W** (t) Big Cheese Photo/Jupiterimages. (ml) Digital Studios. (mr) D. Hurst/Alamy. (b) Purestock/Alamy. **378W** (tl) Red Cloud Stamp image reprinted with permission of the United States Postal Service. All Rights Reserved. (tc) Red-headed Woodpecker Stamp image reprinted with permission of the United States Postal Service. All Rights Reserved. (tr) Luis Munoz Marin Stamp image reprinted with permission of the United States Postal Service. All Rights Reserved. (ml) Digital Stock. (mr) Eastern Bluebird Stamp image reprinted with permission of the United States Postal Service. All Rights Reserved. (b) Mount St. Mary's University Stamp image reprinted with permission of the United States Postal Service. All Rights Reserved. **379W** (t) Jeff Greenberg/PhotoEdit, Inc. (b) S. Kirchner/PhotoCuisine/Corbis. **380W** D. Hurst/Alamy. **381W** Andrew Paterson/Alamy. **382W–385W** Big Stock Photos and PhotoDisc. **384W** Reuters/Larry Downing. **386W** Tom Bean/Corbis. **387W** (t) Front cover from "When I Was Puerto Rican" by Esmerelda Santiago. Used by permission of Vintage Books, a division of Random House, Inc. (b) Corbis. **389W** Marty Snyderman/Corbis. **390W** Franz Marc Frei/Corbis. **391W** Jeff Greenberg/Alamy. **392W** Photos courtesy of the Fredericksburg Theatre Co., Mary Washington College, Department of Theatre and Dance, Fredericksburg, VA. **393W** (l) Photos courtesy of the Fredericksburg Theatre Co., Mary Washington College, Department of Theatre and Dance, Fredericksburg, VA. (r) Tetra Images/Getty Images. **394W–395W** Leong Kin Fei/iStockphotos.com. **396W** Bruce Dale/Getty Images. **397W** Corbis. **398W** Christie's Images/Corbis. **400W–401W** Linda/zefa/Corbis. **403W** Lawrence Manning/Corbis. **407W** Photodisc/Getty Images. **408W** Anthony J. Hall/iStockPhoto. **411W** Big Stock Photo. **413W** David Young-Wolff/PhotoEdit. **415W** Stockbyte/Alamy. **416W** (tl) Gisela Grob/zefa/

Corbis. (tml) PhotoDisc. (tmr) PhotoDisc. (tr) Anthony Nex/FoodPix/Jupiterimages. (ct) Photodisc. (cbl) Antar Bayal/Illustration Works/Corbis. (cbm) PhotoDisc. (cbr) PhotoDisc. (b) Stockbyte. **417W** © Comstock Images/Jupiter Images. **428W** (tl) Metaphotos. (tml) C Squared Studios/Getty Images. (tmr) David Toase/Getty Images. (ctl) David Toase/Getty Images. (ctm) Alex Grimm/Reuters/Corbis. (ctr) Big Stock Photo. (cbl) Big Stock Photo. (cbm) Steve Cole/Getty Images. (cbr) Duncan Smith/Corbis. (b) PhotoDisc. **480W** Gisela Grob/zefa/Corbis. **481W** Nation Wong/zefa/Corbis. **482W** Richard Hamilton Smith/Corbis. **483W** Digital Zoo/Digital Vision/Getty Images. **485W** (l) Norbert Schaefer/Corbis. (r) David Cook/www.blueshiftstudios.co.uk/Alamy. **486W** Gisela Grob/zefa/Corbis. **487W** Worldwide Picture Library/Alamy.

Fine Art

406W Cover art for *Dear America: The Winter Of Red Snow—The Revolutionary War Diary Of Abigail Jane Stewart* by Kristiana Gregory: Valley Forge: March, 1777 © The Granger Collection, New York. Greuze's The Woolwinder © The Frick Collection, New York.

Illustrations

iv, vi, viii, 14W, 44W, 94W Martin O'Neill. **62W, 93W** Steve Bjorkman. **140W, 156W** Craig Phillips. **315W** Samuel A. Minik. **375W** Winifred Barnum Newman. **376W** Norm Bendell. **388W** Kris Wiltse. **402W** Jessica Secheret. **404W** Jessica Secheret.

Additional Acknowledgments

Within this collection of strategies resides the work of hundreds of teachers and students from all over the world, products of the work of their teachers. While it is impossible to thank every one of these by name, there are special individuals who have directly contributed to the philosophies and practices in this program.

Thank you to Cathy McFeaters, Cynthia Péna, Laura Lott, Laura Gunn, Amy Stengal, Dottie Hall, Tracy Winstead, Jeff Anderson, and Jayne Hover, public school teachers who have shared countless conversations with me about experiments and discoveries in our classrooms, exchanging ideas and results with gusto and delight.

Thank you to Linda Stubbs whose experiments and discoveries with the target lesson have provided us all with a perfect-fit strategy for some students who despair of ever fitting.

Thank you most of all to Barry Lane, who has not only shared classroom tools like snapshots and thoughtshots, but has devoted his adult life to modeling and supporting, from the easiest part—adding resources to our students' arsenals or tool belts; through the work—building daily in our students the muscles with which to hoist up these tools and wield them expertly; and into the magic— breathing into our lessons the spirit of curiosity, humor, and greatest of all, compassion.

Editorial

Linda Alders, Amy Barbour, Lisa Berti, Chris Beem, Michael Beets, Renee Biermann, Ela Aktay Booty, Janine Boylan, Susan Buntrock, Karen Cardella, Kristin Cozort, Darin Derstine, Amanda Gebhardt, Toni Gibbs, Trudy Gibson, Nadine Guarrera, Margot Hanis, Rachel Hansen, Fred Ignacio, Anne Kaske, Robin Kelly, Phillip Kennedy, Sarah Kincaid, Jennifer Kleiman, Jennifer Krasula, Joel Kupperstein, Phil Kurczewski, Mary Catherine Langford, Julie Larson, Kathleen Laya, Dawn Liseth, Daphne Liu, Nancy Lockwood, Jennifer Loomis, Kathleen Maguire, Cheryl Marecki, Andrew McCarter, Joyce McGreevy, Mimi Mortezai, Kimberly Mraovich, Amy Ostenso, Barbara Paulsen, Juan Quintana, Katrina Saville, Debbie Saxton, Thomas Schiele, Anastasia Scopelitis, Elizabeth Sengel, Heather Subba, Lin Sullivan, Seija Surr, Honor Teoudoussia, Jennifer Tetzloff, Joy Triche, Marietta Urban, Sharon Ursino, Beatrice Villar, Nora Whitworth, Virginia Yeater, Brown Publishing Network, Chapman Publishing Systems, MetaArts, Morrison BookWorks, Rainbow Creative Concepts, Words and Numbers

Art, Design, and Production

Marcia Bateman, Christy Caldwell, Andrea Cockrum, Kim Cockrum, Jen Coppens, Wendy Crockett, Denise Davidson, Alicia DiPiero, Carol Do, Darius Detwiler, Donna Jean Elam, Michael Farmer, Chanté Fields, Kathryn Glaser, Raymond Ortiz Godfrey, Raymond Hoffmeyer, Annie Hopkins, Karen Hunting, Jeri Gibson, Rick Holcomb, Cynthia C. Lee, Ernie Lee, Jean-Marie McLaren, Douglas McLeod, Mary McMurtry, Melina Meltzer, Rick Morrison, Russ Nemec, Marian O'Neal, Andrea A. Pastrano-Tamez, Leonard Pierce, Deborah Reed, Cathy Revers, Stephanie Rice, Scott Russell, Susan Scheuer, Janet Sandbach, Jeanne Stains, Sumer Tatum-Clem, Andrea Erin Thompson, Andrea Troxel, Donna Turner, Ana Vela, Alex von Dallwitz, AARTPACK, Inc., Brown Publishing Network, Chaos Factory & Associates, GGS Book Services, Rainbow Creative Concepts, Thompson Type, Vertis, Inc., Visual Asylum